GREENE COUNTY, TENNESSEE WILLS, 1783–1890

Compiled by Goldene Fillers Burgner

Southern Historical Press, Inc.
Greenville, South Carolina

Please Direct All Correspondence and Book Orders to:

Southern Historical Press, Inc.
PO Box 1267
375 West Broad Street
Greenville, S.C. 29602

ISBN # 0-89308-203-1

Printed in the United States of America

WILLS

The man owned everything as these wills show. He even willed his wife her clothes, and what she brought with her "when she married me."

In these abstracts I have tried to include the flavor, showing what each person received and revealing what seemed to be the mood of the maker and as time progressed the changes that had come about. The quilts of the eighteen sixties, windmills of the seventies and eighties are all very interesting to me.

In the Name of God, Amen - I Goldene Fillers Burgner of Greene County, State of Tennessee, being sick and weak in body, but of perfect mind and memory, thanks be to God; calling unto mind the mortality of my body and knowing that it is appointed for all men once to die, do make this my last will and testament; that is to say principally and first of all, I recommend my soul into the hands of Almighty God that gave it, and my body I recommend to the earth, to be buried in a decent Christian manner. At the discretion of my executors, nothing doubting but at the general resurrection, I shall receive the same again by the mighty power of God.

Secondly, I give these abstracts to the people who use them hoping that the revealing facts therein will be helpful and gratifying, and that generations yet unborn will find this useful.

So states the first paragraph in all the first wills - By 1890 this was shortened but still said the same thing. Later it was left out altogether.

GREENE COUNTY TENNESSEE RECORDS

Greene (now Tennessee) was formed in 1783
from Washington (now Tennessee). Washington
County was formed in 1777 from the District
of Washington. It was roughly the territory
west of Wilkes County, North Carolina, between Wilkes and the Virginia line, which
had been allowed three representatives in
the General Assembly of North Carolina in
1776.

Sullivan (now Tennessee) was formed in 1779
from Washington County. Part of Washington
(Tennessee) was annexed to Wilkes County,
North Carolina, in 1792.

TENNESSEE

TENNESSEE
AT THE BEGINNING OF
1790
Showing Approximate County Divisions
within Present State Boundaries

NATHAN ALEXANDER   20 May 1823
Rev. Nathaniel Alexander, Preacher of the Gospel. Father, James Alexander
Senr. of Madison County, State of Tennessee. To Rev. Charles Coffin,
manuscripts, papers and philosophy of the mind. Executors: Rev. Charles
Coffin, W. David Farnsworth. Witnesses: Edw. P. Hale, Joseph Wilson.
                              Signed: Nathaniel Alexander

ELIZABETH (GOUDY G.F.B.) ANDERSON   24 Dec. 1800
To grand daughter, Mary Farrel, my chestnut cupboard. To grand daughter,
Elizabeth Farrel, my bed and bed clothes. To my daughter Isabel, all
other property and a legacy left me by my brother, John Goudy in the state
of Pennsylvania. Executors: Son-in-law, John Kelsey and daughter, Isabel.
Witnesses: John Blair, Sarah Kelsey.   her
                       Signed: Elizabeth X Alexander
                                          mark

THOMAS BRANDON   30 March 1786   State of Franklin
Wife: Jane. Son: Thomas. To daughter, Mary, ½ land on Lick Creek, one
bay mare, if recovered, and one cow. Stepson: William English.
Executors: Daniel Kennedy and wife. Witnesses: Thomas Brandon, Rebecca
Brandon, Dan Kennedy.   his
                       Signed: Thomas X Brandon
                                       mark

JAMES BOWERS   31 March 1789
Auphen Mitchell 5 shillings, Elizabeth Clavens? 5 shillings, John Bowers
5 shillings, Richard Bowers 5 shillings. Two young children: William and
Meavey. William to have the cattle, one big pot and skillet pots.
Meavey to have the sheep. To Richard Bowers a young filly named Peppergin.
To wife Kissa Bowers, two mares. Executors: William, son and wife Kissa.
Witnesses: Isaac Davis, Thomas Bailey.
                              Signed: James Bowers

THOMAS BRANDON   1789
To wife, Jane, and son, Thomas, plantation I now live on, equally divided.
To daughter, Mary, ½ plantation on Lick Creek (if recovered), one bay mare
and one cow. To son, John, the other half of plantation on Lick Creek.
Stepson: William English. Executors: Daniel Kennedy, Wife Jane.
Witnesses: Robert Allen, Mary Allen, Aaron Hughes. his
                       Signed: Thomas X Brandon
                                       mark

JACOB BROYLES   10 Dec. 1798
To daughter, Delilah Prather, 1/3 of plantation I now live on, her choice
of two horses or mares, 2 cows and calves, 2 steers. To daughter, Keziah
Williamson, bed and bed furniture each. Wife: Elizabeth. To sons,
Ezekiel, Lewis, James, Jeremiah, John, plantation after wifes death. At
wifes death, all children to share equally. Executors: Thomas Prather,
James Broyles. Witnesses: John Bird, Ephraim Broyles, Matthias Broyles.
                                               his
                       Signed: Jacob X Broyles
                                       mark

RACHEL BANNET (BENNETT ?)   April 1820
All debts to be paid. Daughter and Executor: Ellen Bennet. Witnesses:
Henry Dyche Jr., Jane X Dyche, Ruth Dyche. Dated: 17 Dec. 1817.
                       Signed: Rachel Bannet

THOMAS PARSONS BROWN   12 July 1821
Of Abbeville District, State of South Carolina.
To appoint guardians for my children: Harriet P. and John L. Brown, for

the purpose to carry them to the State of Maine immediately after my
death, there to be educated. Mother: Harriet Devan. Wife: Nancy Brown.
Witnesses: Peter Dillon Senr., Thomas Brown, Peter Dillon Junr.

Signed: Thomas Parsons Brown

ALEXANDER BARRENS   2 April 1821
To wife, Nancy Barrens, all my household furniture, the chest and con-
tents, flax on hand, all corn, meat and provisions, one sow and 5 shoats.
To son, Ganey Barrens, one cow named Luck. Children: Cornelius Barrens,
John Barrens, Ellender and Mary Barrens. All the rest sold at auction
and equally divided. Executor: John Maltsbarger. Witnesses: Cornelius
Newman, Cornelius Smith.   his

Signed: Alexander X Barrens
                                                          mark

MARGARET BALY   5 July 1805
To only daughter, Sarah, one roan mare, 4 head cattle, bed and furniture.
Sole Executor: David Moore. Witnesses: David Moore, William McAmish,
Willet M. McAmish.   her

Signed: Margaret X Baily
                                                          mark

ISAAC BAKER   19 January 1818
To wife, Hannah, plantation and 3 negro men, Charles, Lege and Jenny,
also my mulatto woman Dine, horses and household furniture. To children:
Nancy, Elizabeth and James, to have furniture to set up housekeeping. To
Nancy, negro girl Dine. To Elizabeth, negro boy, Enoc. To son, John,
one share less $100. To son, Isaac, one share less $600. Children:
Rebecca Farnsworth, Jacob, Polly Allen. To John and Delilah Baker -
children of son William Decd., one equal share. Executors: William
Houston, John Gragg. Witnesses: James Houston, William Daniel. Dated:
31 December 1817.

Signed: Isaac Baker

JOHN BELL   30 May 1816
Wife: Elizabeth. To son, James, 100 acres of land. To son, George, 100
acres of land. To son, Wilson Allen, $30.00 at end of schooling. To
youngest son, Samuel, to have the rest. To daughters, Katherine and Mary
Ann, $5.00 each to be enjoyed forever. To grand daughter, Elizabeth
Dixon Bell, one horse, saddle and bridle. Executors: wife Elizabeth, son
James. Witnesses: Thomas Doan, Alexander Henderson.

Signed: John Bell

JOHN BRITT   July Sessions 1823
To wife, Mary, goods, chattels, land and wagons until she remarries, then
everything to my children. Mary's children by me. My 5 children by my
first wife. Dated: February 7, 1821. Witnesses: John Billingsley Senr.,
William Jackson, William Basket.

Signed: John Britt

SAMUEL BROWN   October Sessions 1826
Wife: Hannah
Children: Thomas H., Solomon, Catharine.
Executors: Father, Thomas Brown, Father-in-law, Solomon Beals.
Witnesses: Aaron Hammer, Elihu Beals, William Brown. Dated: June 6, 1825
Sons Thomas H. and Solomon to have all the lands and saw-mill. Daughter
Catharine to have $75 each from her brothers.

Signed: Samuel Brown

HANNAH BAKER   Proven October 1826
To daughters, Polly Allen and Rebecca Farnsworth, 2 negros Dian and
Anderson. Indigent Isaac Baker, $46.00. Judgment on Martain Cline
$12.00. To son, John Baker, negro man, Ismel. Executor: Son-in-law,
Daniel Allen. Witnesses: A. Hunter, Abraham Farner. Dated: 5 Aug. 1826.

Signed: Hannah X Baker
                                                      her mark

JOHN BLACKWOOD   14 June 1789   Greene County, State of North
Carolina. To daughters, Elizabeth and Mary, 5 shillings each. To wife,
Ann, the plantation. Children: William, Ann, Andrew, Martha. Executors:
Wife, Ann, Jones Kendrick. Witnesses: James Kendrick, John Young.
                         Signed: John Blackwood

JOHN BANNAT   20 August 1801
Wife, Rachel Bennat, to have everything her lifetime, Thomas ?. Sons
and daughters. Executor: Wife, Rachel Bannat. Witnesses: Samuel Wilson,
Ephraim Wilson, John Garvin. Will dated: August 5, 1801.
                         Signed: John Bannat

PETER BURGNER   July 1824
To wife, Elizabeth, everything her lifetime - then sold and equally
divided. If Jacob should die - Daniel to have his part. Daughters:
Elizabeth, Polly, Sofiah Burgner. Sons: Jacob F., John C., Henry, Peter
Junr., Daniel, Christian. My apple orchard land on Horse Creek adjoining
Hayle, Capps, Prather and John Broyles. Sons John C. and Henry have
taken their liberty since the age of 15 years. Executors: John C.
Burgner, Jonathan Waddle. Witnesses: Adam Painter Junr., John S. Broyles,
Simeon Broyles. Dated: 31 May 1824.
                         Signed: Pater Burgner

JOHN BOWMAN   Proven January 1810
Wife: Elizabeth Bowman. Oldest daughter: Ruthanne Horn. Oldest son,
Andrew Bowman, to have $6.00 - no more. Sons: Jacob, Daniel. Daughters:
Elizabeth Johnston, Catranenah Bowman, Betsy Bowman. To grandchild,
daughter to Andrew Bowman, equal part. Grand-daughter named Betsy.
Executors: James Jack, Jacob Bowman. Witnesses: W. Wilson, Joseph
St.John, Aaron Bowman.   his
                         Signed: John X Bowman
                                         mark

LEWIS BROYLES   October Session 1804
To wife, Mary, my plantation. To daughter, Sarry, negro girl, Mary. To
daughter, Elizabeth, negro boy, George. To son, Jacob, 225 acres on
South bank of Horse Creek. To son, Lewis, my gun and shot bag. To
daughter, Mary, negro boy, Jupitor. Son, James, to have upper plantation
on Horse Creek. Lewis to run off land. Executors: Wife Mary, son James.
Witnesses: Alex Prather, Thomas Prather, John Broyles. Dated: 11 October
1803.
                         Signed: Lewis Broyles

Lewis Broyles was a Private in the Revolutionary War - Washington County
and Sullivan County, North Carolina. Pension vouchers from Broyles
Settlement on Little Limestone in Washington County, Tennessee. This
Lewis Broyles, Rev. Soldier's grave is under a corn crib near Philadelphia
Church, Washington County, Tenn. Told to me by Bobby Broyles, basketball
couch, 1976. G.F.B.

HUGH CAV ENER (CAVNER)   July Sessions 1825
To wife, Jane, $10 per year for sugar and coffee. Son, John, to cut her
firewood. To grandson, Hugh Cavner, all bench tools. To grandson, Isaac,
my die pot and skillet. Grandsons: William Cavner, William McAmish. To
son John, collection of Hymns and confession of Faith. To grand-daughter,
Jane McAmish, $100. Daughter: Margaret McAmish. Witnesses: Joseph
Bullen, John W. Wilson.
                         Signed: Hugh Cavner

BARNET CRABTREE   25 April 1825
To wife, Peggy Crabtree, 1/3 of all estate and Mansion House. Six sons:
William, John, Barnet, Henry, Daniel, James. To sons, Daniel and James,
$60 each at age 21. Wagon to be shod - son, John, to have ½ of it.
Daughters: Polly Babb, Anney Babb, Susanna, Peggy and Betty Crabtree.
Executors: Daniel Kerby, Peggy Crabtree. Witnesses: Michael Bright,
John Crabtree. Dated: 25 April 1825.
                         Signed: Barnet X Crabtree

PEGGY CROSBY   6 March 1808
My youngest sister, Jinny Crosby, my negro girl Hannah. Witnesses: John
Glascock, Vincent Jackson, Mary X Jackson.   her
                                    Signed: Peggy X Crosby
                                                    mark

ROBERT CRAWFORD   August Session 1797
Executors: William Brotherton, Thomas Randolph. Children: Adam, Nicholas,
George, Peter, John, Catrene, May, Elizabeth, Mary, Susannah, Barbara.
Dated: 17 May 1797. Witnesses: James Anderson, William West Jurat.

ROBERT CRAWFORD   1794
Wife: Isabella. Executor: Benjamin Crawford. Two sons, William and
Alec, to receive land equally. Children to receive reasonable education.
Dated: 20 October 1794. Witnesses: Alec McFarland, John Kilgore Jurat.
                            Signed: Robert Crawford

WILLIAM CARSON   September 25, 1787
Wife: Sarah. Son: _____. Executors: David and John Carson, wife
Sarah. Witnesses: Alexander Galbreath, John Carson Junior.
                            Signed: William Carson

WILLIAM CRAVENS
Wife: Ann? To son, Robert, land east fork of Little Chuckey. Raised
William Houston from childhood - to get land on _____ Little Chuckey.
Executrix: Wife, Nancy. (2 wives?) Dated: 14 March 1796. Witnesses:
Adam S. Shields, John Sanders, Jonathan Lucas?, Samuel Wyatt Junr.

JACOB COUCH   August Sessions 1797
Children: Adam, Nicolas, George and Peter Couch, John Couch, Catrine, May,
Elizabeth, Mary, Susannah, Barbara. Dated: 17 March 1797. Witnesses:
James Anderson, William West Jurat.
                            Signed: Jacob X Couch

HUGH CAMERON   August Session 1796
Greene County, Southern Territory
Wife: Elizabeth. Executors: Wife, Elizabeth, Robert Crockett. Dated:
2 January 1795. Witnesses: Andrew English, James Beaty Jurit.
                            Signed: Hugh X Cameron

URIEL CROSBY   October Session 1821
Wife: Elizabeth. Children: John, Peter, Edward, David, Jeremiah, Rachel
Melone, Naomi Acres, Marjey Melone, Ruth Brown, Mary Casteel, Marget
Casteel. Executor: David Key. Dated: 26 April 1811. Witnesses: Peter
X Casteel, Zachariah X Melone.

URIEL CROSBY   April Session 1799
North side of Lick Creek below Skipper's Creek
Wife: Susanna. Children: George, Thomas, William, Susanna VanPelt,
Frances Murray, Anne Jackson, Sarah Crosby, Elizabeth, Mary, Lydda,
Peggy Rebeah?, Nancy, Jane and William Crosby. Executors: Sons George
and Thomas Crosby. Land on Lick Creek. Dated: 15 February 1799.
Witnesses: Thomas Wyatt, James Hayes, Robert Warren.
                            Signed: Uriel Crosby

GEORGE CONWAY   1800
To sister, Mary Mitchell, my gold ring, small sword, 3 horses Mark
Mitchell took to South Carolina. To Mark Mitchell, rifle gun. To James
S. Conway, plantation below the mouth of Lick Creek. To Henry Conway,
Junr., 2 years schooling and lots in town of Greeneville and Newport.
Dated: 6 October 1800. Witnesses: William Dewoody, John Johnston.
Executors: Henry Conway, Mark Mitchell, George Duffield.
Stock of cattle in the possession of my father.
                            Signed: George Conway

WILLIAM CONWAY   January Session 1802

To son, Christopher, 130 acres at mouth of Lick Creek, running up the river. To son, William, land on river. To son, Henry, land below Whites Ford on Lick Creek. Son: James. Daughter: Molly. Wife: Jane. Grandson: William Hogan. Dated: 4 June 1801. Executors: Sons, William, Henry and Christopher. Witnesses: Robert Rodgers, David Proffitt.

Signed: William Conway

EDMUND CRUMP   October 1801

Sons: Isaac, Benjamin, Edmond. To daughter, Margaret, a feather bed. To daughter, Nancy, cow and calf, a feather bed. Till Nancy gets well. Till Edmond comes of age. Dated: 9 September 1801. Witnesses: Edmund Strange, Richard Huges, John Bell.

his

Signed: Edmond X Crump

mark

ABRAHAM CROSSWHITE   6 December 1801

Wife: Mevy (Mary?). Children: John, George, Sary Moser, Milly Wheeler, Lucy McRunnels (McReynolds?), Polly Fillips. French ___lber? John Slaughter to be paid $1.00. Executors: Wife ___, Joseph Porter, John Carder. Witnesses: Samuel Gragg, Joseph Porter, Elizabeth Porter.

Signed: Abraham Crosswhite

WILLIAM CRAWFORD   27 July 1803

Wife: Margaret. To daughter, Eliner, two cows when she is in need. To son, Samuel, one dollar. Children: Eliner, John, James, Samuel, William. Sons-in-law: Hamilton Neal, Robert Benham? Dated: 23 March 1803. Executors: Margaret Crawford, Cornelius Newman. Witnesses: John Woolsey, Shadrach Morris, Allen McDonald.

Signed: William X Crawford

JOHN CLUTS (CLOTS ?)   2 April 1804

Wife: Christina. To son, David, one horse beast worth 25 pounds. Other children. Executors: Robert Guin, Giles Parman Esqr. Dated: 28 November 1803. Witnesses: Thomas Peel ?, Hugh Wilson.

Signed: John X Cluts

SUSANNA CROSBY

To daughter, Anne Jackson, negro girl Hannah. To daughter, Lydda Davis, negro woman Lucy. Children: Anne Jackson, Lydda Davis, George, Thomas, William, Susannah VanPelt, Frances Murray, Sally Davis, Elizabeth Crosby, Mary Briant, Peggy Crosby, Rebeckah Smith, Nancy and Jane Crosby. Negros to be appraised and then divided. Executors: George Crosby, James Guthrie, James Hays. Dated: June 14, 1806. Witnesses: John Glascock, Phillip Rader, Rebeccah Rader.

Signed: Susanna Crosby

MATTHEW COX   23 February 1807

Wife: Ann. Children: Leah, Ann, William, son Eliakim, Samuel, Gene, daughter Mehalah. William has received 18 pounds, seven shillings more than the others. Executors: Daniel Carter, William Cox, James Goodin. Witnesses: Isaac Armitage, John X Ross, William Jones.

Signed: Matthew Cox

JOHN CARDER

Wife, Dorcas, to have everything to freehold as she wishes, until she remarries, or at her death all to be equally divided between all my children. Executors: Dorcas Carder, Amace Harold. Dated: 14 May 1809. Witnesses: David Snodgrass, William Jolly, John Jacques.

Signed: John X Carder

LEVY (LEVI?) CARTER

Wife: Susanna. Sons, Joseph and Elijah to receive nothing until all the rest of my children get $60.00. Witnesses: David Key, William James. Dated: 5 December 1809. Christopher Kerby.

Signed: Levy Carter

ZACHARIAH CASTEEL   October Session 1821
Wife, Elizabeth, to have unmolested use of my plantation during her
natural life or widowhood. Children: John, Peter, Edward, David,
Jeremiah, Rachel Melone, Naomi Acres, Marjey Melone, Ruth Brown, Mary
Casteel, Marget Casteel. Executor: David Key. Dated: 26 April 1811.
Witnesses: Peter Casteel, Zachariah X Melone.
                         Signed: Zachariah Casteel

WILLIAM CROSBY   27 October 1817
Wife: Elizabeth. All my children. Executors: Wife, Elizabeth, George
Crosby, Coleman Smith, James Landrum. Dated: 6 September 1817.
Witnesses: Thomas L. Hale, John Smith, Jonathan Davis.
                         Signed: William Crosby

WILLIAM CLEMONS   1785
County of Greene, State of North Carolina
To Ruth, my wife, 5 shillings. To Mary, my daughter, all monies and cow
and calf due me from Joshua Gest. Executor: Shadrach McNew. Witnesses:
Robert Orr, Henry Willis, Abraham Hunt.
                         Signed: William X Clemons

FRANCES DELANEY   1784
Greene County, State of North Carolina
To wife, Agnes, all property, horses, hogs, debts and movable effects.
Children: John D., Mary, James, Jane, Daniel, Agnes. Executors: sons,
John, James. Witnesses: Philemon ____?, Henry X Hough, John Delaney.
                         Signed: XXXMarks ? Delaney

JAMES DELANEY   1784   Greene County, State of North Carolina
To wife, Elizabeth, and her heirs and assigns forever everything inc
puter and holloware. Three daughters: Margaret, Jane, Sarah, lawful
begotten heirs. Executors: Wife, Elizabeth, Jacob Smelser of Greene
Co. North Carolina. Dated: 8 October 1784. Witnesses: Anne Yoham ?,
Mary Mekenney, Joseph (Hind ?).
                         Signed: James X Delaney

ADAM DUNWOODY   1794
Greene County, Washington District, South of Ohio
To wife, Esther, land in Knox County on Clinch River. Children: Ester,
Margaret, James, Billy. To James - land on Big Limestone in Washington
County. To Billy - land in Washington and Greene County. Children to
be educated in a gentle manner. If negro, Cuff, behaves himself, he
shall have his freedom after 1 year. Executors: James Montgomery Senr.,
James Dunwoody, Thomas McMackin. Dated: 11 June 1794. Witnesses: Samuel
Dunwoody, Thomas Rogers.
                         Signed: Adam Dunwoody

CHARLES DOTSON   August Sessions 1797
Wife, Mary, to have a childs part. Children: Edmon, Oldest son John,
Moses, Charles, Jemima Dotson, Marthew Roberts, Sarah Coile, Rebecca,
Catrine, Elizabeth, Rivn ??. To daughters, cow and calf each. To son,
Moses, 10 pound good money. Grandson: Daniel Dotson. Twe hundred acres
of land in Richmond County, State of Old Virginia, to son, John, and 10
pounds lawful money. Dated 21 June 1797. Witnesses: Thomas McMackin,
Ezekiel Frazier.
                         Signed: Charles Dotson (his mark)

JAMES DINWIDDIE
To wife, Isabel, a gentel living. Sons and Daughters: 4 children: Thomas
and Mary Carson, Robert and Elizabeth Rankin, David and Jean B. Rankin,
Valentine and Agnes Seveyor (Sevier). Grand-daughter: Ann Dinwiddie
Wilson. Land in Campbell County, Virginia. All children to have negros.
Executors: Robert Rankin, Valentine Seveyor. Dated: April 19, 1800.
Witnesses: James Dinwiddie Jr., Mical Burgar, Samuel Ray.
                         Signed: James Dinwiddie

JAMES ONEAL DALEY 5 December 1839
Wife, Nancy, to have 1/3, her children an equal share. Executors: Sons,
John and Hiram Daley. Dated: 8 April 1820. Witnesses: Patrick Anderson,
Catharine Daily.

Signed: James O. Daily

JOHN DELANEY July Sessions 1823
Children: Anna Davis, Elizabeth Paulsell, John, Easter decd., Margaret
decd. (her daughters, Pegg and Ruth), David, Jacob, Sarah Gann, (her
daughters, Jennie, Pamelia), Isaac, Ruth Gann, Jinny Kennedy (her
daughters, Emeline and Maria), Daniel, Wesley. Twenty dollars to
Methodist Preaching, $2.00 per year for 10 years. Executors: Sons, John,
David, Jacob, Isaac, Daniel and Wesley Delaney. Dated: 22 June 1822.
Witnesses: Thomas Doan, Gravener Marsh Junr., William Stanfield.

Signed: John Delaney

JESSE DAVIS April Sessions 1823
To wife, Sarah, plantation I purchased from William Ford and the entrys
I made to it. Also negroes Cesar and Mary, when they are 21 years old,
they are to have 2 good suits and set at liberty to be forever free.
Children: Betsey Davis, Fields Davis, John, Jesse, Thomas, Hannah, Nancy,
Samuel Davis. Mother: Sarah. Negroes to learn a trade and be set free
at 25 years. Negro men to learn blacksmithing. Executors: James Jones,
Hugh Carter. Dated: 16 April 1823. Witnesses: Henry Yeakley Junr.,
Isaiah Jones, James Jones.

Signed: Jesse Davis

THOMAS DAVIS October Sessions 1826
Son, John, to have land south side dry fork of Camp Creek, granted
September 20, 1789 - 200 acres. Son, James H., is to have another grant
given 12 January 1793 - 200 acres. Children: William, John, James H.,
Nancy Hickson, Patience Kennedy, Polly Alexander, Betty Dyke, Sally B.
Holland. Executors: Son, James H. Davis, Jacob Dyke. Witnesses: Stephen
Brooks, Archibald McAfee.

Signed: Thomas Davis

SAMUEL DUNWOODY July 1827
To wife, Marthen, as long as she bears my name. Children: Peggy Beard,
William, Adam, Esther McSpaddin, Polly, Ibby, Anny Ervin. To Peggy Beard,
$10 when Ann is sold. To son, William, 200 acres land. To son, Adam,
200 acres land. To daughter, Esther, $50.00. To daughters, Polly, Ibby
and Anny Ervin, all movable property. Son, P. W. McClean, to have land
on Delaney's Branch. Executors: Two sons, William and P. W. McClean.
Dated: 15 August 1827??? Witnesses: Lofton Sherril, Adam Dunwoody.

Signed: Samuel Dunwoody

JOHN DODD SR. 2 August 1847
Wife: Sarah (formerly Sarah Stonecypher G.F.B.). Son, Thomas, to care
for my sife, and have all land and possessions. Son: John. Each lawful
heir to have $1.00. Executors: Thomas Dodd, James White. Dated: 4
February 1843. Witnesses: Israel Olinger, Phillip Keller.

Signed: John Dodd

ALEXANDER ERWIN 1789
Wife: Rachel. Children: Samuel, George, James, William, John, Nathaniel,
Rachel, Margaret. To son, Samuel, a horse. To son, George, a horse. To
sons, William and John, land where I now live. To son, Nathaniel, land
in the Cove. To daughters, Rachel and Margaret, featherbeds. Dated: 16
October 1789. Executors: _____. Witnesses: David Eagleton, David
Caldwell, James Gillaspy.

Signed: Alexander Ewing

THOMAS ELLIS   4 March 1861   Of Berkley County, Virginia
Wife: Rebecca Jane. Children: Barberry, Nancy Ann, Rebecca Jane, Mary
Matilda, Elizabeth. Son-in-law, Obediah M. Wright, guardian. David
Ellis, my brother, guardian. Executor: Wiley Campbell. Dated: 23
November 1860. Witnesses: James McCollum, Jacob F. Morrison.
                         Signed: Thomas Ellis

ANDREW ENGLISH, son of John English   1795   Greene County
South of Ohio.   Wife, Agnes, full and free use of all property.
Children: John, Thomas. Executors: Wife, Agnes, father-in-law, Thomas
Robison. Dated: 11 March 1797. Witnesses: Andrew English Senr., James
Beaty.   Signed: Andrew English

THOMAS ELLIS   1788
Of Berkley County, State of Virginia
Wife: Magdalena, to have 1/3 entire estate. Children: Rowland, Susannah,
John, Thomas. To Rowland, 10 pounds money of Pennsylvania. To Susannah,
5 pounds like money. To John and Thomas, remainder of my estate, each to
pay his sister 3 pounds. Executors: Sons, John and Thomas. Dated: 17
October 1788. Witnesses: John Cameron, William Frymysion??
                         Signed: Thomas Ellis

JAMES ENGLISH   25 April 1804
To Son, Andrew, plantation he and I now live on, also my still by his
paying each of his brothers-in-law $10. To Michael Rawlings, land on
Clinch River. To Son-in-laws, Phillip Cole and William Finley, thirty
pounds appraisement. Executors: Son, Andrew English, son-in-law, Michael
Rawlings. Witnesses: John Woolsey, John Robertson. Dated: 10 March 1802.
                         Signed: James English

HENRY EARNEST SENR.   to Col. Henry Earnest   22 May 1809
Children: Betsy Evans, Mary Wells, Sarah Warren, Rebecca and Levina
Earnest, Peter. Wife, Mary, to have back room of my dwelling house. To
Betsy Evans, 33 and 1/3 dollars. To Mary Wells, 33 and 1/3 dollars. To
Sarah Warren, 33 and 1/3 dollars. To Rebecca and Levina, 33 and 1/3
dollars, bedding, cow and calf. To son, Peter, land on Nolichucky River.
Son, Peter, to care for my wife, Mary. To Grandson, Henry Brooks, a
horse. To Grand-daughter, Polly Brooks, a cow and calf. Executors:
Felix and Henry Earnest Junr. Dated: 25 February 1803. Witnesses:
Thomas Doan, Jacob Reese, Ezekiel X Stanberry.
                         Signed: Henry Earnest

ANDREW ENGLISH SENR.   27 January 1818
To Wife, Sarah, her clothes and bed clothes she has made since living
with me, $300 and plantation, $25 per year. To Son, Alexander, 300 acres
land. To Daughter, Mary Robison, $25 per year. To Mary's son, Joseph
Robison, pair of overalls. To Children of daughter, Elizabeth Walker
decd., $200. To Children of son, Andrew decd., $50. To Children of son,
John English, $50. To Rody Kinkade, $200. Dated: 15 December 1817.
Witnesses: Samuel Caldwell, John Robertson, Rody English, Alexander
English.   Signed: Andrew English

PHILLIP EVERETT   1 April 1850   Bond $200.00
Wife: Margaret. Sole Executrix: Wife, Margaret. Dated: 27 January 1838.
Witnesses: G. Wells, Michael Fillers.
                         Signed: Phillip X Everett

FELIX EARNEST   4 July 1842
Wife, Sarah, to have everything as long as she is my widow. At wife's
death all land to sons, personal property to daughters. Children: James,
Thomas, Lewis, Benjamin, McKendree and Harvey. To Son, Henry's lawful
children, $1 each (Henry decd.). All my daughters. Executors: James
Oliphant, Henry Earnest Senr. Dated: 23 July 1838. Witnesses: A. G.
Fellers, T. W. Earnest.
                         Signed: Felix X Earnest

JOHN FRESHOUR SENR.   2 March 1801
Wife, Eave, to have everything as a widow. To Daughters, Mary, Susannah,
Margaret, 8 pounds apiece. To Daughter, Elizabeth Rader, land, but dont
give it to Peter Rader but he settel on it his lifetime. To Sons, George
and John, land adjoining Hutchison. To Son, Jacob, 60 pounds. Other
children: Eve Stephens, Catrin Winters, Magdalene Foute, Mary Freshour.
Executors: Wife, Eve, John Freshour, Joseph Winters. Witnesses: John
Lescollet, Zogren Grag??, Giles Parman.   his
                         Signed: John X Froushour
                                         mark

ANDREW FOX   28 November 1819
To Wife, Sary, home place as a widow. Sons: Andrew, Henry, Lewis, Jesse,
Jacob, Ezekiel, James, Isaac. Daughters: Elizabeth Howel, Nancy Johnston,
Polley Broyles. To Son, Andrew, land adjoining Barnhart. To Son, Henry,
land next to river. To son, Lewis, a horse. Remainder to be divided
between all children. Executor: Henry Earnest Senr. Dated: 28 November
1819. Witnesses: Daniel Guin, Abraham Gfellers.
                         Signed: Andrew Fox

MICHAEL FRAKER   January Sessions 1822
Wife, Margaret, to live with son, Adam. Children: John, Adam, Frederick,
Rebeccah Smith, wife of Henry Smith. Their Children: John and Michael
Smith. Son-in-law: Ninsy Hare. Each of my children to receive $1.
Settlement with my children made 20 August 1813 shall stand. Executor:
Sons, John and Adam. Dated: 9 October 1821. Witnesses: Robinson Loyd,
Thomas Loyd, Jacob Reaves.
                         Signed: Michael Freiker

HENRY A. FARNSWORTH
Wife: May. One third money put on interest for wife. Brother, Samuel,
to get 1/3. Sister, Martha Johnson, to receive interest on other third.
Sisters: Jane Bell, Margaret Alexander, wife of George Alexander.
Executor: Robert A. Crawford. Dated: 12 June 1859. Witnesses: A. R.
Anderson, Phillip Willet. At wife's death, negro Hannah and her children
to be sold.
                         Signed: Henry A. Farnsworth

DAVID GAMMEL (GAMBLE)   10 October 1801
Greene County, District of U.S.
Son: Hughey. Daughters: Jean, Mary, Elizabeth, to get bedding and house-
hold furniture. All rest to be divided equally between 4 children.
Executors: John Blair, David Rankin, Overseer. Witnesses: James
Galbreath, James Pennington, William McClis??
                         Signed: David Gammel   1790

ROBERT GAMBLE   Greene County, North Carolina
To Wife, Elizabeth, one third. Children: Sarah, William, John, Robert,
Andrew, Elizabeth. Executors: Wife, Elizabeth, William Wilson. Wit-
nesses: Joseph Bogel, George Temple. Dated: May 22, 1784.
                         Signed: Robert Gamble

ROBERT GRAGG   1793
Greene County, Tennessee, South of the River Ohio.
Children: John S. William Gragg, Abigail Gragg, Betsey Gragg, Robert,
Samuel, Thomas, Henry. To Son, John S., a horse, cow and calf. To Son,
William, a horse, cow and calf, my rifle gun and shot gun, big pot and
crock. John and William to work together and John make all decissions.
To Daughter, Abigail, ½ her dresses, cow and calf. To Son, Robert, my
Big Bible. To Son, Samuel, my sword, money from Virginia. Sell my stud
horse named Shakespeare for 25 pounds Virginia currency and give money to
daughter, Betsey. Pay Colonel Kelly. Sons: Thomas, Henry, Samuel and
Robert, Benjamin Crow, George Malcom and Joseph McMurtry, an equal share
of all remaining of my estate. Executors: Sons, Samuel and Robert.
Witnesses: Benjamin Crow, Junr., William Wall. Dated: 23 May 1793.
                         Signed: Robert Gragg

ROBERT GRAY   18 October 1797
To Wife, Jane Gray, lifetime estate with house and firewood brought to
door. Children: Youngest son, Edward, John, Sarah Buchanan decd., Mary
Sharp, Jean Gray, Agnes Mesc??, William, Robert. To Son, Edward, land I
now live on. To Son, John, 20 shillings. To Children of daughter Sarah
Buchanan decd., 20 shillings. To Daughters, Mary Sharp and Agnes Mesc??,
20 shillings. To Daughter, Jean Gray, Furniture. To Sons, William and
Robert, 5 pounds. Executors: Sons, William, Robert, Edward. Witnesses:
Abner Gray, M. Collier.   Signed: Robert Gray

HERMANUS GRAY   October Sessions 1798
Wife, Rachel and my children - to receive property equally divided when
children become of age. Executors: Edward Gray, my brother; Henry Cain.
Witnesses: Benjamin Williams, Jacob Gray, John Thorleton.
                                   Signed: Hermanus Gray

ABSALOM GRAY   April 1802
To Wife, Mary Gray, all real and personal property. Grand-daughter, Mary,
daughter of son John, to have everything at wife's decease. Executors:
Wife, Mary Gray, Jacob Gray. Witnesses: Isaac Conlee, John and Isaac
Conlee. Dated: 22 January 1799.
                                   Signed: Absalom Gray

JACOB GASS
To Wife Mary, 113 acre plantation to have and to hold 11 years, 4 months,
13 days. Also still and vessels. At her death to William for 9 years,
5 months, 17 days, then divided equally with Jacob. Wife, Mary, now with
child, if child is a boy, still to be his. To Daughter, Jane, one
spinning wheel. To Daughter, Margaret, black cow and calf. Children:
William, Jacob, Jane, Margaret, Sarah, Susanna. Children not to be bound
out. Mother: Mary Gass. Executors: Brothers, John and James Gass.
Witnesses: John McCurry, John Eason, William McCage. Dated: 18 June 1799.
                                   Signed: Jacob Gass

DANIEL GUIN   26 July 1803
Daniel McDonald Guin, son of brother Robert Guin, to have all my estate.
Sister, Jane Guin, to have $100. Executor: Brother, Robert Guin.
Witnesses: Robert Jameson, Even Evens, John Eason. Dated: July 16, 1803.
                                   Signed: Daniel X Guin

YOUST GERG (GEORGE)   19 February 1804
    I, Youst Gerg of Greene Co., Tenn., I am very sick of body.....I give
to my beloved wife, Catharine, during her lifetime and the time of her
widowhood (he mentions rye, wheat, corn, pork, fat, salt, and flax), one
pair of new shoes and the mending and half-soals...1 cow and the food for
the cow of 1 acre of meadow, but my son hereafter mentioned is to mow
and make it and haul it home for her in the stable...1 gallon of whiskey
and $1 for pounds of good wool...and she shall have the privilege of the
new dwelling house, the lower or the upper room which she shall choose
the best, and the   of the springhouse...(other household items and a
horse and saddle are mentioned) to my sons John Gerge and William Gerge,
my plantation which contains 218 acres to be equally divided amongst
them. The old plantation where the new house is and all the buildings to
my son, John Gerge. John is to pay yearly 25# in good trade until he has
paid the amount of 200# and the other   I give to my son William....
Son William to pay, after he arrives to his lawful age, 100# that is to
say in five years. Yearly 20# in good trade (he mentions farming equip-
ment, cattle, etc. to the two sons)...after the house and barn are
finished, the remainder of   shall be equally divided as follows:
the 200# amongst seven children namely, Margaret, wife of John Crum,
Elizabeth, the wife of Emanuel Parman, Catharine, the wife of Jacob
Fellow, Julianne Gerge, Salome Gerge, Eva Gerge and Michael Gerge. After
my wife's death, her clothes to be given to my daughter Eva...Executors:
Balzar Floag, Martin Lintz. Witnesses: Charles Smith, Michael Gerdner,
John Crum.

                              Signed: Youst Gerge
German for George (Yarrick)   (Signed in German)

DAVID GIRDNER   Weak in body, sound in memory.
To lawful wife, Rachel, all personal estate, rent and income coming from
Robert Gregory for plantation I now live on. To Son, Michael, $4 from
farm. To Oldest Daughter, Catharine Love, $166 1/3 from money due from
Robert Gregory. To Children of 2nd daughter, Christina Cluts decd.,
$2.00. Executor: Stephen Brooks. Witnesses: William Hall, Sarah X Hall.
Dated 3 October 1809.   Signed: David X Girdner

JAMES GUIN   July 1824
Wife: _____. Children: John, Evans, James, Elizabeth. To Sons, John and
Evans, I have made an obligation - 30 acres adjoining Adam Ely, 10 acres
to John, 20 acres to Evans. To Son, James, all land between Martha Glass
and above tract to John and best pair of oxen. To Elizabeth's daughter,
Ede, my wife's part at her death. To Elizabeth's son, Harvey, one years
schooling. Executor: Son, John. Witnesses: Nathaniel Magill, Joseph
E. Bell, Jacob Albricht?? Dated: 28 May 1819.
                     Signed: James Guin

SARAH HAWKINS (FORMERLY SARAH BABB)
To Oldest son, A. C. Babb, all bee hives I die posessed of. To Oldest
daughter, Margaret J. Brooks, wife of W. P. Brooks, clock, cooking stove
and safe. To Daughter, Martha A. Babb, bureau, full leaf table and bed.
To Youngest daughter, Sarah E. Babb, Father's estate, table, bed and cow.
Former husband, Samuel Babb - divorced, not to be allowed anything.
Executor: S. R. Brooks. Witnesses: Thomas Broyles, Ja? eb Brooks.
Dated: 8 December 1885.   Signed: Sarah Babb

EDMUND HENDRIX   7 May 1866 $1,000
To Mother, Judith Hendrix, my farm I live on and 1 years support. Two
sons, N. J. E. Hendrix and Ely E. Hendrix, to receive equally all money.
Executor: William Morelock. Witnesses: Charles Bright, David W. Bright.
Dated: 12 April 1866.   Signed: Edmund Hendrix

WILLIAM HOUSTON SENR. (Rev. Soldier GFB)
Funeral expenses and debts to be paid.
To daughter, Polly, $1000 due me on note of George W. Foute, Cain Broyle
and Alfred Hunter, now in hands of Joseph Houston - to be invested in
land. To Elizabeth, wife of son Howell, $1400 note on money loaned him
and $600 interest to be paid her in 1 year after my decease to guardian
Stephen Huff, then $150 per year with other monies I might give. To
daughter, Orphy, servants Lydia and Amanda, $1490 which I loaned her
husband, Joseph Horton, to pay for Foute Possession which he bought at
auction May 1841.
To son, William, 200 acres land belonging to my father, James Houston
decd., and a portion of 80 acres granted me by State of Tennessee, 50
acres land farmed by McCoys, 31 acre tract I purchased of Capt. John
Parmons?. To William, my red bird sorrel mare and if he lets the
Brumfield or Wills set use mare, she is to be sold and money equally
divided between my heirs.
To son, Warren, 294 acres and 106 acres granted me by State of Tennessee
and another 20 acres grant on both sides Cove Creek. Servant, Dicey, to
be set free. Warren to have interest in Paint Mountain Turnpike and
$150 to paint my dwelling and finishing barn. No one to own servant,
Iram, except Jacob Stephens, who owns his wife.
Executors: George Jones merchant in Greeneville and Joseph Horton.
Witnesses: John A. Park, Jacob Stephens. Dated: 5 June 1841.
                   Signed: William X Houston

JOHN HENDERSON   Probated 23 June 1826
Executors: Son John, son-in-law Merryman Payne.
To daughter Elizabeth Chapman, slave Lucy and her increase, at Elizabeth's
death Lucy to go to grandson, John Chapman. To son, Samuel, 45 acres
adjoining George Masoner and formerly to Jno. Wilson. To daughter, Jean
wife of William Kilgore, $500 as she needs it. To daughter, Lide, wife
of John Kilgore, $500 as she needs, if not used to go for support of her
son, Thomas Kilgore. To daughter, Sarah Hall, wife of William Hall. To
daughter, Mary, wife of Jacob Rinehart, 67 acres - then to her son John

Rinehart. To daughter, Dorcas, wife of Merryman Payne, my negro boys
Tom and Need. To son, John, 800 acres I purchased from Benjamin Armstrong
and George Gordon. To daughter, Charlotte, wife of Henry Hennegar, 100
acre plantation I purchased of Anderson Walker and 30 acres of Samuel
Walker. To daughter Bathsheba, wife of Joseph Craigmiles, their sons,
William and Pleasant Craigmiles, two negroes. To daughter, Abigail, wife
of William Grant, all land deeded me by George Gordon adjoining Busler
Nelson, also negro boy Manners. William Kilgore, son of James, to learn
to read at an English school, rite and cifer thru rule of 3 at expense of
my estate. Test: Peter X Masoner, John H. Kilgore, Samuel Kelly.
Dated: 7 August 1824.   Signed: John Henderson

ABSALOM HAWORTH   22 January 1827 $3,000
Personal property to be sold and proceeds divided equally to wife and
six daughters. Land in County to 5 sons. Wife, Mary, to live on tract
going to Howard. Wife: Mary. Six Daughters: Rachel Haworth, Elizabeth
Davis, Mary Doan, Sarah Buler, Hannah White, Anna Haworth. To Oldest
son, Absalom, land conveyed to me 19 October 1791, by William Morrow,
southside of the Nolichuckey River. To Second son, Nathaniel, Third son,
West, Silas and Howard - land granted to me by North Carolina, Grant No.
989, 26 December 1791. Sons Absalom, Nathaniel and West Haworth to pay
my 6 daughters $100 each. Executors: James Jones (sawyer), Henry Earnest
Senr., Washington Henshaw. Dated: 16 September 1823. Witnesses: V.
Sevier, M. Payne.   Signed: Absalom Haworth

ROBERT HOOD   1784
All property to remain as is until youngest child is 21 or Elizabeth
remarries. Wife: Elizabeth. Children: Nathaniel, John, William, Mary,
Sarah, Jinnet Hood. Executors: Anthony Moore, David Coplin (Copeland)
Dated: September 5, 1784. Witnesses: James Tate, Andrew McPheron,
Jo____??   Signed: Robert Hood

DAVID HOPKINS   November 1789
Wife: Agnes. Children: Mary, Ann, Rebecca, Mary White, to receive a mare
and her increase. Neighbor: William Bigham. Witnesses: George Hopkins,
John Craig.   Signed: David Hopkins

JAMES HENDERSON   Incomplete, part of page torn off.
Sick and weak in body but perfect mind and memory.
To Wife, Hannah, one bay horse 4 years old. To son, John A. Brown, over-
coat, saddle and gun. Executors: Samuel Henderson, Samuel McEmmy (McAmey
GFB). Witnesses: John Gilliland Senr., Jno. McFarland Junr. Dated: 15
August 1793.   Signed: James Henderson

JEREMIAH HARRISON   15 September 1793
Of Greene County, Southwest Territory
Wife, Catharine, to receive all my worldly property as long as her
mortal life and at her death to be equally divided between these children.
Children: Esther, Nehemiah, Josiah, Mary, Elenor, Abigail, Amos, Jane,
Elizabeth, Isaiah, Bathsheba, Margaret, Ruth and Grace Harrison.
Executors: Son, Isaiah Harrison, Samuel _arored?? Witnesses: George
Green, William Wallace, Abel Richardson.
                    Signed: Jeremiah Harrison

JOHN HUGHES   7 July 1795
Greene County - Territory South of the River Ohio
Wife, Sarah, and son, Aaron, to receive all my estate her lifetime, then
to him. Executor: Daniel Kennedy. Witnesses: Dan Kennedy, John
McDonald.   Signed: John J. Hughes

JOHN HOPTON   1796 September 5
To my oldest son, John, 10 shillings for his birthright. Five pounds to
Methodist Church. Remainder of estate to be divided between children:
John, Stephen, Abner, Enoch, Aron, Mary Border, Ann Boyd. Executor:
Adonijah Morgan Esq. Witnesses: Dan Kennedy, Lewis H. Morgan, Jeremiah
Laney.   Signed: John Hopton

REBECCA HAY
To brother, John Robinson, 10 shillings to buy a good book; his sons,
Alexander - Dr. Watts Psalms and Laws; and John - Gospel Sonnets. To
children of sister, Jennet Nelson decd., her son David - Bostons Fourfold
Slate; and her son John - one large Bible. To sister, Hannah Robinson,
A Dead Faith Anatomized, 2 blankets and silk hankerchief; her daughters,
Hannah - one fan; and Sarah - one pair silver sleeve buttons. To sister,
Mary Hutson, one good cap and silk hankerchief. To Rachel Kerr, daughter
of James Kerr, my brother-in-law, (cant read). To Hannah Kerr, tin
kettle. To Sarah Kerr, furniture and chest. To Rebecca Robinson, all
my body clothes. To Sarah Robinson, side saddle. Reuben Hay Nelson, son
of sister Jennet. David and Mitchell Robinson - brother John's youngest
sons. Rebecca Hay and Sarah Robinson Nelson - daughters of sister Jennet.
Isabel Kerr, daughter of sister Hannah. Executors: James Kerr, Samuel
Robinson. Dated: 13 March 1797. Witnesses: William Bell, William
Hutson X his mark.   Signed: Rebecca *R* Hay
                                                 her\mark

JOHN HAWOOD SENR.
To Wife, Hannah, 100 acres land with improvements and orchard. To two
youngest daughters, Patty and Johanna, 100 acres. Executors: Wife,
Hannah, daughter Joanna. Dated: 12 August 1797. Witnesses: Andrew
English, John Woolsey, Elizabeth English.
                                Signed: John Hawood Senr.

JAMES HUTCHISON   April 1800
Wife, Elizabeth, to have everything, if she remarries only a childs part.
All my children, not named, to have reasonable education. Executors:
Wife, Elizabeth, John Gragg. Dated: 21 September 1798. Witnesses:
Benjamin Craig, Thomas Hutchison. Signed: James Hutchison

JOHN HARMON   1798
John Harmon now of Tennessee, late of Pennsylvania.
To Jacob Misemer, a wagon and gears, 150 pounds due me in Pennsylvania.
Executor: Jacob Misemer. Dated: 26 December 1798. Witnesses: William
Wilson, Henry Miller, Adam Miller.
                          Signed: John Harmon
                          (Signed in German)

JOHN HARMON, late of Pennsylvania, now of Tennessee.   1837
Children: Peter Harmon, his sons John and William; Benjamin, his son
James, daughter Nancy. Three sons: John, Peter, Jacob Harmon. Daughters:
Milly Brown, Margaret Reynolds. Executors: Thomas S. Arnold, Charles
Gass. Dated: 16 November 1837. Witnesses: Elim Carter, William C.
Carter. On Bond: my old friend, Major John Harmon - Thomas D. Arnold.
                          Signed: John Harmon

JOSEPH HIXSON
To Wife, Susannah, all lands, negros, stocks, household furniture.
Children: Andrew, William, Timothy, Joseph, Ephraim, John, Susannah
Davis, Benjamin, James. To sons, Joseph and John, 70 acres. To son,
Benjamin, negro boy Abraham. To son, James, negro girl Nance.
Executors: Wife, Susanna, Sons, Joseph and Ephraim. Dated: 26 November
1803. Witnesses: Alex Prethero, Green X Right, Thomas Prather.
                          Signed: Joseph Hixson

JAMES HENRY   28 April 1834 $1,000 Bond
Children: Nathaniel M. Henry, all my children. Executors: Loving Wife,
son, Nathaniel. Dated: 3 February 1833. Witnesses: M. Love, James Guin,
____?____ (in German)   Signed: James Henry

WILLIAM HANKINS SENR.   25 April 1821
To Wife, Hinness, one small spinning wheel, others - note on John Newman,
bed and bedding, six chairs, 3 pots, 2 chests, 1 table, firedogs etc. she
brought when I married her. To eldest daughter, Mary Callahan, 85 cents.
To daughters, Isabella Martin, Euphamy Neely and Jenny Hankins, 84 cents

each. To sons, William and John E. Hankins, 200 acres I now live on purchased of Joshua Kidwell. To daughters, Peggy, Polly and Betsey Hankins, all my moveable property. Executors: William and John E. Hankins, Joshua Kidwell. Dated: 23 October 1811. Witnesses: William Jackson, Margaret M. Jackson (in Blount Co. - aged)

Signed: William Hankins

PHILIP HALE   January Sessions 1820
To Wife, Catharine, I give everything moveable and portion of land to Patrick Henry Hale inc dwelling her lifetime, childs part of negroes. Children: Patrick Henry Hale, George Hale, Hugh Douglas Hale, Joseph Hale, Phillip S. Hale (a minor), Thomas S. Hale, Sarah Neilson, Eliza D. Keith, Catharine D. Hale. To son, George Hale, land in Knox County. Other boys to have land on both sides Nolichucky in Greene County, 750 acres. Daughters to have all other property. Executors: Wife, Catharine, son, George. Dated: 22 April 1814. Witnesses: Colman Smith, Joseph H. Neilson.

Signed: Phillip Hale

JAMES HAYS
To Wife, Rachel, household furniture, horse, saddle, bridle, cow and 2 sheep. At her death all to be equally divided between children. Children: George Hays, Isabel Newman, Mary Lawson, James, Alexander, Sarah Roddy??, Nancy Hartley, William Hays, Jean Brandon. Dated: 31 May 1816. Witness: Simon Pope.   Signed: James X Hays

his mark

JAMES HOUSTON   24 September 1820 $5,000
I give to Hannah Baker, John Houston, William Houston and John Horton, all property except what I shall otherwise give. To George Jones, one negro boy named Marshall and no more. To Absalom Houston, one negro girl, Tildey, and one negro boy, Mitchell, and no more. To Polly Russell, mulatto girl named Jane. To grand-daughter, Rebecca Russell, daughter of Polly, horse, saddle and bridle. Executors: William Houston, John Horton. Dated: 18 April 1820. Witnesses: Andrew Patterson, Joseph Horton, John Freshour Senr., Frederick Cutshall.

Signed: James Houston

JAMES HENRY   13 June 1806
To son, Robert, my plantation with all profits. To sons, James and John, $70 each to be paid by Robert in Trade. To daughter, Elizabeth Shields, $40. To daughters, Agnes Nelson, Mary Nelson and Margaret Cochran, $30 each. To grand-daughter, Polly Nelson, daughter to Joe Nelson, my brindle cow. Debts due me by David and Thomas Watson. Executors: Robert Henry of Greene County, and Col. John Blair of Washington County. Dated: 13 June 1806. Teste: James Dinwiddie, William Kelley, Jonathan Naff.

Signed: James X Henry

DAVID HOLT   (Revolutionary Soldier GFB)
To Wife, Isabella, my present wife and I agreed that at death neither of us would claim anything except what we had before marriage, but I want money I borrowed of her repaid without interest. To daughter, Lucy, wife of Seyburn Jewel, land where they live. To daughter, Sally, bed, chest and bureau. To daughter, Polly, furniture. To son, Joseph, bed and furniture, $100 a year until everything settled. To daughter, Nancy, a cow. To sons, John P. and David R., a cow each. Nancy is the wife of Anthony Moore. Daughter, Elizabeth (not capable), in care of Sally. Executors: My son, Joseph Holt, David Rice. Written: 16 December 1836. Witnesses: Henry A. Farnsworth, James M. Wright, John M. Clawson.

Signed: David Holt

JAMES JOHNSON   Territory South of Ohio   1791
To Wife, Margaret (formerly Denison GFB), personal estate during her widowhood. To son, Thomas, the plantation where I now live. Executors: Wife, Margaret, Alexander Prethero. Written: 24 January 1791. Witnesses: Dan Kennedy, Shad X McNew, George X McNew.

Signed: James X Johnson

THOMAS JOHNSTON
To Wife, Elender, all real and personal property. Children: Mary, John, Sarah. Executors: Wife, Elender, Thomas Collier. Written: 9 August 1806. Witnesses: David Hays, Robert Hays, John Collier.
                              Signed: Thomas X Johnston

JOHN JONES   26 April 1819 $1,000
To Wife, Jane, 1/3 estate. To sons, Phineas, Thomas and James, land at Jane's death. To daughters, Susanna Reese, Deborah Pickering, Mary Thompson, Hannah Robertson and Rachel McCollum, personal property at Jane's death. Executors: Wife, Jane, son, Phineas. Written: 12 February 1819. Witnesses: John Mauris, Michael Bright.
                              Signed: John Jones

JOSEPH JONES   26 April 1826
To Wife, Joanna, one cow. To son, Samuel, 7 head hogs, 2 cows and calf. To son, Caleb, $2.50. To son, Thomas, $2.50 with one dime more. To son, Joseph Jones, 8 hogs and $2.50. To daughters, Polly Farmer, Susy Casteel, Sara Brumley, Anna Jones and Elizabeth Jones, $2.50 each. At Joanna's death, her property to those who take care of the old woman. Executor: Jeremiah Casteel. Written: 20 April 1826. Witnesses: David Kay, Isaac Harmon.   Signed: Joseph X Jones

JAMES JACK   Will contested July 1836
To oldest daughter, Barbary Carret, $10. To Sarah Cogburn, land where she now lives for 20 years, then to John Jack my grandson, son of John Jack my son. To oldest son, Jeremiah Jack, plantation of John and George Vansandt. John Jack and his son James. John's daughters, Margaret and Jeane. John's son John to have Vinzant's Mill Place of 160 acres. Grandson, William, son of John. Sarah Cogburn's gals: Margaret and Sarah. Robert Jack and Samuel Jack, sons of John. Abraham Jack. Great grand-children: Sarah Gibson and Elizabeth Youngblood. Executors: James Jack my grandson, Abraham Jack. Written: January 1829. Witnesses: Joseph Hutchison, John Love, Conrad Girdner, Phillip Henkel.
                              Signed: James Jack
Son James Jack. John Jack to get John Vanzandt tract. Vanzandt Mill Place purchased from George Vanzandt. 7 July 1835 Jeremiah Jack was to appear at Circuit Court daily to answer a charge of ARSON against him. Witnesses: Henry Dyche J.P., J. Dickson.

JOHN JUSTICE   5 March 1855 $500 Bond
To Wife, Thurzene Senr., everything her natural life or widowhood. Children: Richard, James, Mary, Nancy, Martha Justice, John, Alfred and Thurzene. To sons, Richard and James, $500 each. To daughters, Nancy, Martha and Thurzene, everything they claim. To sons, John and Alfred, all my lands. Executor: John Crabtree. Written: 18 July 1854. Witnesses: Henry M. Richards, Barnet Crabtree.
                              Signed: John Justice.

JOHN KIRK
To grand-daughters, Mary and Margaret Kirk, daughters of my son Joseph decd., $100 each. To grandsons, James, John, Henry and Joseph, sons of my son Joseph decd., all my land. To son, John, $50 if he does not bring suit against estate, for $50 I borrowed and paid him and he lost note. To daughter-in-law, Barbara Kirk, widow of Joseph decd., to have where she lives her lifetime. Witnesses: George Crosby, Joseph Davis, Abel Minl g h?? Written: 13 June 1855.
                              Signed: John Kirk

PETER KING   1788   Greene County, State of North Carolina
To sons, Peter and Johnson, land and 20 shillings each. To daughter, Mary, side saddle. To daughter, Sarah, horse and side saddle. To sons, William and Jonathan, land on Flat Creek north side of Holston River. Jonathan also to have $100 and negro, Mary. To son, Benjamin, negro girl, Judith. Daughters, Elizabeth and Rachel. To Wife, Mary, my plantation. Executors: Peter my son, and friend Jones Kendrick.

Witnesses: Edward Hughes, Jones Kendrick, Margaret Kendrick.
Signed: Peter X King
his mark

JAMES KENNEY   23 January 1821 $2,000
To Wife, Rebecca, I gave her or hse has taken $78, 2 feather beds, beds, dresser, plates, teacups, saucers etc., 1½ bushels fruit. All my heirs of lawful age. Land on Flat Creek, north side of Holston River. Executor: Daniel Kenney. Written: 25 September 1820. Witnesses: William Babb, William Maloney, John Maloney.
Signed: James Kenney

CHARLES KILGORE
To Wife, Martha, 2 negro girls, land etc. during her widowhood. Children: William, Mary Culbason, Rebecca Sherl, Martha Walker, John M., Sarah Smith Henderson. To daughter, Mary Culbason, negro named Delilah. To daughter, Martha Walker, 2 negro girls. To son, John, $150. To son, James, one negro and plantation. Son-in-law, Joseph Walker, unreasonably holds negro girl, Philis - Son, William, to use all means to recover her. To daughter, Sarah, negro boy. Executors: Son, John M. Kilgore, John Gragg. Written: 6 June 1822. Witnesses: William Gragg Junr, _____ in German.
Signed: Charles X Kilgore

WILLIAM KESTERSON SENR.   April 1821
To grandson, Henry Kesterson, all my land and improvements (80 acres), if he leaves it goes to William. Sons: William and John Kesterson. To grand-daughter, Nancy, daughter of William, $15. Daughter: Nancy Bowlin. Executor: Son, William. Written: 5 April 1819. Witnesses: Edward Conway, Thomas L. Hale.
Signed: William Kesterson

WILLIAM LESTER   August 1792
To Wife, Jean Lester, 1/3 real estate, all personal property. To son, John, 1/3 land adjoining Joseph White. Sons, William, Joseph and Jennet to have schooling. To daughters, Elizabeth, Isabella and Sarah, 20 pounds, horse and cow each. Executors: Wife, Jean, William White. Written: 5 November 1791. Witnesses: Samuel Moore, Joseph Lester.
Signed: William Lester

MARGARET LARKIN   1795   Widow
Children: James Larkin, Agnes Kennedy, Margaret M. Laughlin, James M. Laughlin, Elizabeth Kennedy. To son, James, an obligation to me and interest. To daughter, Agnes, bedding and wearing apparel. To daughter, Margaret, rest of property. Executors: My brothers, James and Andrew English. Written: 10 March 1795. Witnesses: Robert Crocket, Phillip Cole.
Signed: Margaret Larkin

JAMES LOVE   State of Tenecy, South of the Ohio.
To Wife, Ann Love, ½ property. Children: James Junr., Sarah, Ann. To son, James Junr., land, horse, saddle and bridle. To daughter, Sarah, horse, saddle and bridle. To daughter, Ann, bed and furniture. Executors: Wife, Ann Love, James Brown Senr. Written: 9 October 1796. Witnesses: James Brown Junr., Jonathan Sevier.
Signed: James Love

THOMAS LOVE   23 April 1810
Wife, Dorothea (insane). Children: Mary, wife of George Gordon, William Love, Ann Cravens, Lucy Evens, Frances Evans, 2nd. son Phillip, Martha, Charles, John. To son, William, and daughter, Lucy Evans, $400 each. To son, Charles, and daughter Marth, a portion each. To son, John, land near the Big Spring, adjoining Sheffey. To Ann Cravens, $100. To grand-son, Thomas Evans who is weakly, a negro girl 3 years old. I have confidence in son-in-law, Robert Evans, husband of Lucy, and give Lucy 5 slaves. George Gordon owes me and I have his 5 slaves as security, them to go to his wife, my daughter Mary. Son, Phillip left the state ten years ago, if he shows up he gets an equal part. Pay all my debts. Executors: Sons, William and Charles. Written: 9 April 1810. Witnesses:

16

Merryman Payne, Samuel McKenney, John Sheffer.
                        Signed: Thomas Love.

JAMES LOYD   October 1822
To Wife, Elizabeth, a mare and cow. To son, Thomas, land where I now
live to care for wife Elizabeth. To son, John, 100 acres where he lives.
To daughter Betsey Shields, a cow. To daughter, Peggy McMackin, a $25
saddle. To daughters, Polly, Nelly, Kitty and Sally, a horse, saddle and
bridle each. To son, Abel, 100 acres adjoining Joseph McMackin.
Executors: John Allison, Samuel Kennedy. Written: 4 October 1828.
Witnesses: James, John and Thomas McMackin.
                        Signed: James Loyd

JOHN LAUDERDALE SENR.   22 July 1822, probated $4,000
Wife: Margaret. Children: Rebecca, Charity, Vina, Margaret, Elizabeth
McKeenah, William, Jane Sharp, Robert, Washington, George, Mary Freeman,
Agnes Masoner, Sally Hale, John Lauderdale, Ann Girdner, James, Samuel.
Wife Margaret and daughters, Rebecca, Charity and Vina, to hold land 5
years. Daughter, Margaret is deceased, her part to go to Charity. To
sons, Washington and George, $60 each. Daughter, Mary Freeman, to use
her part herself only. Son, Robert, to have $100 more than the rest.
Executors: John M. Kilgore, William McBride Esq. Written: 9 June 1822.
Witnesses: Henry Thomson, John Russell.
                        Signed: John Lauderdale

MARTIN LINTZ (LINTS)   April 1823 $1,000
To Wife, Elizabeth, land southside of the Camp Creek road. To son,
George, plantation at Elizabeth's death. To sons, Jonathan and Martin,
plantation I bought of William Myers. To son, Abraham, $200. Five
daughters: Polly, Peggy, Sally, ? , ? . To daughter, Sally, a bed, a cow
and a calf. To Polly's daughter, Lavina Girdner, $50. Executors: Son,
Martin, Son-in-law, William Snyder. Written: 12 January 1823.
Witnesses: Emanuel Parman, Michael Fillers.
                        Signed: Martin Lintz

JACOB LINEBAUGH   25 July 1826 $5,000
To son, Daniel, all loose property at my death. Children: John, Jacob,
Catharine Coffman, Elizabeth heafly??, Mary Keller, Rosanna Keller, I
have given them all I intend to give them. To my grandson, Jacob Keller,
son of my daughter Mary Keller, I give an allowance for his own use.
Executors: Son, Jacob Linebaugh, grandson, Jacob Linebaugh, son of Jacob.
Written: 15 April 1826. Witnesses: Daniel Olinger, Barbary Linebaugh.
                        Signed: Jacob Linebaugh
This will was contested by Ben Keller and wife, David Keller and issue.
Suit was made up (compromised).

NANCY LACKLAND   27 October 1826 $200
Children: Ann Lackland and James Lackland, to get all divided equally.
Executors: Ann Lackland, James Lackland. Written: 22 August 1826.
Witnesses: Samuel Brewer, Anny Holt, David Moore.
                        Signed: Nancy Lackland

WILLIAM LANE   3 April 1871 $100.00
Wife: Susan. Children: Abraham Lane, Rebecca White, Mary Dodd, Samuel
Lane, Alexander Lane, William Lane, Jane Starnes. Grand-daughters, Sarah
and Susan Gass. Son, Abraham, to get all real and personal property if
he takes care of me and his mother, Susan. All other heirs to get $1
apiece. Executors: Abraham Lane - his sec. Michael Bright, Alexander
Smith. Written: 14 January 1871. Witnesses: William Crumley, John Ray
Crumley.   Signed: William Lane

SAMUEL MEHAN McAIGHAN (MAYBE McKEEHAN)   11 March 1785
Greene County, Franklin State
To Wife, _____, 1/3 real and personal estate. My three children,
Margaret, James and Mary, to get rest of estate. Money from service to
be saved and used to buy salt and other necessarys. Executors: Wife and

Henry Farnsworth. Witnesses: Benjamin Jameson, James Mkeghan. The whole of my children.   Signed: Samuel McHighen

HUGH McCLUNG   21 October 1786
Greene County, State of Frankland. To Wife, Elizabeth, a sufficient maintenance her lifetime. To son, _____, 10 shillings. To daughter, Sarah, 10 shillings. To daughters, Elizabeth and Susannah, 10 shillings. To my grandson, John Gibson, all my land and tenements. Executors: Wife, Alexander Wilson. Witnesses: Andrew Martin, Alexander Wilson, John Wilson.   Signed: Hugh McClung

WILLIAM MESSEY   2 March 1789   On Little River, Greene County
To James Gillespie Senr., who takes care of me, land on Little River. To James Gillespie Junr., my clothes. Sister: Nancy. Witnesses: David Caldwell, James Ewing, James Gillaspy.
                          Signed: William X Messy

ADAM MORROW   1794
To Wife, Isabel, my whole estate as a widow. Five daughters. Three sons, James, John and Ebenezer, to get land. Executrix: Wife, Isabel. Written: 25 February 1794. Witnesses: James Kerr, William H. Hutson.
                          Signed: Adam Morrow

ENOCH MURRAY   25 July 1799
To Wife, Frankey Murray, everything as a widow. Equal division between all my children (not named). Land in Kentucky. Executors: George Crosby, Thomas Crosby, Wife Frankey. Written: 25 July 1799. Witnesses: Sally Crosby, William Crosby, Lydia Crosby.
                          Signed: Enoch Murray

JAMES McKEEHAN
To Wife, Hannah McKeehan, all estate real and personal forever. Executrix: Hannah McKeehan. Written: September 2, 1805. Witnesses: Robert Guinn, Phillip Swatsell, John Bennet.
                          Signed: James McKeehan

ALEXANDER McALPIN
To Wife, Ginney McAlpin, 1/3 forever, use as advisable. Children: Robert, Henry, John, David, George, Peggy, Sally, Nancy, Dyanah. Executors: Robert Guin, John Farnsworth. Written: November 1, 1805. Witnesses: Henry Farnsworth, Hezekiah Balch. Signed: Alexander McAlpin

WILLIAM MAGILL   Farmer
To Wife, Jean Magill, household furniture, 2 cows, 2 steers, mare, side saddle, bridle and negro woman named Jude. Children: Samuel, William, James, Robert, John, Hugh, Charles, Elizabeth wife of Thomas Walker. To sons, Hugh and Charles, plantation where I now live. Children to receive cattle equally divided. Executors: Son, Hugh and Charles Magill. Written: 19 July 1806. Witnesses: Nath. Callahan, William Shields, James Shields.   Signed: William Magill

HENRY MOSES
Wife, Elizabeth, to have all as a widow, 1/3 if she remarries. All my children. Executors: John Renner, Jorge Neese. Written: 23 January 1808. Witnesses: Roger Browning, Johannes Welty, Rebeckah Browning.
                          Signed: Henry Moses

NICHOLAS MASE
To Wife, Ann Mase, everything to raise all my children. Witnesses: Elijah Willoughby, John Willoughby.
                          Signed: Nicholas Mase

SAMUEL MAGILL
To: Margaret Shannon, Robert Magill, Agnes, Mary, Matthew, Elizabeth Magill, the whole of my plantation. To Jean, wife of Henry Thompson,

one heifer and one milk cow. To Dorcas Shannon, one milk cow. To son,
Robert, one bay mare and one rifle gun. Robert to pay girls worth of
150 bushels corn. To daughters, all household property to equally
divided between them. Executors: Charles Magill, Henry Thompson.
Written: 23 September 1809. Witnesses: James Magill, Hugh Magill.
Signed: Samuel Magill

ADAM MYERS (MOYERS)   25 January 1824 $500.00
To Wife, Mary, to have farm, buildings, water and timber her life or
widowhood. Property to be divided in two equal parts - East side to go
to son, John and his heirs. West side to go to children of son, William
decd. Children: John, William (deceased), Phoebe Roberts, Polly Bullard
(deceased). All personal property to be divided in 5 parts between my
wife and 4 children. Executors: Alexander Armstrong, John Rodgers.
Written: 7 December 1816. Witnesses: Nathaniel Smith, Christopher
Miller.   Signed: Adam ⋀ Moyers
                                             his mark

ISAIAH McNEES
To Wife, Esther, everything forever. Children: Lydia, wife of John
Doster (Foster), Martha, wife of John Steal, Samuel, Susannah, wife of
Henry Yeakley. To daughter, Lydia, $2.00. To grand-daughter, Deborah
White wife of Frederick White, and daughter of my daughter said Lydia
Doster, $120. To daughter, Susannah Yeakley, tract of land, 134 acres,
if they pay wife, Esther, 6 bushels wheat, 11 bushels corn yearly. If
they do not comply - land to be sold and divided between others.
Executor: Samuel McNeese. Written: 10 February 1818. Witnesses: Edwin
Grubs, Samuel Gar??unt (Gaunt).   Signed: Isaiah X McNeese
                                               his mark

JAMES McMACKIN   22 January 1821
To Wife, Mary, cow called Swan, Calf called Star and her support from
land. Oldest sons, Thomas, James and John, to have land in Caintucke,
Butler County on the waters of Green River, 200 acres deeded from
William McMackin. Son, James, to have land I live on bought of Thomas
Kennedy. Three youngest children: Nancy, William and Peggy, to be
schooled and get a horse saddle and bridle. Executors: Brother, Thomas
McMackin, George H. Gillespie. Written: 30 October 1820. Witnesses:
Isaac Hope, Thomas Haws, Conrad Haws.
                         Signed: James ⋀ McMackin
                                     his mark

JOHN McPHERAN   23 April 1821 $1,000
To Wife, Elizabeth, full possession as my widow, to pay my debts. To my
nephew, James Logan, to live with my wife, single or married state, and
care for her unless she marries - then she gets 1/3 household furniture.
To my neice, Peggy McPheran, daughter of William McPheran, if she stays
with my wife, to have cow and calf and feather bed. Executors: Joshua
Kidwell, John Gass. Written: 30 January 1821. Witnesses: James, Andrew
and Samuel McPheran.   Signed: John McPheran

THOMAS McMACKIN SENR.   23 October 1821 $2,000
To Wife, Sarah, plantation during her life or widowhood, also household
furniture and negroes, all sheep and ½ the hogs. To son, Thomas,
plantation I live on, 176 acres. To William McMackin, son of my son
James decd., $50 and a horse. To son, Andrew, 2/3 of a 300 acre tract.
To son, John, the other third. To daughter, Martha McFarland, $50 and
a horse beast. To daughters, Nancy Wilson, Mary Reed and Betsy Scruggs,
$50 each. Executor: Son, Thomas. Written: 7 February 1821. Witnesses:
John Doan, Samuel Duncan, Thomas Haws.
                         Signed: Thomas McMackin

WILLIAM McPHERAN   2 April 1822
To Wife, Susanna, to have everything to raise and school my children til
they reach the age of 21 - then give them a horse, saddle, cow and calf.
At her death children to share equally. Written: 3 August 1821.

Witnesses: James Guthrie, Henry Rader, Isabella Guthrie.
                              Signed: William McPheran

WILLIAM MYER   28 April 1823 $1200
To Wife Nancy, one good bed, ½ kitchen and household furniture. After my
decease all loose property to be sold and equally divided 5 ways to those
listed below; Children: Rachel, Adam, Gabriel; Elizabeth Gable, daughter
of Magdelene Kochers. Daughter, Rachel, to have other half of kitchen
and household furniture. Executors: Barnard Gable, John Cook. Written:
5 September 1821. Witnesses: Fredrick Ricker, John Ricker.
                              Signed: William X Myer
                                               his mark

HUMPHREY MELONE   23 July 1823 $800
To Wife, Temperance, 1/3. All the rest to be equally divided between
children. Children: John, Priscilla, Nancy, Ellender, George, Abraham.
Until children become of age. Executors: Ezekiel Carter, Henry Bell.
Written: 17 June 1822. Witnesses: John Carter, Meshach Carter.
                              Signed: Humphrey Melone

JOSEPH MILBURN
To Wife, Mary, my estate after debts are paid. Executors: David Rankin
Esq., Gravenor Frieze. Written: 31 October 1825. Witnesses: Hiram
Daily, Borah Fisher, Jacob Frieze.
                              Signed: Joseph Milburn

GRAVENOR MARSH   23 July 1832 $2,000
To Wife, Hannah, whole plantation, tools, cattle, sheep, horses, poultry
etc. At her death to be divided. To grandson, Gravener Likens, 100
acres land inc house, black man Mace, sorrell mare and wagon. Children:
Henry, Gravenor Junr., James, Hannah Likens (deceased), Ann Howell, Lydia
McNeese. To sons, Henry and Gravenor Junr., balance of my land equally
divided. To son, James, $1.00. To grand-daughter, Elizabeth Marsh,
daughter of Gravenor, chest of drawers and cow. To grandson, Gravenor
Roberts, $10.00 when he is 21 years old. Children of Hannah Likens,
decd., $7.00. Executor: Gravener Marsh Junr. Written: 31 July 1826.
Witnesses: David Moore, Benjamin Gray, Thomas Doan.
                              Signed: Gravener Marsh

ABRAM (ABRAHAM??) MARSHALL   23 April 1827 $200
To Wife, Martha, all land, cattle, personal property for her use in
raising my children. After her death I give this to son Abram. To
daughter, Ruth, saddle, bridle and calf. To sons, John and Isaac, have
received enough, so after my wife's and son Abram's death - everything to
be equally divided. To son, Jesse, $150. To son, Joseph, $140. To
Daughter, Martha, $75.00. To Son, Simon, $150. To daughter, Rachel, $75.
To son, Thomas, $150. Daughter, Elizabeth Crumley. Executors: Sons,
John and Jesse Marshall. Written: 5 March 1827. Witnesses: Aaron
Hammer, James Jones.   Signed: Abram Marshall

WILLIAM McAMISH
Wife: Elizabeth McAmish. To son, Samuel, 200 acres granted me by the
State of North Carolina. To son, George, and grandson, William, son of
James McAmish, rest of old tract adjoining David Rankin, Seyburn Jewel
and David Holt. Other children: John, Isaac, Adam, Robert, Thomas,
William, Betsy McPheran, Jenny McPheran, Peggy Hope, Polly Gass, each to
receive $1.00. Written: 24 April 1826. Witnesses: David Rice,
Heironemus Dyche.   Signed: William X McAmish
                                       his mark

THOMAS MURPHEY   7 December 1857 $1,000
To be buried on my own plantation and my grave snugly wound in with brick
or stone. All property to be sold and divided between: Betsy Kennedy and
her sons, John and James; Margaret Morrow and her sons, John, Thomas,
James and Joseph. Executors: William West, Dr. William Cavinder.

Written: 17 April 1857. Witnesses: William Johnson, E. H. West.
Signed: Thomas Murphy

WILLIAM D. McCLELLAND   Land one mile north of Greeneville.
To Wife, Janetta, old place south of Greeneville can be repurchased, she
should be close to church and school. Children: Joseph, Oliver (decd.).
Son, Joseph, to have education. Note on David Fry. Note on Capt. Vise.
Note on Lt. Kinder. Others to be collected. Claims due me from the U.S.
Government for my services as Captain Major V.C. - refer to Officers of
the Dept. of the Ohio. My wife should collect the amount due our son,
Oliver, from the U.S. Govt. (Several U.S. Officers named. GFB). Wife
should keep and carry my cold watch. Joseph should keep and carry
Oliver's gold watch. Robert Carter to sell 5 horses I bought of Absalom
Gray. Written: 4 August 1864. Witnesses: G.H. Evans, S.P. Crawford.
Signed: William D. McClelland

CORNELIUS NEWMAN   1 May 1823 $6,000
To Wife, Mary, plantation, household goods, livestock, her lifetime, also
one negro boy. After her death to go to son Jacob. Children: Jacob and
Rebeckah (single). To Clair and John Hardin, one negro. To Joseph and
Honor Bowman, negro girl. To Rebeckah Newman, negro boy, horse and 2
cows. Executors: Jacob Newman, John Hardin, Joseph Bowman, Rebeckah
Newman. Witnesses: Robert P. Pickens, Jesu Blankenbeckler, Abram X
Galle Moon.   Signed: Cornelius Newman

Acknowledged the 28 October 1821 - his finger was sore and his hand
trembled very bad. Earl Newman. Ex. Bondsmen: Michael Myers, E.
Rutherford.

JOHN OLINGER   27 January 1823 $10,000
TO Wife, Nancy, the plantation I live on as long as she lives and 1/3
proceeds from plantation etc. and $200. Children: David, John, Silvanus,
Israel, Elizabeth, Anna. To son, David, where he lives and entry I have
made. To son, John, plantation where my wife is to live and get 1/3, a
mare called Bird, saddle and bridle. To sons, Silvanus and Israel,
plantation I bought of Joseph Carter. To daughters, Elizabeth and Anna,
Mill place - mills to be rented. To Mary Ohlinger, $300. Executors:
Two sons, David and John Ohlinger. Written: 6 January 1823. Witnesses:
John Mauris, Philip Henkel.   Signed: John Ohlinger

JAMES PATTERSON
To Wife, Martha, plantation and household furniture. Children: James,
William, Andrew, Nathaniel, Janey and Nancy. To son, James, 191 acres
known as Cedar Lick. To son, William, land where he lives. To son,
Nathaniel, 150 acres and sisters to live with him. To daughter, Janey,
1 bay horse and 2 cows. To daughter, Nancy, a horse and 2 cows.
Executors: James and William Patterson, Cornelius Newman. Written: 3
March 1804. Witnesses: James Brown Junr., James Brown.
Signed: James Patterson

BENJAMIN PICKERING
To Wife, Rebeckah, all real and movable estate. To sons: Samuel, Ellis,
Enos, Benjamin, Johnathan and John, $5.00 each. To daughters: Rebeckah
and Mary Elizabeth, $5.00 each. Executrix: Wife, Rebeckah. Written: 2
August 1806. Witnesses: John Jones, Ellis Ellis.
Signed: Benjamin Pickering

JOHN RUSSELL   3 February 1862 $1200
Wife: Elizabeth. Heirs: Hezekiah Russell, Margaret Smith. Executors:
Wife, Elizabeth, son-in-law Hezekiah Smith. Written: 10 January 1862.
Witnesses: F.H. Greenway, James D. Wykel. Ex. Bondsmen: Alfred Brumley,
George Greer.   Signed: John X Russell
                                          his mark

JAMES RODGERS
Wife, Margaret. Children: Joseph, John, Samuel, Thomas, Sarah, Margaret,

Jean. Ten pounds Virginia money. Executors: Wife, Margaret, David Fleming, Samuel Fuzune?? Written: 5 July 1794. Witnesses: John Dinwiddie, John Armstrong.   Signed: James Rodgers

JOHN RICHARDSON   18 August 1794
Territory of United States, South the River Ohio.
To Wife, Susannah, still, feather beds, cows, horse or mare etc. her lifetime. Children: Johnathan, Obediah, Elizabeth, Mary - my youngest children: Joseph, Jesse, Siller (Priscilla). To sons, Johnathan and Obediah, land to be divided between them. To daughter, Elizabeth, feather bed, 2 cows and calf. To daughter, Mary, one cow, one heifer and steer. To son, Joseph, $5.50 he owes me. To son, Jesse, 2 cows. To daughter, Siller, one cow. Executors: Wife, Susannah, Isom?? Piquey?? Written: 18 August 1794. Witnesses: John X Price, Mary X King, John Gass.
                              Signed: John X Richardson
                                          his mark

JAMES REGISTER   1799
To Wife, Deborah, everything, all real and personal property for her support four my children. To son, Francis, land after death of wife and a rifle gun. Executrix: Wife, Deborah. Written: 3 December 1798. Witnesses: Andrew English, James ◯ Crawford.
                              his mark
                              Signed: James Register

JOHN REAVES (REVES)   April Sessions 1803
To Wife, Elizabeth, whole estate her lifetime. To daughters, Milly and Martha, 80 acres land inc house, spring and orchard. All the rest of my children. Executors: Wife, Elizabeth, Henry Deck Senr. Written: 8 March 1801. Witnesses: George Washington Woods, Henry Dyke Junr., Frederick Hail.   Signed: John X Reaves
                                          his mark

DAVID RANKIN SENR.
To eldest son, James, $1, black suit and cupboard. To eldest daughter, Mary Williams, $1 and her mothers cloak. To Second son, Robert, 200 acres land, 100 acres land adjoining William McAmis and books. To Third son, David, 10 acres cleared land. To Second daughter, Ann Rankin, $200. To Third daughter, Elizabeth Rankin, $200, $38. To Fifth daughter, Jane Rankin, $230, $38. To grandson, David Wilson Williams, $50 when he is 21. To grandson, David Rankin, $50, ¾ of my books. Executors: Two sons, Robert and David Rankin, Written: 7 February 1802. Witnesses: Thomas Doon (Doan), James Dinwiddie, David Moore.
                              Signed: David Rankin

JOHN RYAN   April Sessions 1826 $2500
To Wife, Christian Ryan, $75, horse, saddle and bridle. Children: James, Martha Hunt, Robert, Joseph, Polly Fulkerson, Sarah Glasscock, Jane and Letty. To son, James, $200 current money of Tennessee. To daughter, Martha Hunt, negro Boy Billy. Wife, Joseph and Robert, to get 2/3 after payment of debts. Martha, Polly, Sarah, Jane and Letty, to get 1/3. Executors: Jesse Hunt, Christian Kelly?? Written: 17 May 1824. Witnesses: Samuel Caldwell, Alexander Caldwell.
                              Signed: John Ryan

JACOB READER (RADER)   22 July 1822 $1200
Wife, Elizabeth, to get equal part. Executors: Wife, Elizabeth, John Etter. Written: 18 May 1822. Witnesses: Turner Sharpe, James Guthrie.
                              Signed: Jacob Rader

JAMES ROGERS   26 April 1821
To son, John, 1 wagon and gears, household furniture, 8 horses. To son, William, One dollar. To daughter, Elizabeth, wife of Hugh Williams, $1. To daughter, Mary, wife of Samuel Coldwell, $1. To daughter, Marthew, wife of James McPheran, 100 acres of land in the hands of John Woolsey and $1. Executor: Son, John Rogers. Written: 18 December 1807.

Witnesses: Cornelius Newman, James Patterson.
                    Signed: James Rogers

DAVID ROLLINGS   October 1827
To Wife, Nancy Rollings, landed estate, goods and ½ geese as widow or
wife. Children: Nathan, Enoch, Polly, William, Ruthy Shelton (alias
Rollings), John, Orpha Lamb. To son, Nathan, all land, but to pay Enoch
$25. To daughter, Polly, 2 cows, 2 sheep and ½ geese. To son, William,
his book account of $13 and $10. Daughters, Ruthy and Polly, to divide
equally sale money. Son, John, and daughter Orpha, have received theirs.
Executor: Samuel Lotspeich. Written: 4 June 1823. Witnesses: Samuel
Kelly, G. Wells.   Signed: David X Rollings
                                         his mark

LUKE SHAWLEY (LUKE ABE SHAWLEY)
To Wife, _____, 1/3 profit of clear lands. To son, Micah, land - pay
George 20 pounds in trade. To son, George, smith tools. To sons, John
and Fretherick, 20 pounds each. To son, Adam, 20 pounds. Executors:
Wife, _____, George Emmett. Written: 13 August 1792. Witnesses: Henry
Earnest, John Muris (Mauris), Charles 𝘉 Dobson.
                                      his mark
                          Signed: Look Abe X Shawley
                                               his mark

WILLIAM SITTON   October 1823
To Wife, Susanna, all personal estate her natural life. Children, sone
deceased. To grand-daughter, Susanna Sitton, now lives with me, cow and
calf, 2 sheep and $20 in money for her schooling. Executors: Abraham
Cottel, Henry Earnest. Written: 3 August 1823. Witnesses: Thomas Doan,
Benjamin Gray, John Gray.   Signed: William Sitton

ADAM SMELSER   24 October 1822
To Wife, Mary, and six children she has had by me: George, Henry, Samuel,
William, David, Barbara Fry, to receive personal property from sale.
Executors: Son, George, Wife, Mary. Eight children I had by my first
wife: John, Adam, Betsey, Elley, Hannah Winkle, Fredrick, Jacob, Susanna
Good and Joseph, to have plantation near James Henry. Executors of this
part: Son, Joseph and Nicholas Elley. Written: 24 August 1822.
Witnesses: Joseph Brown, William McClelland.
                          Signed: Adam Smelser

SAMUEL SHERRILL   1791
Wife: Alta (alha or maybe Orpha, GFB). Land on French Broad _____ ?? may-
be Sevier County, too dim. GFB Witnesses: Ben Yamoney??, Jesse Byrd,
W. Sherrill. Trustees: Andrew Berd, Moses Moor. Written: 17 August 1791.
                          Signed: Samuel Sherrill

GEORGE SLAGLE   April 1826
To Friend, Loucindy Anderson, all my personal possessions, smith tools
to be sold and debts paid. Two sons Loucindy Anderson had by me, one
named Peter and the other (Elbert) or George. Executor: Washington
Henshaw. Written: 5 March 1826. Witnesses: J.W. Davis, John Kennedy,
John Davis.   Signed: George X Slagle
                                            his mark

HENRY SHIELDS   April 1827 $1,000
Wife: Esther. To youngest son, John, 100 acres - he comes of age in 1831.
To son, William, land on Kentucky Road. To daughters, Peggy, Alphie and
Nancy, 300 acres land adjoining William. To daughter, Polly, a mare,
saddle and bridle. To daughter, Jane, $640. Daughter, Rachel wife of
John Guin. As long as children behave themselves, they shall live in a
family capacity. $300 due estate from Royal Stokely. My Patent lands.
Sixteen acres land in Washington County, this state - adjoining Winkle,
Glaze. Executors: William Shields, James Biggs, Henry Henegar, John
Shields. Written: 16 January 1826.
                          Signed: Henry Shields

23

ISAAC TAYLOR
To Wife, Mary, negros. To daughter, Catisey, 3 negros. To daughter,
Margaret, 2 negros. Executors: John Severe of Washington County, Adam
Meek of Hawkins County. Written: 16 October 1790. Witnesses: Thomas
McCollum, George Twinley, Manning Srimers??
Signed: Isaac Taylor

JOHN THOMPSON   1797 April 8
Wife, Elizabeth, gets everything her lifetime - ½ to revert to Polly.
Daughters: Polly Marriett, C_____. Son: David. To grand-daughter,
Elizabeth Stuart, 10 pounds. Executors: Wife, Elizabeth, Son, David.
Witnesses: Robert McCall Junr., J. Lusk.
Signed: John Thompson

MARY TEMPLE   Probated and contested Monday 23 October 1820.
To son, Thomas, servant, chest, 2 chairs and a cow. To son, James, cupboard and 2 chairs. To daughter-in-law, Jinney, widow of William Temple
deceased, largest pot, hooks, churn, cotton cords. To daughter-in-law,
Isabella, widow of Josiah Temple, check reel, 2 tackles and churn. To
grand-daughter, Mary K. Robinson, daughter of Thomas Temple, a servant.
To grand-daughter, Peggy Temple, daughter of Thomas, one feather bed. To
grand-daughter, Jenny Temple, daughter of Thomas, one dutch oven. To
grand-daughter, Sally Temple, daughter of Thomas, a smoothing iron. To
grandson, James H. Temple, son of William, one riding horse. To grand-
daughter, Mary K. Temple, daughter of William, one bed and furniture. To
grand-daughter, Maria, daughter of Josiah Temple, deceased, one coffee
mill. To heirs of my deceased son William. Grand-daughter, Mary E.R.
Temple, daughter of John Temple. To Jenny, one dish. Executors: Son,
Thomas, Valentine Sevier. Written: 22 January 1818. Witnesses: V.
Sevier, Eliza Temple.
Signed: Mary Temple

This will was exhibited by Thomas Temple and contested by James Temple.

GEORGE THOMPSON
To Wife, Mary, plantation as long as she lives. Children: Mary, Jane.
To daughter, Mary, I gave a cow. Executors: Mary Thompson, Jacob Bowman.
Written: 7 May 1807. Witnesses: Walter Clark, Elizabeth Bowman X her
mark.
Signed: George Thompson

NICHOLAS TROBAUGH   26 October 1818 $6,000
Wife, Elizabeth, not to suffer for anything. Children not named. Land
to be sold and children receive 2/3 equally divided. Executors: George
Trobaugh, Frederick Trobaugh. Henry Moyer, bondsman. Written: 9 October
1815. Witnesses: A. Sevier, Joseph Holt, Josiah Clawson.
Signed: Nicholas X Trobaugh
his mark

JOHN WOOLSEY   Probated January 1819 $5,000
To Wife, Sarah, 15 acres land, $30 in silver, a mare, saddle and bridle.
To eldest son, John, Thomas, Mary wife of Andrew English, Sarah wife of
William Osburn, to receive $1 each. To son, Samuel, $150, 50 acres
adjoining Andrew Dobkins. To sons, Israel and Frethias, land adjoining
Simon Pope on Pyburn's Creek (50 acres each). To son, Oliphar, 60 acres,
my book debts. Turner and Rebecca Smith. David and Priscilla Logan.
Executors: Israel and Oliphar Woolsey. Test: John Crawford, Johanna X
Dobkins, Cornelius Newman, Andrew Dobkins.
Signed: John Woolsey

ZEPHANIAH WOOLSEY   May 9, 1801
To Wife, Sarah, dwelling, peach, apple and cherry orchard. To daughter,
Sarah Brasure, $5. To son, Stephen, 50 acres lard. To son, William,
170 acres land. To son, Nehemiah, 170 acres land. Executors: Sons,
William and Nehemiah Woolsey. Test: William Mott, James Huston, James
Williams.
Signed: Zeph. Woolsey

JOHN WALKER SENR.   18 February 1796
To Wife, Mary, negro wench and child. To son, Thomas, to have all my
movable property. To sons, Anderson and Daniel Walker, to get land
equally divided. Michael Blue, my son-in-law. Executors: Son, Daniel
Walker, Charles Killgore. Written: 18 February 1796. Witnesses: James
Brown Senr., John Walker, Joseph Walker.

                                    Signed: John X Walker
                                                   his mark

JAMES WALKER
To Wife, Lean (Jean), bay mare, furniture, cattle and body cloths. To
oldest daughter, Betsey Lyle Walker, yearling filly Shakespeare, heifer
Calico. To daughter, Jenny Patterson, yearling heifer. To minor
children to be educated. Executors: Samuel Wear, William Lowery.
Written: 12 May 1791. Witnesses: Floyd Nichols, Barbara Welelan??, Ann
Nichols.   Signed: James Walker

SOLOMON WILHOIT   April Sessions 1824
...being in a low state of health of body but of perfect mind and memory
...to my beloved wife Caty Wilhoit, horses, cattle, pigs, plantation,
etc...the Mansion House with all others on the plantation for her sole
use during her life (also mentions loom, wagon, her side saddle, six
steel store of geese, household and kitchen furniture)...kitchen utensils
to my beloved daughters Jemima, Peggy and Susannah Wilhoit...to beloved
son Simeon a horse and a riffel gun (that I purchased from Moses Hughs,
Jr.) and $15.00 when he comes of age;;;to my beloved sons Billy and Isaac
Wilhoit $75.00 each...to my beloved daughter Jemima, a cow and calf and
$10.00 when she comes of age...to beloved daughters Peggy and Susannah
Wilhoit, $25.00 each when they come of age...my bound man Henry now a
slave, give and bequeath to him his freedom having served Jacob Dych for
a period of three years from 4 February 1822...all property not specified
before to be sold and money divided amongst my beloved children: James
Wilhoit, Betsy Cartee, John Wilhoit, Phillip Wilhoit, Caty Williams,
Sally Stanberry, Polly Hank, Solome Wilhoit, Rosmonah Dych, Christiana
Rymble, Samuel Wilhoit, Jemima Wilhoit, Simeon Wilhoit, Peggy Wilhoit,
Billy Wilhoit, Isaac W. Wilhoit and Susannah Wilhoit. Friends Stephen
Brooks or George Wells to be executors...signed Solomon Wilhoit.
Witnesses, Lewis Ball and John Cook. A catasil to this will giving other
items to his wife is dated 16 March 1824 and witnessed by Gabrial (x)
Myers and Lucinda (x) Capshaw.

JAMES WEEMS   27 July 1819 $6,000
To Wife, Hannah Weems, 200 acres land. To son, John Weems, land where
William Grubbs now lives. To son, James Weems, land that goes to Hannah.
Wife, Hannah, now pregnant - if the unborn child is a son, to get rest of
land. If the unborn child is a girl, to have land as personal estate.
Executors: Wife, Hannah, Brother, George Weems. Written: 24 May 1819.
Witnesses: Henry Keller, John Weems, William Grubs X his mark.
                                    Signed: Non-Cupative

FREDERICK WHITTENBURG   October 1804
To Wife, Margaret, to have 317 acres land until Peter comes of age.
Sons: William, John, Peter, James. Daughters: Margrethe Brooks, Mary,
Elizabeth Harrison, Sariah, Susanna and Rachel Whittenburg. Land granted
me 27 April 1795, No. 1333? Lant grant No. 1123 dated 12 January 1793,
I give to wife and 6 daughters. To oldest son, William, $1.00. To
Second son, John, 200 acres. Third son, Peter & To fourth son, James,
land of my wife when they come of age. To daughter, Mary, a mare, 3
sheep and 4 hogs. To daughter, Sariah, a horse and saddle. To daughters,
Susan and Rachel, 2 cows and 3 sheep each. Executors: Isaiah Harrison,
Stephen Brooks. Written: 13 July 1803. Test: John Whittenburg,
Elizabeth Harrison, Sariah Whittenburg.
                                    Signed: Frederick W Whittenburg
                                                       his mark

RICHARD WOODS   June 3, 1805
To Wife, Sarah, 50 acres land, negros, mares, cows - to Richard at her

death. Sons: Washington, Richard Manzor. Daughters: Elizabeth and
Sarah Woods, Ginnet Neilson. To son, Richard Manzor, 100 acres land.
To daughters, Elizabeth and Sarah, bed, spinning wheel, saddle and bridle.
To 3 daughters, entry on Duck River to be equally divided. Executors:
Wife, Sarah, James Galbreath. Written: 3 June 1805. Witnesses: John
Hull, George Jameson, Henry Dych Senr.
Signed: not signed

JOSEPH WHITE   11 July 1805
To Wife, Jennat, all movable property. To son, William, land on Lick
Creek cleared by John Baker. To son, David, 1/3 my land on Lick Creek.
To son, Joseph, land. To daughters, Ann, Catharine, Jebel (Isabel?) and
Elizabeth, 10 pounds to be paid by sons. Executors: Sons, David and
Joseph. Teste: James Glass, Sarah X Glass.
Signed: Joseph White

THOMAS WOOLSEY   April 6, 1797
Wife, Phoebe, to remain here as long as she is my widow. At her death
to be sold and divided equally. Still, vessels and gun to be sold to
pay debts. Daughters: Phebe, Ruth, Sarah, Mary Ann. To son, Gilbert,
100 acres on Little Lick Creek. Executors: Giles Parman, Frethias Wall,
Wife, Phoebe. Written: 6 April 1797. Teste: Zeph Woolsey, Stephen
Woolsey, Mary X Woolsey.   Signed: Thomas V Woolsey
his mark

SARAH WOODS   Proved October Sessions 1819
To son, Richard, negro man Cyprus. Son-in-law, Frederick Ortto. Written:
26 April 1818. Witnesses: James M. Wyly, Jally Woods.
Signed: Sarah X Woods
her mark

HENRY YEAKLEY   24 April 1826 $200
To Wife, Susannah, 130 acres and 20 acre grant during her natural life.
Children: Samuel, Mary Maines, Henry, Isaiah, Elizabeth, George, John,
Jacob, Joseph, Malikiah, Ann, Lydia, Sarah. Sons, Samuel, Henry and
Isaiah, have their parts. To daughter, Elizabeth, $50. What is left to
be sold at wifes death and given to 9 last named children. Executor:
Son, Henry. Written: 20 December 1825. Witnesses: James Jones, Samuel
Ma??neer, John Frees.   Signed: L_____ in German.

NEHEMIAH PETTIT   17 January 1824
Boys to be larnt to read, right and cypher to the rule of three. To
Wife, Susannah, 1/3 estate real and personal property. Children: Rachel
wife of James Scoot, Ruth wife of John Witt, Nancy, John, Joel, Enoch
and Margaret Pettit. Children by my first wife _____. To daughter,
Rachel, $100. Executors: William Carter, Thomas Hale. Written: 17
January 1824. Witnesses: Joseph Davis, Joana Davis.
Signed: Nehemiah Pettit

CATHARINE PHILLIPS   8 May 1872
Son, Thomas Phillips, to have everything for taking care of me.
Written: 8 May 1872. Witnesses: E.M. Drake, William Farmer.
Signed: Catharine Phillips

JOHN RUSSELL   10 January 1862
To Wife, Elizabeth, land and property as long as she lives. Then to my
heirs: Hezekiah Russell and Margaret Smith. Executors: Son-in-law,
Hezekiah Smith and my wife, Elizabeth. Written: 10 January 1862.
Signed: John X Russell

JAMES RODGERS   5 July 1794   State of Tennessee, South of River
Ohio. Wife, Margaret, to have use of plantation during her widowhood
for support of my children. To son, Joseph, 150 acres land and 5 pounds
Virginia currency. To sons, John and Samuel, the plantation I live on.
To sons, Thomas and James, 50 pounds Virginia currency each.

To daughter, Sarah, a mare, saddle and bridle. To daughter, Margaret, 15 pounds Virginia currency to purchase a horse, saddle and bridle. To daughter, Jean, one negro girl named Hannah. Executors: Wife, Margaret, David Fleming, Samuel Frazier. Test: Thomas Rodgers, Joseph Dinwiddie.
Signed: James Rodgers

Book 2

ABRAHAM DYER   29 January 1828
To Wife, Ruth, everything as my widow. At wife's death or marriage everything equally divided. Children: Abraham, Samuel, Jacob, Rachel, Polly, Nancy, Elizabeth, Sally. Executrix: Wife, Ruth. Written: 18 July 1822. Witnesses: Nancy Pettit, Samuel D. Dyer.
Signed: Abraham Dyer

JAMES JOHNSON
To Wife, Abigail, and daughter, Hannah, all my household and outdoor stuff, part of 200 acre tract. Debts to be paid. Children: Joseph, Benjamin, William, Barton, Hannah Johnson, Susanna Squibb, Mary decd. Hannah's son David. To son, Joseph, land adjoining Thomas Ripley. To son William, $1 to be paid by Benjamin, he had his part and disposed of it. To son, Barton Hannah, 50 acres with his part in my 200 acre tract. To daughter, Hannah, saddle and bridle. To daughters, Susanna Squibb and Mary decd., they got their part when married, Susanna to have $1. Executors: Solomon Beals, son of Isaac Beals, Aaron Hammer. Written: 27 September 1824. Witnesses: Benjamin Gray, John Gray, William Likens?
Signed: James Johnson

JOHN MAURIS   29 April 1828 $5,000
To Wife, Martha, all her wearing apparel, saddles, bed and bedstead and land where John Reeser lives. Land to be sold, Martha to get interest on money. Children: Mary, Rebeckah, Elizabeth, Ann, Hannah, Sarah, Leah, Ratchel, Easter. Daughters: Rebeckah wife of Benjamin White, Hannah wife of John Dinwiddie and Sarah wife of John Reeser, their parts never to come into hands of their husbands but to be put on interest for my grandchildren. Grandson, Jonah White, minor. Executors: Abraham G.Fellows, Charles Bright Esq. Written: 22 January 1828. Witnesses: Michael Bright Senr., Peter Earnest, Isaac Earnest.
  (Large Sale - inventory on record with Will. GFB)
Signed: John Mauris

WILLIAM ALEXANDER   28 July 1828
Children: Thomas, Stephen, George, William, Mary, Anna, Barbary and Elizabeth. To sons, Thomas and Stephen, and daughters, Mary and Anna, to have plantation where I now live. Mary to have all household furniture. To son, William, $300. To daughters, Barbary and Elizabeth Lackland, $5.00 each. Executors: Sons, Thomas and Stephen. Written: 20 September 1819. Witnesses: Stephen Brooks, William Alexander.
Signed: William X Alexander
                        his mark

PETER BURGNER JUNR.   26 July 1828
To Wife Eve, whole estate, if she remarries all is to be divided between the three children to be educated. Children: William, Mary E. Burgner. Executors: Wife, Eve, Brother Jonathan Waddel. Witnesses: William Painter, William G. Waddel, Immanuel X Good.
Signed: Peter ⋏ Burgner
                        his mark

CONRAD BARNHART   Sale 12 November 1828
(DAR Conrad was born 1750 in Germany. Joined the Revolution in Cumberland Co., Penn. Married Barbara GFellers. GFB)
To Wife, Barbara, houses and furniture, well and bucket, cow and calf. Children: Matthias H., Felix, John, Adam, Andrew, Conrad, Jacob, Abraham, Henry, Catharine, Barbara Harmon, Elizabeth Boweny, Margaret Snapp, Sarah Fox, Polly Seadon, Susan Seadon. To son, Matthias H., a young black mare.

To son, John, Fifty dollars. Book accounts to all my children. Gave
money to all his children, 6 cents to 15 dollars. Executors: Felix
Barnhart, Abraham G.Fellers. Written: 14 April 1828. Witnesses:
Lawrence Earnest, Robert Morrison, William X Newberry.

Signed: Conrad X Barnhart
his mark

GEORGE RIGHTSEL
To Wife, Barbara, all property during her life or widowhood - then my
children to share equally. To step-daughter, Lizzy Wagoner, living? on
the plantation as long as she is single, then a good bed, cow and choice
of my stock. Children: Kisanah, John, Barbara, William, Ann, Hotren?,
and George, to have residue of my estate. As she gives property to them
it is to be appraised by 2 freeholders. Sole Executrix: Wife, Barbara.
Written: 1 May 1803. Test: Henry Shields, Charles Lowry.

Signed: George X Rightsel

WILLIAM REESE   31 July 1816
To son, Moses, 136 acres land on Sinking Creek. To son, William, has
received his legacy. To son, James, has received his legacy. To son,
John, plantation where I live purchased from Isaac Jones - daughter,
Margaret Lane gets ½ or he pay her for it. To my beloved wife, Charity,
the plantation. Grandchildren, Samuel and Mary Grady to receive $1 each.
Daughter: Mary Haworth. Grandson, Jonathan. Executrix: Wife, Charity.
Witnesses: Aaron Coppock, Samuel McNeese, Thomas Brown, Enos Ellis.

Signed: William X Reese

MARGARET SHURLEY
To grand-daughter, Nancy Shurley, daughter of Elizabeth Click, bed,
furniture, cow and calf. Household furniture to be sold and divided
equally between my 2 sons, Adam and Frederick. Executor: Adam, my son.
Written: 19 October 1795. Witnesses: Stephen Brooks, A. Gillespie.

Signed: Margaret X Shurley

JANE LAMONS
To son, William, 1 shilling. To daughter, Gain Coffman, 50 acres land
and all movable property as long as she lives then to her daughter, Mary
Coffman. Executors: John Ferguson, Samuel Ferguson. Written: 13 April
1803. Test: John Woolsey, Cornl Newman.

EQUILLA SHERRILL
To Wife, Lucindy, and grand-daughter, all household furniture. To son,
Elisha, a black mare. Land and movable property to be sold and divided
equally between: Wife, Lucindy, Elisha, Allenlow, Abraham and Isaac
Sherrill, and daughters, Huldah Wilson, Rachel Loyd, Ruth Payen, Margaret
Wilson, Vilet Hutchison and grand-daughter Lovina. Executor: Giles
Parman. Written: 19 January 1805. Test: Andrew Hixson, Ann X Hixson,
Johann Hixson.   Signed: Equilla X Sherel

CHARLES SMITH
To Wife, Margaret, horses, hogs, cattle and land her lifetime. To sons,
John and Robert, 20 pounds each. To daughters, Ann Smith, Margaret and
Jenny Smith, 10 pounds apiece. Property to be divided between James,
Charles, Daniel and William Smith. Written: 13 December 1797. Witnesses:
Henry Conway, Sarah Conway, Richard _____.

JOHN SHAW   19 February 1808
To Wife, Fanny, 1/3 of my estate. To son, John Shaw of Loudon Co., Va.,
a horse and forty dollars. Sons: Benjamin, Joseph, Jesse and daughter,
Betsey. Executors: Wife, Fanny and son, Benjamin. Test: Thomas Love,
William Sharp.   Signed: John Shaw

CHARLES SMITH   20 August 1812
Wife, Mary, to have everything. To son, Benjamin, a mare, saddle and
bridle. To son, Charles, bay horse and new saddle. To son, George, a
horse and bridle. Charles and George to learn to read and rite. Other

children: Mary, Jacob, Molly wife of Adam Wartenbarger, Michael.
Executors: Sons, Frederick and Jacob Smith. Test: Leonard Dell, Jacob
and Penny Bowman.   Signed: Charles Smith

JAMES SCOTT   20 October 1818
To Wife, Mary, everything during her life or widowhood - at her death,
land to go to two sons, James and Elijah, and they are to pay son, John
two hundred dollars each. To daughter, Peggy Davis, one dollar. Other
children: Elizabeth, Ruth, Polly, James, William Alexander. Executors:
Joseph Davis and John Glascock. Witnesses: Joseph Smiley, William
McPheran.   Signed: James Scott

ROGER BROWNING   17 August 1825
To Wife, Rebeccah, everything as a widow, 1/3 if she remarries. Children:
Nathan Browning, Lola Dewes, Lina Dayton, Elizabeth Elkins, Rebecca
Cooper, Benjamin Browning. To son, Nathan Browning, ten dollars. To
daughter, Lola Dewes, fifteen dollars. To daughter, Elizabeth Elkins,
fifteen dollars. To daughter, Rebecca Cooper, one hundred dollars. To
Son, Benjamin Browning, lower part of my plantation. Executor: Benjamin
Browning. Witnesses: Johannes Bannet?, Henry Tobey, Jeremiah Brenner?
                             Signed: Roger Browning

GEORGE EASTERLY   July Sessions 1828   Bond $3,000
Children: Conrad, Jacob, Phillip, George, Casper, John, Moses, Catharine
Curton, Marget, Mary Maloy, Magdalene. To Conrad, large German Bible.
To sons, Jacob, Casper, John and Moses, ten shillings silver each. To
son, Phillip, farming utensils. To daughters, Catharine Curton, Marget,
Mary Maloy and Magdalene, one hundred pounds each. To son, George,
book Truth of Christianity. Executors: Phillip and John Easterly.
Written: 15 April 1811. Witnesses: Phillip D. Maroney later of Blount
County, Henry Burkhalter, later of Marion County.
                        Signed: George G Easterly
                                       his mark

WILLIAM WALL   Inventory January 24, 1827 - 26 January 1829 $600
Wife, Peggy Wall, to have everything her natural life, then to her
daughter. Daughter, Sarah Carr, a cow and calf. Wife, Paggy Wall, her
daughter, Delila Garret and her son William Wall. Grand-daughter, Nancy
Dyke. Peggy's son, William Wall. Executors: John Gragg Senr., William
Chapman. Witnesses: William Chapman, Henry Netherton.
                        Signed: William X Wall
                                        his mark

CHRISTIAN BURKEY   1 January 1829
To Wife, Polly, all real and personal property as my widow. When Joseph
is 21, equally divided. Children: John, Susannah, Christian, Mary,
Delila, Joseph. Executor: William Missinger. Witnesses: Henry Dyke,
George bails??, _____ (German) Had Pa. money.
                        Signed: Christian X Burkey
                                        his mark

DAVID BOLES
To Wife, Elizabeth, all estate during her widowhood, if she remarries -
she gets an equal part. Children: Sarah, Jesse, Jacob, George, John,
David, Daniel, Elizabeth, Polly Aaron??, Joan. Executors: Wife,
Elizabeth, Sons, Jesse, Jacob. Written: 4 January 1829. Witnesses:
Henry Dyke, Josiah Harrison, George W. Hall.
                        Signed: David X Boles
                                        his mark

SARAH REED   27 April 1829 $500
Children: Rachel   , Solomon, Sarah, Edward, Matthias, Meriah,
Mathes,. To daughter, Rachel, my saddle. To son, Solomon, frying pan.
To daughter, Sarah, bed, sheet and bed stand. To son, Matthias, my
Delph ware, shore fire dog and washing tub. Rachel and Sarah to get
indigo cloth. Executor: Son, Matthias. Written: 9 December 1828.

Witnesses: John Catching, Samuel D. Dyer.

Signed: Sarah X Reed
her mark

JAMES WRIGHT   30 June 1829 $2,000
To be buried in graveyard at Harmony Meeting House. Wife, Hannah, to
have everything her lifetime. To son, John, 100 acres, house and improvements. To son, James, to pay my funeral expenses, debts and cost of
sale - then he gets home tract. To sons, Robert and Samuel, land on
Lick Creek with sawmill and entry adjoining land. Daughter, Nelly, to be
equal. Executor: Wife, Hannah. Written: 16 February 1829. Witnesses:
James Patterson, David Alerson Junr. (Allison G.F.B.)

Signed: James Wright

URSULA TARRANT
To brother, Henry Tarrant, my share in 170 acre tract and the tract Lewis
Wills deeded to us, but do not dispossess my father and mother during
their natural life. To sister, Elizabeth Tarrant, bed and furniture. To
sister, Jenny Bruner, formerly Jinney Tarrant, five dollars. Executor:
Father, Henry Tarrant. Written: 30 April 1828. Witnesses: Thomas Bailey
Junr., George Johnston.   Signed: Ursula Tarrant X her mark

DANIEL CARTER   27 July 1829
To Wife, Sarah, furniture, cups, saucers and all the delf she brought
here, a looking glass, 2 bales spun cotton, 6 pounds wool. Two cullard
children, daughters of Clara who was emancipated by John Carter decd., to
be set free when 21 years old. Two sons, Elisha and Ellis, to get all
land. Three daughters, Polly Keller, Sophia Pogue and Jemima Williams,
to get personal property, debts and demands by note. Sons-in-law, Henry
Keller and Thomas Williams, to get one dollar. Polly Keller and Jemima
Williams part to go to their children. Executors: Elisha Carter, Jones
Weems, Ellis Carter, George Weems. Written: 27 June 1829. Witnesses:
Jesse W. Haile, George Kenney, Abram Weems.

Signed: Daniel Carter

JOHN WHITE   27 July 1829 $1,000
Five sons, Robert, John, David, Johnathan and Enoch, to get land if they
can agree. Four daughters, Elizabeth, Kindness, Leah and Melinda, to
have household and kitchen furniture. Executors and Bondsmen: Robert
White, Cornelius Smith Junr., William Craddick. Written: 19 May 1829.
Witnesses: William Craddick, Henry X White.

Signed: John White

JEREMIAH LANEY   27 July 1829 $1,000
To Wife, Elizabeth, all perishable property and 82 acres land. At her
death all to be divided equally. Children: Mary Nelson, Ephraim Laney,
Elizabeth Murray, Susanna Nelson, Hannah Cotter, John Laney. Executors:
Wife, Elizabeth, Washington Hinshaw. Written: 27 April 1829. Witnesses:
Stephen Cannon, Susanna Cannon.

Signed: Jeremiah ⋂ Laney
his mark

PETER DILLON SENR.   27 July 1829
To Wife, Elizabeth, Mansion house, garden and orchard, ½ stock, furniture.
Two sons, Garret and Thomas, land on Sinking Creek - to furnish their
mother 2/3 of what she might need. To sons, William and Peter, 200 acre
tract I live on. Six daughters: Lydia, Sarah, Phebe, Susanna, Jemima and
Elizabeth, to have furniture equally divided. Lydia to have use of
Mansion house. Executors: Sons, Garret, William. Witnesses: David
Stanfield, Aaron Hammer, Britton Feas??

Signed: Peter ⌡s Dillon
his mark

GEORGE COCHRAN   28 July 1829
Children: John decd., Samuel, Ann McCrain, Jameson, Robert, George,
Caroline Dunlap, Peggy Henry, Martha Mitchell, James and Marchel decd.

To son, Samuel, 100 acres joining Busters. To daughter, Ann McCrain, fifty dollars. To son, Jameson, one hundred fifty dollars. Son, Robert, to have $150 less than the rest, my other children to receive equally whats left. Grand-daughter: Polly Dunlap. To his legal heirs $150. Bury me between wife and son. Pale graves with mulberry paling and locust posts. Executors: John Dunlap, Thomas Magill. Written: 16 April 1829. Witnesses: Stephen Brooks, William Hall, James Pearce. Other Executors: Sam Alles, A. Wilson.

Signed: *[signature]*

JOHN GUIN   29 July 1829 $4,000
Ten children: James, Jane, Esther, William, John, Peggy, Hercanes, Robert, Andrew, Alpha, (sister Elizabeth). Son, James, to pay notes of thirty dollars to James Guin Senr. for my land. My wife to raise children on land. Executors: Son, James W. Guin, John Shields. Written: 19 January 1829. Witnesses: Enos Guin, James C. McBride.
Signed: John Guin

JAMES GUTHRIE   25 April 1832 $5,000
To Wife, Isabella, ½ reap and personal estate during her natural life. Son, James, to get wife's part. Step-children: Susannah Patterson and Joseph Trotter, to have everything in case James dies. Mother: Susannah Guthrie. Executors: Wife, Isabella, Andrew Patterson. Written: 2 February 1824. Witnesses: Andrew McPheran, Helbert Arnate?
Signed: James Guthrie

SAMUEL PICKERING $1,000
To Wife, Nancy, one horse, one cow, all my bees, grain etc. for hers and son, George's, support. Children: George, William L., Thomas, Rebecca Nixon, Hannah, Elizabeth, (Rebecca wife of Robert Nixon – her son, John Pickering). To son, William L., land and plantation. To daughters, Hannah and Elizabeth, ten dollars each. Executors: Wife, Nancy, Enos Pickering. Written: 22 July 1829. Witnesses: James Jones, Rachel X Jones.   Signed: Samuel Pickering

FREDERICK DEWITT
Wife, Frances. Children: Susanna Wilson, Elizabeth, Sarann, Frederick, son Berzilla, Milla and Martin, to receive one hundred dollars each. Martin has already received his. Executors: Wife, Frances, Bond on James Forness of South Carolina. Written: 2 February 1829. Witnesses: David Good, William George, Jacob F. Brooks.
Signed: Frederick Dewitt

WILLIAM BLACK   12 November 1829
To Wife, Elenar, use of farm her lifetime, then to be divided between three daughters: Elizabeth, Marthy and Rachel Black. To daughter, Susannah Black, featherbed, mare and cow and 105 acres land. To daughter, Margaret Pettit, featherbed, mare and cow and 100 acres land. To son, Joseph, ½ Susanna's part. Executors: Joseph Black, William Senter. Witnesses: Christopher Sloan, Charles Lowery.
Signed: William Black

JAMES JONES   3 February 1820 $4,000
To Wife, Rachel, everything forever except one cow. Brothers: John and Aaron Jones. To brother, John, six dollars in trade. Sister, Mirrian Brown, wife of Thomas Brown – their children: Mary, James and John Brown. Brother: Evan Jones. Elihu Osburn stays with me, I give his brothers and sisters 1/5 part. Sister: Catharine Campbell – her son David. To Manumission Society of Tennessee – promoting equal justice, ninety six dollars in 16 installments. Brothers-in-law: John and Thomas Ellis. Executors: John Marshall, Aaron Hammer. Written: 8 August 1824. Witnesses: Abraham Crumley, William Lane.
Signed: James Jones
My interest in printing office now in operation in Greeneville, Tennessee to Manumission Society.

CHRISTOPHER LOTSPEICH   No Date

To Wife, _____, all property, horse, saddle and bridle. Sons: Samuel, Ralph decd., John, James and William. Daughters: Elizabeth Hoover, Mary Walker, Sarah Whittenberg, Barbary Broyles, Susanna Pardoe, Rachel Earnest decd. and Rebecca Farnsworth. To children of son, Ralph decd., five hundred dollars. To daughters, Elizabeth Hoover, Mary Walker, Sarah Whittenberg, Barbary Broyles and Susanna Pardoe, five hundred dollars each. To daughter Rebecca Farnsworth, four hundred dollars. To children of Rachel Earnest decd, five hundred dollars. To grand-daughters, Eliza J. and Susanna Wells, fifty dollars each. To my Negros, their freedom. Executor: Stephen Brooks. Witnesses: Josiah Harrison, Caleb Harrison.   Signed: Christopher X Lotspeich

FREDERICK CUTTSHALL   Probated 26 April 1830

To Wife, Catharine, 10 acres and dwelling house and as much personal property as she chooses and all money after debts are paid. Two sons, John and Christian to have deeds to land, windmill, tanning tools and lanyard. To daughter, Elizabeth, wife of William Mysinger, 100 acres where she lives. To daughter, Christenah McNew, 58 acres. To daughter, Margaret, wife of Michael Sane, one hundred and fifty dollars. Executors: Sons, John, Christian. Witnesses: Phillip Henkel, John Ricker.
                    Signed: _____ German

ROBERT CAMPBELL   4 December 1809

County of Washington, State of Tennessee. To Wife, Margaret, house and reasonable maintenance off the land. To son, Carrick, plantation I live on. To daughters, Ruth and Sarah, each a horse and saddle worth one hundred dollars. To daughter, Jinny, ¼ part household furniture. To son, George, thirty dollars. Witnesses: William Blair, George Wallace, Joseph Blair.   Signed: Robert Campbell

JOHN CRUM

Gun and things might do without to be sold and pay me debts. To Wife, Margit, to have land and property her lifetime but not to waste it. Sons, Michael and John, if they dont like the land when of age, sell and divide it. Executors: Frederick Gottschall, Peter Ricker. Written: 4 June 1810. Witnesses: Giles Parman Senr., Joseph Parman. Signed: *Jorenne B Porum*

DENNIS HARTY   October Sessions 1810

To Wife, Jemima, all my pewter, unmolested use of all cleared land, except that where Daniel Harty lives and works. To son, Jacob and Daniel, plantation at death of my wife, Jacob to get house. Sons-in-law, Robert Casteel, Moses McCoy and George Miers, to receive $1.50 each. Grand-daughters, Rebecky Myers and Anna Miers, eight dollars each. Grand-daughter: Elizabeth Myers. To William McCoy and Abner Johnson, everything equally divided not allready specified. Executors: David Robertson, David Keys. Written: 19 August 1810. Witnesses: Elijah Billingsley, John *ER* Ross his mark.   Signed: Dennis X Harty
                                                  his mark

MARGARET ROGERS

To daughters, Sarah, Margaret and Jane, all body clothes and 2 pewter dishes and 2 pewter plates. Margaret also to receive a heifer. Sarah Kelley (formerly Rogers) to keep and nurse my daughter Jane. Jane to get a quilt and featherbed. To son John's wife, Jane, my fowls. To sons, James and Thomas, one school Bible. Executors: Son, John Rogers, William Kelly. Written: 1 September 1809. Witnesses: Jacob X Kelley, Margaret ✓ Rogers.   Signed: Margaret X Rogers

JANE GUIN   26 April 1816 $1,000

To Brother, Robert Guin, one hundred dollars not yet collected. To John Guin, son of Hugh, a milk cow. To Jane Bell Guin, daughter of Robert Guin Esq., bed and clothes. Brother: James Guin. To my Mother, _____, house and furniture. Executors: Robert Guin Esq., my brother. Written: 5 July 1810. Witnesses: Joseph Hamilton, David Thompson.
                    Signed: Jane X Guin

HEZEKIAH BALCH
To be buried at Harmony Meeting House. To Wife, Anna, 1/3 of estate, her clothes, mare and saddle. To son, Elijah W., 2/3 of estate, my clothes and ½ my books. College to get water from the spring. Money due me from John McKinney and John McCampbell, trustees and students of the college. Executors: Elijah W. Balch, John Russell Esquire. Written: 9 October 1809. Witnesses: Thomas Mitchell, Charles Coffin.

Signed: Kez   ah   Balch

HERONOMUS DECK   Executors qualified 11 July 1811
Wife: Margaret. Henry and Jacob Deck to be sole executors. Margaret to have real estate during her natural life. Eldest son, Henry, to remain and clear land for 5 years - then it is to be sold and divided between all my heirs. Daughter, Margaret, to have 100 pounds. Five children: Henry, Margaret, Christina, Mary and Jacob. Test: Michael Woods, Henry Dyche. Written: 31 December 1810.

Signed: Heronomous Deck

LEVI CARTER
To Wife, Susanna, all my property her lifetime. Sons, Joseph and Elijah to receive no more until the rest of my children get sixty dollars in trade. Executrix: Wife, Susanna. Written: 5 December 1809. Witnesses: David Key, William Jones, Christopher Kirby.

Signed: Levy Carter

MARTHA GILLESPIE SENR. (Marthew)   24 April 1811
To daughter, Jane King, ½ clothes and yarn. To grand-daughter, Marthew King, grey mare, saddle and bridle. Jane Hays, Marthew Gillespie, daughter of James Gillespie. Daughter: Elizabeth. To son, John, a horse. To sons, George and Allen, fifty dollars each. Son: James. To grand-daughter, Marthew Gillespie, daughter of Thomas Gillespie, ½ wearing apparel. Grandsons: Thomas and George King, sons of daughter Jane King. Executors: Son, James, Grandson George Gillespie. Written: 28 May 1810. Witnesses: Samuel Dunkin, Thomas McMackin.

Signed: Marthew X Glispie

ROBERT ALLEN*   Substance of Will of Robert Allen decd.
As found by a jury, written by me. Robert Guin
Probated 25 July 1811.   Written: 4 February 1811.
Wife, Martha Allen, to have two negroes, Prusey and Letty her lifetime, then to my first wife's children. My first wife's children: Robert, James, Reuben Allen, Polly Lemmon, Fanny Farnsworth. To Son, Robert, eighty dollars. To son, James, one hundred and forty dollars. To daughter, Fanny Farnsworth, one hundred dollars. Plantation under the care of wife and son, Daniel Allen. To Daniel Allen, 250 acres off home place going up river to where Jeremiah Smith lives known as Cove Spring, and a negro boy named Simpson. To son, Samuel, 250 acres, lower part of plantation and negro boy named Love. To daughter, Margaret Allen, 1/3 household furniture and a negro. Wife Martha Allen to remain and be supported by profits from my plantation. Son-in-law, Samuel Lemmon, to get a negro boy. To son, John Allen, a horse.

Signed: Robert Allen
Taken from Book 1, page 46. Original Will not in book.

SCHOOLFIELD MADDOX (MADDUX)
To Wife, Susanna, all estate her lifetime. Children: Alexander, Thomas, Dorcas, Mary, Sally, Betsy, Rachel. To sons, Alexander and Thomas, land equally divided. My five daughters to get personal estate. Executors: Wife, Susanna, Sons, Alexander and Thomas. Written: 30 July 1811. Witnesses: Alexander Williams, John Shaven r?, Thomas Prater.

Signed: Schoolfield X Maddux

THOMAS McCULLOUGH
To Wife, Mary, all property to dispose of as she pleases after all my debts are paid. Executors: William McPherson, Ralph Parks. Written: 10 September 1807. Witnesses: Jacob Miers X mark.

Signed: Thomas X McCullough

OLIVER SMITH   January 1812
Wife, Mary. Children: Mary and Stephen. If Stephen does not pay what he
owes Elizabeth Cook, pay from estate and take from his part. Executors:
William Wall, John Gragg. Written: 31 August 1808. Witnesses: John
Harris, William Gragg.   Signed: Oliver Smith

JOHN GILLESPIE   27 April 1812
To Wife, Barbarah, negros, dwelling house and 1/3 farm during her widow-
hood. To son, George, all the rest of my estate. Brother: James. To
John, son of brother James, ½ land coming from King - left me by my
fathers will if it should ever be obtained, and horse worth 25 pounds
Virginia currency. Executors: Son, George, Brother, James. Written: 22
November 1811. Witnesses: Jacob Rader, _____?
                            Signed: John X Gillespie
                                           his mark

ANTHONY KELLY
To Wife, Elizabeth, 1/3 personal estate then to my 3 children. Three
children: William, Margaret, Mary. To son, William, 100 pounds. Step-
children, John Kid, Eliner Gaut and Elizabeth Grant, to receive two
shillings each. Executors: William Kelly, my son and William Kelly, my
son-in-law. Written: 20 April 1801. Witnesses: James Dinwiddie,
Alexander Armstrong.   Signed: Anthony Kelly

JOHN WEEMS
To Wife, Kitty Weems, to have all as my widow. Son-in-law, John Young,
to work plantation, support my wife and get plantation at her death.
Sons: George, Thomas, William, James. Son, George, owes me 60 pounds, he
is to pay William 5 pounds. To son, James, 6 pounds 6 pence. To four
daughters: Elizabeth Baley, Agnes Young, Kitty Bowers and Sally Duguar
(Dugger) GFB, to have property not herein mentioned. Executors: John
Gass, John Young. Written: 18 February 1812. Witnesses: Jacob Smith,
Alexander Matticks, John Gass.   Signed: John Weems

PHILLIP BABB SENR.   25 January 1843
Step son, Robert Antrim. Step son-in-law, Jesse Davis, to have all not
already given. All my children (not named) to get one dollar above what
I have already given them. Executors: Robert Antrim, Jesse Davis.
Written: 6 January 1843. Witnesses: John Coulson, Robert Daniel, Thomas
Manis?   Signed: Phillip B Babb
                                                 his mark

DAVID ROBINSON   26 April 1813
To Wife, Peggy, profit on land where I live adjoining David Wilson, a
horse, bridle and furniture. Children: William, Betsy, James, Jane and
Polly. Son-in-law: John McGaughey. Sons, William and James, to have
reasonable schooling - at Peggy's death land to be divided between them.
To son, James, my rifle gun and pouch. Daughters to get ten dollars
each. Executors: Wife, Paggy, Son, James. Written: 19 January 1813.
Witnesses: Robert Dobson, John Cavener, William Wilson.
                            Signed: David Robinson

ADAM G.FELLERS   27 April 1813
To daughter, Barbara Barnhart, twenty four dollars. To daughter,
Catharine Waggoner, two dollars and her children nine dollars. To
daughter, Nancy Rimal, six cents. To son, John G., six cents above what
he has received. To son, Abraham G., six cents. To sons, Jacob G. and
Henry G., six cents each. To daughter, Eve, five dollars. Executors:
Son Abraham G., son-in-law Conrad Barnhart. Written: 12 December 1812.
Witnesses: Thomas Doan Senr., William Lotspeich, Samuel X Mauck.
All other property to be sold and divided equally. Catharine's children
to get her part.
                            Signed: *Adam Gfeller*

JAMES GRAHAM   27 April 1813
To Wife, Sarah, dwelling and land southside Nolichuckey River, household
furniture, cattle and grain etc. To youngest son, Joseph, 130 acres
southside Greene County, but Sarah has profit her lifetime. To sons of
my son George, James and George, one hundred dollars each. Children of
John decd., 6 cents. To sons, Charles, James, Thomas and William, six
cents each. To daughters, Mary, Sarah, Elizabeth, Jane, Margaret and
Ruth, six cents each. Land in Washington County to be sold. All the
rest of property to be sold and divided between my daughters. Executors:
Henry Earnest Esq., John Lotspeich. Written: 24 March 1813. Witnesses:
John Hughes, Absalom Hayworth, Jacob X Fellows.
                                 Signed: James Graham

JONATHAN EVANS SENR.   27 April 1813
To Wife, Hannah, McPharlands place on Nolichuckey River and 1/3 movable
property - at her death to go to youngest son, James. To eldest son,
John, one dollar, having received his part. To son, Evan, one dollar,
having received his part. To son, Robert, land I purchased of James
Brown and land I purchased of William Brumley. To sons, Johnathan and
William, an equal portion. To daughters, Hanna and Peggy Evans,
plantation on Little Chucky that I purchased of Alexander Stewart.
Executors: Wife, Hannah, Son John. Witnesses: Robert Evans, Edmund
Garret, Charles Love.   Signed: Johnathan Evans

THOMAS PRATHER   26 July 1813
To Wife, Delilah, everything her lifetime to raise my children.
Daughter: Polly Painter. Children: Elizabeth, Cathren, Mary, Nancy,
Delilah, Johnathan, James Jeremiah, Abigail. To daughters, Mary, Nancy
and Delilah, when they marry have property equal to Polly Painter. Each
child to receive marriage portion at wife's death. Sett property and
divide equally. Executors: Wife Delilah, Sons Johnathan, James and
Jeremiah. Written: 30 March 1813. Witnesses: William Brown, John
Broyles, John Bird Senr.   Signed: Thomas Prather

GEORGE ELY   27 July 1813
To Wife, Elizabeth Ealy, to live on plantation her natural life - at her
decease furniture to go to daughters. Children: Adam, George, Nicholas,
Mathias. To son, Adam, 82 acres. To son, George, 51 acres and six
months schooling. To son, Nicholas, 3 sheep. I give to Jacob Smelser
and Michael Koble (Cobble), one horse each. Executor: Son, Michael Ealy.
Written: 25 May 1813. Witnesses: William Snyder, Ellen Snider, one in
German.   Signed: George X Ely
                                                his mark

BENJAMIN FARNSWORTH   Proven 27 July 1813
To Wife, Polly, all real and personal estate. Children: Thomas, William,
Alexander, George. Executors: Wife, Polly, David Farnsworth. Written:
26 March 1813. Witnesses: P.W. Jameson, Robert McAlpin, David
Farnsworth.   Signed: Benjamin Farnsworth

CHARLES SMITH   27 October 1813
Wife: Mary. Children: Benjamin, Charles, George, Mary, Frederick, Jacob,
Molly wife of Adam Wattenbarger, Michael. To son Charles, a bright bay
horse and saddle. To son, George, horse, mare and fifty dollars.
Charles and George to be learned to rede and rite. Executors: Son,
Frederick and Jacob Smith. Written: 20 August 1812. Witnesses: Leonard
Dell, Jacob Bowman, Penny Bowman.
                                 Signed: Charles Smith

PETER RICKER   24 January 1814
Wife, Peggy, to have all her widowhood, then to be sold and divided
equally. Children: John a minor, Eve Smithers, Peggy Guinit, Jacob and
George Ricker, Polly Fann, Frederick Ricker, Rachel Willet, Martin, John,
William and Huldah Ricker. Son, John, to receive a horse. Executor:
George Wells. Written: 9 September 1813. Witnesses: John ____(German),
Solomon Wilhoite, John Cook Senr. Signed: Peter Ricker

JOHN POGUE   26 April 1814

To Wife, Nancy Pogue, hole tract of land and movable estate. To son, Th
Thomas, 50 acres adjoining Thomas Pogue. To sons, John, Farmer, William
and Howell, 50 acres each. Howell's sister, thirty dollars in good
traid. Amongst my living daughters - land on Lick Creek. Executors:
Wife, Nancy, Thomas and John Pogue. Written: 6 January 1814. Witnesses:
John Price, Benjamin Williams.   Signed: John D Pogue
                  his mark

JAMES C. BELL   25 July 1814

To Wife, Sally M. Bell, mare, saddle, bridle, 2 cows, 1 bed, spinning
wheel and chist. To my son, David M., whatever part of my father's
estate is due me. To my daughter, Polly Ann, all my clothes except one
Regimental Coat and cocked hat which is to be sold. Executors: Wife
Sally, Father, William Bell Senr. Witnesses: James Kerr Senr., Samuel
Leming, James Kerr.   Signed: James C. Bell

JACOB MISSIMER   2 July 1814

To my friend and brother, John Missimer, all my personal estate to be
freely possessed. Executors: James Shields, Nehemiah Pettit. Written:
5 January 1814. Witnesses: Fred Cleaver, Joseph Smelser, Ruthey X
Scott.   Signed: Jacob X Misimer

JOHN REYNOLDS   Tuesday 25 October 1814

To Children: John, Sally, Betsey, David, have received their part. The
rest to go to Wife, Mary Elon??. To sons, Reuben and Jesse, all perishable property to take care of me and my wife and son, Vinson. Executors:
Reuben and Jesse Reynolds, friends. Written: 8 August 1814. Witnesses:
William Malone, John X Malone.   Signed: John Reynolds

MICHAEL GIRDNER   25 January 1815 $5,000

Wife, Huldah, to have everything during her natural life. Children:
Conrad, Sally, George, Nancy Gurdner. From Huldah's note - son, Michael.
Executors: Wife, Huldah, Conrad Girdner, James Allen. John Farnsworth
also served. Written: 12 October 1814. Witnesses: Jacob Lince, Martin
Lintz.   Signed: Michael Girtner
                        (written in German)

GEORGE COOK   27 January 1815

Children: Henry, Sarah Harget, Elizabeth Cook, George, Nancy, Jacob, John,
Christian Cook, Mary Meloy, Eve Hutchison, Margaret Nees. To Son, Henry,
to have where he lives and three hundred dollars. To daughter, Sarah
Harget, 30 bushels corn, 1 share in iron factory. To daughter, Elizabeth
Cook, 125 bushels corn. Son, Jacob, note for $111.00 be deducted from
his part. To Joseph Hutchison, husband of daughter Eve, note for $50.00
deducted. Eve Hutchison's 6 children. To daughter Mary wife of James
Meloy, three hundred dollars. To daughter, Margaret Nees, plantation at
Pilot Hill. To Adam Nees, shares in iron factory. Executors: George
Cook, John Gragg. Written: 21 January 1815. Witnesses: Gilbert McCoy,
John Love.   Signed: George G Cook - his mark

EBENEZER MORROW   24 July 1815

To my brother, John Morrow, the whole of my estate. Executors: Thomas
Murphy, John Morrow (above). Written: 19 December 1813. Witnesses:
Robert Carson, Thomas Kennedy.   Signed: Ebenezer X Morrow
                              his mark

MICHAEL NEHS (NEAS)   25 July 1815 $2,000

To Daughters: Dolly wife of Henry Raush, Eve wife of Philip Harpine,
Elizabeth wife of Michael Dittamore, all real and personal estates to be
divided equally. Sons: John and Adam, have received their full share.
Son, John, has kept and nursed me for several years - to have house clock.
Everything left to be sold and divided between my daughters. Executor:
Grandson, George Nehs. Written: 8 May 1815. Witnesses: John Neese Junr.,
John Runner.   Signed: Michel X Nehs

JOHN WILSON   25 October 1815 $3,000
To Wife, Margaret, and four daughters, Polly, Betsey, Nancy and Peggy, a
decent and comfortable living on the plantation where I reside. To my
son, John Wear Wilson, land adjoining Hugh Cavender and John Balch. To
my son, Alexander McClung Wilson, 80 acres adjoining William Brannon and
Thomas Russell. To my son, Henry Newton Wilson, 100 acres adjoining
Kerr. To my son, James Calvin Wilson, residue of land. Executors: Wife,
Margaret, eldest son, John. Written: 10 July 1815. Witnesses: James J.
Wilson, Josiah Clawson, Jno. Russell.
                        Signed: John Wilson

JOSEPH NEWELL   22 January 1816 $500
To Wife, Margaret, all my estate during her natural life, then to be sold
and divided equally. Children: Rachel, Sally, Joseph, John, William, and
David Newell. Executors: Joseph Van Pelt, John Newell. Written: 30
April 1814. Witnesses: Nathaniel ⟨S⟩ Nupton, Thomas X Hurley, Joseph
X Newell Junr.   Signed: Joseph Newell.

JOSEPH RUNELS   23 January 1816 $400
To Wife, Christiner, 1/3 real and personal estate, then to children.
Children: Joseph, John, Catey, Elizabeth, Nancy, Samuel, Mary Rebecca.
To my sons, Joseph and John, whole of my estate - 150 acres land.
Executors: William Hendry, Phillip Babb. Written: 18 June 1815.
Witnesses: Dutton Lane, Leonard Starnes, Christopher Houts.
                        Signed: Joseph ⟨⟩ Runnels - his mark

JINNY GUIN   23 January 1816
To my son, James Guin, one hundred dollars. To my son, Randolph, fifty
dollars. Grand children: Peter Robinson Guin, son of Robert Esq. decd.,
one hundred dollars; Eliza Betsey, daughter of James Guin, ten dollars;
James, son of Hugh Guin, ten dollars. Great grand-daughter, Jenny
McDonald Guin, daughter of John, ten dollars. Grand-daughters: Alphiar,
Nancy, Eliza Jane Bell, Peter Robinson, Eliza Guin children of Robert
Guin Esq. decd. Executor: Son, James Guin. Written: 3 May 1814.
                        Signed: Jinny X Guin
                                    her mark

ABEL LOYD   22 April 1816 $1,500
To Wife, Hannah, all household furniture, mare, sheep, cattle, hogs and
land all her life - to bring up my children in a genteel manner - at her
death my four sons, Thomas, James, John and Able, to get land. Three
daughters: Mary Loyd, Betsey Fraker and Sarah Carter, to get the rest.
To daughter, Mary Loyd, 13 pounds 11 shillings. Grand-daughter: Lavina
Loyd. Executor: Wife, Hannah. Written: 28 March 1816. Witnesses:
Thomas Loyd, John Loyd, David Carter, Hanah Loyd.
                        Signed: Abel Loyd

BENJAMIN JAMESON   22 July 1816
To Wife, Jane, all profits of the plantation where I now live her lifetime. At her death everything to be sold and divided. To my son, Robert,
100 acres land. Executors: Wife, Jane, Robert Guin. Written: 13
December 1807. Witnesses: John McKeehan, Ephraim Wilson.
                        Signed: Benjamin X Jameson
                                        his mark

BENJAMIN YEATES   22 April 1816 $3,000
To Mariah Frances Yates, her grandmother;s side saddle, scarlet cloak and
fifty dollars. To Samuel Francis Yates, Rebecca Yates, riding saddle,
wearing clothes and sixty dollars. Richard, Nicholas and Johannah Weems
to equally divide the rest. Executor: Thomas Self. Written: 29 November
1815. Witnesses: Turner Sharp, James McFarland.
                        Signed: Benjamin X Yates
                                        his mark

WILLIAM CAVENER   22 April 1816
At Camp Teheforte, a private soldier in Captain William McClelland's

Company, 7th Regiment U.S. Infantry. Beloved brother and sister, John and Margaret Cavener, to get pay and bounty lands due me, plus any other property. Written: 11 September 1814. Witness: A.G. Goodlie (or Goodlet?), Surgeon 7th Juss??? Signed: William X Cavener
his mark

ADAM BROYLE 23 April 1816
To Wife, Mary Magdalena, ¼ of 144 acres land, at her death to son, Elias, 12 hogs - 9 out hogs and 3 in a pen. To my son, William, 50 acres adjoining a road leading from Henry Reynolds to Waddels Mill to Aaron Hoptons. To my sons, Thomas and John, ten dollars each. To my daughter, Polly, ten dollars. To my daughter, Nancy B., 1/3 value of land. To my daughter, Sally, 1/3 value of land. To my daughter, Nancy, eighty-eight dollars. Executor: Samuel Broyles. Written: 10 April 1816. Witnesses: James H. Davis, Susanna Person. Signed: Adam 7 Broyles - his mark

MARGARET McELROY 25 April 1816 $1,000
To grand-daughter Marthan? Shirley, daughter of Adam Shirley, to get land and plantation where I live. Son, Adam, to get land until Marthan becomes of age. To grand-daughter, Nancy Shirley, black mare and cow. Daughter: Margaret Emmert. Sons: Michael, George, John and Frederic Shirley. Executors: Son, Adam Shirley, George H. Gillespie. Written: 1 April 1816. Witnesses: Thomas Doan, Isaac Gollet, George H. Gillespie.
Signed: Margaret Muckleroy

JACOB KINSER SENR. 22 July 1816
To Wife, Easter, all possessions as long as she lives and stays a widow. To my son, George, 100 acres land. To my sons, Henry and Adam, 150 acres land. All my children to be equal. Executors: Jacob Kinser Junr., Peter Cobble, Bdn. John Cobble, Henry Missemer. Written: 29 February 1816. Witnesses: Lewis M. Hays, George Kinser, Adam Kinser.
Signed: Jacob Kinser

EPHRAIM WILSON 23 July 1816
Executors on Bond: Stephen Brooks, Hugh Wilson, Frederick Dewitt.
To Wife, Agnes Wilson, all my estate to dispose of as she sees fit. Children: Jane McAmish, her daughters Nancy and Jane McAmish; 2nd daughter, Mary Moore, her daughters Nancy and Jane Moore. Sons: James and Hugh. To grand-daughters, Nancy and Jane McAmish, one negro. To grand-daughters, Nancy and Jane Moore, a negro and her increase forever. To my grandson, Ephraim Wilson, son of my son James, a negro boy. All property to be sold and divided at Agnes's death. Executors: Stephen Brooks, Son, Hugh. Written: 30 January 1816. Witnesses: Frederick Dewitt, Christopher Bradshaw. Signed: Ephraim B Wilson - his mark

THOMAS McCOLLUM 28 October 1816 $300
To Wife, Nancy, everything during her widowhood inc crop now growing. And my children. Have sails to get forty dollars to put roof on house. Executors: Wife, Nancy, David Morrow. Written: 19 August 1816. Witnesses: L.B. Hawkins, Thomas Roberson, Edward Murphy, James McCollum.
Signed: Thomas McCollum

MAJOR TEMPLE 29 October 1816 $600
To Wife, Mary, I give the use of my dwelling, servants, wearing apparel, one hundred dollars, a horse and 3 cows. Children: Thomas, James and heirs of my son John, Jinny wife of John Berry, heirs of my son William, Daughter-in-law, Isabella, wife of my son Josiah Temple deceased. To son, James, 200 acres land - not to be unreasonable with servants and provide for wife, Mary. To daughter, Jinny twenty dollars. To the heirs of my son William, twenty dollars. To daughter-in-law, Isabella, ½ grain crop. Executors: Sons, Thomas and James Temple. Written: 8 August 1816. Witnesses: Josiah Clawson, Christopher Bradshaw.
Signed: Major Temple

JOHN MISSIMER 28 January 1817 $4,000
To Wife, Mary, all my estate - at her death it is to be equally divided

between children: William, Sally, Catharine, Hezekiah, Susanna, Peter and heirs at law. If my wife is pregnant, this child to be included with heirs. Executors: Wife Mary, Martin Lintz, George Andes. Written: 6 January 1817. Witnesses: James Shields, Henry Missimer, Peter Cobble.
Signed: John ⟶ Missimer - his mark

BENJAMIN VANPELT   28 April 1817
To Wife, Mary, all household goods, chattels, book debts and notes. To my daughter, Hannah Harrison, a featherbed. To my son, Benjamin, 2 cows. To my daughter, Mary Jones, a featherbed. To my son, Joseph, 2 beds, horses and one cow. Executors: Wife, Mary, Son Joseph, John Baley. Written: 26 December 1816. Witnesses: Thomas Conway, George H. Hynds, James Graham.   Signed: Benj. Vanpelt

JACOB FREES   29 July 1817
To Wife, Katherine, full use of dwelling house and kitchen during her widowhood and sufficed support. To son, David, until he is 21 a horse and cow. To my sons, Michael, George, Jacob and John, 100 acres land each. Michael's land joining Johnson Small and Ripley. To my daughters: Elizabeth Grubbs, Mary Fries, Rebecca Fries and Anna Stanfield, one hundred dollars each. My book in German Language. Executors: Son Jacob, Son-in-law Edwin Grubbs. Written: 16 February 1817. Witnesses: Thomas Doan, Samuel Mainess, Gravener Marsh Junr.
Signed: Jacob Frees

JOHN SNAPP   26 July 1830 $5,000
To Wife, Elizabeth, use of mansion house, part of barn and stables. At age 21, boys to get a bed. At age 18, girls to get a bed. Children: Mary Susannah Chester, John H. Snapp, Madison C. Snapp, Harrison G. Snapp, Woodford A. Snapp, Matilda D. Snapp (has an infirmity), Peachy K. Snapp, Newton S. Snapp, Alexander A. Snapp, Minerva, Elizabeth I., Casanders and Camiola T. Snapp. Harrison G. has been going to Washington College. All children to have equal shares. Negros to be sold except Lucky, who gets her freedom. My black man, Moses, at Capt. Henry Cook's in Alabama. (Wife Elizabeth, was Elizabeth Cook - GFB). Executors: Samuel Snapp, W. P. Chester Junr., Son Madison C. Snapp. Written: 6 July 1830. Witnesses: Henry Earnest, Enos Pickering, F. A. Gillespie, Jno. Smith.
Signed: John Snapp

JOHN NEHS (NEAS)   6 April 1846 $4,500 estate
To wife, Elizabeth, Two hundred dollars in silver, 100 acres land, garden, spring and springhouse. To sons: John, George, Adam, Phillip and Jonas, 200 acres land each. Jonas' mind is not strong enough to bargain, my executors are to look after him, his land adjoining Philip Henkel. Daughters: Catharine wife of Jacob Ottinger, Elizabeth wife of Adam Bible, Margaret wife of John Aly (Ely?), Susannah wife of Henry Ottinger, Eve wife of Lewis Ottinger and Magdalene, to receive equal parts of revenue received from sale of moveable property, money, notes, bonds and bank accounts. Magdalene to receive One hundred dollars more than the rest. Executors: Sons, George and John Nehs. Written: 19 June 1830. Test: Jacob? Ottinger, _____ Nehs - written in German.
Signed: John ++ Nehs
his mark

JAMES ROBISON   25 October 1830 $2,000
Wife: Jane C. Robison. To my sisters: Hannah Robison, Rachel Robison and Jane Robison Kelly, Fifty dollars each. To my sister, Polly Kelly, Fifty dollars after the death of my wife. Jane Robison Kelly and Helden Cammel Kelly, children of James Kelly, to get my land at my wife's decease. Written: 22 September 1830. Witnesses: John Robison, Washington Henshaw,
Signed: James Robison

SAMUEL DOAK   Greene County, lately of Washington County.
To Wife, Margaretta, to have decent maintenance and live with sons. To my sons: Johnny Whitfield Doak and Samuel Witherspoon Doak, all movable property. To my daughters: Julia and Lucinda Doak, Jane Rice, Nancy and

Polly Montgomery, right and title to all property I gave them when they left home. To my step-son, Alexander McEwen, a mare, saddle and bridal. Executors: Sons, Johnny W. and Samuel W. Doak, David Rice. Written: 30 December 1818. Witnesses: James Galbreath, Samuel Robinson, James Patterson, George Bell. Signed: Samuel Doak

ISAAC WHEELER   25 April 1831 $500
Executors and Bondsmen: Hezekiah Slatter, Christopher Lightner, Elijah W. Headrick. To my sons, James and Jesse, all land my mother lives on after her death. To Wife, Elizabeth, houses and plantation during her widow-hood. To my son, Isaac, a mare and saddle when he comes of age. Mother: Margaret Wheeler. Daughters: Jemima Wheeler Mills and Lyda Wheeler Slatten, personal property at wife's death. To grand-daughter, Sidney Wheeler, a cow and calf when 16 years old. Witnesses: Alexander English, Abraham X Moore, Jno. Vinsant. Signed: Isaac Wheeler

RUTH BAXTER   25 April 1831
Son: Barnet Baxter. Written: December 20, 1830. Witnesses: John X Ritter, David Ritter, Thomas Collier.
                              Signed: Ruth (3) Baxter

THOMAS MITCHELL   25 July 1821
John and Thomas, my younger sons, to have where I live for taking care of father and mother. Blanchy and Polly, my two youngest girls, to live with John and Thomas while single - at marriage to have as much as Jenny. Other children: Jenny Williams, Samuel, Seery (Sarah), Andrew, Lucy and William. Samuel to give his counsel to family. Written: December 2, 1820. Witnesses: M. Lincoln, Joseph Brown, John A. Brown.
                              Signed: Thomas Mitchell

SAMUEL GAUNTT   21 October 1831 $2,000
To Wife, Susanna, land west side of Sinking Cree, ½ profit of Grist Mill, 2 barrell of flour and Eight dollars annually to be paid by Malachai. Children: Samuel Kelley Gauntt, Karrenhppock Evans (daughter), Malachai Gauntt, Esther W. Garret, Publias Gauntt (son). To son, Samuel, Five dollars. To daughter, Karrenhppock, desk and book case. To son, Malachai, where he lives on west side of Sinking Creek inc Mill and sawmill. To daughter, Esther, loom and spinning wheel. Grand children: Lydia, Abigail, Joanna, Kerenhappock, Hannah, Beulah, Rual??, Julien, Naomy, Bathsheba Garret. Executors: William Johnson (of James), Son Malachi Gauntt, Isaac Earnest. Written: 20 June 1831. Witnesses: K. T. Crane, Felisse W. Wells, Thomas J. Earnest, Thomas Templeton.
                              Signed: Samuel Gauntt

MARY ALEXANDER   23 January 1832
To Thomas Alexander, son of Thomas, my brother, 100 acres being an undivided part where I now live. To: William K. Alexander, son of Stephen Alexander; William Alexander, son of George Alexander; William Alexander, son of William Alexander, balance of my hogs, cattle, pots and loom. To Catharine, wife of John Alexander, one reel. To Eliza, daughter of Stephen Alexander, one spinning wheel. Elizabeth, daughter of Thomas Alexander. To Polly Walker, on stand of bed curtains. To Elizabeth Gray, daughter of Thomas, a cupboard. To Elizabeth Park, furniture. Executor: William King Alexander. Witnesses: Henry Jess, Thomas Alexander, son of William. Signed: Mary X Alexander
                                                        her mark

NATHAN DAVIS SENR.   23 July 1832 $4,000
To Wife, Nancy, ½ land and personal property. To my son, Nathan, the other half. To my daughter, Betsey Wisecarver, Fifty dollars to be paid by Nathan. To grand daughter, Permely D. Tooles, one bed and furniture. Executor: Son, Nathan Davis. Written: 5 June 1826. Witnesses: Daniel Bryan, Joseph Davis.   Signed: Nathan Davis

VALENTINE CATRON   23 July 1832   October 1832
To Wife, Eve, all land and personal property as my widow plus power to

buy and sell. As children come of age – not named. Executor: Wife Eve,
son-in-law Jacob Baughard. Witnesses: Jacob Harmon, Johnathan X Abel.
Signed: Valentine Catron

THOMAS BAILEY SENR.   25 June 1830
To Wife, Elizabeth, competent support her lifetime. To daughter, Catharine
Duggar, Five dollars. To son, William Baily, Thirty dollars. To son,
Thomas Baily, all real and personal estate after paying other legatees.
To daughter, Elizabeth Strong, one cow. To grand-daughter, Elizabeth
Baily, One hundred dollars. Grandson, James P. Baily. Executor: Thomas
Baily. Witnesses: Jones Weems, John Weems, William Patton.
Signed: Thomas Baily

ROBERT HILL   24 July 1834 $1,000   of Cocke County, Tenn.
To Wife, Elizabeth, 1/3 of estate including dwelling house, northside
Nolichuckey River. Sons: John White Hill and William D. Hill, to have
landed property if they pay my daughters, Priscilla and Jane, $1000 each
at their marriage – to pay in yearly installments. Daughters: Priscilla,
Jane, Penelope West decd. To grandson, Robert West, house and lot in
Russellville, Jefferson County. Executors: John Hill, John B. Grigsby
M.D. and John White Hill. Written: 31 January 1829. Witnesses: Robert
McFarland Junr., John Rightsell, Alexander McFarland.
Signed: Robert Hill

LEWIS BALL   12 May 1832
To Wife, Huldah (Huldah Beach, widow of Michael Girdner – GFB), to have
lands she had before I married her and money owed me by James Allen in
Greene County Court. Negroes to be set free. To Thomas Ball, Painte
Mountain land, then to his sons, John and Lewis. Four daughters: Susanna
Coulter, Martha Holland, Ann Ball and Elizabeth Saymaker, if still alive
to divide whats left. Son: John Ball to have my island tract of land
then to go to Green Ball. Executors: Hugh Holland, James Colliz??
Written: 12 May 1832. Witnesses: William Ashley, Ann Ball, William
Houston, Jacob Stephens.   Signed: Lewis Ball

CHRISTIAN BIBLE   22 October 1832
To Wife, Margaret, dwelling house, well and milkhouse, 2 pare shoes, ten
bushels corn yearly as long as she keeps my name. To my oldest son,
John Bible, 100 acres land. To son, George, where he lives. To son,
Adam, tract of land. To son, Jacob, 80 acres land. To son, Abraham,
tract of land. To son, Isaac, old plantation. To son, Lewis, 100 acres.
To two grand children, daughters of Christian Bible decd., Elizabeth and
Ann, land on Wolfe Creek. To daughter, Elizabeth, wife of Isaac
Crezelius, 50 pounds in traid. To daughter, Mary, wife of Jacob Easterly,
50 pounds in traid. To daughter, Catharine, wife of Phillip Easterly, 50
pounds in traid. To daughter, Sarah, wife of Jacob Bartle, 50 pounds in
traid. Each to be paid by my sons. One hundred acres land I bought from
Michael Dittemore on Wolf Creek to be sold and divided between all my
children. Youngest sons: Abraham and Isaac. Executors: John Bible,
Phillip Easterly. Witnesses: George Easterly, Lewis X Stolz.
Signed: Christian X Bible
his mark

ANN LOVE   22 October 1832 $1,000
Wife of James Love deceased. Daughter, Nancy Love, all real and
personal property and all due me from the estate of Sarah Cassons.
Witnesses: John and Moses Whittenburg.
Signed: Ann X Love

GEORGE MORELOCK   23 October 1832
Wife: Elizabeth. To sons: Samuel and David, 100 acres each. Son: George
decd. – his children, Enoch, Edward, David, and Polly, Ten dollars each.
Daughter, Ratchel widow of Jacob Light – her children to receive Thirty
dollars equally divided. Son: Jacob decd. – his children: George, John,
Elizabeth, Anny and Crissey, Thirty dollars to be divided equally.
Daughter: Elizabeth wife of Henry Humbert, Five dollars and no more.

Children: Johnathan, Nathan, Hannah wife of Frederick Smith, Sarah Stacy, Anna Morelock, to receive equal parts of final sale. Daughter, Polly wife of Isaac Humbert, to receive Five hundred dollars. Executrix: Wife, Elizabeth. Written: 3 June 1832. Witnesses: Jacob Beals, John X Perry, John McAmis. Signed: George Morelock

JAMES PATTERSON   23 October 1832
James Patterson died 31 August 1832. To Wife, Mary Ann, whole residue during her natural life except servant, Lewis, who is to be set free. Pay Nelson debt first. Executors: Andrew Patterson, David Rice. Written: August 26, 1832. Witnesses: Elizabeth Clawson, Val Sevier.
Signed: Janes Patterson

ABRAM CARTER   26 October 1832
To Wife, Rebecca, Fifty dollars and small spinning wheel the old man bought for her, a side saddle and 10 pounds coffee. Other property to be sold and money divided between my heirs inc Rebecca, my wife. Children: Nancy Weems, Temperance Malone, Elenor Keller, Elizabeth King, Sarah Edmunds. Executors: Ezekiel Carter, John Carter. Will dated: 22 March 1832. Witnesses: John Pogue, Henry Simpson.
Signed: Abraham   Carter
his mark

SILAS VESTAL   28 January 1833
Will regarding slaves. Executors to set slaves free at my death. Executors: Valentine Sevier, Richard M. Woods. Will dated: 4 November 1832. Witnesses: Sally Woods, Elisa Ortto.
Signed: Silas Vestal

SOLOMON BEALS SENR.   30 January 1833
Wife, Rebeckah, to have plantation, at her death it goes to my son, Samuel, he is to pay her 1/3 profits her lifetime. Samuel to have land transferred from Benjamin Iddings by State of North Carolina, also transferred to Iddings by William Berry, John Hays adjoining Jacob Beals. To Son, Stephen, One dollar. To daughter, Elizabeth Grist, Twenty dollars. To grandson, David Grist, Fifteen dollars. To son, Jacob Beayles, one cow. To daughters, Hannah Pratt and Ann Loyd, Twenty-eight dollars each. To daughters, Lydda Underwood, Marth Beals and son, Jacob, to share in 105 acre land sale. Daughter: Jane Collet. Grand-daughter: Jeanne Gribbels. Executors: Sons Jacob and Samuel, Jacob Beals Senr., Son-in-law of Joseph Beals. Will dated: 5 February 1822. Witnesses: John X Fraker, John Fraker, Michael Fraker.
Signed: Solomon Beals

JOSEPH DUNKEN   22 April 1833 $1200
Wife, Polly, to have everything her lifetime or widowhood, then to my sisters: Elizabeth McNeese wife of Ewen McNeese. Nephew: Joseph Smith, my sisters son. Father: Anthony Dunkin. Executors: Samuel McNeese, Gravender McNeese. Witnesses: Michael Bright Senr., Jacob White.
Signed: Joseph X Dunkin

PETER CASTEEL   22 July 1833
To Wife, Susanna, unmolested use of everything her widowhood. Children: Daniel, Edward, John, Washington, Polly, Johnathan, Elizabeth, Peter. To sons, Edward, John and Washington, One dollar each. To sons, Johnathan and Peter, to get land. To daughter, Polly, cow and calf. To daughter, Elizabeth, a red calf. Sons-in-law: Caleb Jones, Samuel Jones. Executor: William A. Hawkins. Will Dated: 17 February 1833. Witnesses: William Sample, Jeremiah Casteel. Signed: Peter X Casteel

JOHN CARTER   22 July 1833
Wife, Christiner, to pay debts and what is left divided between all my children (not named). Will Dated: 6 March 1833. Witnesses: John Price, Benjamin Carter, Mel?? Carter.   Signed: John Carter

ISABEL MORROW   28 October 1833 $500
To my sons, James and John, to get land according to line betwixt them.
To daughter, Nancy, my wheel. To daughter, Lindy, smoothing iron. Grand
children: Lindy and Betsey of James, Adam of John. Executor: Son John.
Will Dated: 9 May 1830. Witnesses: John Bell, Samuel Brewer.
                           Signed: Isabel X Morrow
                                           her mark

ROBERT DOBSON
To Wife, Eleanor, whole of property as my widow, land inc spring house
and loom house on road from Greeneville to Rogersville. Nephews:
Azariah Dobson and Robert Dobson, sons of my brother Samuel Dobson.
Azariah to have my farm, 145 acres - in case he dies property to go to
his brother Robert. Father: Joseph Dobson. Executors: Wife, Eleanor,
Samuel W. Doak. Will Dated: 11 November 1828. Witnesses: George Jones,
William V. Vance, George T. Gillespie.
                           Signed: Robert Dobson

JAMES HENRY   27 January 1835   28 April 1834 $1,000
To my son, Nathaniel M. Henry, Evans land when titles made. All my
children to be taught to read, write and arithmetic. Executors: Loving
Wife, son Nathaniel. Will Dated: 3 February 1833. Witnesses: M. Love,
James Guinn, _____ (German)   Signed: James Henry

PHILLIP HENKEL (Lutheran Minister - GFB)   28 July 1834 $500
To Wife, Catharine, all my estate and at her death it is to be sold and
divided between all my children. Persis to be made even with other
children. Executors: Son Irenius N. Henkel, Son Eusebius S. Henkel,
John Peters, David Buck. Will Dated: 1 July 1832. Witnesses: George
Easterly, George Nease, John Eberl, Phillip Easterly.
                           Signed: *Philip Henkel*

MESHACK HAILE   28 April 1834 $4,000
To Wife, Mary, all land and negroes I possess. Youngest sons: Jackson,
Elijah and James, get $120 each at Mary's death - Elijah and James get
land. The following negroes: Ned worth $400, Thomas $400, John $300,
Washington, $300, Nelson $300, Jesse $200 and Anderson $100, to be
equally divided between these my children: Lewis, Nancy, Charles, Enoch,
Mary and Jackson Haile. Those who take higher price negros to pay to
those getting a lower priced one, making all equal. Son, Mashack to get
$250 in good trade. Slave, Grace, to be set free at 50 years of age.
Executors: Wife, Mary and Son Lewis Haile. Witnesses: Jacob Hacker Jr.,
Andrew L. Harold, Amasa Harrold. Signed: Mashack (?) Haile
                                                   his mark

JOSEPH HENDERSON   28 July 1834 $4,000
My wife and I are weakly and infirm with old age and have consulted with
my children. Loving Wife: Eleanor. To my son, Joseph, 170 acres land.
To my son, Anderson (or Alexander?), $122. My son, George, has his part.
Son, Joseph, has his part. To my son Robert, $1000. To my daughter,
Anny N. Hall, $75 cash. Executors: Alexander Henderson, Joseph Henderson.
Will Dated: 10 September 1829. Witnesses: Michael Bright, Jacob Beals,
John Rees, James Kelly.   Signed: Joseph Henderson

JACOB BEALS   1 August 1834 $3,000   Lanty Armstrong, Sec.
To Wife, Jane, $100 trade consisting of household furniture she brought
with her, plus equal part. To be buried at Nob Meeting House. Children:
Elisha, Martha, John, Polly, Thomas, youngest son Andrew. Elisha, Martha,
Polly and Thomas, each to get a horse worth $100, saddle and bridle.
Five years after my death all to be sold and divided. Executors:
Gravenor McNeese and my cousin Jacob Beals on Sinking Creek. Will Dated:
3 June 1834. Witnesses: John Loyd, William Milburn, Samuel Beals.
                           Signed: Jacob X Beals

                                    43

JAMES DILLON   27 October 1834 $50.00
Brothers: Garret, William, Peter. Sisters: Jemima Smith, Lydia Dillon.
To sister, Jemima, $50 on interest. To nephew, Isaac Dillon, $20.
Brothers-in-law: John Stanfield, John Rees, George Smith, Levi Babb,
Johnathan Hayworth, $35 to be equally divided. Executors: Brother Garret,
Brother-in-law John Rees. Will Dated: 8 March 1834. Witnesses: Joseph
Henderson Junr., George Henderson, Alexander Hencerson.
                              Signed: James X Dillon
                                              his mark

ANN HAWORTH   27 October 1834 $800
To my mother, Mary Haworth, note I have on her for $9.00. Five sisters:
Rachel, Elizabeth Davis, Mary Doan, Sarah Coyle, Hannah White. Brother:
West Haworth. Executor: West Haworth. Will Dated: 3 June 1834.
Witnesses: John Oliphant Senr., Silas Haworth.
                              Signed: Ann Haworth

EDMOND BOLING SENR.   27 October 1834
Wife, Polly, to have everything to raise my children, until William C.
Boling reaches the age of 21 - my wife to have equal share if living.
Six sons: John, James, Joshua, Edmund, Valentine King Boling and William
Cannon Boling. Executors: Wife Polly, Nicholas Dunigan. Will Dated: 17
September 1834. Witnesses: Joseph Davis, John Wood, John Bryan.
                              Signed: Edmond X Boling
                                               his mark

HENRY REYNOLDS SENR. $500
To Wife, Charity, 50 acres land including dwelling house, all personal
estate, all money in hand and out of hand. Children: David, land where
he lives; Ellender Reaves, land where she lives; William; Joseph, land
to join James Kelly's; Richard, land to join Ellender's. Land to be
divided by Henry Reynolds Junr., George Reaves, Hezekiah Hughes. Other
children: Henry, Pattsey, Sally, Ellender, William, Joseph, Richard.
Executors: Henry Reynolds, Benjamin Reaves not requiring security. Will
Dated: 8 January 1835. Witnesses: Hezekiah Hughes, George Reaves, Henry
Reynolds.   Signed: Henry X Reynolds
                                              his mark

JOHN HORTON   26 ____ 1835 $500
To Wife, Nancy, Farm where I live, 10 slaves, all stock during her
natural life. If I outlive her the above goes free and simple to son,
William after my death. To children of my daughter, Jemima decd., Five
dollars. To daughter, Tabitha, Five dollars. To daughter, Polly, Five
dollars. To son, Joseph, the Hutchison place. To daughter, Nancy, two
negroes. To daughter, Hannah, two negroes subject to sale. To daughter,
Edah, remainder of Hutchison place. Daughter, Tabitha Jamison, to have
a featherbed. Children to share in debts if any. Executors: George W.
Foute, William Horton, John X Freshour. Will Dated: 14 January 1835.
Witnesses: James A. Patterson, A. Kennedy, Samuel Smith.
                              Signed: John Horton

SAMUEL McKENNEY
To Wife, Sarah, use, benefit and profit of the farm, 1/3 livestock. To
son, Samuel, horse and cow, land adjoining Frethias Wall's Mill near
McMurtreys Branch. To son, Alexander, land adjoining Robert. To
daughter, Ellener Ottinger, $100 paid by Alexander. To daughter, Jenny
Bordon, $100 paid by Robert. To daughter, Anne Ottinger, $100 paid by
Samuel. Daughter: Rebecca. Son: Robert. Executors: George Cook, John
Gragg. Will Dated: 6 February 1820. Witnesses: Claudius Buster, Elijah
Borden, George X Masoner.   Signed: Samuel McKenney

SARAH DAVIS   27 January 1835   Bond $250
Children: Elizabeth Weems, John, Fields, Jesse, Nancy McAmis, Hannah
Davis, Thomas. To daughter, Elizabeth, Five dollars. To son, Jesse,
Thirteen dollars. To daughter, Nancy, Three dollars. To daughter,
Hannah, Nine dollars. To son, Thomas, Thirteen dollars. Jesse Davis

                                  44

lives with John Davis. Thomas Davis lives William McAmish Junr. Fifty dollars due me from William Brown. Land to be rented until youngest child is 21 years old. Executors: Son John, Son Fields Davis. Witnesses: Abel Conovan, William McAmish Senr., Samuel Davis.

Signed: Sarah Davis

SAMUEL ROBINSON   27 January 1835 $2,000
Oldest sons, James and John, have their portions. Two oldest daughters, Hannah and Rachel, horse worth $60 and profits on Wilson Place. Youngest daughter, Margaret-her daughter Hannah Jane Milburn, good suit of clothes. Margaret Milburn;s son Samuel R. Milburn, suit and Five dollars. Younger sons, Samuel E. and William B., all remaining estate. Executors: John McGaughey, Samuel W. Doak. Will Dated: 29 August 1832. Witnesses; Felix Oliphant, John Kerr, Elizabeth Kerr, Harriet A. N. Kerr, John Bell, Silas Dobson, John Robinson.   Signed: Samuel Robinson

ABEL McINTOSH   27 January 1835
To my son, Jesse, 96 acres adjoining George Crosby and Joseph Davis, negro boy and two girls. To my daughter, Susannah Woods wife of David Woods, $80 trust. Emancipate negro Milly. No executor - each one take tneir part. Will Dated: 7 August 1833. Witnesses: Hugh D. Hale, Joseph Matthews. Handwriting of Daniel Bryan.

Signed: Abel McIntosh

JOHN LOVE   28 April 1835 $500
To Wife, 1/3 in fee simple. To my children, 2/3. Interest in Buckland Estate in Virginia - mortgage made to Thomas Hunton of Farquehar. Land in Jackson County, Tennessee which Charles I. Love manages. Will Dated: 4 October 1828. Witnesses: _____ Dickson, Samuel Wheeler, Vincent Jackson.

SAMUEL ELLIS   27 July 1835
To Wife, Kezia, all remaining personal estate not to be divided until her death. Children: Nehemiah, Jesse, Mary Pakins, Hannah, Johnathan, Mordecai, Samuel. To son, Nehemiah, smith tools. To daughter, Mary Pakins, Twenty dollars in trade. To daughter, Hannah, ½ personal property. To son, Johnathan, property where he has erected a dam for working the tilt hammer in his shop adjoining Galbreath and David Rankin. To grand-daughter, Hannah Hammer, Five dollars in trade. All other land to be divided between my wife and other children except Johnathan. Executors: Aaron Hammer, Son Nehemiah Ellis. Witnesses: John McAmis, William Johnson, William Alexander.

Signed: Samuel Ellis

ISAAC HAMMER   25 January 1836 $10,000
To Wife, Rachel, $150. Twenty-five hundred dollars to Society of Friends of New Hope (Quaker). Land in Washington County to Brothers and Sisters and children of my former wife. Brothers: Jacob, John, Joseph and Johnathan decd. Sisters: Barbara Range, Elizabeth Kelley and Mary Bogart. Former wife's children: Jacob, John, Daniel, David, Joseph Bowman and Catharine Miller, to receive money from sale of a tract of land. Personal property of Rachel's former husband. Executors: Aaron Hammer, John Marshall. Will Dated: 2 February 1835. Witnesses: George Jones, William Dickson.   Signed: Isaac Hammer

POLLY KELLEY   27 January 1836 $500   Non cupative will.
At home of Alexander and Margaret Baily where she took sick. Neice: Mary Jane Farnsworth gets everything, absolutely all. Executor: Thomas Farnsworth. Will given oral: 10 January 1836. Witnesses: Alexander and Margaret Baily, George Wells.

JAMES COURTNEY   25 April 1836
To Wife, Sarah, all property. Children: James, Martial, Lucy Marshall, Elizabeth Holdaway, Agga Hurley, Sarah Hurley, Polly Hurley, Jane Pettitt - one dollar each. Son, Fielding, shall have all my estate real and personal at Sarah's death. Grand children: Sarah P., Twenty dollars

and featherbed; and Jeremiah Mangrum, Twenty dollars. Executors: Sons:
Marshall and Fielding Courtney. Will Dated: 16 September 1833. Witnesses:
George Murray, Thomas X Stroud, James I. Senter, Jacob Haun.

Signed: James X Courtney
his mark

ELLIS PICKERING   25 April 1836 $1,000
To Wife, Deborah, all land during widowhood. To my sons: Nathaniel,
Ellis and Levi, each to get a horse when they are 21. My sons: Enos,
Phineas, Johnathan and Benjamin, have received theirs from me. 27 ½
acres to Enos - rest of land to 6 other sons. To my daughters, Jane,
Mary and Rebeckah, to get personal property at wife's death. Executors:
Brothers: Enos and Johnathan Pickering. Will Dated: 19 February 1836.
Witnesses: William Johnson, Henry Thompson, Aaron Hammer.

Signed: Ellis Pickering

JOHN HENDERSON SENR.   May 3, 1836
To Wife, Margaret, all personal property until William is 21, then a
childs part, then to be divided between my three daughters. Notes on
John amount to $200. Children: William, Alexander, Elizabeth, Mariah
Henderson, Margaret Cates, Robert and John S. Henderson. Newton, son of
daughter, Elizabeth. William and Newton to be schooled as much as
possible. Will Dated: 23 December 1833. Witnesses: R. Merry?, Robert
Henderson.

Signed: John X Henderson

JOHN BRANDON   4 July 1836
To Wife, Dianer Brandon, plantation plus hogs, cattle, sheep etc., but if
she takes up with any other man - the above property to be sold and
divided. Several children (not named). Administrators: Father, Thomas
Brandon and Thomas Brownlow Junr. Will Dated: 12 December 1835.
Witnesses: Stephen Hicks, Thomas Brandon, Unicey X Brandon.

Signed: John Brandon

THOMAS WILLIAMSON   1 August 1836
Wife, Kizzia, in case she intermarries she only gets 1/3 personal
property - rest to be sold and divided between my 6 daughters. Children:
Thomas W., Delilah, Jeremiah, John, Elizabeth, Polly, Kezziah, Tabitha,
Sara. My three sons have their part - to have no more. Executors: son,
Jeremiah, Washington Hinshaw. Will Dated: 1 June 1836. Witnesses:
Johnathan Prather, John Nelson.   Signed: Thomas Williamson

DAVID RANKIN   1 August 1836
Wife, Jain, to use everything as a widow. To son, Lewis, where he lives
and a negro boy. To son, William D., a negro boy. To son, James, three
lots in Raytown. To daughter, Isbel Wast??, a negro man. To daughter,
Polly Ann Rankin, ½ Lacklin place. To daughter, Batsay Jain Rankin, the
other half of Lacklin place. To son, John, lot where tanyard is. To
son, Robert, $1500 in traid and note on Smith Harvey Hankins. To
daughter, Nansay, where Pleasant Morrison now lives. To daughter,
Malinda, where Isaac Keeny lives. To daughter, Adeline Rankin, 150
akors. Executors: William Jonson, John McAmish. Will Dated: April 15,
1836. Witnesses: Warner Peters, Nancy X Ray.

Signed: David Rankin

WATSON DUDLEY   5 September 1836
To Wife, Ellender, house and truck patches, if she leaves without cause
it is to be sold and divided. To daughter, Patsy Dudlee Varner, 50
acres in gap of mountain on Broils road, rest to be divided between
grand children. Grand children: Patsy, Polly, Caroline, Elizabeth,
George, Watson Varner, George Watson Dudlee, John, Bartley, Sally,
Elender, Polly Ann and Solomon Dudlee. (Some would have to be children-
GFB). Watson Varner, George Watson Dudlee and John Dudlee to have $20
more than the rest. Executors: Jacob Stephens, Joseph Hutchison.
Will Dated: 12 July 1836. Witnesses: Jacob Stephens, John Love.

Signed: Watson X Dudlee

SETH BABB   5 September 1836
To Wife, Mary, use of house, 1/4 orchard and meadow, one mow of barn and
one stable, 1/4 profits of sugar trees. Children: Hiram, Err, Seth,
Ruth, Mary, Hulda, Rhoda, Nancy Lowe Babb. To son, Hiram, jains suit of
cloths. To sons, Err and Seth, farming tools. Daughters to receive one
dollar each. To grand-daughter, Martha Babb, daughter of Rhoda Wickes
formerly Rhoda Babb, Twenty-seven dollars. Executors: Two sons, Err and
Seth Babb. Will Dated: 4 August 1836. Witnesses: Abner Babb, Hugh
Carter Junr.   Signed: Seth Babb

JAMES COTTER   3 October 1836
To Wife, Rebecca, land adjoining Asa Gray. Youngest son, Abel Cotter,
to get land at Rebecca's death. Sons: Abener and John Cotter, died in
Indiana - their heirs $100. Rebecca Gass daughter of William Brown and
Catharine Cotter, William in Indiana. Other children: Polly wife of
William Couch, George, James Junr., Samuel, Hugh, Margaret, Rachel,
Rebecca Morelock, Nancy Cotter. Executors: Adam Humbert, Samuel Hunbert.
Will Dated: 8 July 1831.   Signed: James Cotter

ELIZABETH PETERSON   3 October 1836
Niece: Sarah Lunsford, Nephews: Elbert Lunsford and Joseph Lunsford, to
each a sheep. Joseph to get a Bible. Executor: Jesse Lunsford. Will
Dated: 3 April 1836. Witnesses: John McAmis, Sarah Baly.
                      Signed: Elizabeth X Peterson
                                         her mark

WILLIAM JOHNSON   3 October 1836
To Wife, Elizabeth, all lands to raise children till they are 21. Nine
children: John, Enos, Caleb, Isaac H., Matilda, Mary, Mahala, Jane and
Rebecca. Executor: David R. Johnson. Will Dated: 6 September 1836.
Witnesses: John McAmis, Barton Johnson.
                      Signed: William Johnson

JOHN HULL   7 November 1836
To Wife, Mary, everything during her life. Children: Peggy Trobaugh,
Charlotte Hull, John Hull, Mary Dyche decd. Daughter: Peggy Trobaugh,
wife of David Trobaugh, her part to go to her children - David to get
one dollar. Daughter: Charlotte Hull, to receive $50 more than the rest
for faithful service. Grand-daughter: Mary Miller, daughter of Mary
Dyche decd. Grand children: William and Anna Charlotte King, to get
their mother's part - to their dad, Stephen King, One dollar. Grandsons:
John and Allen Dyche, One dollar each. Executors: Adam Bible, son John
Hull. Witnesses: Thomas Arnold, D ull B itte??
                      Signed: John X Hull - his mark

WILLIAM G. FARNSWORTH   29 September 1836
To Wife, Mary, land and proceeds to raise my two children until the
youngest is 15 years of age. Father-in-law: Silas Dobson. Two children:
Alexander D. and Margaret Louisa Farnsworth. Executor: Silas Dobson.
Will Dated: 27 September 1836. Witnesses: John Link, Henry A. Farnsworth,
Silas Dobson.   Signed: William Farnsworth

REBECCA PICKERING   5 May 1824
To my son, Johnathan, 30 acres land. Sons: Samuel, Ellis, Enos, John
and Benjamin to have remaining land. Four grand daughters: Mary, Heta?,
Rachel and Elizabeth Neal, daughters of my daughter Rebeckah decd., wife
of Henry Neal, to have 1/3 household furniture and wearing apparel. Her
other daughters: Mary and Elizabeth Johnson. Executors: Sons, Samuel
and Johnathan Pickering. Will Dated: 5 May 1824. Witnesses: James
Jones, William Pickering.   Signed: Rebeckah Pickering

WILLIAM BEALS   26 November 1836
To Wife, Rachel, plantation adjoining Thomas Self etal. oldest daughter,
Mary. Other five children: Sarah, Hannah, Daniel, Abner and Elizabeth.
Executors: Jacob Beals, Jacob Ellis, Adam Bible. Will Dated: 26 November

1836. Witnesses: Thomas Self, James McDaniel, William McDaniels.
Signed: William Beals

MOSES REES   23 January 1837
To my sons, William and Solomon, Three dollars each. To son, James, 60
acres adjoining William. To son, Moses, 60 acres adjoining Jesse
Wright. To daughters, Ann, Catharine and Margaret, Fifty dollars each.
To daughter, Charity, Fifteen dollars. To daughter, Lida, a bed, saddle,
and cow. Daughter: Mary. Executors: Son-in-law John Wright, Son,
Solomon. Witnesses: Jesse Wright, John Rees.
Signed: Moses Rees

ROBERT HENDERSON
Slave, Benjamin, to be emancipated and to have 3 horses, hogs and tools.
To my neice, Anna H. Hall, $120. Four nephews: Alexander, George, Joseph
and Robert Henderson, sons of Joseph Henderson decd. Executor: Alex
Henderson. Will Dated: 19 November 1836. Witnesses: Daniel Delaney,
Franklin M. Hutchison.   Signed: Robert ⟋ Henderson
                                          his⟍mark

ROBERT GRAY   10 March 1837
To my daughter, Elizabeth, 40 acres acjoining Pickering. To daughter,
Mary, 100 acres land and Twenty-five dollars cash. To son, Robert, all
the balance to support my wife in bread, meat and necessarys. Wife:
Catharine Gray. Executors: Son Robert C. Gray, Asa Gray. Will Dated:
March 10, 1836. Witnesses: Michael Bright Senr., Joseph Fraker.
Signed: Robert Gray
Signed by Michael Bright because Robert Gray had lost his eyesight.

BENJAMIN GRAY
To Wife, Matilda, all lands etc. to raise my children. Unfinished work
to be finished - hats sold, also my hatting tools. Children: Mary Jane,
Louisa, Pollyann. Polly Ann, wife of Enos Johnson, is a girl I raised -
to share equally. Executors: David R. Rankin, John Rankin. Will Dated:
29 January 1837. Witnesses: John Marshall, William Likens, David S.
Wood.   Signed: Benjamin Gray

JACOB HORNBARGER
I'm old and infirm and destitute of my eyesight. Children: Jacob, Polly
Miller decd., George and Delilah. To my son, Jacob, Mill Place adjoining
Morelock, Ellis, Bales, McAmis and Henderson. To my son, George, big
wagon and gears, new wagon. To my grand-daughter, Mary Young, Five
dollars. To my daughter, Delilah McCurry and her husband Joseph McCurry
with whom I make my home - I give her land on Sinking Creek. Set slaves
free and protect them from being imposed upon. Executors: John McAmis,
Asa Gray. Will Dated: 9 May 1837. Witnesses: V. Sevier, George W.
Foute.   Signed: Jacob Hornbarger

JAMES TRAIL   4 May 1834
Grand-daughter: Susan Trail, daughter of Archibald Trail. Daughter:
Elizabeth Voiles. All my children. Judy Scot, wife of Elijah Scot, to
have equal share with each one of my children. Executors: Enoch Ward,
James Matthews. Will Dated: 4 May 1834. Witnesses: Jacob Haun, George
Ward, Marshall Courtney.   Signed: James X Trail
                                                his mark

ELISHA CARTER   23 March 1837
To Wife, Margaret, 1/5 part as my widow. Four sons: Anderson the oldest,
Benjamin 4th, Melton Thomas Carter youngest, 2nd son Daniel. To eldest
daughter, Nancy, one nag valued at $75 and $200 cash. Two younger
daughters, Susanna and Jemima, share equal to Nancy. Land on Lick Creek
to be sold. Daniel to be appointed Executor. Will Dated: 23 March 1837.
Witnesses: John Olinger, John Kenney.
Signed: Elisha Carter

HIRAM LINDSEY
My Mother, ____, to have negro, then to go to William M. Williams and
Farmer Pogue, also land, shares and stock. To children of Jacob Myers,
bed and bed clothes at my mother's death. Will Dated: February 12, 1837.
Witnesses: Robert D. Self, Alfred ____.
Signed: Hiram Lindsey

ROBERT RANKIN
Wife, Elizabeth, to have use of my house. Children: Polly, Thomas, James,
Anna West. Land and debts to two sons: Thomas and James - to pay Fifteen
dollars per year to wife and Polly each. Daughter, Polly, at my wife's
death, $500 if single stay with my wife, horses, saddle and bridle. To
daughter, Anna West, Five hundred dollars. Executors: Two sons, Thomas
C. and James Rankin. Witnesses: David Rice, Elijah Tame??
Signed: Robert Rankin

GEORGE G. CRAWFORD (DR. GEORGE G. CRAWFORD)
To Wife, Elizabeth, personal property. Executor: Brother-in-law, William
S. Gillespie. Will Dated: 23 September 1837. Witnesses: John Maloney,
Benjamin Lyon??
Signed: G. G. Crawford

William Gillespie died - George F. and Allen Gillespie served as Executors.

THOMAS COULSON   3 October 1837
Plantation to sister Mary's sons: William and Thomas Coulson. To sisters,
Hannah Loyd and Sarah English, to get money from 2 milch cows. To
sister, Susannah Pearce?, 6 bushels wheat, cotton and wool cords. To
sister, Rachel Coulson, and brother, Enoch Coulson, Fifty dollars each.
Brother: Elijah Coulson. Executors: David Bright, Hale Baxter. Will
Dated: 13 September 1837. Witnesses: Cornelius Smith Junr., Alfred Hays,
Robert Hays.
Signed: Thomas X Coulson

WILLIAM BROTHERTON   February 5, 1838
Wife, Jinny Brotherton, to have land - then let it go to Harvey Hale and
4 sons: William, Ogburn, John and Alexander. To heirs of my son Benjamin
Brotherton, One dollar each. To heirs of Esther Hale, One dollar each.
To heirs of John, James, George and Henry Brotherton, One dollar each.
Executors: Beverly Smith, Jinny Brotherton. Will Dated: 17 February
1837. Witnesses: Peter Couch, John Couch Junr.
Signed: William X Brotherton

JACOB SMELSER   5 March 1838
Wife, Elizabeth, gets all after funeral expenses and debts are paid.
Son, John, to have my bay horse and pay George Andes and Andrew Reader
Sixteen dollars. Children: Polly, John, Katherine, Margaret, Eliza Jane.
Children to share equally. Executors: Wife, Elizabeth, Adam Ealey.
Will Dated: 14 January 1838. Witnesses: William H. Gasscock, Jacob
Missemer, Daniel X Lechner.   Signed: Jacob X Smelser

JACOB GARRET
To Wife, Barbary, all land during widowhood. Children: Sarah, Elizabeth,
Margaret, Magdalene, John decd. William Jacob Garret, son of my son
John decd., to have an English education. Daughter Margaret's son,
Jacob Kennedy, to share with his mother and have a common English educa-
tion. Executors: Jacob Stephens, Samuel L. Stephens. Will Dated: 29
January 1838. Witnesses: Joseph Horton, Samuel Freshour.
Signed: Jacob Garret

WILLIAM ROSS SENR.   Buried at Mr. Bethel
To son, James, all land where I live fee sinple, all household and
farming utensils and 1/4 of the servants. To daughter, Nancy Cuncan, and
son, William, servants. To daughter, Jane Bullen, servants and One
hundred dollars. To son, John, Ten dollars. To son-in-law, John S. Reed
and my daughter, Grace (now deceased), Ten dollars. To John Grimes and
my daughter Polly, Ten dollars. Son-in-law, Thomas Batt, Ten dollars.
To Grand-daughters, Jane, Malinda and Elizabeth Batt, Jane Moore, Fifty

dollars each. Executors: Sons, William and James Ross. Will Dated: 19 July 1831. Witnesses: David Rice, Robert Rankin.
                                    Signed: William Ross
This Will was contested by John Ross.

WILLIAM CONWAY   13 January 1838
Negroes to be liberated and stay in Tennessee. Executor to go to Tenn. Legislature, if no results, send them to Liberia at my estate's expense. Help negroes until they by their labor can provide for themselves. Land on Nolichuckey and Lick Creek. Land to children of my nephew, William C. Hogan - 258 acres. To William Conway Hale, son of Eliza Hale, 50 acres and my share in Fish Trap opperated by Thomas L. Hale. Thomas L. Hale's wife, an orphan child, taken in by me and raised by myself and decd. wife as our own - 52 acres northside of Lick Creek. To Sarah Porter Hogan, daughter of William C. Hogan, bed, bedsteads, etc. To Anne David, friend of my wife, one of my best beds. To James Carmichael Davis, son of Ann Davis, Five hundred dollars. To Margaret Hale, daughter of Eliza, a feather bed. To Desdemona White, wife of Capt. White of Jefferson County, feather bed and furniture. To William Conway Maloney, secretary and book case. To Massy Hill, a watch. To Pierce B. Anderson, a walking cane. Legace to James C. Davis, to be put on interest. Executors: Pierce B. Anderson, Massy Hill, of Jefferson County. Will Dated: 13 January 1838. Witnesses: William O. Scruggs, Frederick Scruggs, James H. Jones, Thomas L. Hale.
                                    Signed: William Conway

SAMUEL McNEES
To Wife, Lydia, 177 acres with profits her natural life. To son, Isaiah, above land at Lydia's death if he supports and cares for her, if not it goes to my son, Gravener. To son, Gravener, land where he lives - 223 acres. To daughter, Elizabeth Carter, One hundred dollars. To daughter, Jane Crumley, Two hundred dollars. Daughters: Leddra and Rachel J. McNeese. Daughter-in-law, Charity McNeese wife of son Marmaduke decd., to have money. Daughter-in-law, Elizabeth McNeese widow of James, One hundred dollars. Notes on Miller Sexton. Executors: John Marshall, Aaron Hammer. Will Dated: 28 January 1838. Witnesses: Thomas Pierce, Jesse Ellis.   Signed: Samuel McNees

WILLIAM HENDRY   24 July 1838
To Wife, Sally, 1/3 real and personal estate as my widow. To sons, Thornton and Joseph, Fifty dollars each. Heirs of Eli Hendry. To daughter, Mary Ann Beagels, One hundred and fifty dollars. To daughter Sally McCray's heirs, One hundred and fifty dollars. Grandsons, Marshall and Eli McCray, have received Seventy-five dollars. To daughter, Nancy McAfee, Three hundred dollars. Executor: Charles Bright. Will Dated: 24 June 1838. Witnesses: Jacob Starns, Thornton Hendry, Joseph Hendry.
                                    Signed: William Hendry

HUGH MAGILL
To Wife, Mary, plantations, tools, stock, household and kitchen furniture as long as she is my widow. Children: Elizabeth wife of James Glass, Jane wife of Nathaniel Henry, James H., William, John, Hugh, Hetty or Esther, Mary, Lorinda and Charles Magill - equal parts after paying each of my deaf and dumb children Thirty dollars. Executors: Nathaniel Henry, Wife Mary. Will Dated: 7 March 1838. Witnesses: John Walker, James Magill.   Signed: Hugh Magill

ELIZABETH BRYAN   October 12, 1838
To grand-daughter, Elizabeth Horner, 50 acres inc house and spring. Three sons: John, Josiah and Daniel Bryan, to get remaining land equally divided. To daughters, Anna Hurley and Rebecca Drace, personal estate. Will Dated: 12 October 1838. Witnesses: Christopher Haun, George Murray, Matthias Wright.   Signed: Elizabeth X Bryan

JOHN HARMON - Repeat from Book 1.

NATHANIEL HAWORTH   7 January 1839
Wife, Anna. Children: Hannah, Eliza, Absalom Duffle, James Jackson,
Haworth. My small children - if my wife brings forth a boy. Daughters,
Hannah and Eliza, have their legacy. To son, James Jackson, where I
live. Wife, pregnant. Executors: Wife, Anna. Will Dated: 6 December
1838. Witnesses: Thommy A. Oliphant, William G. Lightner.
                            Signed: Nathaniel Haworth

WILLIAM BROWN   23 March 1835   Town of Greeneville
Wife, Violet Brown, to stay on with my friend Valentine Sevier. To
Valentine Sevier - all property not given to my wife. Surplus money
after wife's death - to 3 churches in North America - Presbyterian,
Methodist Episcopal, Cumberland Presbyterian. Executors: Henry Earnest
Snr., Valentine Sevier. Witnesses: Richard West, Ja Britton.
                            Signed: William Brown

EDWIN GRUBS   4 February 1839
To Wife, Elizabeth, all land for her benefit and disposal forever.
Children: David, Samuel, Martha, Catharan, Jesse, John, Amos, Mary,
Elizabeth, Rachel, Lydia, Hannah - each Three dollars as they come of
age. Executrix: Wife, Elizabeth. Will Dated: 18 December 1824.
Witnesses: Robert Evans, James Jones, John Grubs, Amos Grubs.
                            Signed: Edwin Grubs

JOHN PRICE   4 March 1839
To Wife, Mary, wagons, sheep, 10 hogs to butcher this year, sell no corn
till May or June. To son, William, slave by paying One hundred dollars
into the estate. Son, Rickerson, is sickly. To son, Alexander. To
daughter, Lucinda Dell, slave and Fifty dollars. To daughter, Nancy Ann
Jones, negro and her increase to remain free of deeds of trust. To son,
Josiah, Four hundred and fifty dollars. To daughter, Elizabeth, Four
hundred and fifty dollars. Son, John decd., his children: Mariah,
Abraham, John,, 5 girls. Old Miss Milton to live with my wife her life-
time, then with any one of my children at my estate's expense.
Executors: Sons, Rickerson and Alexander Price, Jesse W. Haile, James M.
Brotherton. Will Dated: 26 October 1838. Witnesses: Reuben West, Robert
Jeffers, Joseph Hendry.   Signed: John Price

ANTHONY DUNCAN   May 1839
To daughters, Sarah and Elizabeth, Forty dollars in current bank notes
each. To daughter, Mary White, and Jacob White her husband, Ninety
dollars. To daughters, Jane and Margaret, One dollar in bank notes each,
they have their portion. Mary and Jacob to care for me and receive
balance of estate. Executor: Jacob White. Will Dated: 20 February 1839.
Witnesses: Cornelius Smith Jr., Jesse Lely??
                      Signed: Anthony X Duncan

WILEY JANE (JEANS)
To Wife, Mourning, movable assetts after debts are paid. Sons: Joseph
P. and Wiatt, to get land at Mourning's death if they pay my grand-
daughter, Manurvy Jane Jean, Twelve dollars each. Daughters: Sarah
Milburn, Elizabeth Oliphant. Daughter-in-law, Polly, widow of James
Jeans. Executors: Abraham G. Fellers, Aaron Hammer. Will Dated: 14
October 1837. Witnesses: Uriah Harrold, James A. Shaw, Alexander X
Carroll.   Signed: Wiley Jeans

JACOB LINEBAUGH   3 June 1839
To Wife, Lucinda, beds, clothing, 2 cows, 11 sheep. Two sons: Daniel and
Frederick, to be educated. Executrix: Wife, Lucinda. Will Dated: 27
February 1835. Witnesses: Henry Dell, Jacob Dell.
                      Signed: Jacob C} Linebaugh
                                his mark

WILLIAM C. CARTER   5 August 1839
Enough personal property to be sold to pay debts. Wife, Margaret, gets
whats left her widowhood. Little daughter, Rachel, to marry and have

place where I live - to have Welch Farm. Brother: Hamilton Carter, gets
Welch Farm if Rachel should die or wife marries. Brother: Charles Carter,
gets where I now live. Executors: Andrew McPheron, John Armitage. Will
Dated: 9 May 1839. Witnesses: Charles Gass, Elim X Carter.
                              Signed: William C. Carter

HENRY HENEGAR   4 July 1832
Wife, Charlotte, to pay debts and have all property I have given - at her
death to be divided. Daughter, Elizabeth Hays, has received One hundred
dollars. To son, John H., and daughter, Charlotte McBride, One hundred
dollars each. Executrix: Charlotte Henegar. Will Dated: 4 July 1832.
Witnesses: William N. Craigmiles, William Kilgore.
                              Signed: Henry Henegar

AGNES FARNSWORTH
Notes on David Farnsworth and Thomas Reynolds to be collected and divided
with money from sale. Children: Jeremiah, Robert, George, Malinda
Lotspeich wife of James, Dorcas, Diana wife of Thomas Gillenwater. Son,
Jeremiah, to have colored man, Tennessee. To daughter, Malinda, bed,
underbed sheet, pillows and counterpain. All children to get colored
man or woman. Executors: Jeremiah Farnsworth, James Lotspeich. Will
Dated: 3 April 1839. Witnesses: Christopher Winters, George Wells.
                              Signed: Agnes X Farnsworth

JOHN WALLACE
To my adopted daughter, Amanda McGinnis, Five hundred dollars. To step-
daughter, Martha M. Mercer, my horse. Step-son: Elbert F. Mercer.
Executors: Elbert F. Mercer, John Armstrong. Will Dated: 3 May 1839.
Witnesses: Abraham Naff, Joseph Armstrong, Samuel Rankin.
                              Signed: John Wallace

SAMUEL McKENNEY   27 April 1835 $200
To Wife, Polly, 1/3, 1/2 personal property, land willed to me by my father
on waters of Caney Branch. Six Children: Susan, Lane, Alexander, Nancy,
Elizabeth and Barnabas to receive the rest. Executors: Alexander
McKenney, James Woods. Will Dated: April 6, 1835. Witnesses: Samuel
Jackson X McKenney, Hiram Gable, Hugh Stuart.
                              Signed: Samuel McKenney

JOSEPH REYNOLDS
To Wife, Mary, all personal property during her widowhood, then to be
sold and divided. To my son, Vincent, land, and he is to give us yearly
100 bushels corn, 10 bushels wheat, 20 bushels oats, and keep us in firewood. All my heirs. Executors: Wife, Mary, William Standly. Will
Dated: 7 December 1837. Witnesses: Charles Gass, Thomas Davis.
                              Signed: Joseph Reynolds X his mark

NANCY MYERS   5 November 1839
To my sons, West, William and Jacob, Five dollars each. To daughter,
Ingy Day, Five dollars and a cow and a sheep. To daughter, Nancy Bryant,
all furniture, clock and money. Other children: Polly Frazier, Viney
McCullough. Executor: William M. Williams. Will Dated: 27 August 1839.
Witnesses: George Bell, E. R. Self.

                              Signed: Nancy X Myers

ISABELLA BUSTER   2 December 1839
To my son, John, One hundred dollars. My daughter, Jane Walker wife of
John, to see that my black woman, Dill, is set free and receive just
wages for her work. Grand-daughter, Martha Hale, to have choice of
cattle. Executors: Anderson Walker, Samuel Gregg. Will Dated: 1 October
1839. Witnesses: Samuel Cochran, Marshall W. Gragg.
                              Signed: Isabella X Buster
                                          her mark

ALEXANDER HENDERSON   6 January 1840
My brother, Joseph, to keep slave, Jesse, and pay my estate sixty dollars

each year, and care for him - then set him free and give him $100. Brothers: George and Robert, to manage my store. To my cousin, Eliza W. Hutchison, One hundred and fifty dollars for caring for me. Executors: Brother, Robert Henderson, Jeremiah Moore. Will Dated. 23 November 1839. Witnesses: William Stanfield, James W. Galbreath.

Signed: Alex Henderson

THOMAS BROWN
To Wife, Meriam, all land, cattle and furniture. To my daughters: Margaret, Rachel, Ruth and Polly, personal property. To daughter, Betsey, my gray mare. Two grandsons: Thomas and Solomon Brown, son of Samuel Brown, to have six acres. Four sons: Isaac, William, James and John Brown, to have land and One hundred and fifty dollars. Executors: Sons, Isaac and William Brown, Son-in-law Thomas Beals. Will Dated: 5 December 1839. Witnesses: Joseph H. Earnest, Isaac Brown, William Brown.

Signed: Thomas Brown

THOMAS McAMIS 3 March 1840
To Wife, Jane, all I have during her natural life and at her death to be divided between son, Thomas W., and daughters, Nancy and Jane McAmis. Other children: Polly Farnsworth, James McAmis, Betsy Hall, Sally Ross, Peggy and John McAmis, to receive One dollar each. Executrix: Wife, Jane. Will Dated: 1 June 1830. Witnesses: Ephraim Wilson, John McAmis.

Signed: Thomas McAmis

PLEASANT THOMASON 6 April 1840
To Wife, Lavina, pay debts and get the rest her widowhood, then to be equally divided between all my children. Children: Milton, Matthew, Liza, Perlina, Timothy, Bury, Nancy, John I., Lucindy Hendrix. Executors: Wife, Lavina Thomason, Son, Milton Thomason. Will Dated: 9 August 1839. Witnesses: Joseph P. Jane, Thomas A. Oliphant.

Signed: Pleasant Thomason

EDWARD MOORE
Wife, Nancy, has everything, at her death it is to be divided between my children. Wife, Nancy, should remain single. Will Dated: 31 October 1837.

Signed: Edward Moore

ROBERT HENRY
To Wife, Hannah, 1/3 land, dwelling and kitchen for her support and to raise my four youngest children and educate them. Two youngest sons: Robert and William, whole of my lands in Greene County. Two youngest daughters: Melinda and Jane, horse, saddle and bridle worth Eighty dollars, cow, bed and featherbed. Servant, Bill, to be set free. Second wife's children. Executors: Abraham Naff, John Miller. Witnesses: Johnathan X Naff, Thomas Cremer.

Signed: Robert Henry

PHILLIP BIBLE 21 December 1837
Wife: Margaret. To my son, Jacob, all my lands to take care of my wife and daughter in my dwelling - if my wife and daughter should marry, Jacob is released from her support. Daughter: Margaret. Executors: Jacob Bible, Anthony Hankins. Witnesses: A. Rankin, John Bowers.

Signed: Filip Bibl
Phillip Bible

ABRAHAM GALLEMORE June 1840
Wife, Sarah, to have all, if she remarries a child's part. Children: beginning with the oldest: Jane, Abraham, Russel, Annah, Claburn, Fanny, Theny, Sarah, to receive equal parts. Executors: Wife, Sarah, James Melven. Will Dated: 3 November 1826. Witnesses: Joseph Melven, John Caruthers, David X Stevens.

Signed: Abraham X Gallemore
his mark

JOHN GASS SENR.   4 September 1845 $10,000
To Wife, Betsey, 270 acres where we now live, furniture, stills, mills
during her widowhood. At Betsey's death negroes under her command to be
set free and given $100, and moved to a Free State to free forever.
Children: Agnes King, George, Jain Farnsworth, Poly Y. Balch, Margaret
Ross, Nancy Ann Doherty, Martha Weems, John - stock in railroad company,
bank stock etc. to educate children on the bounds of Gass School District
forever. When my children left I prochened them off. Some made poor use
of it. Son John bad manager. To grandson, David Gass, if he gets
religion and is baptised to get horse worth $80 to $100. To son, H. B.
Gass, 300 acres. Grandsons: William A. Hankins and John Marvey Ross,
land near Blue Spring. My grave between my 2 wives. Have Gass Graveyard fenced - Gass Meeting House reorganized by old Calvinistic Presbyterians and give it to Cumberland Presbyterians. To grandson, William,
son of John, to have my clothing. To George Gass, son of John, a horse
worth $50.00. Executors: Valentine Sevier, Alexander Williams, Betsey
Gass my present wife, William Ross my son-in-law. Will Dated: 1 March
1837. Witnesses: A. W. Stephens, James Brown, George Jones.
                     Signed: ⟨signature⟩ John Gass
Mr. Gass thought his place worth $12,000 - It was a rather large estate -
270 acres with several smaller tracts, a store, still houses etc. This
Will was challanged by son-in-law, William Ross, and resulted in much
litegation.   G.F.B.

MALACHI CLICK   3 August 1840
To Wife, Rebecca, 1/3 property as my widow. Son: George, left country.
Sons: Nathan, Samuel, Malachi and Washington, to have all land. Malachi
to have One dollar more. Daughter: Polly Magee. My wife also gets 2
pots, pot hooks, half dozen plates, shugar bowls, set tea cups, saucers
and cream jug, knives and forks. Executors: Washington Hinshaw, Wife
Rebecca. Washington Hinshaw, wife and family - one years provisions.
Witnesses: William Ripley, Martin Click Junr., Martha Click.
                     Signed: Malachi X Click
                                      his mark

DANIEL KELLER SENR.   3 August 1840
Wife, Christena Keller, pay a debt I owe Weems estate, gets 1/3 of the
rest. To son, Daniel Jr., a bay mare. To son, Isaac, a horse. To son,
Phillip, school land and pay Sara Jeffers $100. To son, Abram, upper
tract. To daughter, Mary Wurcland? (Wineland?), 1/5 debts due me. To
daughter, Elizabeth Keller, land on Gap Creek. Daughter: Sayra Jeffers.
Executors: Phillip Keller, John Weins (Weems). Will Dated: 6 June 1840.
Witnesses: Joseph Bradley, James X Jeffers.
                     Signed: Daniel Keller

JOHN MACE
To Wife, Milly Mace, all estate to raise my children. Executors: Wife,
Milly Mace, William Willoughby. Will Dated: 15 July 1839. Witnesses:
James G. Guthrie, Henry X Mase.
                     Signed: John Mace

DANIEL KEY
To Wife, Temperance, personal property to dispose of as she thinks proper.
Executors: Wife, Temperance, John Olinger. Will Dated: 30 June 1840.
Witnesses: Jacob Gass, Samuel Keller.
                     Signed: Daniel Key

JACOB RENNER
Wife, Mary Magdalena, rent farm and have children educated. Executors:
John Bowers, Phillip Neas Junr. Will Dated: 7 October 1840. Witnesses:
(German) Neas, Philip Bower.   Signed: Jacob X Renner
                                                  his mark

JACOB EARNEST   2 November 1840
Wife, Mary, provided for. Land to be sold Fee Simple and pay debts, then
divided. Children: Robert W., Henry L., Mary E., Lydia J., Earnest,

Felix W., Thomas J., Maria Wells, Ruth F. Barren, Martha L. King.
Executors: Barton L., Henry L., Earnest Earnest and son-in-law Humphries
Wells. Will Dated: 3 August 1840. Witnesses: Henry Earnest, Joseph W.
Earnest.   Signed: Jacob Earnest

HUGH MALONEY
To son, W. Conway Maloney, 1/2 farm on Chucky River. To son, Thomas F.,
1/2 farm on Chucky River inc an island. To daughter, May, Ten dollars.
Sons, Thomas and William get personal estate. Two sons by last wife:
James and George Maloney, Ten dollars each. Executors: William Smith of
Little Chuckey, W. Conway Maloney. Will Dated: 3 October 1840.
Witnesses: Christopher Cooper, Zephas Johnson.
                          Signed: Hugh Maloney

JAMES SHIELDS   26 June 1834
I hope we meet again in happy mansions and join the happy spirits of
those gone on and those who will come hereafter in passing the etarnel
great three in one.
To Jane - my dearly beloved wife of 51 years - to have money and property
and pay my debts, to have books and surveying instruments, set her slave
free. To William now living in Missouri, $100. To son, James, 100 acres
land in Hawkins County on Whetstone Creek. To son, Melton, daughters,
Joana and Lea, $150 each. Daughters, Esther decd., Joana, Lea, sons
James, Daniel, Samuel and Melton to have $1200 owed me by Christopher
Cook and his son Samuel. To son, Henry, all my land on Lick Creek with
mills and improvements, blacksmith tools, silver watch, to pay son and
daughter, Milton and Joanna, $150 each - Henry is to provide, norish
and assist my wife in her declining years.
To be buried by the side of the field.
Set my slave woman, Soffee, free 1 May 1841 and if she should have
increase before that time, set it free at 21 years, give her provissions.
That negro's soul is as precious in God's sight as my own. I hope you
see the evil of the practice of slavery and let the oppressed go free.
My father, William Shields of Fredrick County, Maryland - I was named
executor of his Will with my brother, John Shields - the distance was to
grate and I sent John my relinquishment. I got 28 pounds, 13 shillings
and 4 pence - John died. I gave my receipt - no settlement has been
made. See that estate is settled and divide my part. Executors: Two
sons, David and Henry Woods Shields.
                          Signed: James Shields

CODICIL 9 January 1838 - Debt on Cooks is dissolved as they gave up land.
Soffee had a female mulatto child 19 July 1835 named Jain, which mulatto
I give to my wife to sell or dispose of as she thinks proper until Jain
is 21 years old and at that time she is to be set at liverty.

ROBERT HAYS   4 January 1841
Wife, Jane Hays, is heir of Sarah Glasscock decd., who had land in
Washington County, her share to be collected. To youngest son, Thomas,
200 acres land where I live on Long Fork of Lick Creek. To eldest son,
Charles, land on Long Fork of Lick Creek. To son, John, a bay horse etc.,
I have given him 75 acres land. To daughter, Margaret wife of James
Rogers, $400 to be paid by Thomas. To daughter, Susanna wife of Robert
Smith, $400. To grand-daughter, Margaret daughter of Charles Hays, $25
to get her a saddle. Executors: Nathan Morelock, Charles Hays. Will
Dated: 7 November 1840. Witnesses: Richard Fincher, Andrew Hays,
Cornelius Smith Junr.
                          Signed: Robert Hays - his mark

DAVID MORELOCK
Wife: Judy. Children: William, Thomas, Samuel, Sarah, Anna, Henry,
Matilda, Martha, Elizabeth. At wife, Judy's death William to have $40
more than the rest. Executors: Son, Thomas Morelock, Samuel Peters.
Will Dated: 12 February 1841. Witnesses: John McAmis, Jacob Beals,
Michael Maltsberger.   Signed: David Morelock

ROBERT EVANS   1 March 1841
To Wife, Frances, her sufficient support her natural life and at her

decease there is to be an equal division. Seven Children: Charles, James, John, Robert, Thomas, Mary, Susan. To son, Charles, $300. Son, James, has received his part. To son, John, island sawmill place. To son, Robert, $1000. To daughter, Susan, $500. Executors: Two oldest sons, Charles and John Evans. Will Dated: 11 May 1840. Witnesses: Thomas R. Marshall, William Partin.

Signed: Robert Evans

JONATHAN HUMBERD   1 March 1841
To Wife, Sarah, personal estate. Son: Mark (no right) to be kept and cared for on my plantation. Other heirs. Executors: Miller Saxton. Will Dated: 4 January 1841. Witnesses: Hugh Carter, William Ford.

Signed: Johnathan X Humberd

REBECCA RIMAL   NON CUPATIVE   18 September 1830
Witnesses: Elizabeth X Broyles, Polly X Mauk. Signed: 6 October 1840. She came to home of Alexander Broyles - stayed 5 weeks, surprised by sickness - breathes no more. Polly Mauck's oath affirmation - she a Quaker.
February 20, 1841 - the following summoned: Jacob Seaton and wife Sally Rimal, Betsey Rimal Miller, Polly Bird formerly Polly Rimal, John Williamson and his wife, formerly Dorcas Rimal.
                                    TO
Jacob, Isaac, John, and George Rimal, John Good, John Fillers and Betsey Fillers, Asa Baily and Delilah Baily, Jacob Good. Administrator of estate, Jacob Seaton. Polly Mauk, wife of Samuel Mauk, Washington Co. Polly Mauk swore Rebecca Rimal wanted her girls to have her effects because her sons had got their share. Witnesses: Thomas McAdams, J. Pearce.   Signed: Polly X Mock
                                            her mark

SOLOMON FORTUNAL
Father: Sugar Fortunal to get 1/3. Brothers: Wyly and Moses, to get 1/3 each. Wyly and Moses to use their part to support our father, Sugar, if he needs it. Executors: Lee Bullen, James Robinson. Will Dated: 25 March 1841. Witnesses: David M. Dobson, Daniel Beals.

Signed: Solomon Fortunal

RACHEL BEALS   3 May 1841
To daughter, Hannah, my man and 5 sheep, 20 geese. Children: Hannah, Daniel and Elizabeth, have the care and charge of Mary. Executors: Adam Bible, Jacob Beals. Witnesses: Benjamin Shaffer, Henry Shaffer.

Signed: Rachel X Beals

THOMAS MALONEY   2 August 1841
To Brother, William Conway Maloney, all real and personal estate. Executors: William Conway Maloney, Christopher Cooper. Will Dated: 22 July 1841. Witnesses: William T. M. Outlaw, A. C. Maxwell, William Brown.   Signed: Thomas Maloney

JESSE REEVE   6 September 1841
Wife, Ann, to get 2/3 - sell what she does not need. To sons, Thomas Jefferson and Jesse Smith Reeve, my plantation in Cocke County. Son, Jesse Smith Reeve, to have note on Henry and Isaac Earnest for $200 and the family Bible at the old lady's death. To son, George Washington Reeve, use of 1/3 plantation. Daughter, Elizabeth Wall decd, daughters ____. Executors: Son, Jesse Smith Reeve, son-in-law Isaac Earnest. Will Dated: 12 July 1841. Witnesses: James Biddle, James Fox.

Signed: Jesse Reeve

JOHN McCOLLUM   6 September 1841
Wife, Sarah, to have profits of land as long as she is my widow. Children: Marina wife of Daniel Bruner, Sarah wife of Joseph Milligan, Mary wife of William Ford, Mahala wife of Samuel Bruner - their children: James C. Archibald, John, Jacob C. Bruner, Margaret - son Archibald. Daughters: Marina, Sarah and Mary to receive $100 each. Margaret's son,

Archibald, to have a horse and $100 at age 21. Executors: Wife, Sarah McCollum, James McCollum. Will Dated: 19 April 1841. Witnesses: Charles Bright, James C. Doty.   Signed: John McCollum

SAMUEL CALDWELL   4 October 1841
My part of money from land in Pennsylvania to be equally divided. Wife not named. To son, Thomas, land on Clear Fork of Lick Creek. To my daughter, Nelly, house worth sixty dollars. To daughter, Mary, wife of Terry White, use of my sawmill for 6 months. Sons: Alexander, Andrew, James, John. Daughter: Elizabeth. Executors: Sons, Thomas and Alexander Caldwell. Will Dated: 22 September 1841. Witnesses: Andrew English, Jacob Holtsinger.   Signed: Samuel X Caldwell

WILLIAM BLEVINS   5 October 1841
To Wife, Elizabeth, land on headwaters of Lick Creek formerly belonging to Isaac Tunnell. Executrix: Wife, Elizabeth Blevins. Will Dated: 28 June 1841. Witnesses: Andrew English, John E. Deatherage.
                    Signed: William ——Blevins
                                   his mark

HANNAH EVANS   1 November 1841
To Children: John, Evin, Robert, Johnathan, William, James C., Hannah wife of Charles Love, One dollar each. To daughter, Peggy Ann Evans, all my real and personal estate. Executors: Evin Evans, William Evans. Will Dated: 27 April 1821. Witnesses: Thomas Magill, Nathaniel Magill, James Magill.   Signed: Hannah Evans

PHEBE REES   3 January 1842
Just debts to be paid - son, Peter, gets balance. Sons: Peter and David. Other children to receive One dollar each. Executors: Peter Rees. Will Dated: 8 December 1841. Witnesses: John Collet, Jesse Wright.
                    Signed: Phebe —— Rees

JOSEPH WHITE
To Wife, Margaret, all during her widowhood - after her decease to 6 sons, land adjoining John Whitehead, Hail Baxter and Cornelius Smith Junr. Sons: Isaac, Abraham, Jacob, Cornelius, Washington, Joseph. Daughters: Elizabeth White and Mary, wife of James Thompson. Son, Isaac, to have 6 acres. Son, Joseph, to have $60. Executors: Charles Bright, Hail Baxter. Will Dated: 18 June 1841. Witnesses: John Baxter, William Ross.
                    Signed: Joseph X White
                                   his mark

SAMUEL WILHITE   7 February 1842
To son, John, 3 surveys land. To son, James, Two dollars. Daughters: Susanna Glaze, Mary Massengill and Sarah Williams to have balance of my estate. Executors: Son, John Wilhite, James F. Broyles. Will Dated: 27 August 1832. Witnesses: Isaac Earnest, Washington Hinshaw, G. T. Banor
                    Signed: Samuel Wilhoite

ANGUS McCOY
Land on Newport Road to be sold and pay Dr. James Woods and Dr. Wyet. My three sisters: Jane, Katherine and Nancy, will finish paying my debts if necessary, they get land. After their death, land to go to my nephew, John McKay. Brother: George McKay. Executor: Dr. James Woods. Will Dated: 17 October 1840. Witnesses: John Eberle, Marshall W. Gregg.
                    Signed: Angus McKoy

CHRISTOPHER HOUTS   8 March 1842
To son, Jacob, 100 acres land where I live. To daughter, Magdalean, 50 acres. To daughter, Mary, land adjoining Samuel Bowman. Daughter: Barbary Bruner, living in Indiana. Grand-daughter: Susanna Ellis. Grand-daughter, Barbary Houts, 120 acres on Lick Creek. Sale Well next to mountains. Executors: Jesse Ellis. Will Dated: 11 September 1840. Witnesses: Samuel Bowman, John Weems.

FREDERICK TROBAUGH   8 March 1842
All notes and accounts to be collected. Children: John, George, Henery,
William, Samuel, Elizabeth French, Anna Ailshie, Allen. Should John
Trobaugh never return or have heirs, his part is to be divided among the
heirs. Executors: Sons, George and William Trobaugh. Will Dated: 4
February 1840. Witnesses: Charles Gass, William Dunwoody.
                              Signed: Frederick Trobaugh

DAVID KEYS (KEY)   6 June 1842
To Wife, Mary, old Pilgrim mare. Children: Eldest son John, Peter, Mary
Luster wife of Reuben, Elizabeth Harmon wife of John, Lucinda Burrows
wife of Peter Burrows, son Alfred Key. Eldest son, John, to have a mare
and no more. To daughter, Elizabeth Harmon wife of John, 4 shares of 395
acres, they having bought 3 shares. To son, Alfred, remaining 3 shares.
To son-in-law, Peter Burrows, all he owes me. Alfred and John to support
Mary. Executors: Son, John Key, John Bryan. Will Dated: 17 May 1842.
Witnesses: John Olinger, Matthew Cox.
                              Signed: David X Key

HENRY FOX   4 January 1849 $1600
To Wife, Sarah, plantation as a widow. Two children: Andrew Jackson and
Jacob Smith Fox. Will Dated: 12 June 1841. Witnesses: Isaac Earnest,
Henry Earnest.   Signed: Henry X Fox

FELIX EARNEST - Repeat from Book 1

JAMES GASS   1 August 1842
To Wife, Polly, plantation and its profits and horses, cows etc. To
George Britton, son of William Britton, one horse, saddle and bridle if
he stays with Polly until he is 21. Daughter, Nancy, to have her support.
Children: Nancy, Charles, Joseph, James, William, Betsy Armitage, Polly
Babb (her children, Emaline, Sally, Harvey, Justice Phillip Babb.), John
M. Gass. Son John M., to have land in Grainger County on Holston River.
Ten first children. Executors: John Armitage, Charles Gass. Will Dated:
30 April 1842. Witnesses: John Hay?, William Ross Senr.
                              Signed: James Gass

ALLEN GILLESPIE   5 September 1842
To Wife, Sarah, negro girl named Esther now in possession of Rev. Samuel
W. Doak. Children: James W., William S., Polly, Elizabeth Crawford,
Martha H. Tyler, George, Thomas, Robert, Sarah, Allen H., Jude Ann. To
son, William S., $120 I loaned him when he and his wife went to Nashville.
Pay debt to William G. Crawford, husband of Elizabeth. Educate Thomas,
Robert and Sarah. Land on Limestone Creek. I'm in dispute over land in
Virginia. Executors: E. L. Mathes, George Gillespie. Will Dated: 9 June
1842. Witnesses: Jacob Miller, John Falls.
                              Signed: A. Gillespie (German)

DANIEL KIRBIE
Children: Malissa, Polly, Daniel Kirby. To son, Daniel, land to keep his
three sisters in bred and meet and pervisions while they live single and
stay together and he is 21. Executors: John Crabtree, Charley Bright.
Witnesses: Daniel Warner Kirbie, Melissa Kirbie, James Crabtree.
                              Signed: Daniel Kirby

KATHARINE WILHOIT   29 September 1842
(Widow of Solomon Wilhoit - DAR - G.F.B.) Grand-daughter: Nancyann
Myers. I owe Immanuel Parman Thee dollars. Executors: Samuel Wilhoit,
Joseph Hutchison. Will Dated: 29 September 1842. Witnesses: John X
Freshour Junr., David L. Stephens.
                              Signed: Catharine X Wilhoit

JAMES BAXTER   28 January 1842
To Wife, Sarah, to have use of land. To Levi Woodberry, son of Bennet
Baxter, 30 acres land at Sarah's death. Executor: Bennet Baxter.

Witnesses: John P. Holtsinger, Jacob Holtsinger.
                         Signed: James Baxter

JOHN MORRISON   2 January 1843 $1500
Wife, Elizabeth, to have home place during her widowhood, then to go to
son, Wesley Morrison's 3 sons: James Crawford, Archibald Campbell and
John Wesley Morrison. Children: Rebecca, Rachel, Leah, Elijah decd.
(his sons: John Fletcher, Jacob Fleming and Elbert Aiken Morrison), James,
Wesley. To daughters, Rebecca and Rachel, 30 shillings each. Wife's
grand-daughter: Malinda V. Babb. Executors: Son, Thomas Morrison, Thomas
Baly. Will Dated: 1 December 1842. Witnesses: William Jones, Gabriel
Henry.   Signed: John Morrison

MOSES DOTSON
To son, Charles, where I live. To daughter, Mary Oliver, bed and bedding.
Son, Rheuben decd., his heirs to receive $30 paid by Charles. Executors:
Charles Dotson, Grandson, Samuel Abraham Dotson. Will Dated: September
30, 1842. Witnesses: J. B. Yeager?, Isaac Brown, John X Brown.
                         Signed: Moses X Dotson
                                        his mark

ANDREW I. PARRY
To sister, Elmira, $400.00. To sister, Emily D. Snapp, $300. To my
mother the remainder after expenses. To George, my cloes. Dated: 16
November 1842.   Signed: Fairwell - Andrew I. Parry

JAMES MORROW
Wife, Ester, to live in my house with Malinda. Children: Malinda,
Betsey. To Brother, John Morrow, my big coat and saddle. Daughters to
share equally. Executors: John Morrow. Will Dated: 18 June 1843.
Witnesses: Thomas Murphy, Alexander McCollum.
                         Signed: James Morrow

WILLIAM HOUSTON - Repeat from Book 1

DAVID BROWN SENR.
Beloved wife. Sons: Joseph, David Junr., Sylvanus, Jetham, William
Brown. Daughters: Polly Thompson, Marthy Brown, Phebe Tucker, Nancy
Holder. Son John's two heirs. Will Dated: 15 January 1843. Witnesses:
Leonard H. Jones, Richeson X Price.
                         Signed: David X Brown
                                        his mark

MARY KEY
Wife of David Key decd., and daughter of John Keller, my father, now
deceased. To son, Samuel Keller, to have land, money, everything. My
brother, George Keller decd. died without issue - my part and my part of
400 acres on Lick Creek to Samuel. Executor: Son, Samuel Keller. Will
Dated: 13 August 1842. Witnesses: Andrew Dyche, Wylie I. Procter.
                         Signed: Mary X Key
There was a lawsuit testing the validity of this Will brought by heirs
of law of Mary Key, namely: Peter Key, John M. Harmon, James Saunders,
William Ross Junr.

ISABEL CRAWFORD   3 June 1843
To daughter Mary McFarland's heirs, $14 divided between them. To
daughters, Margaret Hall, Rebecca Guin and Lydia Brown, $5 each. Son:
William. To grand children, Amanda, Harriet and Daniel Willet, $100
each. Executor: Son, William Crawford. Witnesses: Marshall W. Gregg,
Samuel Cochran.   Signed: Isabel X Crawford

MICHAEL BRIGHT SENR.   5 December 1842
Opposed by John Maltsberger Sr. and Polly his wife.
My last and first Will. About to take a journey home. To be buried by
my wife. To my three sons: Michael, Charles and David, $2000, to have

59

$1000 more than others for good reasons, they stayed with me to age 26 and helped me with family. To oldest and first born daughter, Polly wife of John Maltsberger, $1000, her husband owes me debts. Daughters: Caty wife of Jacob Stregil?, Sarah decd., wife of Samuel Bowman, Elizabeth wife of Lanty Armstrong, and Rachel wife of Nathan Morelock, to receive $1000 each. Two boys living with me: George W. and James H. Bright - reported eligitimate children of my son David - their teacher owes me, they are to be educated and learn Mechanicks Trade if they want at my expense. My wife and I loved them. George and Alexander Hays to build house. Will Dated: April 17, 1837. Teste: Charles X Fincher, Nathan Morelock, Samuel X Collet.

Signed: Michael Bright Senr.

PHILLIP BABB SENR.   4 September 1843
To Wife, Nancy, land inc orchard, barn and dwelling - comfortable living. To my four sons: William, Abner, Phillip and Samuel Babb, my land equally divided after death of my wife. Daughters: Rebecca, Elizabeth, Rhody and Anna Meriah, to have all surplus property. Executors: Sons, William and Abner Babb. Will Dated: 17 July 1843. Attest: Absalom Stonecypher, John A. Stonecypher, Alexander Brown.

Signed: Phillip X Babb

HENRY MYARS   26 June 1843
To Wife, Elizabeth, $500 from sale of plantation. Children: Polly, Harriet, Rebecca (still with me - underage), William Henry. Daughter, Rebecca, to have as much from personal property as other daughters. Ten children. Executor: Jacob Kerbaugh. Will Dated: 4 September 1832. Witnesses: Charles Gass, John Kerbaugh.

Signed: Henry Myers

ERASTUS EVANS   2 October 1843
To my two sisters: Eusebie and Sarah O. Evans, all my part of my father's estate in Virginia. To my brother: James H. Evans, my part of my fathers claim in estate of Robert Harrison in Virginia. Executor: Daniel Britton. Will Dated: 1 July 1843. Witnesses: Allen Dyche, Casper Easterly.

JOHN GLASSCOCK   6 November 1843 $5,000
Children: William, Keren H. Haile, all my other children. To son, William, $50 to make him even. My son, George, not to share even with other children - by agreement. My slaves to choose their master or mistress. Executors: Jesu Glasscock, William A. Henderson. Will Dated: 17 October 1843. Witnesses: William Rader, Lemuel Crosby (may be Samuel), Jesse Rader, George Kinser.

Signed: John Glasscock

JACOB HARMON   1 January 1844 $9,000
To Wife, Catharine, land, house and 1/2 garden. Sons: Jacob Junr. and John, 540 acres land on both sides of Lick Creek. Daughters: Polly Cutshall, Betsey Bible, Eve Trobaugh, Catharine Sealykness??, Sally Harmon. Grand-daughter: Catharine Trobaugh, daughter of William and Eve. Shields Miller on Lick Creek. Sons to pay daughters at Catharine's death, $1000 each. Executors: John and Jacob Harmon. Will Dated: 8 February 1843. Witnesses: Thomas Self Junr., Thomas Self Senr., Reuben Rader.

Signed: Jacob _frumerm_ Harmon

REBECCA LITTLE (LYTLE)
Children: Eliza Lytle, Albert Lytle, John Lytle, Sarah Fillers. To daughter, Eliza, all land except 50 acres deeded me by Michael Fillers which I gave to son Albert. To son, John, bed and clothing. To daughter, Sarah Fillers, bed and clothing. Executor: Henry Wells. Will Dated: 22 December 1843. Witnesses: George Wells, L. B. Wells, J. P. Wells, proven by Jacob P. Wells.

Signed: Rebeccah X Lytel
                                        her mark

PETER KENT   (Revolutionary Soldier - G.F.B.)
To Wife, Sarah, land and personal property. To daughter, Harriet Johnson,

bed and trunk. The remainder of my estate to grand children: John and Abigail Kent. My pension for Sarah An. Executor: John Freshour Junr. Will Dated: 29 April 1842. Witnesses: Johnathan Easterly, William Gragg.
Signed: Peter Kent

JOHN WISECARVER   4 March 1844 $1,000
Executors on Bond: Samuel Wisecarver, George Jackson, Jacob M. Bewley. To Wife, Elizabeth, tract where we live - daughters to get her part. To son, William, and daughter, Sally, $1.00, they have their part. Children: Polly, Bethena, Samuel, William, Sally, Harmon. Executors: Sons, Samuel and Harmon Wisecarver. Will Dated: 6 January 1843. Witnesses: Thomas L. Walker, George Jackson, Charles Wilkinson.
Signed: John Wisecarver

MERRYMAN PAYNE   died February 10, 1844   Noncupative Will.
Wife, Darcus (Henderson - G.F.B.). She asked for directions. He replied, "all he had was hers". Witness: M. Lincoln.
Signed: Thomas Lane Jr., J. Howard

THOMAS W. EARNEST   1 April 1844   Bond $4,000
To Wife, Nancy D., all profits due me and all she had when we were married. Brothers and sisters to receive One dollar each and all my right in my father and mother's land. Sold goods in Rheatown Company Partners: Henry Earnest, Jesse S. Reeve. Executors: William A. Eakin, John Rankin. Will Dated: 17 February 1844. Witnesses: Jesse S. Reeve, Robert Rankin.
Signed: Thomas W. Earnest

JOHN SIMPSON   6 May 1844
Wife, Barbara, to have all she had plus what I have and profits from same during her life. Children: Nancy Chidester, Robert, Elias B., John, George B., James - each must git an equal share. Executors: Son, George B. Simpson, Micael Basher. Will Dated: 21 March 1843. Witnesses: John Bowman, Martin Basher.
Signed: John Simpson

JOHN CRAWFORD   24 November 1840
To Wife, Dianna, horses, cattle, sheep, land on Lick Creek. To sons, James and William, land on main Lick Creek adjoining Israel Woolsey. To sons, John and Jackson, land on Long Fork of Lick Creek. To youngest sons, George and Isaac, my wife's land at her decease. To sons: Samuel, John and Hamilton, $1.00 each. To my brother, William, 100 acres where he now lives. Three daughters: Nancy, Rhoda and Jane, $1.00 each. Executors: Wife, Dianna, Son, Samuel Crawford. Will Dated: 24 November 1840. Test: William Coulson, Cornelius Mays, Cornelius Smith Junr.
Signed: John X Crawford

MARY DELL   5 August 1844   Bond $6,000
Jacob Smith and Barbary his wife to get slaves. Henry Dell and Joab Dell, my three heirs in this county, home plantation by paying off my note to Ephraim Dell. Ephraim Dell of Indiana. Jacob Newman and Elizabeth his wife, and Lucinda Dell, wife of George Dell decd., living in the state of Missouri, two heirs to be an equal division. Executors: Henry Dell, Jacob Smith. Will Dated: 10 January 1843. Witnesses: Leonard Smith, Henry Smith.   Signed: Mary X Dell

SOLOMON STONECYPHER   2 September 1844
To Wife, Elender, decent maintenance during her natural life or widowhood. Son, Joseph, to get wife's part. Children: Joseph, Susannah wife of Joseph Fincher, Ester wife of William Crabtree, Diartha Stonecypher, Sarry Stonecypher, Ruth wife of Jonathan Thornburg in Indiana, Temperance wife of Jesse Doty, Catharine wife of Thomas Thomason, Henry, Nathan and John Stonecypher. To daughters, Susannah, Ester, Diartha, Sarry and Ruth, $1.00 each. To daughter, Catharine, all residue of my estate arising from sale of personal property. Executors: Samuel Humberd, Joseph Stonecypher. Witnesses: William Ross, Seth Babb.
Signed: Solomon Stonecypher

CHRISTOPHER HAUN   2 September 1844 $7,000
Son, Daniel, has his full share. To son, John, land at the mouth of
Potter's Creek, where he now lives. To daughter, Levina who married
George Jackson, their children: Rebeckah Ann, Dempsey, Caleb, Isaac,
Andrew, Mary, land where I now live, to pay other children money to
make all equal. To daughter, Phebe McMillan, land where they live
deeded me by Benjamin VanPelt. Wife: Rebeckah. Sons: John, Christopher,
Abraham. Daughters: Elizabeth Witt, Mary Ann Black. Executors: Sons,
John and Christopher Haun Junr., Harmon Wisecarver, Samuel Wisecarver,
John Kinnes?? Will Dated: 15 March 1838. Witnesses: Samuel Wisecarver,
Harmon Wisecarver, John Pinnans??
                              Signed: Christopher Haun

HENRY FORD   Proven 2 December 1844
To My mother, ____, notes and balance of personal estate. Brother I
guess William, $1.00. To sister, Polly wife of Samuel Humber, $1.00.
Sister: Elizabeth married Jackson Babb. Executors: Samuel Humber Esq.
Will Dated: 6 November 1844. Witnesses: Charles Bright, Mark Gaunt.
                              Signed: Henry Ford
Jesse Wright entered suit against me in Chancery Court - Mark Gaunt,
Hugh E. Cotter and William Ford my securities to be made harmless.
Malachi Gaunt's children to have land I live on, purchased from Solomon
Stonecypher.

CORNELIUS SMITH   6 January 1845
To Wife, Sarah, plantation on Long Fork of Lick Creek adjoining David
Logan, Charity McNeese and Cornelius Smith Junr. Other land on Lick
Branch of Lick Creek adjoining Job Parrett. Children: John, Cornelius,
Hiram, Aaron Smith, Sarah wife of Job Parrett, Milly wife of Thomas
Thompson, Nancy wife of John Maning, Lydia wife of Jesse Mays, Honor
wife of Peter Mays. To daughter, Sarah, 30 acres, all tracts to have
water. Well where I have been boring for salt and boring tools - if
there is profit it is to be divided equally. Executors: Cornelius Smith
Junr., David Olinger. Witnesses: Turner Smith, John Dodd, David M.
Bright.   Signed: Cornelius Smith

JOHN THOMASSON   3 March 1845
Daughter, Martha Barrum, $6.50. Daughter, Nancy Oliphant, $20.00. Two
grand-daughters: Elizabeth and Nancy White, $1.00 each. Children:
Martha, Barrum, William Thomasson, Nancy Oliphant, Thomas, Howel and John
Thomasson. Executors: Sons, Thomas and Howel Thomasson. Will Dated:
10 March 1843. Witnesses: Ephraim Doty, Lee Walker.
                              Signed: John Thomasson

JONAS McNEESE   3 March 1845 $300
Wife, Ruth, to have decent support from the farm. Children: William,
John E., Samuel, Mary McNeese Ball, Elizabeth wife of Aiden McNeese,
Rebecca wife of Elihu McNeese, Hulda, Mellinda, Mahala McNeese. Land
to be divided between my 3 sons - lines running east and west. Hogs
to be sold for cash during next pork season. Executors: Son, William
McNeese, Wife, Ruth. Will Dated: 3 February 1845. Witnesses: James
Shanks, William Orr, Andrew Logan.
                              Signed: Jonas McNeese

SUSANNAH SMITH   23 September 1844
Daughter, Leuciana Meyer wife of John Meyer - land in Washington County,
adjoining Isaac Hartman, John Blakely - deeded to myself and Solomon
Smith by my beloved husband Nathaniel Smith, also my pension now in
sucessful operation for the services of my husband Nathaniel Smith in
the Army of the United States. Executors: John Meyer Junr., Nathaniel
S. Meyer. Will Dated: 23 September 1834. Witnesses: Jacob Hacker,
John Crawford.   Signed: Susanna X Smith

ANDREW McPHERON   8 April 1845 $800
To Wife, Jane, house, kitchen, spring and springhouse, meat, grain etc.
to support all who live on place with her. Try and keep up the place

and Mill. Children: Martha McPheron, 4 youngest sons; John, Andrew, Samuel, Allen, James, Margaret wife of John Fisher?, Polly wife of John Hartman, Blanchy wife of Joseph Drake, Rebecca Burkey decd., Susanna wife of Samuel McCurry, Thomas McPheron, Elizabeth wife of James McPheron. Martha to be schooled and taught to read the Old and New Testaments. Land on Delaney's Branch in Greene County where Thomas Mills now lives. Executors: James C. Wilson, Allen Russell, John Russell. Will Dated: 8 February 1845. Witnesses: Charles Gass, Amasa Harrold Jr.
Signed: Andrew McPheron

RICHARD M. WOODS   24 June 1845
Wife, Eliza Ann, to have life estate. Children: James C., Sarah Jane Woods. James C. to have my watch and walking cane. Sisters: Elizabeth Ortto and Sarah Woods to have their house and lots their lifetime. Property to be valued and divided as my executors see best. Executors: Maj. James Britton, David Rice, William A. Hankins, Mordecai Lincoln and also guardians of my children, James and Sara Jane. Will Dated: 4 June 1845. Witnesses: V. Sevier, D. Sevier, A. Aiken.
Signed: Richard M. Woods

GEORGE SMELSER   7 July 1845   Non-cupative
Wife: Elizabeth. Children: Adam, Henry, William, Jonathan, Phebe, Malinda, Barbary Ann, Ephraim, Polly, Elizabeth and Margaret. At house of John Harmon where he was sick. Witness: John Fisher.
Signed: Charles Gass, who wrote the Will at Mr. Smelser's direction.

JANE FARNSWORTH   1 December 1845 $180.00
To my son, Solomon, one silver watch. To daughter, Sarah wife of George Lintz, my black woman. Son: Thomas. Rest of my children. Executor: John Perman. Will Dated: 2 September 1845. Witnesses: John Gourley, Thomas Reynolds.
Signed: Jane X Farnsworth

JOHN GASS SENR.   Judgment of Will   3 November 1845
William Ross et al vs. Valentine Sevier and Alexander Williams, Executors for John Gass decd. in Chancery Court, 6 November 1845, Contesting Will - not codicil. Jury: Samuel Parman, William C. Hale, Moses Whittenburg, George Henderson, Jacob Bible, Jacob Hacker, Silas Dobson, Thomas Phillips, Jacob Keicher, William Rader Senr., William Rader Esq. and Thomas Russell of David. Thomas Campbell, Clerk of Supreme Court of Tennessee - Knoxville. Will to stand as John Gass willed, but not the codicil. Will to be recorded in Greene County, Tennessee.

WILLIAM GEORGE   5 July 1846 $8,000
Wife: Elizabeth. Eight heirs: Eliza Harrison, Elizabeth, John Dickson, Samuel Nelson, Narcissus, Margaret, Nancy, Cornelius Wester. Executors: Wife, Elizabeth, Conrad Girdner. Will Dated: 17 December 1844. Witnesses: George Lintz, Alfred Dewitt, (John Link?) - Jeremiah Farnsworth served.
Signed: William George

JOHN HARDIN   5 January 1846 $700
To Wife, Clary A. Hardin, one third real estate. Two youngest sons: Ollayer and Vollentine Hardin, to get home plantation - 130 acres. Youngest daughter: Clary A. Hardin, a house, $40 and other things. Sons: Cornelius, Robert, John, Jacob, Isaac, Marsh and Isaac Harmon, One dollar each. To Bennet and Rebecca Weems, One dollar. To Benjamin and Honor Carter, One dollar. Executors: Cornelius and John Hardin - friends. Will Dated: 28 March 1842. Witnesses: Andrew McPheron, Andrew McPheron, Allen McPheron.
Signed: John Hardin

JOHN NEASE   6 April 1846 $4500
To Wife, Elizabeth, plantation except, Little new field on road and clover field - from Schoolhouse up. To son, Henry, 200 acres where he lives. To son, Phillip, 200 acres where he lives. To son, Thomas, land including 2 fields mentioned before at $5 per acre. To son, Jacob, his

plantation. Poor little daughter, Mary Ann, to stay with Levina if Mary
Ann outlives her mother. Other Children: William and Levina wife of
Jacob Rader. Black boy Eli. Executors: Two sons, Phillip and Thomas
Nease. Will Dated: 9 March 1846. Witnesses: _____ Ness, Joseph X
Renner. Seven hundred acres or more land.

Signed: John Nease

THOMAS BRANDON   6 April 1846
Wife: Nancy. Sons: Endemyon, Thomas, Johnson, William, James, Nathaniel.
Endemyon to have land near the pump. Daughters: Eunice Brandon, Polly
wife of Joseph Dykes, Mary Ann Moore wife of William Moore, Rose Ann
Moore wife of Gabriel Moore, Charlotte wife of William Dobbins, Nancy
wife of James Hamilton. Grand-child: Polly Dikes wife of Joseph Dikes.
Executor: Endemyon Brandon. Will Dated: 10 March 1845. Witnesses:
Elijah Headrick, William Basket.   Signed: Thomas Brandon

REV. C. A. VAN VLECK   4 May 1846
To Wife, Christiana Susan Van Vleck, money, property and evidence of same
for the support of my children. Brother, William A. Van Vleck, to aid my
wife with the business. Executors: Wife, Dr. Alexander Williams, Jacob
Howard. Will Dated: 7 December 1845. Witnesses: V. Sevier, James
Britton.   Signed: Charles A. Van Vleck

JOHN COUCH   4 May 1846
To Baptist Church - 1 acre and spring. 1 acre for graveyard.for the
public forever. If church fails - land to revert to son, Peter. To son,
Peter, 630 acres, stock and money including my windmill. To sons, John
and Jacob, all I have given them. To daughter, Elizabeth Alexander, all
I have given her. Executor: Son, Peter Couch. Will Dated: 25 March
1845. Witnesses: George Kenney, Harvey Hale.

Signed: John U Couch
his mark

WILLIAM WOOLSEY   1 June 1846 $6,000
Executors on Bond: Wylie Kelley, William B. Woolsey, Frederick Dewitt,
John W. Ruble. To Wife, Sarah, all real and personal estate - not to
sell or make waste with it. Children to get it at her death. To son,
Thomas, land on French Broad River, where he now lives. To son, Zephaniah,
decd. - his widow Rachel $5, her children $50. To son, William B., to have
land rent free - but he must keep up fence. To daughter, Hepzibah Woolsey,
One half the cupboard. Other children: Gilbert, Jerusha Woolsey, Marriann,
Sarah and Karenhappuck Woolsey. Daughters to have beds, bedsteads, horses
and land. Executors: Wylie Kelley, William B. Woolsey. Will Dated: 6
May 1846. Witnesses: William S. Ruble, John W. Ruble.

Signed: William Woolsey

SARAH GILLESPIE   7 September 1846 $2400
Sons: Allen, Thomas, Robert. Thomas and Robert to have a bed and a piece
of furniture each. Five daughters: Polly, Elizabeth, Martha, Julia and
Sarah to divide negroes and all remaining estate. Executors: Ebenezer
Mathes, Josiah Yeaker, Allen Gillespie, John Crabtree. Will Dated:
September 3, 1844. Witnesses: M. L. Neilson, Ann Gillespie, Elmira E.
Pierce.   Signed: Sarah Gillespie

JAMES DINWIDDIE   6 July 1846   Bond $2500
Sons, James H., John and William F., have their share, Five daughters:
Elizabeth R., Easter, Pollyann, Jane Frazier, Martha Pierce - to get land
equally divided. Black girl, Dinah, to be free and live with my daughter.
Executors: John Crabtree, Pollyann Dinwiddie. Will Dated: 28 June 1846.
Witnesses: James Dillon, Michael Fraker, Abner Frazier.

Signed: James X Dinwiddie

WILLIAM HALL SENR.   6 July 1846 $16,000   Non-cupative Will
To be buried in orchard, graveyard to be paled. Wife, Polly, to have
dowry and live with one of my girls. Children to have what I gave them -
no fussing. Give clothes to children they fit best. Executors: David

F. Hall, Henry Hall, Jefferson Range, William S. White.

GEORGE JONES   3 August 1846
Wife, Nancy, to stay on place as long as she lives, $1000 in silver, four
servants, horse beasts, my sheep and shears, corn, wheat, cotton, wool
and flax. To daughter, Mary Allen, servant girl named Martha. Mary's
sons, Robert and George Allen, servants. Sons: Mason Jones, James Jones.
Until the Allens come. Property to be equally divided. Executors: John
Ruble, Thomas Jones Esq. Will Dated: 6 February 1844. Witnesses: George
Wright, Amasa Mills, Edward Looney.
                       Signed: George Jones

HENRY THOMPSON   7 September 1846
Property to be equally divided. Children: Martha Thompson, Rebecca
Lauderdale, Margaret Shelley, Pollyann Cochran, Minerva Russell, Samuel
Thompson, Henry Thompson Junr. Nothing to James C. Thompson now decd.
nor his heirs - I gave him his part. Executor: John Sheffey. Will
Dated: 12 February 1845. Witnesses: Daniel Graham, John Russell.
                       Signed: Henry Thompson

GEORGE H. GILLESPIE   7 September 1946 $14,000
To Wife, Ann, dwelling house and personal property. To daughter, Eliza
Ann Bullen, negroes and 70 acres deeded me by Loyd Bullen. To daughter,
Barbara Jane Stonecypher and Betsy Ann Beals, orphan girl I raised - $60
each. If slaves become turbulent, sell them and put money on interest
to raise and educate my grand children. Executors: Two sons-in-law,
Loyd Bullen, Absalom Stonecypher. Will Dated: 6 March 1845. Witnesses:
D. R. Johnson, Thomas Carson.   Signed: George H. Gillespie

MARY HAWORTH   5 October 1846 $200
Son, Howard Haworth, to get remaining property by paying my children,
not named, $1 each. Four daughters to receive beds, bed clothing and
wearing apparel. Executors: Howard Haworth, Isaac Earnest, William
West. Will Dated: 11 May 1839. Witnesses: John Oliphant, West Haworth,
James Biddle, Isaac Earnest.   Signed: Mary X Haworth

WILLIAM BASKET   5 October 1839
To Wife, Mary, lands and tenements. To son, William, 130 acres. To
daughters, Jane Dykes and Nancy Brandon, have gotten a cow and calf,
other daughters to have the same. Daughters: Polly, Lucinda, Eliza and
Matilda Basket. Executrix: Wife, Nancy. Witnesses: Elijah W. Headrick,
Abraham X Moore.   Signed: William X Basket

ELIZABETH McPEARN (McPHERON)   1 May 1848 $800
Widow of James McPheron. Willed everything to William M. and Cassa E.
Morgan. Will Dated: 18 October 1846. Witnesses: Eph Carter, Alexander
Morgan.   Signed: Elizabeth X McPheron

ROBERT SMITH SENR.   4 January 1847
To son, Robert, $50 from sale of land where he lives. To daughters,
Lydia Barnett and Mary Winkle, to have $50 also. Other children: Anny,
Jacob and Samuel. Debt against Andrew Kennady to be collected and
divided. Executors: Sons, Samuel and Jacob Smith. Will Dated: 16
November 1846. Witnesses: George Gammon, J. A. Park, Samuel Shrewsbury.
                       Signed: Robert Smith

SAMUEL RIPLEY   4 January 1847 $8,000
Five sons: David, Andrew, Tylgman, Lafayette and Josephus. Three
daughters: Camaline Hayworth, Sarah Jane and Sharlotte, $1 each. Nancy
Ann and Maloney Sprinkle indebted to me, collect and divide it with the
avobe eight children. Slave, Jefferson, to have Saturday's for himself.
If Nancy Ann should become a widow, she is to have 10 acres with a house
near spring. Executors: Two sons, David and Andrew Ripley, Joseph H.
Earnest. Will Dated: 13 December 1846. Witnesses: John Squibb, James
Fox, Joseph H. Earnest.   Signed: Samuel Ripley

ISAAC HARMON   4 July 1847 $1,000
Children: Juicy Province wife of William Province, Thuzy Price wife of
R. Price, John M. Harmon, Emma Samples wife of William Samples, Peter
Harmon, Elizabeth Beekner wife of Abraham Beekner - already have their
parts. To son, Amacy Harmon, land on Lick Creek and one half one still.
Son, Isaac Harmon, to have nothing. To daughter, Peggy Ann Couch and her
husband John, one half of 50 acre tract near Casteel Mill. Daughters,
Peggy Ann Couch and Mary Ann Shelley, to have 100 acre Knowles Place.
To son, William A., my home tract and part of 400 acre entry. Executors:
William A. and Peter Harmon, my sons. Will Dated: 25 November 1846.
Witnesses: Michael Myers, Jane Smebs??
                            Signed: Isaac Harmon

JOHN CARTER   1 March 1847
Wife, Elizabeth, gets everything. Nothing to be taken away from her by
children. Will Dated: 7 September 1837. Witnesses: Benjamin Carter,
Allen Carter, Ezekiel Carter, Vincant Anderson.
                            Signed: John Carter.

JOSEPH ALLEN   1 March 1847
To Wife, Margaret, 521 acres land on Sinking Creek. Twelve slaves to be
emancipated May 1, 1851. All my children (not named) to share equally.
Executors: Robert Rankin, Abraham Naff. Will Dated: May 6, 1846.
Witnesses: J. A. Cox, James X Simpson, V. Sevier. Sons-in-law: John
Simpson, Samuel Conley.   Signed: Joseph Allen

PALSER HAWK   5 April 1847 $2400
Son: Barnabas. To grandsons, David and William Winkle, sons of daughter
Catharine wife of Jacob Winkle, plantation whereon I now live to be
equally divided between them at their father, Jacob Winkle's death and
their mother Catharine. Grand dhildren: William, John and Elizabeth
Hawk, $50 each. Grandson, child of Barnabas Hawk, five dollars. I give
to Frederick Ricker no more - I gave him and his wife Elizabeth $75,
they gave me a receipt. Will Dated: 27 November 1846. Executors: Jacob
Winkle, David X Bird, Joseph Hutchison, Moses Whittenburg.
                            Signed: Palser X Hawk
                                             his mark

JOSEPH L. HAYS   5 April 1847 $4,000
To Wife, Mary, windmill, plantation and personal property. Sons: George
and Aloana Hays, to get land at Mary's death or marriage. Daughters:
Ary, Emeline, Abigail, Nancy, Martha Jane, Mary Elizabeth and Ruth, $100
each to be paid by sons. Executors: George Hays, Robert C. Cray, John
Crabtree, Gravener McNeese. Will Dated: 2 January 1847. Witnesses:
John Crabtree, G____ Wnee g??

JOHN GREGG   7 June 1847 $3,000
To Wife, Hannah, plantation, rents and profits and $10 worth of books
from my library. Children: Marshall W. Gregg, George A., Elijah, Rebecca
Chambers, John, William, Ann wife of Jacob Kelly. To son, Marshall W.
Gregg, land adjoining George Brown and John Keyes, he owes me $856.2½.
To daughter-in-law, Susan C. Gregg, interest on money, but I want
Alexander Logan of Indiana to aid her. Put Ann Kelly's part in her own
hands and not pay Jacob Kelly's debts. I give and bequeath to Elmira
Jack $15.00. Eignt grand children: heirs of Samuel Gregg, Eliza Ann,
Susan Esther, Hannah Jane, John, Margaret Amanda, Harriet Adeline,
George and Finly - $450. To Greeneville College - book "Rise and Fall
of Roman Empire". Executor: Son, Marshall W. Gregg. Will Dated: 26
December, 1844. Witnesses: Samuel Cochran, Samuel Henry.
                            Signed: John Gregg

JACOB SMITH   5 July 1847
To Wife, Barbara, land on north bank of Lick Creek. Children: Leonard,
Thomas, Henry, Rebecca wife of Jacob Wattenbarger, John, Barbara Ann,
Hannah - land adjoining Joseph Williams. Heirs of Mary Dell decd.
Thomas Weems - up Camp Creek. The Jacob Linebaugh land, formerly owned
by Joseph McCurry - to John, adjoining Henry Tarrant, Joseph Williams,

Wyly Campbell, James McCollum. Witnesses: Thomas Bailey, Thomas N. Weems,
James Williams.   Signed: Jacob Smith

CATHARINE EVERHART   7 June 1847
Children: Elizabeth Brotherton, Henry Brotherton, David Everhart, Eve
and Benjamin Vaughn, Nicolas Everhart, Thomas Berry, Mary and Beverly
Ford, James Everhart, Anna and Leonard Smith, Jacob, Emanuel and Thomas
Everhart - one dollar each. To my son, Thomas Everhart, all balance of
my estate at my death. Executor: Leonard Smith. Will Dated: 7 September
1844. Witnesses: George Smith, Henry Smith.
                           Signed: Katherine X Everhart

JACOB BRUNER   4 October 1847
To Wife, Margaret, $150 and a childs part of personal property. Sons:
Jacob, Henry, Elias, Daniel, Samuel, George and Othniel, to divide money
on interest after my wife's part is taken out. Daughters: Polly Messer,
Betsy Starnes, Margaret Baily - equal part of personal property except
money on interest. Sole Executor: Joseph Bruner, my son. Witnesses:
William Crumley, Jacob Everhart.   Signed: Jacob Bruner

JOHN BOWMAN   14 September 1847
To sister, Mary Calvert and her children, $1000. Children of sister
Barbary McConnell decd., to be put in hands of John or William McConnell,
and to receive $1000. To my step mother, $1. Children of Elizabeth
Simpson decd., to be put in the hands of Elias Simpson and John Simpson,
and to receive $1000. Brother, George, to receive $1200. To half
brother, David, $15.00. To half brother, Elias, $1.00. To Sarah Brooks
(crippled), $50.00. One thousand dollars to African Missions (Methodist)
- to be paid to Rev. Samuel Patton and Rev. David Fleming. Put tombstones at my father's and mother's graves. Executors: L. A. Cox.
Witnesses: Jonathan R. Collins, William A. Eakin, Henry Smith. Codicil
Witnesses: Charles Loyd, Robinson Loyd.
                           Signed: Ell Bowman

WILLIAM GASS   6 December 1847 $200
To daughters, Polly and Nancy Gass, my home plantation until Nancy is 21
then to be divided between my son, John M., if he comes back, all my
children. Children: Polly, Nancy, John M., Joseph, William, Alexander,
George and Sarah Keys. To son, Alexander, a clay bank colt. Executors:
Sons, Joseph and William Gass. Will Dated: 28 June 1847. Witnesses:
George W. Gass, Kinchen S. Harvey, Joseph Gass, William Gass.
                           Signed: William Gass

WILLIAM JONES SENR.   6 March 1848 $2,000
To Wife, Mary, all lands and personal property as long as she lives or
can manage. Daughter, Nancy decd. wife of George Wright - her children,
William and Martha Jane Wright, $150 to be divided. Sons: Elliot and
Isaac Barton Jones. Two youngest sons: Lemuel H. and William Jones to
pay $150 each to Martha Jane Wright. If grand-daughter, Martha Jane
Wright stays with my family, she gets $50. Daughter: Polly Goodin.
Mahala Holston who lives with me to have $10.00. Executor: Elliot Jones.
Will Dated: 21 March 1847. Witnesses: Wylie I. Proctor, Henry Simpson,
John G. Weems.   Signed: William Jones

MARY RADER   6 March 1848 $100
To daughter, Elizabeth Rader, bed furniture etc. and 1 set red flower
earthen plates. To daughter, Lucinda Colyer, my blue mercer cloak. To
daughters, Catharine Altom, Esabella Guthrie, Emaline Jenkins, balance
of my wearing cloths. Executor: Son-in-law, William Rader. Will Dated:
2 April 1847. Witnesses: Lemuel Crosby, Jesse Rader Senr.
                           Signed: Mary X Rader

JOHN CAVENER SENR.   8 February 1848
Wife, Phebe, to have articles in Cocke County and what she brought when
we got married. To son, William, my bureau. To son, Hugh, my falling
leaf table. - To daughter, Nancy Harmon, 20 acres land. Sons: John,

Thomas and George to have the plantation I live on, 100 acres towards
Andrew Johnson's land - John to have management of farm. Anna Reese
staying with me. Grand-daughter, Nancy Emeline, daughter of my son
Isaac, to have 2 sheep. All heirs to sign a quit claim to John Armitage
of all interest my first wife, Susan, had to a piece of land. Executor:
John Cavener. Will Dated: 27 December 1847. Witnesses: William West,
Henry Harmon.   Signed: John Cavener

SARAH ANN KENT   3 April 1848 $100
To daughter, Harriet Johnson, all household furniture and all money. To
grand-daughters: Nancy Jane Johnson, a side saddle; and Sarah Johnson, a
cow at death of my daughter Harriet. Sons: John, James L. and William
S. Kent to get $1 each. Daughters: Elizabeth Johnson and Nancy Harrel
to get $1 each. To grandson, William Reynolds, son of Thomas Reynolds,
$1. Will Dated: 13 October 1846. Witnesses: Jesse Holt, Washington
Keys.   Signed: Sarah Ann ⤫ Kent

SAMUEL McPHERON   1 May 1848 $800
To brothers: Andrew and Allen, land my father, Andrew, willed me. To
sisters: Blanche McPheran Drake and Martha McPheron, pereshable property
my father willed me. Executor: Brother, Andrew. Will Dated: 23 March
1848. Witnesses: John Harmon, Jacob Harmon.
                        Signed: Samuel McPheron

DAVID OLINGER   5 June 1848 $2500
To Wife, Rachel, household and kitchen furniture, horses, sheep, hogs,
cattle to remain on farm and at my wife's death to go to my three
daughters. Children: Mary Ann Ragan, Nancy, Eliza, John, Jesse and
David. Son, John, to have farm, but must give his mother decent support
and pay other two sons $200. Finish a schoolhouse I started. Executor:
Son, John Olinger. Will Dated: 29 May 1847. Witnesses: James Tunnell,
Robert Campbell.   Signed: David Olinger

GODFREY SAYLOR   3 July 1848
Two sons and five daughters living with me. To eldest daughter, Eliza-
beth, 30 akars. To daughter, Rebecca, 30 akars adjoining Elisha Carter.
To daughter, Catharine, 30 akars. To Nancy, Hannah, Mary and Lydia, 30
akars. To son, John, 41 akars. To son, Joseph, 30 akars which I
purchased from Joses Mills and Adam Lonas. Two hundred and thirty-six
akars of school lands to go to my seven children living at home. My
Shugar camp to grand-daughter, Martha Melinda Saylor, daughter of Jacob.
To daughter, Sarah wife of David Brown, $30. To son, George, $30.
Grandsons: John and David deceased, sons of David, $30. Executors: Son,
John Saylor and daughter, Rebecca. Test: Frederick Smith, Joseph Hendry.
                        Signed: Godfried Saylor

SAMUEL BEALS   3 July 1848
Samuel Beals of Solomon. To sons: Caleb, James, Jacob and Stephen, $1
each, having given to them already. To three daughters: Rebecka, Ebby
and Martha Beals, 1/3 of wheat raised by John Prat, James Beals and H. D.
Fraker. To son, Jacob, a horse brute and sow. Sell and divide what is
left. Executors: Charles Bright, John Crabtree. Will Dated: 15 June
1848. Test: Hiram D. Fraker, Samuel Has.
                        Signed: Samuel X Beals

ROBERT MALONEY   3 July 1848
To Wife, Catharine, plantation where we live and all personal estate.
Children: Valentine, Robert, Mariah, John. Daughter, Mariah, to be
made equal with other girls. To son, John, 11 acres. Two hundred acres
on Chuckey Mountain on headwaters of Dry Fork of Camp Creek and 25 acres
southside Chucky River adjoining Pierce's Island, to be sold, pay debts
and divided. Executors: William C. Maloney, Valentine Maloney. Will
Dated: 15 May 1848. Witnesses: Charles Gass, Dawson Pitt.
                        Signed: R. Maloney

ELIZABETH CARTER   3 July 1848
To grand-daughter, Nancy Carter, all property for waiting on when I was
not able to wait on myself. Executor: Ephraim Carter of Jacob. Will
Dated: 15 March 1847. Witnesses: Charles Gass, Vinsant Anderson.
                         Signed: Elizabeth ⟋⟍ Carter
                                        her mark

SIMON POPE   6 November 1848 $8,000
To Wife, Rebeckah, household furniture, negro girl, horses, $100, 2 cows,
10 sheep, 500 pounds pork and bacon, 100 bushels grain and all my real
estate as my widow. All my Brother, Williamson Pope's children, $7 each.
All my real estate to Samuel E. Northington and Reuben West, son of John
West. Jesse Northington, my brother-in-law's children, John Pope's
children, Elizabeth Pettitt's children, Feribie Pope's children in
Alabama, and my brother Wiley Pope and his children living in Muscogee
County Georgia - my money. Executor: James Shanks. Will Dated: 30
September 1848. Witnesses: Thomas English, Hiram Smith, Allen English.
                         Signed: Simon Pope
Rebecca Pope dissented - saying this will was entirely unsatisfactory to
her. She paid the costs of entering the dissent 6 November 1848.

JAMES SMITH
To Wife, Sarah, real estate and personal property, if she should marry
she is to take only what she brought when she married me. Three youngest
sons: Jeremiah, William and David to have land and pay darters $200. To
two darters: Margaret and Elizabeth. Last five children - first four
children. Executors: Wife, Sarah. Will Dated: 27 December 1843.
Witnesses: Andrew Andes, Daniel Laughner.
                         Signed: James Smith

RICHARD M. JOHNSON   4 December 1848 $5,000
Wife, Elizabeth, to sell enough property to pay debts and to have the
rest her widowhood. Sons: Phillip, John and Solomon, to have land on
Knoxville Road near Blue Springs after death of widow, and to pay
daughters $100 each. Daughters: Anna, Sally, Barbara, Maria, Polly and
Catharine Elizabeth Johnson. Executors: Son Phillip, Wife Elizabeth.
Will Dated: 5 November 1848. Made on his death bed - signed by witnesses.
Witnesses: John Harmon, Phillip Henry Bible, George Lonas, Frederick
Wampler.

JOHN BROYLES   6 November 1848
Horse Creek. Written 26 August 1845.
To son, David, land conveyed me by Matthias Broyles and Joseph Sharp
below mouth of Jeremiah Prather's spring branch, also half of Tennessee
Grant Nos. 18148 - 92 acres, and 16778 - 30 acres. To son, Ozey R.
Broyles, land. Sons: Jacob F. Broyles, Nathaniel B. Broyles and Jack
Broyles, have their portions. Five daughters: Mary Wilhite, Elizabeth,
Lucinda, Elender and Frances A. Broyles to receive equal parts. David
and Ozey to support my wife and me. Executors: Jack F. Broyles, son-in-
law John W. Wilhite. Witnesses: George W. Foute, Jacob F. Broyles.
                         Signed: John Broyles

BENJAMIN WILLIAMS   5 March 1849 $6,000
Wife, Priscilla, to take her choice on what she needs for her little
flock. Daughter, Polly Walker, to get $80 more than the rest. Three
youngest son, to have 12 months schooling and learn and get into a light
trade, then they are to have a good overcoat. Other sons. Executors:
Farmer Williams. Will Dated: 7 October 1848. Witnesses: Elliott Jones,
Lemuel Jones. Correction - Gabriel F. Page.
                         Signed: Benjamin Williams

JAMES D. DICKSON   2 April 1849   Bond $6,000
Wife, Eliza A. Dickson, to have enough to buy a comfortable house and
lot sufficient to live and raise my children. At her death it is to be
sold and divided. Executors: Brother William (S. or G.) Dickson,
brother-in-law William West. Will Dated: 12 February 1849. Witnesses:
A. R. Anderson, John Dunlap.   Signed: J. A. Dickson

JOHN MARSHALL
To my wife, _____, real and personal estate as my widow. Three youngest
children: Eli, Richard and Mary. Son, Eli, to care for place and get one
half at wife's death, until he is 25 years old. To son, David, $65.
Executrix: My wife. Witnesses: D. R. Johnson, John Squibb.
                              Signed: John Marshall

GEORGE COURTNEY SENR.   October 1849
To Wife, Elizabeth Courtney, all my property and estate, then to be
divided between my children. Children: Decia, Eliza, John, Sarah,
Stephen, Marshall and Mourning. Son, Marshall, to be made even with
others. Grandson: George W. Courtney, son of James. Executors: Sons,
John and Stephen Courtney. Will Dated: 3 April 1849. Witnesses: William
Courtney, Fielding X Courtney.   Signed: George X Courtney

DAVID LOGAN   2 July 1849 $3,000
To Wife, Priscilla, lands, mare, saddle and blanket. To daughter,
Priscilla, to have possession of one of my dwellings if she marries, also
one half kitchen furniture - land on Lick Creek near Loss Mountain (490
acres) to go to other children. Children: Jane wife of William Stanley,
Susannah decd. wife of John Dodd - their daughter Mary Jane Dodd, Andrew
Logan, David Logan, James Logan and Margaret McBride decd. Executors:
Wife Priscilla and son Andrew. Will Dated: 25 September 1846. Witnesses:
William Orr, John Bales. Final Executors: Andrew Logan, Joseph Rogers,
Syl Ottinger.   Signed: David Logan

MARY KEY   Repeat   Will to stand.
The contested case was tried in Circuit Court, June Term 1849, Hon. I. W.
Luckey Judge, Presiding. Jury: John Link, Andrew Miller, Warner Peters,
Charles Lovett, William G. Morris, Joseph Galbreath, Joseph Johnson Esq.,
Thomas L. Hale, Adam E. Dinsmore, John Fraker, John Walker and Leander
Dinsmore. Plaintiff to recover against defendants - Peter Key, John M.
Harmon, James Lenders and William Ross Jr.
I give and bequeath to my son, Samuel Keller, all my property real,
personal and money including 400 acres my father purchased now in hands
of John Ross and John S. Reed and my part in brother, George Keller's,
estate. He died without issue.

JOHN BOWERS SENR.   6 August 1849
To Wife, Mary Magdalena, all land during her widowhood, if she does well
- if she does not do well, sell black man, Anthony, and put money on
interest for her use. Sons: John, Phillip, Peter, Moses. Daughters:
Polly Renner, Catharine Neas, Sally Neas, Barbara Trobaugh, Peggy Renner,
Elizabeth Neas and Regner Freshour. To son, John, 473 acres where I live
and to pay other children $2700. To son, Phillip, 150 acres I bought of
John Stephens. To daughter, Polly Renne, one half acre for a barn lot.
Barbara Trobaugh and Peter Renner's part goes to their heirs - because
they do not live as becometh Christians. Regina Freshour a widow.
Executors: Son Moses Bowers, John Bowers, Michael Neas. Will Dated:
October 24, 1846. Witnesses: John Link, Samuel H. Shrewsberry, W. A.
Girdner, William Girdner.   Signed: John Bowers - in German

WILLIAM CRADDOCK   3 September 1849
To Wife, Rebecca, gray mare, all cattle, sheep, hogs, bridle and saddle
her widowhood. At her death everything to be sold and money to be put on
interest for three youngest sons: William, Robert and David, equally
divided. My other children: John, James, Madison, Newman, Melinda,
Charity, Lucinda, Rachel and Rebecca - I have given their part. If
needed sell personal property to pay my debts. Executor: Joseph McCall.
Will Dated: 16 June 1840. Witnesses: Cornelius Smith Senr., David M.
Bright.   Signed: William X Craddick

PHILLIP EVERET - Repeat.

JACOB WHITE   12 April 1844
To Wife, Mary, all household and kitchen furniture her life then to sons:

Joseph and William. William also to get all my notes and money to support Mary. Sons: Joseph, William and Eli. To son, Eli, 300 acres on Cedar Branch. Daughters: Elizabeth McNees, Matilda wife of George Jennings, Selina wife of George Maltsberger, Jane wife of Jonathan Pickering, each to receive one dollar. Executors: Sons, Eli and Joseph White. Will Dated: 12 April 1844. Witnesses: Charles Bright, Daniel White, Jesse Ellis.   Signed: Jacob X White

OSILLAR R. TARRANT   3 June 1850
To Patsy Jeffers, one note I hold on her and $3 when collected. To Fanny Jeffers, a cupboard. To daughter, Elizabeth Tarrant, $2. To daughter, Rachel Carter, balance of all I possess. Will Dated: 15 January 1850. Test: Samuel X Carter, Joseph Bradley.
                          Signed: Osillar R. Tarrant

ABRAHAM SNIDER   1 July 1850
To Wife, Catharine, real and personal estate her natural life. To son, Jacob, one half land, great coat. To son, David, other half of land. To son, John, $80. Sons to furnish wife with firewood and do milling for her. Daughters: Barbara, Elizabeth Russell and Martha Jane Snider. Grand-daughter: Catharine Russell of William. Land adjoining Hesekiah Russell. Executors: John Dunwoody, John Walker. Will Dated: 23 March 1847. Test: Daniel Graham, Joseph M. Snider.
                          Signed: Abraham / Snider - his mark

GEORGE ALEXANDER   5 August 1850
To daughter, Isabella Jane (Jaynes), personal property, land on Middle Creek adjoining Henshaw. To daughter, Jane Newberry, land on Middle Creek. To daughter, Elizabeth Parks, $5 to be paid by Isabella. To daughter, Ann Creamer wife of William Creamer, land. Daughter: Mary Smith. To son, William, land. To son, Lorenzo, 87 3/4 acres southside Nolichuckey River. Son: George deceased. To grandson, William Alexander, son of George decd., land on Middle Creek. To grandson, Alexander, son of Ann Creamer, land. Land conveyed to me by Hixson on Cove Creek including 131 perches in Oar Bank deeded to me by Daniel Allen and George House. Executors: Phillip Hinshaw, Joseph Jeane. Will Dated: 1 February 1850. Witnesses: William S. McGaughey, Thomas Alexander, Washington Hinshaw.   Signed: George X Alexander

MARY ANN HOUTS (MAGDALENE)   5 August 1850 $1,000
Nephew and Niece: Rolente and wife Mary Ellis, all land from my father, Christopher Houts decd. Executors: Rolente and Jesse Ellis. Will Dated: 19 January 1843. Witnesses: Gabriel Henry, James McAmish, James Linebaugh.   Signed: Mary An X Houts

SAMUEL REEVES   5 August 1850 $1600
Wife: Ann. To sons, Thomas and Samuel, land to be divided betwixt my two sons. To daughters, Margaret and Catharine Reeves, personal property. Executors: Wife Ann, Josiah Harrison. Will Dated: 25 March 1850. Witnesses: Jacob K. Jones, Thomas Murphey.
                          Signed: Samuel Reeves

JACOB BIBLE   5 August 1850
Wife: ____? To daughters, Margaret and Susannah, residue of land at death of their mother plus $200. To son, William, 92 acres land. To sons, Isaac, Andrew, Noah and Jacob, 85 acres land each. Sons to pay my wife 60 bushels corn yearly. If Andrew and Noah stay with my wife they are to pay her. Executors: Noah Bible, Andrew Bible. Will Dated: 25 May 1850. Witnesses: Abraham Bible, _____ Maloney.
                          Signed: Jacob Bible

WILLIAM A. CARSON   2 September 1850
To Wife, Mary Matilda, $200, house and kitchen furniture. To my father $300 until daughter, Marthew Rutleg Carson comes of age. Sister, Louiza, and brother, David to have $75 to come back to daughter at their death. To Hamilton and Esther Hays, $5 each. To Marthew and Thomas Carson, all

71

my clothing. Executors: Father and Thomas Carson. Will Dated: 10 August
1850. Test: Silas C. Shanks, William R. Reynolds.
                              Signed: William A. Carson

JACOB LINEBAUGH   4 November 1850 $2500
To Wife, Sarah, home place, cattle etc. as is. Children: James, Mary
Williams. Allen Williams to pay Samuel Linebaugh for a bay mare to care
for note Samuel holds on son James and myself. Executors: James Line-
baugh, my son. Will Dated: 27 September 1850. Witnesses: Thomas Baily,
John Siver??   Signed: Jacob Linebaugh

JOHN BIBLE   4 November 1850
To Wife, Elizabeth, land where I now live. To son, David, land after
mother's death after paying two grand children: James and William Fry
$76, $90.66 2/3 cents in trade when they are 21. Grandson, Thomas Fry
to have land to support his grand-mother until he is 21. Executors:
Christly and David Bible. Will Dated: 2 August 1844. Witnesses:
Abraham Bible, W. Conway Maloney, John Bower of Chris.
                              Signed: John Bible

JAMES PICKENS   6 January 1851 $3,000
Non-cupative Will made at home of Sarah Fink in Sullivan County.
Daughter, Lilli Baxter, to get everything. Executor: William Mullinnise.
Bondsmen: Elijah W. Headrick, Samuel Walker, James Shanks, Nathan
Morelick. Will Dated: 28 September 1850. Signed: John Duncan, James L.
Halse, Witnesses.

JAMES BROTHERTON   3 March 1851
Wife: Rodah Brotherton. To son, James M. Brotherton, 150 acres plantation
where I live to care for my wife and I. To grandsons: Andrew I. and
William Brotherton, one corner cupboard, bed and bedding. Executor:
George Kenney. Will Dated: 29 July 1850. Witnesses: Alfred Couch and
James D. Kenney.   Signed: James † Brotherton

JOSEPH KENNEDY   3 March 1851 $4,000
To Wife, Ann, all deeded land her natural life, five negroes, accounts,
debts. To daughter, Martha Malissa Kennedy, good house. To children:
Hannah E. Mercer, Nancy Ann Bowman, Sophia B. Armstrong and Samuel R.
Kennedy, to have all property at my wife's death shear and shear alike.
Executors: Brookins Campbell, R. A. Thompson. Will Dated: 26 November
1850. Witnesses: Thomas P. Robertson, John C. Powell.
                              Signed: Joseph Kennedy

WILLIAM A. HANKINS   3 March 1851 $4,000
Executors to settle all my debts and debts due me. Land for use of
widow and children. To children: Hanry M., Polly Ann and Sarah M. and
if there should be another they are to have a good English lerning at
the expense of my estate. To son, M. A., blacksmith tools. To son,
W. P., rifle gun, one holster to Richard the other to Henry. To son,
J. C., family Bible. Slaves to go to a free state and be free forever.
Executors: John C. Hankins, Richard M. Hankins, William C. Hankins. Will
Dated: 3 July 1850. Witnesses: R. J. Kidwell, J. E. Kidwell.
                              Signed: William Hankins

MORDECAI LINCOLN   5 May 1851 $20,000
To Wife, Sophia W. Lincoln, brick house, profits from tanyard. Children:
Perlina E. Grace and John C. Lincoln, deceased, received $4000 money from
land I sold in Hardy County, Virginia. Grandson: Mordecai Lincoln Barton
gets land in Carter County, Tennessee near Fish Spring. To daughter,
Mary Sophia Lincoln, ground joining the Adademy, all slaves and property
in Greeneville. Executor: W. R. Brown. Will Dated: 12 March 1851.
Witnesses: Thomas Lane, William West, James Britton, William M. Lowery,
B. M. McDaniel.   Signed: M. Lincoln

MARY GILLESPIE   17 July 1851 $6,000
Two dollars each to Neices and Nephews: Sarah E. and Mary K. Easterly,

Archibald D. Nelson, Sarah E. Nelson, Robert Tyler, Minerva Tyler, Ann
W. Williams and Thomas A. Gillespie. Sisters: Judean Easterly, a fine
yellow shawl; Martha Tyler, a white shawl; Sarah Nelson, a black veil;
Elizabeth Crawford, all the rest of my estate. Brother: Allen H.
Gillespie, to get my negro to pay debts. Executrix: Sister, Elizabeth
Crawford. Will Dated: 18 October 1850. Witnesses: Jacob Miller Senr.,
John Miller.   Signed: Mary Gillespie

ARCHIBALD BABB   16 March 1851
To Wife, Lucinda, remaining after debts are paid. Father to take land I
bought from brother, Phillip Babb, and sisters and pay my executor in
bank notes. Executor: Er Babb. Witnesses: James C. Babb, Joseph Bruner.
                              Signed: Archibald Babb

THOMAS SELF   7 July 1851
Wife, Elizabeth, to have farm and bond I hold on Claburn Self. To John
Hunter, $2. Four daughters, Letty Hunter, Elizabeth McDaniel, Sarah
Jane Burkey, Mary wife of John McDaniel, one bed each. Delilah Jane,
daughter of James McDaniel and Susan his wife decd., $2. To Claburn
Self, John Burkey and Jacob Harmon, $2 each. John Burkey, plantation
where Lewis Morgan lives. To William McDaniel, place where he lives.
Land between Big Spring and McDaniel's. Executors: Harrison and Thomas
Self. Will Dated: 8 May 1850. Witnesses: Joseph Hawkins, Joseph Cobble,
Nathan Hawkins Junr.   Signed: Thomas Self Senr.

CATHARINE HAUN   1 September 1851 $500
James Wright, William Matthews, those who take care of me get property.
Executors: James Wright, John Wright, Jacob Haun. Will Dated: 7 March
1850. Witnesses: John Courtney, Nicholas Dunnagen.
                              Signed: Catharine X Haun

JACOB LINEBAUGH   5 May 1851 $10,000
To Wife, Christina, 1/3 including 25 geese, chickens, cows, horses etc.
To son, Henry, 200 acres on Lick Creek. To youngest son, Elihu, the
homeplace. Son, Jacob, has his part. Sons: Samuel and Daniel, $100 in
trade each. Daughters: Elizabeth wife of Humphrey Malone, Barbara wife
of Stephen Rhea, Susan wife of Enoch B. Morelock, Sally wife of David
Morelock, Rachel wife of Ladon Holder, Melinda wife of David Everhart,
Christina, Caties was wife of Samuel S. Hawkins (her children: Henry,
Sally, Rachel, James, Jacob and Jane Hawkins), Polly's children - she
had been married to Samuel McNeese (their children: Elihu, Jane, Henry,
Sally and Jacob McNeese). Daughters to receive $200 each. Executors:
Sons, Henry and Elihu. Will Dated: 25 March 1848. Witnesses: Charles
Bright, Michael Bright.   Signed: Jacob Linebaugh

HENRY RADER   1 September 1851 $2400
Wife, Catharine, to remain on premises her natural life - to have use of
land and slaves to support her. The slaves to be set free. To son,
Henry, $1. To son, John, $62. To daughter, Elizabeth Bowers, $132. To
daughter, Rachel Basinger, $110. To son, Casper Rader, $35. To
daughter, Catharine Smith, $93. To daughter, Isabella Smith, $95. Son,
David, gets nothing. Daughter: Mary Lauchner. Executor: Son, William
Rader. Will Dated: 21 December 1846. Witnesses: William Rader,
Valentine S. Rader, Bondsman William Rader of Jacob.
                              Signed: Henry Rader of Henry

EPHRAIM BROYLES   6 October 1851
To Wife, Grace, interest from $500, possession of house her lifetime,
then it is to be divided equally between my four children. Four children:
Matthias Broyles, Eve wife of George Kindle, Sally wife of Jacob Dulaney
and John I. Broyles. Executors: John I. Broyles, Col. Henry Earnest.
Will Dated: 19 March 1828. Witnesses: J. Nelson, William Brown.
                              Signed: Ephraim X Broyls

HENRY FARNSWORTH   6 October 1850
I bequeath to daughter Marthy the tract of land I now live on during her

natural life then to her children: Robert?, Margaret I., Henry Allen,
Mary Elizabeth, Samuel Alexander and Thomas Doud. To daughter, Jane G.,
$300 to be lade out in land to have her lifetime - if no children - land
to go to Henry A. Farnsworth and Samuel A. Farnsworth my sons and
children of my daughter Margaret Alexander decd. No division to be made
until the death of myself and wife, Frances. Will Dated: 24 March 1849.
Test: Britton X Johnson, Mary X Johnson.
Signed: Henry X Farnsworth

CLEMENT REYNOLDS   1 October 1860 $3,000
To Wife, Margaret, all property her lifetime while single. All my
children. Executor: Vincen Anderson. Will Dated: 9 August 1850.
Witnesses: James L. Carter, Sparling Bowman.
Signed: Clement Reynolds

ABSALOM STONECYPHER
To Wife, Sarah, all she needs for support - the rest to be divided. Son,
Samuel, to pay and divide his note to me between others. Daughters:
Betty, Sarah and Rebecka to divide balance. Three sons: Henry, John and
Jacob have their share. Heirs of Absalom Stonecypher Junr., born and
unborn all lands. To Sarah Stonecypher, daughter of Alexander Stone-
cypher decd., $50. Executors: Wife Sarah, Absalom Stonecypher Junr.,
son-in-law Joseph Bruner. Will Dated: 3 January 1845. Witnesses: Hugh
Carter, James Washington Carter.
Signed: Absalom /M/ Stonecypher
his mark

THOMAS C. RANKIN   1 December 1851 $10,000
To Wife, Elvira, whole plantation with cattle and tools, except tanyard,
to support and educate my children. To son, James B., $900. To son,
Robert, the tanyard. To son, Alexander, upper plantation. To son,
Charles, $300. To daughters: Mary Elizabeth, Julia and Amanda Jane,
horse saddle and bridle and all other money from sales etc. Brother:
James. Executors: John McGaughey Senr., Son James B. Will Dated: 18
October 1851. Witnesses: James D. Rankin, James Jane. Executors on
Bond: James B. Rankin, James D. Rankin, James MacDowell.
Signed: Thomas C. Rankin

JOHN COGGBURN   1 December 1851
To Wife, Malinda, all perishable property, if she should die my land is
to be rented for support of my children. Five youngest children: Highram
I., Martha M., Mary E., Nathan W. and Harriet Livenia. Executors: Wife
Malinda, Gabriel E. Page. Will Dated: 4 June 1851. Witnesses: Marshall
W. Gregg, Samuel Henry.   Signed: John Coggburn

SAMUEL ALLEN   2 December 1851
Wife, Elizabeth, to have plantation her widowhood then to three sons:
William, James and Samuel. Daughter, Rebecca Carolene to get household
furniture, hogs, 5 cows, wheat, oats and corn, also $1200. Negroes to
be sold. Four children before named. My interest in Farnsworth Tract
to be sold. Executors: Wife Elizabeth, Samuel H. Shrewsberry. Will
Dated: 24 September 1851. Witnesses: Robert A. Crawford, Robert Allen.
Signed: Samuel X Allen
his mark

ALLEN WILLIAMS   2 February 1852 $3,000
Executors on Bond: Nathan Dodd, Thomas Bailey, Robert Rankin, Joseph
Henderson, Samuel Lain. To Wife, Polly, plantation and mill, household
furniture, cattle, grain, hay, poultry, pork and beef - at her death to
sons, Thomas Dawson and Jacob Washington Williams. To daughter, Betsey
Alvira Williams, $400. Jacob to pay Betsey $400. Thomas to pay Betsey
$100. Executors: Nathan Dodd, Thomas Baily. Will Dated: 26 December
1851. Witnesses: Joseph Henderson, Thomas Dodd Junr.
Signed: Allen Williams

JOHN ENGLISH   1 March 1852 $9,000
Wife, Easther, to have profits from home farm, land on Lick Creek - farm

74

near Snapp Ferry Road. Children: Melinda, Rhoda, Andrew, John, Elizabeth Shields and Agnes English - Lick Creek Farm. To daughter, Melinda,
horse, saddle and bridle. To daughter, Rhoda, bed and furniture. To
son, Andrew, crosscut saw. To grandson, John son of Andrew, my saddle.
Executor: Andrew English Esq. Will Dated: 2 January 1852. Witnesses:
James Shanks, Reuben West.   Signed: John English

RACHEL HAMMER   5 April 1852 $2,000
To Nancy Pickering, daughter of Hannah Pickering, who now lives with me,
$50 with interest when she is 18. All other property land and personal
to Hannah Pickering, who now lives with me. Executors: Aaron Hammer,
Jacob Ellis, Jacob Beals, John Marshall. Witnesses: Jacob Ellis, Jacob
Beals, Abner Beals.   Signed: Rachel X Hammer

SOLOMON BEALS   5 April 1852
To Wife, Catharine, balance during her natural life. To son, Joseph, 50
acres - to take care of my and my wife and pay Elihu $100. Son: Elihu.
Daughters: Charity, Hannah and Rachel to get household and kitchen
furniture. Executors: Son Joseph, John Marshill. Will Dated: 8 February
1846. Test: Aaron Hammer, Jacob Ellis.
                     Signed: Solomon Beals

SUSANNAH SMITH   5 April 1852
Two sons: William D. and Isaac D. to have all my property and money.
Daughter, Lavina Stephens, my saddle. Executors: Sons William D. and
Isaac D. Smith. Will Dated: 14 August 1851. Witnesses: William H.
Smith, Christian Bible.   Signed: Susannah -+- Smith

JACOB WATTENBARGER   5 April 1852 $3,000
Executors on Bond: Abram Weems, Thomas Baily, Wyley Campbell. Wife ___.
To son, Joel, land where he lives. To daughters, Hannah and Nancy, beds,
furniture, cow and calf and $14.00. Land adjoining Grassy Creek. Son:
Samuel. Executors: Joel Wattenbarger, Abram Weems. Will Dated: 31
December 1851. Witnesses: Joseph Bradley, John Cooter, Henry Brubaker.
                     Signed: Jacob X Wattenbarger

JOHN McCURRY   5 April 1852 $500
To grand children, Isabel and Milly Hayworth, my furniture. Son Joseph
decd., his heirs $1. To sons, John and Robert, $1 each. To son, James,
30 acres land. To daughter, Annie McCurry married to Makes L. Fiels,
$1. Other property to be sold and divided. Executor: Son John McCurry.
Will Dated: 23 March 1852. Witnesses: James McCollum, Isaiah M. Stewart.

JOSEPH HUFF (HAUFF)   7 June 1852 $900
Wife, Margaret, to use and distribute furniture of every kind, 7 sheep,
horses, cows etc., wheat to be cleaned. Children: Elias, Barbary Rader,
Sally Welty, Peter and Elizabeth Welty, Andrew Jackson and William Huff.
(Elias Welty has inability). Executors: William Hauff, son-in-law
William Rader, William B. Hudson, Alfred Brumley. Will Dated: 20
February 1852. Witnesses: William B. Hutson, Cla?na? Kifer.
                     Signed: Joseph X Hauff

ALEXANDER WILLIAMS   6 September 1852
To Wife, Catharine D. Williams, real and personal estate to dispose of
as she thinks proper. Will Dated: 10 April 1843. Witnesses: Jeff
Henderson, J. J. Mitchell.   Signed: Alex Williams

CAROLINE DUNLAP   6 September 1852   Bond $600
To son, George, remainder of land. To son, John M., $50. To daughter,
Eliza Amanda, 2 good beds and cupboard. To children, Edward and Polly,
one years maintenance. To son, William, 10 acres land. Other children:
Henry, Margaret, Jane, Grace (may be Jane Grace wife of William Grace -
G.F.B.), Sarah Compton. Will Dated: 29 July 1852. Witnesses: Samuel
Cochran, Turner D. Kelley.   Signed: Caroline X Dunlap

JOSEPH RUNELS
Wife: Leah??. To son, John, 50 acres where I now live to keep us our lifetime. Executor: John Runels, son. Will Dated: 30 August 1850. Witnesses: Leonard Starnes, John Melone.
Signed: Joseph —|— Runels
his mark

JANE BROTHERTON   23 April 1852
To daughter, Easter Patterson, all wearing clothes. To James Barnes family, $1. To Alexander Barnes family, $1. To Wesley Runyans, Robert Robison and Absalom Barnes, $1 each. To servant, Phillip, rest of estate. Executor: George Kenney. Witnesses: Alfred Couch, James M. Brotherton.
Signed: Jane X Brotherton

JACOB HARDIN   6 December 1852 $600
Wife, Abigail, to have decent support to raise my children. My children (not named) to receive equal shares. Executors: Abigail Hardin, John Maltsbarger, John Kidwell. Will Dated: 15 November 1852. Witnesses: Cornelius Newman, Y r i s?? Tadlock.
Signed: Jacob Hardin

JOHN ROBINSON   6 December 1852 $8,000
Amongst all my sister, Peggy Milburns children, their share of land. To John Robinson Low, son of Hugh Low, $200 when he becomes of age. To Mt. Bethel Church Old School Congragation, $100, Bible and Hymn book. To Ruth R. and Polly Kelley, daughters of James Kelley, a bed each. To Alexander Ruth, daughter of Miller Gallion, a bed. To Sarah Kelley, daughter of Samuel Kelley, $25,00. To Jane Parsons, daughter of Robert Parsons, $25. Slaves to be freed and given $100. Stock in East Tennessee and Virginia Railroad to be paid, if work goes on, to Presbyterian School. Executors: John and Richard McGaughey. Will Dated: 22 October 1850. Witnesses: James P. McDowell, Daniel Kennedy.
Signed: John Robinson

ANDREW DOBKINS (DOBBINS?)   6 December 1852   Bond $500
To Wife, Joana, all lands and personal property. Girls to get balance of land and each have water. Children: William, Rebecca, Polly, Dorcas, Rachel, Patsy Arnold. To son, William, $50. To daughter, Patsy Arnold, $10 in trade. Executor: William Jones. Will Dated: 18 December 1850. Witnesses: George and Henry Monteith.
Signed: Andrew X Dobkins

CHRISTENA PETERS   7 February 1853 $300
To daughter, Polly, $15 above half the money now on hand. To son, Jacob, half after above taken out. Daughter: Catharine. Executors: John Freshour (Chucklehead - GFB), Jacob Peters. Will Dated: 8 January 1853. Witnesses: M. G. Sprinkle, James Renner. Bondsman: Joseph Runner.
Signed: Christina Peters

NICHOLAS EALY   7 February 1853 $500
Wife: Elizabeth. After my wife's death, land to go to John Ealy. Children: Sarah Lamb, Joseph Ealy decd. - children, Anna Champlin, to receive money from sale. Executors: George Washington Ealy, John Ealy. Will Dated: 29 May 1852. Witnesses: James Shaw, Joel Bowers, Thomas Russell.

JOHN STEPHENS   Probated 7 March 1853 $4,000
I give and bequeath to William Freshour one fourth of my estate, both personal and real. The balance equally divided between Andrew Freshour and M. O. Jenkins. Executors: Andrew Freshour, M. O. Jenkins. Will Dated: 25 November 1851. Witnesses: Joseph Hutchison, Joseph Freshour. Ex. Bondsmen: John Love, Samuel H. Shrewsberry.
Signed: John X Stephens

EZEKIEL CARTER SENR.   7 March 1853
To Wife, Martha Carter, 300 acres and personal property for her support.
To daughter, Hyla wife of Jeremiah MacMillan, 100 acres where she now
lives. To son, John Carter, 200 acres where he lives. To son, William
Carter, 300 acres where I live. Other children have their portion.
Executors: Abraham and Ezekiel Carter. Will Dated: 2 January 1852.
Witnesses: William R. Brown, James P. MacDowell, V. Sevier.
                                           Signed: Ezekiel Carter

MICHAEL BASINGER   14 August 1846
To son, Phillip, 116 acres. To son, Isaac, 80 acres and grist mill
adjoining Henry Feazel. To children, Jacob, George, William, Betsy
Porter, Sally Champlin, all the rest, debts and demands against my
estate. To Mary Goslin with whom I'll stay the rest of my life, 97
acres. Executors: Phillip Basinger, Thomas Starnes, William Ealy.
Witnesses: Michael Dearstone, Isaiah Dobson, William Wolaver.
                                           Signed: Michael X Basinger

JAMES HISE   7 November 1853
To Wife, Polly, one half land Adam Cashada lives on then to daughter,
Eliza Jane's heirs. To son, Henry, Dobson tract - 80 acres, plus $100
when he becomes of age. To son, John, other half where Cashada lives,
plus $100 when he becomes of age. To daughter, Elizabeth, 67 acres land.
To daughter, Maryann, 223 acres where I now live. To son, Isaac, 95
acres. Daughters: Anna Cashada, Martha Jane. Land on Paint Creek Ridge
adjoining state line to be sold to raise money. Profits from Gourley
Bridge. Executors: David R. Johnson, Samuel Shrewsberry, Stephen Lawson.
- but they were Mary X Hise . Will Dated: 7 June 1858. Executors:
John Parman, Theron F. Price, J. B. Bird, D. R. Johnson refused to serve.
Witnesses: Abraham Hughes, George Hughes.

WASHINGTON HINSHAW   4 April 1853 $2,000
To Wife, Jane, what she brought here with her, $100, house, kitchen and
garden. To son, Levi, to have slave, Tom, who is to set free when 25
years old. To son, Phillip, my book. To daughter, Maria Alexander,
$100 in bank notes. Children: William, Nancy Harrison, Rebecca William-
son and Ruhama? Lemming to have $120 each. Land on Middle Creek to
River, grist mill and sawmill. Executors: Levi Hinshaw, A. W. Howard,
Joseph P. Jane, Thomas Davis. Will Dated: 10 March 1848. Witnesses:
David Rice, S. M. Doak, J. P. Janes, James F. Broyles.
                                           Signed: Washington Hinshaw

ELIJAH COULSON   6 October 1853
To Wife, Mary, all furniture, house, stock etc. to manage the farm.
Children: Deborah, Sarah, Elizabeth, Susan, Nancy Ann, Rachel, Samuel
and Elija. To daughters, a horse, saddle and bridle each. To son,
Samuel, 82 acres land. To son, Elija, land where I now live. Executors:
Charles Hays, George M. Dery. Witnesses: George W. Bright, Thomas Hays.
                                           Signed: Elija Coulson

JONATHAN NAFF SENR.   5 September 1853 $800
Wife: Elizabeth. Step son-in-law, John Smith, to get land to take care
of wife, Elizabeth. Executor: David R. Johnson. Will Dated: 24 Sept.
1851. Witnesses: A. S. Johnson, Joseph Shields. Ex Bondsmen: A. S.
Johnson, John Smith.   Signed: Johnathan X Naff

EZEKIEL CARTER   5 September 1853
To Wife, Martha, all land until youngest child comes of age or her widow-
hood, then she gets one third - other two thirds to be divided equally
between my four children. Four children: Alexander W., Tallitha C.,
Samuel L., Joel M. Executors: Samuel Miller Senr., John E. Carter.
Will Dated: 25 July 1853. Witnesses: John Malone, Elbert S. Car?
                                           Signed: Ezekiel Carter

JACOB REESER   3 October 1853
Wife: Elizabeth. To children, John, Jacob and Elizabeth Graham, $120.

To sons, Isaac I. and Archibald M. 245 acres where I now live - they are
to pay debts and support wife, Elizabeth. To son, W. F. Reeser, 50 acres
where he lives. Daughters, Martha C. and Mary S. Reeser, each to have a
saddle, bridle and $25. Executors: Son, Isaac I. and Archibald Reeser.
Will Dated: 19 November 1851. Witnesses: I. I. Yeager, George T.
Gillespie.   Signed: Jacob Reeser

ALEXANDER BROWN   3 October 1853
To William Brannon, with whom I now live, real estate, all personal
estate in fee simple for taking care of me. To Mary Brannon, eldest
daughter of William, bedsteads and bedding. To Margaret Brannon, second
daughter, and Caroline, third daughter of William, each to have bedsteads
and bedding. To John Mason, nephew - son of James Mason, $50.
Executors: Blackstone McDaniel. Witnesses: John Maloney, L. I. Drake.
                              Signed: Alexander Brown

THOMAS CARSON   3 July 1854
Children: Lewiza, Easter, Maxwell, David, William decd's legatee, Martha
R. Carson. To Lewiza and David, all my affects to take care of me.
Martha R. Carson to have $1. Will Dated: 30 December 1853. Witnesses:
James McMackin, Robert Smith, Henry Mathes, Robert Taylor.
                              Signed: Thomas Carson

ER BABB   7 February 1854
To Wife, Elizabeth, house, furniture, one half of barn, one half of
orchard below milkhouse, cows, calves etc. To Elder son, Andrew Jackson
Babb, Gaston land. To Second son, William Carrol Babb, land near Babbs
mill. To son, Samuel Houston Babb, tract I gave my wife, at her death.
To son, James Wyly Babb, land near Babbs Mill. To daughter, Martha wife
of Samuel White, beds, cows etc. to make her even with other daughters.
Six daughters: Martha, Polly Na___?, Lucinda Broils, Matilda, Caroline,
Margaret, Jane. Sons to pay my wife every third bushel corn and wheat.
Executor: A. J. Babb.   Witnesses: William McA is William McAmis.
                              Signed: Er Babb

JAMES H. EVANS   4 April 1854 $2400
To Wife, Polly, overplus after sale for her benefit and to raise my
children. Land in District 7 to be sold to pay debts. Children: Sarah,
Rebecka, Mehalah, Narcissa, William, Franklin Page, James Watson Evans.
Father, William Evans, estate in Harrisonburg, Rockingham County,
Virginia. Mother Rebecca Evans, formerly Rebecca Harrison. Executor:
Elliot Jones. Will Dated: 9 March 1854. Witnesses: A. W. Howard, John
Burkey, Henry B. Harrison.   Signed: James H. Evans

SUSANNA PIERCE   3 July 1854 $100
To daughter, Polly Pierce Coulson, 6 acres adjoining Charles Hays. To
daughter, Nancy Simmons, $1. Executrix: Polly Coulson. Will Dated: 5
March 1854. Witnesses: Charles Hays, Franklin X Conly, Enos Pickering.
                       Signed: Susanna X Pierce
                                      her mark

VALENTINE SEVIER   1 May 1854
Sons: Robert, James and Charles decd. (his children), these have their
part. Daughters: Mrs. McCorkle, Mrs. Jones, Betsey Cunningham, Jane
Vance, $7 each. To Daughter, Susan, $800. To son, David and Joseph,
$1000 each. To sons, William and Edward, $300 each. To Wife, Vinera
C., to have my dwelling, gardens etc. Two little sons, Charles L. and
Henry V., $2000 each. Executor to pay my part of notes to Deaderick
and Sevier Business pay to D. A. Deaderick Ex. pf his fathers estate.
Slaves to be taught to read the Scriptures and be free at age 21.
Executor: David Sevier. Will Dated: 9 January 1854.
                              Signed: Valentine Sevier

PHILLIP BOWERS   10 May 1854
To Wife, Sarah, Cogburn tract, adjoining Joseph Renner, as long as she

remains my widow. Son, Philemon, to pay wife, Sarah, $100 a year for 11 years. Executors: Wife Sarah, William Girdner. Witnesses: Andrew Rader, Phillip Neas. Signed: Phillip ⌇ Bowers
                                                              his mark

WILLIAM WILLOUGHBY   30 July 1852 $2500
Property to be sold at private sale, children to have equal parts except William Ray and wife, who are to have $160 less than the others since I have given to them. To Wife, Elder, her dower where Enoch Willoughby now lives. Lucy to receive $200 in trade. Ex. and bondsmen: John Willoughby, Jacob Myers. Will Dated: 13 May 1854. Executor: Brother John Willoughby. Witnesses: William M. Williams.
                                 Signed: William Willoughby

NICHOLAS EVERHART   3 July 1854 $6,000
To Wife, Anna, all lands and property her widowhood, if she marries she shares no longer. Executors: Anny Everhart, George Kenney. Will Dated: 22 October 1853. Witnesses: John R. Young, James M. Brotherton, Thomas Morelock, Alfred Couch.   Signed: N. Everhart

PHILLIP COOTER   13 April 1853
To Wife, Sarah J. E., furniture, wool, sheep, flax, mare and sow etc.. 218 acres land. Minor children of wife, Sarah: Peggy to have a mare and 2 cows, and Alexander W. to have 2 cows, horse, gears and mattox, oats and fodder. Children of wife, Sarah: John, Bernard, Polly. Executor: Bernard Cooter. Witnesses: John Saylor, Samuel Morelock.
                                 Signed: Phillip X Cooter
                                              his mark

ABRAM WHITE   7 August 1854 $100
Ex. and bondsman: Henry White, Loyd Bullen. To Wife, Nancy, $1 and her maintenance, at her marriage or death the above and household furniture to go to daughter, Sarah. Son, Henry, to have land when Sarah marries, all farming tools. To daughter, Sarah, loom, corner cupboard and all furniture. Children: Henry, Sarah, Mary McLaughlin, Margaret White, Willie White, Samuel White, Elizabeth Barham, Nancy Taxton (Paxton?), Abram White, Lucinda Barham. All other children to get one dollar. Executor: Son Henry White. Will Dated: 4 May 1850. Witnesses: Loyd Bullen, Edmund Hendrix.   Signed: Abram White

JOHN MALTSBERGER   4 September 1854 $2,000
Sons, Phillip and David to have whole of plantation. Sons, Michael, John each to have $1. Each daughter to receive $100. Daughters: Catharine wife of Jacob Bowman, Susanna wife of Alexander McCollum, Sarah wife of William Miller, Rebecca wife of Valentine McNew, Deborah wife of Lewis Tadlock, Martha wife of Azariah Doty. Daughter, Rachel's children to receive $100. John Jones, son of my daughter Polly.T To Jane Petter, one of daughter Polly's children, married to Frederick Petter, $50. James M. Tadlock, son of my daughter Elizabeth, $50. Keep the old gray mare. Use money to pay my debts. Executors: Sons, Phillip and David Maltsberger. Will Dated: 9 August 1854. Witnesses: Charles Bright, A. W. Brabson, Nathaniel Pickering.
                            Signed: John ─┼─ Maltsberger

LEWIS STUTTS   2 October 1854
To Wife, Barbary, whole sale contents of my property. Heirs: Catharine, John, Elizabeth, Sarah, Anna, Susannah decd. Executors: Abraham Bible, Daniel Knipp. Will Dated: 4 March 1849. Test: Christian Bible, S. Harrison Bible.   Signed: Lewis ⊬ Stutts
                                              his mark

TURNER SMITH   6 November 1854
I'm to be decently buried and my just debts are to be paid. To Wife, Rebecca, all real estate and buildings, furniture, wheat, corn, bacon or pork on hand. To daughter, Loucinda, land adjoining English and Woolsey - at her death it is to go to grandson, John Marion Rush. David and

Martha Rush to live on land and pay Lucinda one third grain. To son,
Israel, land and tools. Other children: Robert, Fethias and Member
Smith, each to receive $25. Rebecca to pay Elizabeth Loyd $25, also
pay Martha Rush. Executor: Israel Smith. Will Dated: 22 September 1854.
Witnesses: James Shanks, David A. Forrester, William Crawford.
                                    Signed: . Turner Smith

JEREMIAH FARNSWORTH   4 December 1854 $15,000
Wife, Mary Ann to have what my executors decide is enough plus all
interest on notes dew me. To son, Humphries, young gray horse. To son,
David, sorrel mare. The two boyls get land. To daughter, Rebecca, to
be made equal at her outfit. To children: Jane Anderson, Ruth Brannon
decd. (her heirs, Mary, Margaret, Caroline, Alfred Brannon), Alfred N.,
and Harriet Reaves, each to receive $100. Son, Wyly to receive $120.
Colored man, Tennessee, entitles to all his earnings. Executors: Wife
Mary Ann, Son Humphries. Will Dated: 5 October 1854. Witnesses: G. F.
Page, Humphries Wells.   Signed: Jeremiah Farnsworth

HEZEKIAH RUSSELL   4 December 1854 $1,000
To Wife, Mary, all property her natural life, wheat, pork and bacon for
one year. To son, William and Archibald, $10 each. Heirs of my son:
John, Jeremiah, James and Polly Ann Smith. To John Lister's wife or
children, have been satisfied. My children to receive equal parts.
Executor: John Sheffey. Will Dated: 8 January 1852. Witnesses: Thomas
Starnes, William Thompson. Ex. and Bondsmen: Jacob H. Ackerman,
Archibald Russell, John Russell.   Signed: Hezekiah Russell

MARY MAGDALENE HOUTS
Dater, Barbara - all my property my father, Christopher Houts, left me
after his decease. To my grand-daughter, Mary Ellis and her husband
Rolente Ellis, to have property after Barbara's decease. Executors:
Roland and Jesse Ellis. Will Dated: 19 January 1843. Test: Gabriel
Henry, James McAmish, James Linebaugh.
                           Signed: Magdalene X Houts
                                               her mark

RACHEL DAVIS   4 December 1854   Bond $5,000
Children to stay together. The older ones to raise the younger ones.
Husband, James Davis decd. Oldest son, John M., 2nd Samuel B. Davis,
3rd David Davis, 4th Phillip. Four daughters: Luiza, oldest., Mary,
Lydia Annas, Elizabeth Jane. Executors: Phillip Maltsbarger, John
Davis. Will Dated: 8 February 1854. Witnesses: David Bright, Abigail
Hardin.   Signed: Rachel Davis

JOSIAH REN
Two daughters: Elizabeth and Margaret, all my property for their kind
and tender affection for me and my old woman in our feeble and declining
years. Wife: Dicey. Executors: John Shields, Bdn. William Shields,
Thomas Easterly. Will Dated: 24 November 1851. Witnesses: William
Shields, Thomas C. Easterly.   Signed: Josiah ┬ Ren
                                                    his mark

JOHN RENNER SEIGNOR   1 January 1855
Wife, Elizabeth, to have all, her lifetime. To daughter, Sally, and her
two heirs, 250 acres on headwater of Meadow Creek. To the heirs of my
son, Jacob, the plantation where their mother lives. Daughter: Polly.
Son, Henry to pay $100 he owes me. Sons: Peter and William. All heirs
set even at $600. The one that will take the mill shall not be deprived
of water. Executors: Son John Renner, son-in-law, Johnathan Easterly.
Will Dated: 12 January 1848. Bondsmen: John Bowers, Rufus Easterly.
Witnesses: John Smith, Henry Tobey.
                           Signed: Johannes Renner
27 September 1855 - John Renner resigned as executor due to fact that he
had sold his possessions in Greene County and expects to start to Texas
today, with my family and be a citizen of that part of the country for

the balance of my days. Witnesses: Rufus Easterly, William Ottinger.
Signed: John ⤶ Renner

STEPHEN BROOKS   At my residence April 1850
Wife, Margaret, to have income from plantation. Ten lots of land to
children. Two hundred and fourteen acres in Montgomery County, middle
Tennessee to be rented or sold. Sons: William, Asbury, Jacob F., Jesse.
Daughters: Mary wife of John K. Harrison, Charity wife of Henry E. Wells,
Sarah Griffen, Elizabeth, Nancy and Rachel. Executors: Jacob F. Brooks,
William Brooks, Will Dated: 11 April 1850. Witnesses: Samuel Ottinger,
G. F. Page.   Signed: Stephen Brooks

JOHN JOHNSON   5 February 1855 $200
To Wife, ____, all my land and property her lifetime, then to son, Joseph.
To sons, Wiley, Carter, John, Samuel, James and Elijah, $100 each to be
paid by Joseph. Four darters one dollar each. Executors: Son, Joseph
Johnson. Will Dated: 8 November 1854. Witnesses: Lemuel K. Core??,
Oliver Hardin.   Signed: John X Johnson

JOHN JUSTICE SENR.   5 March 1855 $500
To Wife, Thurzene, all property her widowhood, except money, a house and
furniture to each of my children. Children: Richard, James, Mary and
Nancy Justice, Martha, John, Alfred and Thurzene Justice. A rock called
Marble on my land. Executor: John Crabtree. Will Dated: 18 July 1854.
Witnesses: Henry M. Richard, Barnet Crabtree.
Signed: John Justice

ELIZABETH GRUBBS   7 August 1855 $1,000
Plantation to be sold 3 months after my death. Children: Mary Grubbs,
Edwin Grubbs, Catharin Robertson, Jesse, John, Amos decd., Rachel
Johnston, Lydia Yokley and Hannah Freeze. To daughter, Mary Grubbs, 200
acres land. To grandson, James A. Grubbs, horse, saddle, bridle and
martingills. My two grandsons: David and Samuel decd. To children by
my husband's former wife. Executor: Charles Bright. Will Dated: 4
September 1848. Witnesses: Jacob Hacker, Lanty Armstrong.
Signed: Elizabeth X Grubbs
her mark

WILLIAM MOYERS   2 April 1855 $2,000
Son of John Moyers Senr. Brothers: John and Nathaniel. To John, land
to pay back other heirs $300, if he doesnt - land to be sold and equally
divided. Sister: Lucinda. Nephew: Jesse C. Moyers. My mare to my
Mother. Executor: Brother, Nathaniel Moyers. Will Dated: 20 February
1855. Witnesses: Abraham Naff, John Crabtree.
Signed: William Moyers

JOHN DICKSON   7 April 1855   Bond $10,000
To Wife, Sally, after payments of debts - entire estate, if she should
die it is to go to my neice, Matilda Martin. Executrix: Wife Sally.
Will Dated: 26 August 1854. Witnesses: William M. Looney, David F.
Patterson, Robert J. McKenney.   Signed: John Dickson

JOHN M. RODGERS
To Wife, Mary, support off plantation, unenterrupted possession of East
side of my house. To son, James B., a negro boy. To son, John, $400.
To daughter, Mary wife of John Cole, a negro woman, curtains, table
cover of Irish linen. To son, Alexander, $400. To daughter, Rachel decd.
- heirs Isaac and James McCollum, sons of Alexander McCollum, $400. To
son, Joseph, plantation of 200 acres where I now live adjoining Elizabeth
Caldwell, Andrew Logan and others. Joseph's two sons, James and William.
Executors: Wife Mary, Son Joseph. Will Dated: 15 February 1854.
Witnesses: Alexander Robertson, Jesse Doty.
Signed: John M. Rodgers

MINERVA NORTON
To Rachel Olinger, wife of David Olinger decd., $1. Levie Rush $1. Jesse
Rush decd $1. Lewis Rush $1. To William Lane, property on Lick Creek.
William M. Lane was to take care of Mrs. Norton. Executors: Thomas
Baily. Will Dated: 29 July 1854. Witnesses: M. D. Strong, Jacob
Everhart.   Signed: Minerva X Norton

Thomas Baily declined to ser as executor.

WILLIAM WYKEL   4 June 1855 $8,000
Ex. Bondsmen: James D. Wykel, William D. Culver, James Susong. Farm in
Cocke County to be sold and divided. Wife, Jane, to settle my debts and
get all property as long as she lives. Children: George, William S.,
James D., Marshall L., Mary Jane, Elizabeth W., Catharine E., Eliza,
Joseph and John. To son, Marshall L., saddle and bridle. To sons,
Joseph and John, to have home place. Mine and my wife's graves to be
finished with toomstones. Executor: Son James. Will Dated: 6 January
1855. Witnesses: Alfred and James Susong.
                              Signed: William X Wykel

ROBERT RUSSELL   4 June 1855 $4,000
Wife: Margaret. Three sons: Thomas, David and John Russell. Daughter:
Charlotte. Other children. David is to care for wife, Margaret and
daughter, Charlotte if they become disabled. Thomas and John are to
help. Will Dated: 16 May 1848. Witnesses: Charles Gass, Casper
Easterly.   Signed: Robert Russell

THOMAS McCLAIN   6 August 1855 $400
To Wife, Elizabeth, plantation where I live, provissions and profits
from land, then it is to go to Jonathan who is to take care of us.
Children: Jonathan, Daniel, Joseph, George, John, Clark, McNea, Nancy
Harvey, Deborah Henry, Elizabeth Vernon and Murrel. To son, Murrel
McLain, 50 acres on Cany Creek. Executors: Sons Murrel and Jonathan
McLain. Witnesses: James Murphey, James Davis, Michael Maltsbarger.
                              Signed: Thomas McLain

JOHN S. REED   6 August 1855 $18,000
To Wife, Ann, all she brought with her when we married inc $430 note on
Reuben H. Davis and to have sufficient support. Children: Jane wife of
James Moore, Polly wife of John Moore, Lucinda wife of Reuben H. Davis,
Eliza wife of Samuel W. Davis, Nancy wife of George M. Crouch, William
Reed. To daughter, Jane, a negro girl. To son, William, to have 250
acres. Grandson, William R. Reed son of my daughter, Fanny, $1 - all I
intend for him to have. Grandson: Joseph M. Reed. To grandson, James
Reed, $100 for a good English education and learn a good trade. To
grandson, John Reed, $100. To grand-daughters: Grizzy - $50, and Nancy
Reed - $100. Daughters to have negroes appraised and share equally and
pay money to them personally, especially Nancy Crouch - dont let her
husband have it. Executors: Son William, William West. Will Dated: 16
March 1862?? Witnesses: E. W. Headrick, William A. Harmon.
                              Signed: J. S. Reed

MOSES DOTSON   3 September 1855 $200
Sister: Sarah, all land and property - then to go to Brother, David
Franklin Dotson's son Reuben Moses. Brothers: Cornelius and John Dotson.
Sisters: Mary Moon?? (Moor), Jane Ellet. Executor: Brother Cornelius
Dotson. Will Dated: 6 June 1855. Witnesses: John Laney, Peter Dotson.
                              Signed: Moses X Dotson

SARAH REEVE   5 November 1855 $400
To Husband, George W. Reeve, all that is coming to me from the estate of
my father, William Painter decd. Will Dated: 4 January 1855. Witnesses:
Jesse S. Reeve, Charles Earnest.   Signed: Sarah Reeve

JAMES OLIPHANT   5 November 1855 $10,000
Son William L. to have plantation. Daughters, Sally Melinda and Harriet
to have their support. Other children: Nancy, James, Polly Ann. To

daughter, Nancy Russell, $375. To grandson, James O. Hoyal, $375. To grand-daughter, Pollyann Robertson, $375. Interest on money to school my grand children. If negroes get unruly, they are to be sold. Executors: David R. and William L. Oliphant. Will Dated: 18 August 1855. Witnesses: Lewis Rankin, John G. Rankin.

Signed: James Oliphant

ABRAHAM MOORE   3 December 1855 $500   Non cupative
Wife, Mary Moore, to stay on home place and be supported off land. Son, William, to have homeplace and place where Henry Monteeth now lives. To son, Murrell, Mason place and a nursery of apple trees. Other children: Nancy Brandon, Mary Monteeth and James M. Moore, equal share. Sam Gabriel decd. Nephew: Alexander Moore. Henry Monteeth to stay on place. Dated: 20 October 1855. Signed: William X Dykes, William X Moore. This will was made orally, later written and signed: Hanry and Mary Monteeth. This will was in Court - Executors would not bring it in until made to.

ANNIE HAYS   9 January 1856
To daughter, Hester Newland, $5. To daughter, Sarah McCurry, interest on money. To Hiram Guire?, $50. To Abraham Guire, $50. To Elizabeth Bowers, $50. My father's grave to be installed with a good stone wall. Executors: David Bright, S. J. Biddle. Will Dated: 13 August 1851. Test: S. J. Biddle, David Bright, Lyddia Bright.

No signature.

JOHN RECTOR SENR.   30 March 1856 $500
Children by my first wife: Nellie Irving, Deborah Whillock, Nancy Hutts, Rachel Howard, Elizabeth Dunlap, Sarah Guinn, Mary Kibler, Enoch Rector, to receive $1 each. Son, John, land where he lives. Sons, George and Franklin, land where I live. Daughter Jane Rector, bedstead and cupboard. Daughters by last marriage: Susan Dearstone, Harriet Peters, Maria Roberts, Rebecca Peters and Jane Rector, to have money from sale divided equally. Executor: John Davis. Will Dated: 16 March 1853. Witnesses: A. J. Plrece?, Isaac Basinger, Executors who served: Alexander Anderson, Robert Mason.

Signed: John X Rector Senr.

JOHN KERBAUGH
Wife, Elizabeth, to have support from land. Children: John M., William W., (rest of my legal heirs.) Executor: James Davis. Will Dated: 25 November 1855. Witnesses: Charles Gass, Jacob Kerbaugh.

Signed: John X Kerbaugh

SAMUEL COTTER   7 March 1855
To Wife, Susannah, land on Stogdens Creek - Entry No. 3020, and horses, cattle, hogs, tools etc. Children: William, Betsy, Rebecca Beals, James, Jesse, George, Polly, Loyd. Single children to remain with widow. Sell property not needed to pay debts. Executor: Loyd Bullen. Witnesses: Rufus K. Maral?, Hugh E. Cotter.   Signed: Samuel Cotter

WILLIAM ROLLINS SENR.   7 April 1856
To Wife, Rachel, land on Cove Creek adjoining Warren Houston including the graveyard field adjoining William Houston, plus livestock, tools, jugs, bottles, furniture etc. Children: George, David, Greenberry, Enoch, Amy, Nancy, Lydia, Eliza, William, Seth and John Westley Rollins. Executor: John R. Lamb. Will Dated: 28 April 1855. Test: Isaac Seaton, Christopher Mills.   Signed: William X Rollins

WILLIAM THOMASSON   7 April 1856
Wife: Margaret. To son, Valentine, $20 from his mother's part. To daughter, Frances Witt, 1 horse beast and $20. To daughter, Elizabeth, side saddle and $20. To daughter, Mary, side saddle worth $20. Daughters to have as much as Frances got when she left me. Executor: Michael Dearstone. Will Dated: 5 August 1853. Test: James R. Ealy,
  led? Gos X lin.   Signed: William Thomason

ISAAC HORTON   7 April 1856 $1,000
To Wife, Ann, all I got with her by marriage. Money from my land warrant.
All other property to be sold and divided between my other heirs. Will
Dated: 4 March 1856. Executors: Joseph M. Horton, William White, Thomas
Hays. Witnesses: Samuel Peters, Harvey D. Allen.
                          Signed: Isaac Horton

PHILLIP NEAS   5 May 1856 $2,000
To son, Joseph, plantation where I now live to care for me as long as I
live. Youngest son, Andrew, to have other plantation when he is 21. To
son, George, plantation I bought of Joseph Williams where Joseph Lafollett
lives. To son, Phillip, plantation adjoining that I willed George. To
daughters: Elizabeth wife of John Eisenhour, Sarah wife of Jacob Ottinger,
$500 each. Executor: Son, Joseph Neas. Will Dated: 18 October 1852.
Witnesses: Henry Tobey, James Lauderdale. Ex. Bdn.: A. W. Walker, Jacob
Ottinger.   Signed: Phillip Neas

ANN KENNEDY   2 June 1856 $2,000
Wife of Joseph Kennedy decd. I inherited from my father, Robert Allison,
270 acres. My will not to conflict with that of my husband. Ten
Children: Robert A., William H. and David Thompson, Rachel Mercer,
Elizabeth Stuart, Hanna Eliza Mercer, Nancy Ann Bowman, Sophia Armstrong,
Samuel R. Kennedy, Martha M. Creamer. Nancy Ann Stuart, daughter of my
daughter, Elizabeth Stuart. Elizabeth Crawford, Risina McCollum, David
W. Mercer, heirs of Daughter, Rachel Mercer - $200 equally divided.
Balance equally divided. Will Dated: 17 April 1856. Witnesses: Josiah
Conley, Abraham Naff, Thomas P. Prub??e?
                          Signed: Ann X Kennedy

ELIZABETH ANN RADER   2 June 1856 $1,600
Formerly Elizabeth Ann Myers. To my husband, Lemuel Rader, 50 acres I
inherited from my mother and all coming from Jacob Myers, my guardian.
Mother, Mary Myers decd., lying on Gap Creek adjoining my father, Jacob
Myers. To my heirs - all money coming to me in the hands of William M.
Williams adm. of Elizabeth Walker decd. Felix Wells and others.
Executor: Husband Lemuel Rader. Will Dated: 28 March 1855. Witnesses:
William Rader, Cornelius Rader.   Signed: Elizabeth Ann Rader

THOMAS DAVIS   6 October 1856 $1,000
To Wife, Levina, land and all personal property. Executors: Josiah
Harrison, Thomas Jones. Will Dated: 15 May 1854. Witnesses: John H.
Dunsmore, M. K. Jones.

JOHN R. FARNSWORTH   6 October 1856 $1,000
All estate to John Gourley's daughter, Elizabeth. Executors: John
Gourley, Uriah Matthews. Will Dated: 11 August 1856. Witnesses: George
Gammon, Richard Gammon.   Signed: John R. Farnsworth

ANN M. COX   December Sessions 1856
To my sister, Rachel M. Babb wife of Samuel Babb, all my personal
property. Executrix: Rachel M. Babb. Will Dated: 1 August 1856.
Witnesses: Daniel Britton, Isaac Peter.
                          Signed: Ann M. X Cox

JOHN WALKER   5 January 1857
To Wife, Jane, all property during her natural life or widowhood. To son,
David M., my book account against him - if he hands one $300 note on me
which I paid. To sons, Michael W. and D. J., my farm if they pay $125
each to my other children. Executors: Sons, A. W. and M. W. Walker.
Will Dated: 20 June 1853. Test: R. M. Easterly, N. H. Masener.
                          Signed: John Walker

MARY MASONER   5 January 1856 $500
Children: Newton H., James H., Margaret Masoner, Mary Ann Gragg, all
personal property to be equally divided. Executors: Newton H. Masoner,

John S. Love. Will Dated: 14 March 1853. Witnesses: Henry McCoy, James Henager.   Signed: Mary X Masoner

SARAH WOOLSEY   2 February 1857 $1,200
To daughter, Hepsibah Bell (Hessebah), my bay horse and bedstead. To daughter, Jerusha Ruble, yellow heifer, small baker and one half the new bed. To daughter, Sarah E. Woolsey, cows, hogs, furniture and all articles she made. To daughter, Kerenhappech Overholser, red cow, bed-stead, one half new bed. To son, Gilbert, 31 1/4 acres land. To son, William B., black alpaca dress pattern. To son, Stephen, one bed Blanket. Executor: Wylie Kelley. Will Dated: 27 January 1857. Witnesses: H. T. Price, G. H. Price.   Signed: Sarah Woolsey.

RICHARD WILKINSON   5 March 1860 $100
To Wife, Letty, mare, cow, one half my land - at her death to go to son, Richard. Richard also to have other half of land. Children: Richard, Nancy C. Harper. To Nancy C. Harper, 31¼ acres land. Heirs: Jane, Elizabeth, Sarah, Emeline, Martha, William, John, Charles, James - $2 each. Executors: Allen Baker, Ambrose Bible, S. Davis. Letty Wilkinson refused. Will Dated: 25 May 1855. Witnesses: Solomon Matthews, Reuben Wisecarver.   Signed: Richard X Wilkinson
                                                    his mark

JOHN ELLISON   6 July 1857 $500
To Wife, Louisa, all money in and out of hand, all my estate, real and personal during her life - then to be sold. To son, David A., blacksmith tools and rifle. Children: David A., Mary, William, Robert, James, Elizabeth, Jimmason, Margaret Bailey - each to have $5. Witnesses: George Reaves, Washington Reaves, William Elvey?
                               Signed: John X Ellison

JOHN MORROW   7 July 1857 $1,000
To son, Adam, plantation where he formerly lived, purchased from Robert Rankin for $700. To four sons, William, David, Ebenezer and Samuel, plantation where I now live til Samuel is 21 and personal property. To six daughters: Nancy, Mary, Margaret, Elizabeth, Hannah and Isabella, $100 each. Executor: sons William and David. Will Dated: 15 May 1857. Witnesses: William S, McGaughey, James M. Briton.
                                  Signed: John X Morrow

JAMES BROWN   16 August 1857
Wife, Jane, to posess all my landed estate sufficient for use of family, cattle, grain and provisions. Children: John Wilson Brown, William C. Maloney Brown, James Thomas Brown, Emma and Laura Brown. Son, James Thomas Brown, to have land at Jane's death. Daughters, Emma and Laura, to have money on hand or from sale. Executors: David M. Dobson, Robert Brown. Witnesses: John P. Hiltsinger, John Brown.
                                  Signed: James Brown

JOSEPH HAYS   7 September 1857 $1,000
To son, Andrew J., all my lands during his life - his two sons, Joseph and Jackson Hays. Daughter, Barbary, has her part. Executors: Andrew Hays, R. S. Bowman, Charlie Hays. Will Dated: 20 June 1857. Witnesses: Charles Hays, R. S. Bowman.   Signed: Joseph Hays

PHINEAS JONES   6 October 1857 $2,000
To Wife, Sarah, all land, money and effects. To daughter, Rebecca, life-time support, I owe her $100. Son, Alexander, owes me $70. Executor: James Reeves. Will Dated: 21 August 1857. Witnesses: J. G. Reeves, M. S. Temple.   Signed: Phineas X Jones

THOMAS MURPHEY   3 November 1857
To be buried on my own plantation with grave snugly walled with brick or stone. Divide between Betsa Kannada, Marget Morrow and their mother - where William I. Murphey now lives. Betsa Kannada's and Marget Morrow's sons meaning - Thomas, John and James Kannada; John, Thomas, James and

Joseph Morrow. Executors: William West, Dr. William Cavener. Will Dated: 17 April 1857. Witnesses: William Johnson, E. H. West.
Signed: Thomas Murphey

CAROLINE M. FARNSWORTH   2 November 1857 $8,000
Sister, Mary A. wife of Daniel Allen, to have all property including slaves. Sister, Elizabeth wife of Joseph B. Walker, to have my black girl, Emily, and her 3 children. Niece: Caroline Allen. Executor: Daniel Allen. Will Dated: 4 September 1850. Witnesses: James Baker, James L. Todd.
Signed: Caroline M. Farnsworth

ELIZABETH JOHNSON
After debts are paid, my afflicted daughter, Rebecca Johnson, gets the remainder of my estate. Rest of my children have been portioned off. Executors: David R. Johnson, Son John Johnson. Will Dated: 13 March 1855. Witnesses: James seseton??, Alexander Jones.
Signed: Elizabeth Johnson

VINCENT JACKSON   7 December 1857 $1,000
Wife, Clementine, shall have place. To son, Aquilla, 104 acre farm where I live, if he died to go to his wife. Rest of my children have gotten theirs. (Son George in other papers). Executor: George Jackson. Will Dated: 2 January 1857. Witnesses: William Rader, Lemuel Crosby.

ENOS PICKERING   7 December 1857 $4,000
Wife, Mary Ann, to have all my cleared land, all property including washing machine, windmill, feathered fowls and $150 cash, also to have railroad stock. To William and Benjamin Johnson, my wife's sons by a former marriage - all my interest in their grand-father William Johnson's estate. All my children namely: Benjamin, Johnathan, Charity, Elisha, Ellis, William, Hannah, Enos, Elijah, John, David, Ketron, Angeline, Mary Ann, Margaret, Samuel - to divide everything equally. Executors: Son Samuel Pickering, son-in-law Henry Thompson. Will Dated: 3 February 1855. Witnesses: John Hammer, Samuel B. Dillon, Aaron Hammer.
Signed: Enos Pickering

MARTHA CARTER   7 December 1857
Widow of Ezekiel Carter, Decd. Four daughters: Sarah Key, Anna Simpson, Priscilla Pogue, Hila McMillan - to divide my kitchen furniture, also all other property to be sold and divided between my daughters. Rest of my children have their part. Executors: Abraham and Ezekiel Carter. Will Dated: 9 March 1853. Witnesses: Peter Harmon of Isaac, Wylie I. Proctor.
Signed: Martha X Carter

SARAH HANKINS   3 April 1858 $3,000
Son: Alexander Gass, each of his heirs, $1. Son: George M. Gass, one $40 debt. Three grand children: George, Emaline, John A. Britton - $1.00 each. Daughter: Mary F. Weems, her son David F. Weems - one clock and bed. Daughter: Nancy Myers, each of her children - $1.00. Son: John E. Hankins and wife Elizabeth - negroes and corner cupboard. Executor: John E. Kidwell. Will Dated: 23 February 1858. Other Executors: J. G. Gass, S. B. Headrick, James Britton Junr.

Signed: Sarah X Hankins

ALEXANDER ENGLISH   5 April 1858 $5,000
To Wife, Mary English, full and uninterrupted possession, stock and slaves. If slaves become disobedient they are to be sold. To grand-daughter, Melinda Tunnel, $600 I intended to give her mother. After Mary's death all to be sold and money divided between my children equally - including Alexander and Melinda Tunnel. Executor: Andrew English. Will Dated: 7 March 1857. Witnesses: James Shanks, _____ Brandon.
Signed: Alexander English

BARNABAS GABLE   3 May 1858 $1,000
To sons: Barnabas Junr., Elias, William, $1 each with what they have received. One dollar to be halved by their heirs. Children: Hiram,

Elizabeth, Polly, Susannah, Orpha, Catharine, Rachel, Mary Magdalena
Gable - to have an equal part of what is left. Son: Hoker Gable, his
heirs can halve the dollar I give him. Executor: Son Herman Gable.
Will Dated: 25 March 1855. Witnesses: R. D. Browning, W. D. Guinn.

MICHAEL WOODS   7 January 1858 $6,000
To be buried with my children that are buried on the farm where I now
live. My wife is to remain and have support, cattle money etc. her life,
then to go to Samuel and my three daughters. Children: Samuel S.,
Margaret wife of Martin McBride, Jane widow of Henry Boyd decd., Lucinda
wife of James Evans, oldest son James Woods, 2nd son William, 3rd John,
4th Archibald. Sons, James, William, John and Archibald, have their
share. Make Samuel equal to other sons and pay him for his taking care
of my wife and me. Executors: Sons John and Samuel S. Woods. Will
Dated: 25 April 1856. Witnesses: Reuben H. Davis, A. W. Walker.
                           Signed: Michael Woods

JACOB ELLIS   8 June 1858 $500
To Wife, Elizabeth, all movable property that is necessary for her
support. Sell remainder and pay debts. To son, Daniel, 96 acres I
bought of Abner Beals. To son, Abner, part of land I bought of Henderson
adjoining Meeting House lot. To sons, William and Solomon, balance of
this plantation. Other property divided between my four daughters: Lydia,
Mary, Sarah and Martha. Lydia also to have a bed. Executors: Sons
William and Abner Ellis. Will Dated: 24 May 1858. Witnesses: Aaron
Hammer, Ellis Beals.   Signed: Jacob {,' Ellis
                                           his' mark

GEORGE JACKSON   5 June 1858 $32,000
Wife: Jane. Children: Isaac, James V., Mary E. Jackson, Dempsey, Caleb,
Harriet E. Jackson, Sarah M. Jackson. Son, Isaac, to take all land,
slaves and property to support Jane and family until James V. Jackson is
21. When James V. is 21 he is to assume support of my wife, Jane. All
my children are to receive equal shares. (Father Vincent Jackson in
other papers.) Executor: Son Isaac Jackson. Will Dated: 10 May 1858.
Witnesses: William Rader, Lemuel Crosby.
                           Signed: George Jackson

JACOB CRUM   2 August 1858
To grand-daughter, Eliza and her heirs, one negro girl and $300. Property
not named, to be equally divided between my children. Children: Sarah,
Margaret, William, John's heirs, Nancy's heirs. Executors: Lewis Click,
William Crum. Will Dated: 15 July 1858. Witnesses: N. H. Lamb, Jacob
X Keller. Names on Bond: Margaret Thomason, N. H. Lamb, R. K. Waddle,
J. M. Cunduff, Katharine Winkle.   Signed: Jacob Crum

WILLIAM WILLIAMS   2 August 1858 $25,000
To Wife, Eliza, all my real and personal estate her lifetime. Executor:
Felix W. Wells. Will Dated: 6 June 1853. Witnesses: Eliz Garrett,
Nathan Farmer, Felix Wells descinded. Ex. was John G. Weems - his bonds-
men - George Kenney, J. M. Fry, Reuben West.
                           Signed: W. M. Williams

ANDREW STINE   2 August 1858
I give my body to its mother earth. To be buried at St. James Church
burying ground. To my grandson, John Hawk, 250 acres on end of farm
where I live, 2 horses, gearing, clock and delph ware, and he must pay
$25 each to his sisters: Sarah, Mary, Emaline and Susan. To my three
grandsons, Andrew, William and Thomas Hawk - the remainder of my lands.
To daughter, Mary, $50 cash. To daughter, Catharine, $50 cash, my loom
and gearing. John Hawks to support his aunt Sarah Stine. Executor:
Andrew M. Walker. Witnesses: Joseph Ottinger, D. J. Walker.
                           Signed: Andrew X Stine

REBECCA SAYLOR   2 August 1858
To be buried at night. Nephew: Nelson Saylor. My sister, Mary Saylor's

son, to receive 62 acres land, one chest and one big wheel. Will Dated:
30 June 1858. Witnesses: A. J. Carrells, Thomas Weems, John B. Correll.
Signed: Rebecca X Saylor

JANE I. CRAIG   2 August 1858
To daughter, Nancy Craig, my black girl Betsy and her offspring - by
paying my daughter Eleanor Anderson $100. Debts to be paid - what is
left to be divided equally among my children: Nancy Craig, Eleanor
Anderson, Mary Farnsworth, Jane Twitty heirs, James Craig, Samuel and
Robert Craig. To grandson, John Craig that lives with me, $50.
Executors: Son James, Nephew Major S. Temple. Will Dated: 6 March 1849.
Witnesses: T. W. McAmis, Jacob F. Anderson.
Signed: Jane I. Craig

POLLY ANN EVERHART   2 August 1858 $1,200
To my sister, Jane Everhart, my side saddle. To my brothers: William,
Daniel and James Everhart, $1 each. Sister: Elizabeth Lawson. To my
mother, Anna Price, all real and personal estate that I have in my father,
Nicholas Everhart's estate. Executrix: Mother Anna Price. Will Dated:
19 April 1858. Witnesses: George Kenney, William Hawkins.
Signed: Polly Ann Everhart

THOMAS FARNSWORTH   5 October 1858 $1,000
Wife, Rebecca, to have all estate her lifetime - then to go to my son,
William R. Will Dated: 6 July 1838. Witnesses: Washington Harrison,
Robert P. Johnson.   Signed: Thomas X Farnsworth

SOLOMON SMITH   2 August 1858
To Wife, Elizabeth, 67 1/2 acres land in Washington County adjoining
James Million, now belonging to Elbert S. Smith, son of Solomon, and
sufficient support. Plantation where I live equally divided between
my sons: Elbert S., William R., David A. and George W. To daughter,
Susannah, her support during her lifetime. To daughter, Mary, one
bureau and a looking glass. Mary's part to go to her two children,
Alexander and Mary. His wife says she is sadderfide with his will.
Son-in-law: William McMackin. Executor: William Mackin. Will Dated:
8 July 1858. Attest: Nathaniel Moyers, Lucinda Taylor, Robert Taylor.
Witnesses: James McMackin, Solomon Harrison.
Signed: Solomon Smith

JOSEPH HARTMAN   7 February 1859 $3,000
To Wife, Cinthia, all land, money and property where we live. Land in
Washington County and up to $500 to go to Thomas Roberts's wife Jane.
Over $500 to go to Charles Collet. The remainder to my first cousins.
Executors: J. J. Yeaker, George F. Gillespie. Will Dated: 15 September
1858. Witnesses: Thomas Williams, George F. Gillespie.
Signed: Joseph Hartman

JAMES KENNEY   7 March 1859 $1,000
To Wife, Elizabeth, whole amount of my estate - if she should die or
marry it is to go to all my children. Executors: Two oldest sons: George
E. Kenney, Harven W. Kenney. Will Dated: 5 February 1859. Witnesses:
George Kenney, M. B. Crumley.   Signed: James Kenney

LEWIS J. DRAKE   7 March 1858 $8,000
Place good marble toomstones at my grave and enclose it with good iron
bannistry. Executors to put marble toomstones at graves of parents,
Gabriel and Rebecca Drake, and Eliza Flemings (Russell's) grave, pay my
Mason's dues. Land on Warrensburg Road 2 miles from town. Wife,
Catharine, to have profits of all my money or notes - at her death they
are to go to my neices and nephews. Pay $50 to Greeneville Presbyterian
Sabbath School. Executors: Samuel McGaughey, William W. Drake. Will
Dated: 9 February 1859. Witnesses: L. B. McCorkle, James Britton Junr.
Signed: L. J. Drake

SAMUEL SNAPP SENR.   7 March 1859
To Wife, Dianna, use and possession of the east end of my dwelling house
and the room below and above stairs and kitchen, 3 negroes, furniture,
cattle, hogs, cupboards etc. her natural life. Wife to get profits from
estate. Deeds of gift to children: John P., James E., Eliza D. Doak and
Nancy C. Carson. Son: Samuel E. Executors: Sons John P. and Samuel E.
Snapp. Will Dated: 5 February 1848. Witnesses: David Rice, J. A. Park,
Joseph Newberry.   Signed: Samuel Snapp

OBADIAH JOHNSON   4 April 1859
My Wife, _____. To my daughter, Anny, all personal property and growing
grain. To Samuel Dunwoody, my land warrant. Executor: Jeremiah
McMillan. Will Dated: 7 February 1856. Witnesses: John M. Hull, John
Gauntt??   Signed: Obadiah X Johnson
                                              his mark

RICHARD SCRUGGS   4 June 1859
To Wife, Ann, $2000 and a negro girl to be hers, bed clothing she brought
to my house, furniture, stock and provisions. Son, James decd., his
legal heirs $2500. To son, John, $2750. To daughter, Sarah Bayless,
$1300 and negroes. To son, Abijah, $600 since I gave him $4400. To son,
Rufus's legal heirs, $2500. To daughter, Mary Jarnagan's legal heirs,
$3000. To daughter, Martha Webster, $3000. To son, Richard M., I have
given him $6000. To son Frederick, $1800 and personal property and 42
acre Lick Creek Farm. Nephew: John Scruggs. Son: William C., I have
given him $6000. Executors: Sons: Abijah and William C. Scruggs, and
Richard M. Scruggs. Will Dated: 29 November 1858. Test: James C. Larue,
Thomas I. Easterly.   Signed: Richard Scruggs

JOSEPH SHEETS   6 June 1859
To Wife, Mary, all real and personal property then to son William C.
Sheets. To Mariah Davis, whom I partly raised, $100. Executor: Enos
Keezel. Will Dated: 27 September 1858. Witnesses: E. Link, John Parman,
David Dawitt.   Signed: Joseph Sheets

THOMAS McAMIS   5 September 1859
To Wife, Sarah, $200 in money, all furniture, horse, saddle, cow and
rents from land, to get decent support, firewood and milling dove.
Children: Margaret Logan, Elizabeth Porter, Louisa Brummet, Nancy Ann
Rodgers, Loucinda Olinger, Mary Campbell, Martha Crouch, Sarah Baily,
William H., James. Daughter, Margaret, has received her share. Seven
other daughters to receive $700 each and equal part of land at my wife's
death. To son, William H., home tract adjoining Evan T. McNeese, A. J.
Babb, James Gass Senr. and the Poor Farm. Executors: William H. McAmis,
John Olinger. Will Dated: 16 October 1857. Witnesses: William McAmis,
James Jane.   Signed: Thomas McAmis

TURNER D. KELLEY   5 September 1859 $1,500
Wife, Elizabeth, to have everything to raise and school children until
they are 21. Brother: Wyly Kelly. Children: James Luther, Madison M.,
Clark Marion, Milton Columbus, Sarah Josephine (crossed in will), Clayton
Decator, Turner D., Sarah Josephine. Executrix: Wife Elizabeth. Will
Dated: 2 August 1859. Witnesses: Reuben H. Davis, William A. Morley.
                                 Signed: Turner D. Kelley

THOMAS DAVIS   5 September 1859
To Wife, Margaret, all furniture she wants, land with rents and profits
her lifetime, then to go to son, William, for his full share. To
daughter, Cintha Jane Rector, $500. To daughter, Polly, $400. To grand-
daughter, Frances A. Linder, $300. Balance of heirs not mentioned.
Executor: Ephraim Davis. Will Dated: 20 August 1859. Witnesses: James
A. Roberts, James Park.   Signed: Thomas X Davis

JOHN ADAM WATTENBARGER   28 June 1859
To Wife, Mary Magdalene, all property I do not devise, to be hers her
widowhood. Children: Molly Carter wife of John Carter, Eliza Couch wife

of Alfred Couch, Jacob, Charles, Wilson, Sarah Fink wife of William Fink.
To grandson, Alfred son of Wilson Wattenbarger, gun, trunk, $200 and part
of farm to care for his grand-mother. Executors: Wilson Wattenbarger,
James Williams. Will Dated: 28 June 1859. Test: Thomas Bailey, B. M.
Bailey.

HENRY RIPLEY   3 October 1859 $3,000
To Wife, Mary, 25 acres land and balance of movable estate her lifetime.
To daughter, Lucinda Jane Ripley, 25 acres and household articles, beds,
sheets, delf etc. To daughter-in-law, Eleanor widow of my son Thomas,
25 acres land. To daughter, Rachel Pickering, 25 acres land. To
daughter, Phebe Brown, 25 acres. To son, Elcana Ripley, my wife's land
at her death. Executors: Thomas Thomason Esq., son Elcana Ripley. Witnesses: Thomas Ripley, Demetrius B. Ripley. Bondsmen: Elkanah Ripley,
Thomas Thomason, Thomas Ripley, Benjamin Johnson.
                        Signed: Henry Ripley

MICHAEL BRIGHT   3 October 1859
My body to be buried in a decent and funeral manner. Wife departed.
Daughter, Sarah wife of Thomas Bales, has her part, but give her $100
more. Estate to be divided between my two sons, David M. and Michael
L. Bright. Executors: David M. Bright, George W. Bright. Witnesses:
Charles Bright, John Dodd Senr., John Dodson, There were two wills with
no signature being on the first. Signed: Michael Bright

JOHN W. WILHOITE
To Wife, Mary, all property her life. Son, Elbert Milton Wilhoite, to
remain on farm and care for Mary, for which he is to receive a fair
share. Three daughters: Elizabeth A. Park, Frances A. Dosser, Mary Blair
Wilhoite, to have $300 each. Mary Blair Wilhoite to be provided for and
finish her education. Daughter, Caroline T. Dosser decd., her children
to receive $300 each paid by Milton. To son, Washington M. Wilhite, $500
in addition to what he has received. Executors: George B. Park, James H.
Dosser. Will Dated: 15 July 1856. Witnesses: George W. Foute, Isaac
Earnest.   Signed: John W. Hilhoit

MOSES BOWERS   February 27, 1859
To my three children, Andrew S., Mary M., Lavina J. Johnston, 196 acres
divided equally. Negroes to be divided equally between three children.
Wife: Margaret. Witnesses: Samuel Parman, John Guin, J. K. Hancher.
Will Probated: 6 February 1860.   Signed: Moses Bowers

HENRY FEEZEL   5 March 1860   Bond $80,000
To Wife, Nancy Ann, 113 acre Washington Nealy place, $100 yearly and
sufficient support. To sons, Samuel decd. his children, James Martin
and daughter, Conella wife of Russell Pickens, all residents of Missi-
ssippi - $500 each. To son, George W. decd. his heirs, $500 each. To
children: William Anderson, Catharine Jane, James Robinson, Alpha Louiza,
Rachel Elizabeth, Margaret Lucinda, Martha Ann Hester, John Henry, Susan
Elvina - $500 each and to any other children who may be born to George W.
Feezle and his present wife. To heirs of William M. Campbell and
Elizabeth's children: Bluford, George W., Sarah, Martha - $500. To
Henry Feazle son of Jacob H., $200. To Samuel Russell son of John
Russell and Louiza Campbell, $200. To Eli Patton Feezle son of Jacob H.,
$200. To Jacob H. Feezle, his notes of $1300. To George W. Feezle county
of Blount, his several notes. Henry's children: Samuel, George W.,
Elizabeth Campbell in Greene County. Will Dated: 7 January 1860.
Witnesses: John Love, John Brunner.
                        Signed: Henry Feezel

GEORGE WELLS   2 April 1857 $500
I'm in my 86 year, have a sound mind and memory but time is short. Wife,
Mary Wells, to have mansion house, 2 cows, 4 sheep, furniture and Jacob
P. Wells is to pay her 1/6 of all grain grown on land. When Mary dies,
the property is his, also the wagon, windmill, loom and Family Bible. To
son, Henry E., the upper end of the Daniel Nelson tract, he is to pay my
grand-daughter, Eliza McAlpin, $50. He has paid her and has her receipt.

Grand-daughter, Susanna Moore (alias Wells) to get $50 in trade when she needs it and Henry E. can spare it. Sons: Lawrence Wells, B. Wells, Jacob P. Wells. Lawrence Wells has his part. Children: Sarah B. Robinson, Lawrence B. Wells, heirs of Elizabeth Gorley, to receive and divide money from sale. These three heirs to pay our funeral expenses. Jacob Wells to pay to Mary Ann Farnsworth. Rebecca Lotspeich, Sarah B. Robinson - $100 is made as their portionable part of my real estate. Two sons, Humphris and Felix W. Wells have received their parts. Executor: son Humphris. Will Dated: 2 April 1857. Teste: John K. Harrison, William W. Harrison.
Signed: George Wells

JOHN McKEE   6 February 1860
To Catharine Jeremin and Jane Eliza the issue of a former marriage in Pennsylvania, of whom I am the reputed father - $1.00 and no more. To Wife, Elizabeth, $2000 to be put on interest for her support. To Elizabeth's child, Nancy Ellen - $1000. Son: Robert. Executors: wife Elizabeth and son Robert. Witnesses: B. McDannel, John A. Brown.
Signed: John McKee

MARSHEL W. WYKEL   21 January 1860 $1,000
Mother to have my notes - my debts are to come out of them and put toomstones at my grave. Brother: James D. Wykel a citizen of Macon County, Illinois. Brothers and Sisters: William Brannon, Catharine E. Brannon, Eliza Adeline Wykel, William S. Wykel, Jane Wykel, James D. Wykel, William D. Culver, M. J. Culver, George W. Wykel. Brother: John M. Wykel of Harrison County, Missouri. Executor: brother James D. Wykel. Will Dated: 19 November 1859. Ex. Sec.: Alfred Susong, James Susong.
Not signed or witnessed.

JANE TEMPLE   6 February 1860
Put toomstones at our graves. To seven daughters: Mary Robinson, one bureau; Margaret Biggs, a clock; Elizabeth Gallaher, Sarah R. Biggs, Jane Slemmons, Ellen McCord, Isabella Temple - to divide money. Isabella to have a cupboard and carpet. Grand-daughters: Margaret Robinson, Jane Biggs. To grandsons: Thomas T. Robinson, James Robinson, Major D. Robinson, shovel and tongs. Son-in-law: James Biggs. Bounty land to be sold. Twenty-eight dollars to the Brick Presbyterian Church at Timber Ridge, in Greene County, Tennessee. Executor: James Biggs. Will Dated: 16 April 1855. Test: A. Rankin, Elijah Debusk.
Signed: Jane X Temple

JOHN DODD   2 April 1860 $15,000
District 18 - Greene County, Tennessee. Wife, Catharine, to have all estate. To son, John G. and daughter, Catharine, a horse, saddle and bridle. To son, Samuel R., horse, saddle and bridle worth $150 when he is of age. To daughter, Martha M. Sisk, a colt. Sons: James C. and William W. Younger children to be schooled. Cranberry Sisk not to live on Martha's land in case she dies. Executrix: Wife Catharine. Will Dated: 25 February 1860. Witnesses: William Girdner, Henry A. Farnsworth.
Signed: John Dodd

JOHN McCURRY   7 May 1860 $5,000
To Wife, Sarah, all estate. Sarah Elizabeth McCurry alias Reynolds, daughter of John McCurry alias Reynolds, her sisters Catharine and Marseller I. to share with my wife in real estate, if she dies they are to get her part adjoining Joab Dell and John Davis. To my oldest sister: Anna Fields - $50. Oldest brother: James McCurry decd. his heirs $1. To brother, Robert, and sister Nancy Howard, $1 each. To brother, James McCurry - $50. To Sarah Jane Kelley, formerly McCurry, tract of land for a home. To John Briant Kelley, stock in Virginia and Tennessee Railroad. Executor: John David Esq. Will Dated: 6 February 1860. Witnesses: William Crumley, William Lane.   Signed: John X McCurry

ELENDER BLACK   7 May 1860
To daughter, Elender Bowling, all land adjoining Richard Wilkinson, Daniel Kesterson. Executrix: Elender Bowling. Will Dated: 25 August

1859. Witnesses: Solomon Matthews, George E. Scott.
Signed: Elender ⟨⟩ Black

LINZA F. RIPLEY   2 July 1860 $2,000
To Wife, Mary, all furniture and real estate, and stock in Virginia and
Tennessee Railroad. Executors: Wife Mary, Elbert S. Ripley. Will Dated:
15 March 1860. Witnesses: T. D. Cavener, J. M. Colyer.
Signed: Linza F. Ripley

DAVID R. JOHNSON   4 June 1860 $6,000
Mother: Hannah Johnson was and is a part of my family - to have ample
and comfortable support. To Wife, Mary Jane Johnson, entire estate to
raise and educate my children. At my wife's death divide equally with
my 10 children. Three sons to get land. Ten Children: Benjamin Gray,
Louise Caroline, Melissa Adeline, Julia Matilda, James Burton, Sarah
Elizabeth, Kitty Margaret, Martha Ellen, John Rankin and youngest
daughter, infant not named. Executor: Son Benjamin. Will Dated: 18
April 1860. Witnesses: Joseph H. Earnest, Thomas Thomason.
Signed: D. R. Johnson

NATHAN B. JOHNSON   5 June 1860 $8,000
To Wife, Mary Jane, all property I got when I married her and $500. To
my three sons: John A., Joseph B. and William H., balance of estate
divided between them. To Daughters: Youngest Ora, Anna and Virginia,
$500 on interest to cloth and educate them. Land in District 13.
Executors: Azoe Koontz, William Alexander. Will Dated: 21 April 1860.
Witnesses: Jefferson Gfeller, Madison G feller.
Signed: N. B. Johnson

JAMES McCOLLUM   6 August 1860 $4,000
To Wife, Sarah, land, notes and what she brought here with her and $5 per
year. Children: Susan wife of John Milligan, Lucinda wife of Benson
Baily, Jane wife of Wyly Campbell, Mary McAmis, Alexander, John, James,
William. Son, Alexander, has received his part. To son, James, two
shares railroad stock. Daughter, Jane, has received $200. Grandson:
Thomas R. McCollum. Executors: Two sons - James and William S. McCollum.
Will Dated: 5 October 1858. Witnesses: Charles Bright, Simon Marshall.
Signed: James McCollum

GEORGE W. REEVE   6 August 1860 $3,000
Wife: Selina Elizabeth Reeve. Son: Jesse S. Reeve, to receive land.
Executor: Jesse S. Reeve Senr. Will Dated: 1 July 1860. Witnesses:
Stephen Pierce, Elbert M. Wilhite. Bondsmen: Azor Koontz, A. W. Howard.
Signed: George W. X Reeve

JACOB COLLET   4 October 1860
To Wife, Nancy, all my property her lifetime, then to my daughter,
Catharine Pender and her children. My grand-daughters: Martha A. and
Nancy J. Pender. Rest of children provided for. Executors: Jeremiah
McMillen, Peter Harmon. Witnesses: Henry and Paul Bible.

JOHN MILLER   3 December 1860 $2,500
To daughter, Mary Miller McAlister, $300. To sons, Green B. Miller and
Robert G. Miller, the farm. Executor: son G. B. Miller. Will Dated: 30
May 1859. Witnesses: Thomas Williams, John Pence.
Signed: John Miller

ANDREW ENGLISH ESQ.   7 January 1861 $20,000
To Wife, Polly, everything plus sufficient support. Wife to have one
half notes, other half to my brothers and sisters. Alexander and Melinda
Tunnel to have their Mother's share. Land on Lick Creek to my brothers
and sisters. Executor: John D. Hays. Will Dated: 6 November 1860.
Witnesses: George W. McDonald, James Shanks.
Signed: Andrew English

92

WILLIAM GASS   4 February 1861
To my wife and children - land adjoining John Gass. Sell hogs and pay
my debts. Executor: William West. Will Dated: 8 November 1860.
Witnesses: Lemuel Cox, G. H. Cochran.
                                    Signed: William Gass

THOMAS ELLIS - Repeat from Book 1

JOHN REES   4 March 1861
To be buried at our burying ground on my farm where my parents lie. To
son, William, 18 acres land. To son, John, $150 to be paid by Jonathan.
To son, Henry, $300 to be paid by Jonathan. To son, Caleb, $300 to be
paid by Jonathan. To son, Jacob, $300 to be paid by Jonathan. To sons,
Peter and Alfred and daughters, Elizabeth and Margaret - $100 each to be
paid by Jonathan. To son, Jonathan, 180 acre farm. To Wife, Mary, all
personal property to be sold and divided at her death. Executors: My
son Jonath Rees, A. W. Walker. Will Dated: 19 January 1859. Witnesses:
James Ottinger, J. D. F. Jennings.   Signed: John X Rees

WILLIAM DODD   2 April 1861   Bond $28.00
Nine children: Mary Dodd, John, Massa Henry, Sarah Campbell, Adam Dodd,
Elizabeth Dodd, Serena Oliphant, Lucinda Bell, Edward, Rudolphus. Sell
property and divide. Executors: Joseph Henry, John Dodd. Will Dated:
17 April 1856. Witnesses: Benjamin F. Bell, Thomas F. Alexander.
                                    Signed: William X Dodd

BARBERRY STUTTS   Probated 4 March 1861
One half of my estate to my daughter, Elizabeth Stutts. The other half
to my grandson, William Stutts, for his care and attending to me. Test:
Jacob Bible, Isaac D. Smith.   Signed: Barbary X Stutts

ROBERT MASON   3 June 1861 $7,000
Sell stock of goods belonging to store. My father and mother to live and
remain upon the tract of land as long as they live, then it goes to my
sister, Eliza. To brothers: George and John A., all my interest in 6 and
one third house and lots doing business. To Robert Mason, son of John,
$50. Wife and two children: William and Matilda Mason. Andrew J.
Fletcher this day shot me with a pistol while I was in pursuit of my
lawful business. Prosecute him. Executors to be appointed by Court.
Will Dated: 1 May 1861. Witnesses: James H. Rumbaugh, S. P. Crawford.
                                    Signed: Robert Mason
In 1865 August 7 - value was $10,000. Executor: O. B. Headrick.

BENJAMIN CARTER   6 May 1861
To Wife, Rachel, whole of my estate, real and personal. To son, Elbert
S., plantation where he lives. To daughter, Priscilla S. Carter, 46
acres land. To sons, Thomas, Nathan and Henry - to get my home. Nancy
and Jane Henry to get plantation where Edward Hendry lives. Executors:
Elbert S. Carter, son-in-law William Hendry. Will Dated: 29 January 1861.
Witnesses: George Kenny, Joseph McCurry??
                                    Signed: Benjamin Carter

PHILLIP COBBLE   5 August 1861
Wife, Sarah, to be supported decently, to have control of entire farm
her lifetime and $600 in gold and silver. To my four sons: Nathaniel,
Andrew J., Lewis and David - my farm including the big spring, also
Andrew Stutts farm and to pay $500 to my daughters. To my three daughters:
Anna Cobble Rader, Barbara and Elizabeth Cobble - $1000 to be divided.
Land on Little Chuckey. Sister-in-law Elizabeth Stults to live with my
wife Sarah. Executor: Sylvanus Cobble. Will Dated: 1 March 1861.
Witnesses: Valentine S. Rader, James Smith of James, J. K. Hancher.
                                    Signed: Phillip Cobble

PHEBE ETTER   7 October 1861
Daughter, Sarah Keebler, to have all my personal estate and land warrant.

Executor: Jesse Rader. Will Dated: 29 January 1861. Witnesses: Sylvanus
Cobble, Irenius Cobble. Signed: Phebe Etter

ELLENDER OTTINGER   4 November 1861 $500
To daughter, Sarah Masoner, $5 only. To son, Thomas, $5 only. To sons,
William, Henry and Jacob Ottinger, all balance of my property, land,
money, notes etc. to be equally divided. Jacob also to have a bureau.
Executors: Son Henry Ottinger, Joseph Nease. Will Dated: 28 September
1861. Witnesses: Benjamin F. Bell, Joseph Neas.
                          Signed: Ellender X Ottinger

JOHNATHAN PIERCE   6 January 1862 $2,000
To Wife, Sarah, household and kitchen furniture her lifetime, then to go
to son, William M. Pierce. To son, Alexander H. Pierce, plantation where
I now live and all stock and pay all debts. A. H. To support wife, Sarah.
To son, Mountiville L. Pierce, a house when he is 21. Will Dated: 5
December 1861. Witnesses: William Mulliniux, Alex B. Tadlock, Murrell
Moore.   Signed: Johnathan Pierce

JOHN RUSSELL - 3 February 1862 - Repeat from Book 1.

JANE D. MASON   3 February 1862 $500
(Widow of Robert - G.F.B.) Two children: William and Matilda Mason -
after debts to receive all my property, goods, chattels and money. My
children's guardians to be my sister, Mrs. Isabella Ewart and William
B. Rankin, Testatory Guardians. Executor: William B. Rankin. Will
Dated: 4 September 1861. Witnesses: William West, Samuel McGaughey.
Ex. Bondsmen: Elbert Biggs, James A. Galbreath.
                          Signed: Jane D. Mason

ESTHER HENRY   5 March 1862 $1,400
My sister, Margaret, gets my dowry her lifetime, then to my brother,
James. Put tombstones to graves of my father and his family in Timber
Ridge Graveyard. To my Nephew, James son of my brother, Robert, one
shoat and 2 calves. Executors: James Henry, Christian Bowers, Anthony
Rankin. Executors to be appointed by brothers. Will Dated: 13 December
1861. Witnesses: A. Rankin, Margaret X Henry.
                          Signed: Esther Henry

PETER EARNEST   4 March 1862 $120,000
To my son, Joseph H., my mill and plantation worth $4000. To my son,
Nicholas W., 500 acres barren lands worth $3500 with the plantation I
have given him worth $1500. To my son, Benjamin F., plantation where
I now live worth $8000, he is to give the estate $3000. To my daughter,
Nancy Rankin, Lands worth $2000, $600 stock in East Tennessee and Virginia
Railroad, $1000 County Bonds and $900 cash. To my daughters, Mary Ann
Moor, Sarah Ruth Allen decd., Julian Stephens and Catharine Jane McLin-
her son Benjamin Earnest McLin - each to receive $600 stock in Railroad,
$1500 County Bonds and $1200 cash. Executors: Sons - Joseph H., Nicholas
W., Benjamin F. Earnest. Will Dated: 27 May 1856. Witnesses: Isaac,
Sarah, Kitty E., Charles S. and Isaac R. Earnest.
                          Signed: Peter Earnest

ISAAC JUSTICE   3 March 1862 $1,000
Wife, Polly, to have everything, if she should marry she gets full
possession of Milligan Tract. Children: Francis, James, Elizabeth,
Martha, Louisa, to have full possession of all other property. Grand-
children of son Francis, Betty Ann, David, Martha Jane, to remain on
farm with my wife. Daughters: Polly Arnold, Rebeckah McNeese, Margaret
Cradic to have personal property at wife's death. Sons: John, Thomas,
Jacob and William. Executors: Wife Polly, friend John Justice of Thomas.
Will Dated: 11 August 1856. Witnesses: Loyd Bullen, Absalom Stonecypher
Senr.   Signed: Isaac Justice

PHEBE JONES   5 May 1862
To my daughter, Nancy Cox, my feather bed and straw bed that I now lay on,

my wearing cloths and little wheel. To my son, Lemuel Jones, all property out of doors for his own use. Executor: Son-Lemuel Jones. Will Dated: 2 November 1861. Witnesses: Elliot Jones, W. P. Jeffers.

Signed: Phoebe X Jones

DUTTON LANE   5 May 1862 $200
Wife, Susan, to have everything her lifetime. Children: Jane Justis, Keziah Thompson - to share equal at Susan's death. Executor: William Duggar. Will Dated: 1 May 1850? Witnesses: George W. Gass, Nancy Gass.

Signed: Dutton Lane
William Duggar refused to serve as Executor. Wife Susan served.

BETSEY GASS   formerly Betsey Rankin   3 June 1862
To Betsey Jane Bonham, Malinda Rankin, Earnest, Adaline Rankin, John Rankin, all children of David Rankin Esq. late of Greene County decd., and Sarah Elizabeth daughter of Betsey Jane Bonham - five in number, share and share alike. Executors: John Rankin, his sister Jane Bonham, son and daughter of brother David Rankin decd. Will Dated: 25 March 1858. Witnesses: William M. Lowery, B. McCannel.

Signed: Betsey X Gass

JOHN BAYLES
Wife, Sarah, has all land and personal property her lifetime. If she leaves she gets only one half. She is to hire her negroes out for her support. Daughter: Celah Humphreys wife of John Humphreys and her son John Bayles, to have land on Doe River near Elizabethton, land known as the Elisha Humphreys Tract. Three hundred acres at Celah's death to go to John. To son, Barton Bayles - land on the Nolichuckey River, Williams Tract. To daughter, Eliza Cox, land deeded to her and her first husband, William Beard. To daughter, Adeline wife of Joseph Simpson - 200 acres land purchased of Hezekiah Bayles. To son, Luke, 300 acres of my wife's estate at her death. To daughter, Polly Ann Withers, all the residue of my estate. Six children to have railroad stock. To Eliza's son, Ephraim Cox, $500 when he is 21. Executors: Sons-Barton and Luke Bayles. Will Dated: 1857.
Codicil - Luke is diseased (sick), Adeline Withers to serve as Executor.

ISAAC JACKSON   4 August 1862 $2,500
To Wife, Catharine, one third of everything. One fourth personal property to be sold except a pet shoat of my step-mother's. Father: George Jackson decd. Two children: Dorothulea and Thomas gets the rest at 21. Executor: Lewis F. Rader. Will Dated: 18 June 1862. Witnesses: William Rader, Lemuel Crosby.   Signed: Isaac Jackson

JACOB FINK   3 November 1862   Bond $1,000
Children: George W., Michael A., Samuel C., William P., Andrew J., Sarah, Eliza Jane. William P. to fatten hogs on his part and add to estate. To daughter, Eliza Jane, one flax hackle, 2 chairs her mother is to have use of, Wife: _____. Executors: William P. Fink, Wilson Wattenbarger. Will Dated: 24 April 1862. Witnesses: Joseph Brubaker, G. W. Yokley, Henry Brubaker.   Signed: Jacob X Fink

ADAM BIBLE   3 November 1862
To second wife, Elizabeth, what she brought when we were married, house and personal property - if she remarries it goes to son, John. Divide cloth between her children and my children equally. Children: John, Henry, Solomon, Christian, Paul, youngest daughter Rachel, Susan, Elizabeth, Magdalene, Dolly, Margaret. Five sons to get land. Six daughters to have $160 apiece. Youngest daughter, Rachel, to be made equal with those who are married. Executors: Henry and Christian Bible. Will Dated: 11 August 1857. Witnesses: E. F. Mercer, Charles G. Gass.

Signed: Adam Bible

HANNAH ROBINSON   1 December 1862 $1,000
To my brother, William B. Robinson, two notes in hand of Maj. John McGaughey. To my niece, Sarah H. McLain, bedstead with "Ross" spread,

silver tea spoons, unmade calico frock. To my niece, C. Virginia
Robinson, a bureau. My sister, Margaret Milburn decd., her children to
get residue. Executors: William B. Robinson, Lewis Rankin. Will Dated:
8 November 1861. Witnesses: W. S. Oliphant, Samuel S. Doak.
Signed: Hannah Robinson

ELBERT S. FRAKER   2 March 1863
My sister, Martha Malinda wife of Jacob Whitfield, to have everything
including my interest in my father's estate, to pay brother, William, $4.
Brother: William A. Fraker. Brother, Flemming's four children to have
$50 each when they are 21. Brother: Andrew C. Executor: Charles Loyd.
Will Dated: 13 August 1862. Witnesses: John Richard Senr., Cravener
Manes, Michael B. Armstrong.   Signed: Elbert S. X Fraker

WILLIAM PARKER   3 June 1862 $500
Nine and one half acres and everything to John Willoughby. Executor:
John Willoughby. Will Dated: 12 April 1861. Witnesses: E. M. Drake,
Jacob Myers.   Signed: William Parker

JOSEPH BLACK   6 April 1863
To Wife, Elizabeth Ann, $500, mare, saddle, bridle, to remain on farm as
my widow. To sons, William, Lewis, Clark and Christopher - $25 each and
no more. Daughter, Rebecca Ellen Black, has cared for her mother and me,
to have negro Jane and her increase. To Zachariah Hurley and wife Levina
- $1155. To Abram and Phoebe Kirk - $1155. To apprentice, John Dunahoo -
$25. To James and Beersheba Campbell, $100 to stay and work for family.
Executor: William Hawkins. Witnesses: Thomas Russell, D. N. Gass,
William Hawkins.   Signed: Joseph Black

THOMAS KENNEDY   3 August 1863 $2,000
To daughter, Margaret and her heirs forever, house and kitchen furniture,
horse, cattle or hog stock. Slaves to be divided between my grand-
children: Thomas Kennedy Jr., John, James F., Daniel, Mary Jane Kennedy
Farnsworth, Penelope Kennedy, equally as to valuation. Executors: John
Kennedy, Thomas Kennedy Jr. Will Dated: 9 December 1857. Witnesses:
G. P. Snapp, R. F. Russell.   Signed: Thomas Kennedy

ISABEL JANE   3 August 1863 $1,000
To husband, Stephen Jane, all my land and furniture etc. after paying
Jane Newberry $300. Will Dated: 25 July 1863. Witnesses: J. P. Jane,
John Stacy.   Signed: Isabel X Jane

CHARITY McNEES
To daughter, Caty McNeese, for taking care of me, all my personal property
and all that was willed me by my father, Solomon Bales decd., which I am
to receive at the death of my mother. To my other children: Letty Ann
wife of John Barnes, Eden McNeese, Elihu and Solomon McNeese - $1 each.
To my grand children: Hannah McFarlin and Elmiry J. McNeese, daughters of
my son Samuel decd. - $1 each. Executors: John A. Dodd, Dr. John White.
Will Dated: 6 May 1859. Witnesses: Charles Bright, Jacob Bright.
Signed: Charity McNeese

ELIAS CARTER   2 November 1863
To Wife, Rodias Carter, 100 acres plus personal property, at her death
it is to go to my three daughters: Jane Linebaugh, Westy Carter and Lucy
C. Carter. Four sons: Young, Emberson, Alpheus and William R. Carter,
to receive remaining 110 acres of land. Executors: Sons - William R. and
Emerson Carter. Will Dated: 27 May 1862. Witnesses: George Kenney,
Johnathan Brubaker. Executor was Henry Brubaker 18 June 1863 (Civil
War).   Signed: Elias X Carter

ALEXANDER PRICE   2 November 1863 $2,500
To Wife, Melinda Price, all tools necessary to carry on farming, all f
furniture, stock and grain as my widow. My black boy, Jack, to run farm.
At Melinda's death, all to be divided equally. Children: Dau. Artimicy

(Artinincy) Rush, Mary Ann Carter, Lucinda Price, Sarah Johnson, Margaret Jones decd. her children: Nancy Catharine, George Russel; dau. Nancy Katharine Kenney. Daughter, Artimicy, to have $250 currant money. Executor: S. S. Babb. Will Dated: 19 October 1862. Witnesses: T. A. Kite, William A. Price. Signed: Alexander Price

ABNER BEALS   2 November 1863
Wife, Serene, to manage farm as she thinks best. At her death, everything to be divided equal. Children: Sarah, Jane, Mary Ann, Louisa, Enoch, Newton, Jacob, George M., Caroline, Thomas A., Elbert and Nathan. Executor: Brother - John Beals. Will Dated: 17 September 1863. Witnesses: David Ellis, John Beals.
                              Signed: Abner Beals

JOHN W. RUBLE   7 December 1863 $2,000
To Wife, Mary, one third plantation including buildings. To daughter, Polly Price, rest of land and to pay Joseph Ruble $5. To son, William I., farm where he lives and to pay son, Solomon H. Ruble's heirs $5. Executor: William I. Ruble. Will Dated: 20 November 1860. Witnesses: William B. Woolsey, David Parman. Signed: John W. Ruble

JAMES ROBINSON   7 March 1864 $2,000
To Wife, Polly, black mare, saddle and bridle, furniture, clothing, $60 and necessaries, to be supported by all my heirs. To son, Major, bed-stead and bedding. To sons: Thomas and Allen G. - slave and pay to other children: Margaret M. Oliphant, James H., Marianna Moser wife of Robert Y. Moser - their share of slave worth $850. If this is not O.K. try to get slave a job as a section hand on the railroad. Son: John D. Robinson is away, if he returns destitute, assist him. Executors: Major D. and Thomas T. Robinson. Will Dated: 6 August 1863. Witnesses: Thomas Thomasson Junr., William S. McGaughey, Robert Rankin.
                              Signed: James Robinson

IRA PAINTER   1 February 1864 $1,000
I volunteered in the Confederate States Army and knowing the uncertainty of life. Brother: Johnathan F. Painter is to have all my land, money and my share in my Father, Phillip Painter's estate. Will Dated: December 26, 1862. Will made near Vicksburg, Mississippi. Witnesses: L. D. Cavener, J. R. Shelton. Executor: Thomas K. Alexander by the Court. Bondsman: Phillip X Painter. Signed: Ira Painter

JOHN H. MULLINS   4 July 1865 $2,000
To Wife, Elizabeth, to have all estate and pay all trust debts, at her death to go to my brothers and sister. Land in District 17, land in Washington County. Sister: Rebecca Ann Mullins. Brothers: N. C. Mullins, M. B. Mullins, A. Mullins. Executor: Squire Thomas Colwell. Will Dated: 1 April 1863. Witnesses: A. G. Register, Adeline Register.
                              Signed: John H. Mullins

SOLOMON REED   1 August 1864 $2,000
Four eldest daughters: Nancy Esther Profit, Mary Ann Cox, Sarah Elizabeth Scott, Martha Mariah Marshall, to have my lower farm equally divided. To Wife, Margaret Ann Reed, farm where I now live her natural life, then it is to go to my three youngest daughters: Margaret Candace, Sabina Rebecca and Harriet Aramenta. Executor: John C. Dyer. Will Dated: 23 May 1864. Witnesses: Lemmel Crosby, Abraham H. Dyer.
                              Signed: Solomon Reed

JANE BRYAN   1 August 1864
To daughter, Emeline Hurley, to have bed and bedding, 3 sheep, big spinning wheel, 3 big chairs and one of two $40 notes I hold on son, Prior Crittendon, dated 16 January 1864. To daughter, Martha Jane Crittendon, bed and bedding, cow, 6 sheep, loom, gearing etc. and other $40 note on son, Prior. To daughter, Amelia Crittendon, same as Martha Jane and a $30 note on Pryor. To son, Thomas W., $1.00. To grand-daughter, Louisa Jane Hurley, bed and bedding. Executor: Arthur Stroud.

Will Dated: 25 January 1864. Attest: Lemuel Crosby, James Wright.
Signed: Jane X Bryan

WILLIAM D. McCLELLAND   5 September 1864
Wife, Janetta, to keep and cary my gold watch. Son, Joseph, to keep
watch of his deceased brother, Oliver. Wife and son, Joseph, to share
equal. Land on which the family lived 1 mile north of Greeneville, sold
to Dr. S. P. Crawford, can be repurchased. Buy property, church and
schoolhouse greatly desired, so Joseph may have education. NOTES: David
Fry $120, Capt. William Bese 1 Tenn. Cav. $115, Lt. G. W. Kinder 1 Tenn.
Cav. $100. Claims in the hands of Rev. J. P. Holtsinger. Sheriff James
Jones $15. Thomas Day of Gap Creek $8, John W. Brown $8, Pleasant
Fortner $3, George Holtsinger $4, Joshua Coggin of Greene County $30 for
a Spencer Rifle. Two horses bought of Absalom Gray for $225 to be paid
of three horses sold. Capt. Robert Carter to sell said horses. Col.
R. R. Buller, agent, to collect claim due me from U.S. Govt. for my
services as Captain, Major etc. Refer to George Schofield, Cox, Haskell
and other officers of Dept. ot the Ohio as to my efficiencies and devo-
tion to our common cause. Wife to collect of Col. Butler amount due son,
Oliver, as soon as collected from the Government of U.S. Executrix:
Wife Janetta. Will Dated: 4 August 1864. Test: G. H. Evans, S. P.
Crawford.   Signed: William D. McClellan

WILLIAM BROWN   3 October 1864   From two Wills
To second wife, Lucinda, ball mare and carriage and what she brought with
her when we married. Lucinda's daughter, Sally, to be equal with other
girls. Son: Morton V. Brown to take care of step-mother and sister,
Sally, and haul all their part in the barn and crib. To sons, James
C. and Elija A., the Mountain Farm. To son, Richard W., where he lives
on Plum Creek. To son, John H. and his son William S. Brown, where he
lives. To Daughters: Polly Marshall, Margaret Graham, Elizabeth Fields
and Sarah Brown, $300 in notes, judgments and property. One share each
in East Tennessee and Virginia Railroad - I have 10 shares. Executor:
Son - William L. Brown. Will Dated: 18 July 1862. Witnesses: S. S.
Babb, Abraham Carter, Robert Brown.
Signed: William X Brown

JOHN SHEFFEY   3 October 1864
Greene County, 5th District. Wife, Margaret, to be provided for as the
law directs her lifetime. Children: Augustus, William H., Minerva
Cochran, Alfred M., Jane Susong's heirs. Son, William, to have $600
less than the others who share equally. Executor: James Henry Senior.
Will Dated: 27 February 1864. Witnesses: Robert Henry, James Henry.
Signed: John Sheffey

ROLAND ELLIS (ROBERT?)   3 October 1864
To Wife, Polly, all property during her widowhood. Son, David Ellis, has
received a horse, saddle and bridle. Minor Heirs to be made equal to
David when they are 21. Executor: William Jones. Will Dated: 4 July
1862. Witnesses: Alexander Brown, Joseph X White, Abraham Haynes.
Signed: Roland Ellis

ANDREW J. LAFOLLET   7 November 1864 $500
I believe married Mary Bird daughter of Matthias - G.F.B.
To Wife, Mary E., one bed of her choice, one oven and led fire shovel,
pot hooks and one half growing corn and potatoes, all delf, knives,
forks and one wooden bucket. Parents: Joseph and Elizabeth Lafollet, to
get the remainder. Executor: William R. Gibbs. Will Dated: 28 July
1864. Witnesses: William R. Gibbs, John Parman, Humphries Wells.
Signed: Andrew J. Lafollet

JOHN RICHARD SR.   3 October 1864 $1,000
To Wife, Rebeckah, all my lands, furniture and stock of every kind. At
her death or marriage everything to be divided between children: Martha
Isabella, Jane. To son, Henry M., land. To son, John, land and pay his
mother one third her lifetime. To grandson, John William Richard son of
Henry M., $5. Executor: W. F. Reeser. Will Dated: 12 January 1864.

Witnesses: John Crabtree, John Dast??
                    Signed: John Richard

JOSEPH HENDRY   7 November 1864
Children: Serene, Elisa, Lucy, Angeline, William, Edward, Sarah. To my
daughter, Serene, one gray filly. Other daughters to be equal. Execu-
tors: D. G. Correll, son of John E. Hendry. Will Dated: 11 October 1864.
Witnesses: C. B. D. Harold, Anderson X Carroll. Ex. Bondsmen: Peter
Brubaker, A. J. Carroll, Daniel Miller, Anderson X Carter.
                    Signed: Joseph Hendry

DAVID RICE SENR.   7 January 1865 $1,000
To Wife, Isabella as my widow, house, land where I now live with abso-
lute control with $800 to be put on interest for her support and $50 for
taxes if due. Son: David, has deeded land. Children: David, George D.,
Nancy, Catharine, John, Andrew, Mary P., Sallie, Margaret, Benjamin.
Benjamin to care for his mother and single sister, then get the land.
Two hundred dollars each to children: George D., Nancy, Catharine, John
and Andrew. Executors: William B. Robinson, James S. Wilson. Witnesses:
George Hoyal, Andrew L. Harrold.   Signed: David Rice Senr.

MATILDA D. MARTIN   5 June 1865 $2,000
To my two servants, Edmund and Mary, their freedom and $100 each. All
property to go to all the children of John Dickson and Robert Dickson,
formerly of Fayetteville, Tennessee, and John McCurley of Greene County,
Tennessee. Executor: William West. Will Dated: 11 February 1865.
Witnesses: E. W. Headrick, William M. Lowery.
                    Signed: Matilda D. Martin

NANCY K. WINTERS   3 April 1865 $2,500
Wearing apparel to my friend, Mary Dodd. To my son, James, all property
of every kind to be kept by my mother till he is of age - if he dies
without issue, property is to go to Mary Jane McCampbell and her children.
Executor: James G. Reaves. Will Dated: 20 March 1865. Witnesses:
Johnathan Light, E. W. Headrick.   Signed: Nancy K. Winters

THOMAS BAILEY   12 November 1862
To Wife, Henrietta, all my home farm. To son, M. L., where he lives
south of Snapp Ferry Road. To son, G. N., 140 acres where he lives. To
son, B. M., 440 acres. To son, George A., 480 acre home tract at my
wife's death. To daughter, Elly C. Russell, $1000. To daughter,
Katharine M. Baily, 50 acres and $500. Executor: Marion L. Baily.
Witnesses: John R. Young, James M. Odell.
                    Signed: Thomas Baily

HUGH CARTER   2 May 1865
To Wife, Martha Carter, one half home plantation during widowhood. To
James W. Carter, 1600 acres land in District 6, 2500 acres land in Sherl's
Cove. James W. Carter, lawful heir, to serve as his guardian. Eight
shares in Tennessee - Virginia Railroad. To Jacob England, his freedom,
$50 and 50 acres mountain land. My Executors: John B. Hawkins, M. B.
Crumley. Will Dated: 13 June 1863. Test: Thomas N. Weems, Daniel
Linebaugh.   Signed: Hugh Carter

JANE HENNEGAR
Pay lawful then give to my sister, Maria Hennegar - she can divide as
she sees fit. Brothers: John and Francis M. Hennegar, whichever is still
alive. Executrix: Maria Hennegar. Attest: W. B. Hundson, Thomas Love.
                    Jane Hennegar
                    Signed at her request.

WILLIAM COLLET   6 January 1865
Son: James A. Collett, to take possession of all my property. To son,
William Whitley Collett, $1000 for his education. To my eldest daughter,
M. E. Bolton, cow, furniture. To my youngest daughter, Mary Caledonia

Collett, $1000 for her education. Witnesses: W. A. Collett, B. F. Yeager, J. F. Yeager.
Signed: William Collett

EDMUND BAXTER   5 June 1865
To Wife, Martha, some household property. Son: John Newton Baxter, to have where he lives if he supports my wife and me deasently. Son, Samuel N. Baxter and daughter, Susannah, to have nothing since I have provided for them. To daughter, Martha Jane Hays, $300. To grandson, A.G.R. Baxter, all notes on hand, bridle, saddle and 2 years schooling - to stay with grandmother. To Nancy Jane Brooks, $200 out of my wife's portion, until she can leave here honourably. Will Dated: 17 November 1864. Witnesses: David F. Hall, Enoch Hale.
Signed: Edmund Baxter

HIRAM SWANEY   5 June 1865
Four youngest children: Elizabeth A., Eliza G., George W.W. and James S. to stay on place and live of profits of mill and farm. Girls to get $50 yearly. Other children: Bennet B., Albert T., Mary I. wife of James M. Keys, Lavina A. wife of James D. Martin, William H. Home called English Farm - 17 District, 228 acres. Mill on farm and store. Note on J.H. Haze - Security Jesse Robison 63 acres. John Smith Tract in 16 District on Lick Creek. Land in 14 District Washington County with saw and grist mill - sold to Conrad Baser? Executor: Son-in-law - James D. Martin. Will Dated: 10 June 1864. Witnesses: Jacob Hays, Josiah Horner, J.W. Dinwiddie, M.L. Paterson.
Signed: Hiram Swaney

JOHN FRAKER SR.   17 January 1865 $2,000   District 15
Children: John, Michael, Rachel wife of Samuel Davis. Daughter, Rachel, to have her part, then to go to her children. Executors to divide land in 2 parts. Michael to get one part and John the other. Executor: Joseph H. Earnest. Will Dated: 17 January 1855. Witnesses: Thomas Bayless, Jacob Hacker.
Signed: John X Fraker

MASHAC CARTER   20 November 1858
To Wife, Nancy Carter, one third of land plus comfortable support her lifetime. Two sons, George and Josiah Dottery Carter, to divide land equally. Four daughters, Eleanor, Margaret, Nancy Ann and May Elizabeth, to have all personal property. Rest of children have their portion. Executor: Abraham Carter. Witnesses: E.W. Headrick, James Jones?
Signed: Mashac 3 Carter
his mark

WILLIAM G. DICKSON   5 July 1865 $2,500
All I have to be shared equally between my sister, Jane Margaret, and my brothers, Richard West and William G. Dickson?? Executor: Richard West Dickson. Will Dated: 25 May 1865. Witnesses: John I. Mitchell, Thomas Lane.
Not Signed.

GEORGE F. GILLESPIE   3 July 1865
To Wife, Elizabeth, sole control of all my effects, real and personal, pay debts and keep children together. When the children leave home, portion them as she sees fit. Executrix: Wife Elizabeth. Will Dated: 10 December 1864. Witnesses: J.J. Yeager, Dan W. Raines.
Signed: George F. Gillespie

JAMES J. STATEN   15 April 1864
To Wife, Anna, home farm her lifetime, $800 goot bonds. To my eldest daughter, Penelope Ann Whittaker, 12 acres land adjoining S.H. Baxter and Phillips. To daughters, Mary Jane and Martha Ellen, home farm after death of my wife. Executor: William White. Will Dated: 15 April 1864. Test: John Olinger, Gabriel Henry, E.S. Campbell.
Signed: James J. X Staten

MATILDA WEEMS   (CARTER'S STATION)
Children: George J. Weems, Narcissa wife of Thomas N. Williams, John G.

Weems, Minerva Cain, Nancy C. Rush. Son, George J., to be made equal
with other children. They have all due them of my estate. John G. Wemms
and Minerva Cain to have all other household ware. Grand-daughter,
Matilda C. Baily, to have bed and furniture, to be put in hands of Nancy
C. Rush until child becomes of age. Executor: Abraham Carter. Will
Dated: 7 November 1863. Witnesses: James M. Maloney, Elliott Jones.
Signed: Matilda Weems

FIELDEN COURTNEY   4 March 1885   Page 387
To Wife, Margaret, all lands during her widowhood, then to sons, Joseph
and William S. Courtney. Daughters: youngest, Nancy Adeline and Susan
Victory, each a good bed, cow and calf. To daughters, Catharine Hodge,
Ann Wise and son, James Courtney, $1 each. If sons Joseph S. and
William S. should not return (Civil War). Will Dated: 16 October 1863.
Witnesses: Allen Britton, Solomon Matthews.
Signed: Fielden X Courtney

ELIJAH DEBUSK   Page 388
To Wife, Mollie, 60 acres her natural life, then to be sold and equally
divided. Youngest child, Thomas, not of age. Children: Josiah, Andrew
J., Johnathan, Shadrach - have received $100 each. Mentions windmill.
Executor: Shadrach Debusk. Will Dated: 25 December 1862. Witnesses: I.
Biggs, A. Bradford.

WILLIAM ROSS SENR.   23 September 1864   Page 589
To my son, David R., the plantation I live on. Sons, John H., William
and James, have received $1200. Son: George. To daughter, Nancy Ann
Jackson, the black girl and her child, buggy and harness, Wilson Farm,
loom and spinning wheel and pay George $75. Executors: Son - William,
William West. Will Dated: 23 September 1864. Witnesses: Samuel
McGaughey, E.W. Headrick.   Signed: William Ross

ELIZABETH ELLIS   31 March 1863   Page 590
Widow of Jacob. To Rody Crumley, a girl I raised, bed and bedding, 20
pounds feathers, beds, quilts, $15 and other things. Three daughters,
Sarah, Martha and Liddy to share with Rody. Executor: Daniel Beals.
Will Dated: 31 March 1863. Witnesses: Ellis Beals, William _____?
Signed: Elizabeth X Ellis

MILLER SEXTON   26 June 1859   Page 591
To Wife, Nancy Ann, all land and stock her lifetime. Children: Henry W.,
James A., Sarah Ann, Margaret Janes, David Miller Sexton, Martha Meranda
Yeakley's heirs, Elizabeth Jane Martin and her heirs, Sarah Ann Sexton
and her heirs. To sons, Henry W. and James A., $50. To children, Sarah
Ann, Margaret Janes and David Miller Sexton, horse, saddle and bridle,
pewter cups and saucers. Executor: Pleasant A. Witt. Will Dated: 26
June 1859. Witnesses: William Woods Esq., James C. Moore.
Signed: Miller X Sexton

ARCHIBALD McAFEE   6 March 1860   Page 592
To son, John, $100. To son, Michael, $150. To children, Archibald M.,
William K., Sarah Waddle and Jane Rambo, equal parts. My 2 beds and
furniture to be divided. To grand-children, Martha, Van and Rufus
Jennings, $10 apiece. Executors: Rufus Waddle, William K. McAfee.
Will Dated: 26 March 1860. Witnesses: Charles Lovette, Frederick Dewitt.
Signed: Archibald McAfee

SAMUEL WISECARVER   15 April 1859
Wife, Elizabeth Jane, to pay debts and have everything as my widow, then
it is to be divided between my several children. Executor: Solomon
Matthews. Will Dated: 15 April 1859. Witnesses: Enoch P. and George M.
Murray.   Signed: Samuel Wisecarver

JOHN SUSONG SR.   21 May 1861   District 9   Page 593
To Wife, Charity Susong, all property. All my lawful heirs. Son, John

M. Susong to take care of Mother and get 40 acre farm. Executor: Son - Andrew. Will Dated: 27 May 1861. Witnesses: John Sheffey, A.E. Susong.
Signed: John X Susong

GEORGE W. ALEXANDER   Page 594
Wife: Martha. Five children: Laura Margarita, Mary Isabel, Joseph McCall, James Houston and Sarah Elizabeth. Youngest child, Sarah Elizabeth, not of age. My wife lives with my mother. Note on Samuel M. Davis and Balas Jones - $700 in gold. Notes on J.B. Dobson, John Alexander, William and Alexander Laughlin, Jacob Brooks, John M. Colver, Henry A. Farnsworth, James M. Gregory, J.N. Harrison, William Britton, David Britton, Marion and Henry Brooks. My father's estate is soon due. Mother: Sarah Alexander has land on which there is a mill where my brothers, John and William Alexander live. Executors: Thomas K. Alexander, Lewis M. Tadlock. Will Dated: 28 May 1863. Test: John and James G. Alexander. Executors to take monies and buy farm for my wife and children.
Signed: G. W. Alexander

PHILLIP PAINTER   5 March 1866 $1,000   Page 596
To Wife, Martha Painter, all lands during widowhood, and at her death to go to sons, Johnathan and Ira - they are to take care of us. To daughter, Julian Williamson wife of Harry Williamson, land adjoining Thomas K. Alexander and David Morrow, $200. To daughter, Mary Morrow wife of David Morrow, $200. Son, Thomas, has received his share. Executor: Son-Johnathan. Will Dated: 10 March 1860. Witnesses: John Alexander, Thomas Alexander.
Signed: Phillip (S Painter

JEREMIAH HARRISON   3 September 1866 $1,000   Page 597
Son, Benjamin W., to have 50 acres land adjoining John P. Harrison, Henry Brooks, Sary Lintz and David Bird. To Wife, Elizabeth, balance of my land, negroes and their increase. Executors: James Jones, Thomas Jones. Will Dated: 19 January 1857. Witnesses: Michael George, M.P. Lintz, Thomas H. Brooks (writing in German).
Signed: Jeremiah Harrison

LUCINDA PRICE   5 March 1866 $800   Page 598
Put a nice set of tombstones at my grave. Mary Ann Carter, Sarah Johnson and Nancy Katherine Kenney to receive property equally divided. Executor: S.S. Babb. Will Dated: 5 February 1866. Witnesses: William A. Price, T. A. Kite. Ex. Bondsmen: Wylie Carter, Daniel Kenney.
Signed: Lucinda Price

GEORGE REAVES   29 December 1865 $1,000   Page 599
Four daughters now living with me, Sophia, Martha, Nelly and Cyntha to receive my farm of 114 acres and pay to others, $5 each. Sons: William A., James G. Reaves. Daughters: Nancy Ann Rambo and Louise Kirk. To grandson, James Crum, $5. To grandsons, William and John C. Ruble, $2 each. Grandson: George Ruble. Executor: Son - James G. Reaves. Will Dated: 29 December 1865. Witnesses: William Cavener, Thomas Hughes.
Signed: George Reaves

ELI CARTER   6 August 1866   Page 599
My Wife to have full support from my lands during her widowhood. Sons: Stephen E., John, Nathan and Elliott Carter - farm to be equally divided. Four daughters: Melissa Carter, Minerva Malone, Nancy A. Carter and Mary C. Carter. Son-in-law: William Malone. Daughter, Mary C., to receive $150 when Elliott is 21. Executor: Son - Stephen E. Carter. Will Dated: 6 May 1866. Witnesses: George Kenney, Joseph F.A. Maury.
Signed: Eli X Carter

ELISHA LAUGHTERS   1 October 1866 $500   Page 600
To Wife, Ellender C. Laughters, house and lot in Greeneville and all personal property. Executrix: Wife Ellender. Will Dated: 21 December 1865. Witnesses: Joseph Powers, Jacob I. Shackleford.
Signed: Elisha Laughters

JOSEPH S. SHIELDS   3 August 1861   Page 600
Children: William Carter Shields - 110 acres on road Rheatown to Greene-
ville adjoining J.S. Reeve, John Campbell, William Ellis, Samuel Beals
and Samuel Pickering, also to feed and clothe me and my wife our lifetime.
Wife: Nancy. Executor: Jesse S. Reeve Sr. Dated: 3 August 1861.
Witnesses: Jesse S. Reeve Junr., John Y. Elliott.
                          Signed: Joseph Shields

HENRY BROOKS   18 August 1866   Page 601
To Wife, Nancy, 200 acres her widowhood. Executor: Son - Marien W.
Brooks. Dated: 18 August 1866. Test: James Harrison, William Ruble,
James G. Gregory. Gregory on Marien's bond.

JOEL CARTER   Page 602
To Wife, Salina, real and personal estate, notes, accounts, goods and
chattels. Executrix: Wife Salina. Dated: 17 September 1866. Witnesses:
James Hawkins, James M. Maloney.   Signed: Joel Carter

NANCY CRUMLEY   16 August 1866   Page 602
To my daughter, Phebe Catharine, the chest. To my daughter, Sarah Alis,
small dinner pot. To my daughter, Mary Elizabeth, small oven. To my
daughter, Lydia Jane, fire shovel and the Bible. As my daughters come of
age or marry, my beds, bedding etc. My real estate - 33 acres adjoining
John McCurry, Gabriel Henry, to be rented and money used to support my
daughters. Executor: My father - Gabriel Henry. Dated: 16 August 1866.
Witnesses: J.B. Hawkins, M.B. Crumley.
                          Signed: Nancy Crumley

MARY ANN LEMING   5 February 1867   Page 603
To my nephew, Samuel W. Leming, land lying in District 13. To my niece,
Martha L. Leming, a bureau. To my niece, Margaret V. Leming, best bed
and bedsted. To my niece, Emma Leming, fall leaf table. To my sister-
in-law, Rhinemah Leming, all other personal estate. Executor: Nephew -
Samuel W. Leming. Dated: 25 February 1857. Witnesses: James F. Broyles,
J.W. Hinshaw.   Signed: Mary Ann X Leming
                                                    her mark

DANIEL ELLIS   1 October 1886 (on Will) 1866 in Book $1,000
To Wife, Hannah, land and personal property her widowhood, to have and
dispose of as she thinks best. At her death it is to be equally divided
between my Children: Mary Ann, Elizabeth, Jacob, Daniel B., Isaac J.,
Susanna M., John and Howard J. Ellis. Executrix: Wife Hannah. Dated:
16 June 1886. Witnesses: William Pierce, Jonathan Beals.
                          Signed: Daniel Ellis

GEORGE HANNAH   1 October 1866 $3,000   Page 605
To Wife, Elizabeth, all real and personal property. Ten children.
Youngest son: F.B. Hannah, to have $250 more than the others. Executor:
Son - John H. Hannah. Dated: 19 August 1866. Witnesses: Charles S.
Stover, James W. Burger.   Signed: George Hannah

SAMUEL MORELOCK   1 July 1867 $800   Page 606   Dist. 17
To Wife, Rebecca, 81 acres on Clear Creek, waters of Lick Creek and Grist
Mill, and all household goods except a safe - to go to wife's son, David
Craddick (Craddock), plus all tools, stock etc. Let negro run mill.
Children by first wife: William, Jacob, Yancey, Samuel and Wright
Morelock, Sarah wife of John Barnard, Dolly wife of Clabourn Stacy, Julia
wife of John Dykes, Julian wife of Nathan Light, Hannah wife of John
McCurry alias Runnels, son Thomas' daughter, wife of John Coatney - all
to receive $1 each as I have given them all I intend to. Executor:
Samuel B. Baxter. Dated: 13 April 1862. Witnesses: Zachariah S.
Maltsberger, Samuel Crawford, John Crawford.
                          Signed: Samuel Morelock

JOHN RILEY   2 September 1857 $500   Page 608
To Wife, Sarah, all landed estate, personal property and money on hand
during her natural life. To children: Sarah, Mariah, Daniel, Mary Anne,
Elizabeth, Richard - $50 each as they come of age. Divide all equally at
Sarah's death. Executors: Rufus K. Waddle, William Crum. Dated: 28
September 1860. Witnesses: Daniel S. Ricker, Orpha Morton.
                           Signed: John Riley
Sarah Varner wants Will of John Riley (former husband) attended to. John
Winkel was deputized to bring in witness to Will. 31 May 1863

MARGARET A. COCHRAN   4 November 1866   Page 609
To my daughter, Eliza Lauderdale, 1 cow. To my daughter, Martha, 1 cow
and sorrel mare. To my daughter, Sarah, 3 head of cattle. Son: William
decd. Daughters to have my land. Children, heirs of William Cochran:
James, Margaret and Sarah. Witnesses: James Henry, Samuel Cochran.
                           Signed: Margaret A. X Cochran

JOHN CRABTREE   30 April 1867   Page 610
To Wife, Sarah, plantation I live on, 2 wagons, gears, cattle, all per-
sonal property during her widowhood. To my daughter, Ruth Babb, 75 acres
and pay her mother one third. To my grandson, Crawford Crabtree, every-
thing if he stays and cares for his grandmother in a decent way. If
Crawford fails, it is to go to my grandsons, John and Robert, sons of
Barnet and Amanda. Executors: Wife Sarah, A.B. Crabtree. Dated: 30
April 1867. Witnesses: E.M. Tadlock, Alfred Justice.
                           Signed: John Crabtree

WILLIAM TROBAUGH   25 May 1866   Page 611
To daughter, Catharine Cobble - $1. Younger heirs to be made equal with
older heirs. My daughters to have what they made. Remainder of household property to all my heirs. To daughters, Sarah, Margaret and
Elizabeth - each 1/5 of my Wright Tract of land. To son, John's children
1/5 of land. To daughter, Catharine's children, 1/5 of land. To my
grandson, James Trobaugh, 1/8 home tract of land. To daughter-in-law,
Elizabeth Trobaugh - $1. Executor: James S. Stroud. Witnesses: S.
Matthews, Ambrose Bible.   Signed: William Trobaugh

ELIZABETH McLAIN   Page 612
Wife of Thomas McLain decd. To grand-daughter, Sarah Elizabeth daughter
of my son Jonathan, horse and saddle. To grand-daughter, Elizabeth
daughter of my son Joseph, a spinning wheel. To my three daughters,
Nancy Harvey, Deborah Henry and Elizabeth Vernon - my wearing clothes.
To my son, Johnathan and wife Catharine, all household furniture for
their kind care of me. Executor: Son - Murrel McLain. Dated: March 11,
1856. Witnesses: William Niel, Lewis B. Ball.
                           Signed: Elizabeth X McLain

EVAN T. McNESS (McNEESE)   14 September 1865 $1,000   Page 613
To my Wife, Elizabeth, house, garden, spring and use of barn lot and land
where we live. To my first son, Valentine S. McNess - $1. To my second
son, Jacob, 117 acres where he lives. My third son, William decd. his
heirs, Rebecca Ann, Elizabeth Jane and George - $5 each. To my fourth
son, John C. McNess - $5. To my fifth son, Eli McNess, 140 acres to be
sold and kept for his son, Francis Marion. To my daughters: R Murta wife
of William McAmis, Susan wife of John Hyder - $1 each. Executors: Sons -
Jacob and Eli McNess. Dated: 14 September 1865. Witnesses: Charles G.
Rankin, William Stonecypher.   Signed: Evan T. McNess

SAMUEL KELLER   19 May 1863 $2148.20   Page 615
To Wife, Rebecca, first choice of negroes and plantation where I now live
her natural life, then to my son, Samuel Keller. Samuel also to have
Tract on Hawkins Road. To my daughter, Martha Pickens? - land. To my
son, John C. Keller, land adjoining that which his wife inherited. To
my daughter, Rebecca wife of George Lady, land where they live. To my
daughter, Elizabeth Lady, Campbell Tract on Stage Road. To my daughter,
Nancy Maloney, remainder of Campbell Tract. To my son, William E. - land.
Lucinda Davis, Matilda Carter and Polly Cox to be made equal to sons,

John and Samuel. These three were not designated as children - I guess
they were - G.F.B. Mentions landed estate of John Keller and Samuel
Keller. Executors: Sons - John and Samuel Keller. Dated: 19 May 1863.
Witnesses: C. Smith, George Kenney.

Signed: Samuel Keller

WILLIAM INGLE   6 January 1868 $5,000   Page 617
To my daughter, Mary Woods - $300. Sell land given to son, William decd.,
and pay debts. To grand-daughter, Elizabeth Day, $500 at age 21. Exe-
cutor: My son, John Ingle. Dated: 11 August 1866. Witnesses: Farmer
Williams, E.M. Moore.   Signed: William X Ingle

ELIZABETH K. HAYS   9 November 1867   Page 618
To my daughter, Catharine M. wife of George Pickering - 1/2 wearing
clothes, cotton dress pattern and $1. To my other daughter, Mary Ann
wife of A.J. Brumley - 1/2 wearing clothes, cotton dress pattern and $1.
To my son, R.C.G. Hays, all other personal property, a windmill and a
grindstone. Executor: Son - R.C.G. Hays. Dated: 9 November 1867.
Test: James Allen, J.W. Dinwiddie, Louisa L. Kennedy.
Signed: Elizabeth K. Hays

MARY SQUIBB   17 May 1866
To my daughters, Elizabeth Scott and Jane McCurry - double coverlid and
counterpene. To my grand-daughter-in-law, Mary Biddle - one twild
coverlid. To my daughter-in-law, Margaret Morehead - twild blanket for
her use forever. To son, George B. Smith - land adjoining George Click
given my by my father. Dated: 17 May 1866. Test: J.P. Lane, J.M. White.
Signed: Mary X Squibb

STEPHEN CANON   22 December 1867   Page 619
To my son, Patrick Cannon - 75 acres land in District 22 adjoining John
Click and John Bird. He is to pay daughters, Elizabeth Shaw and Eliza
Jane, $100 in trade. Witnesses: Henry H. Jones, James B. Click.
Signed: Stephen X Canon
his mark

BRITTON PHILLIPS   28 November 1867   Page 620
Have our family graves with 4 or 5 more paled in. Four daughters: Mariah
Jane, Margaret Elizabeth, Sarah Manda and Mary Emily - to have all my
personal property and landed estate as long as they are single and to-
gether. Sarah Manda and Mary Emily to have side saddles to make them
even. Executor: John T. Smith. Dated: 28 November 1869. Witnesses:
John Phillips, Benjamin Middleton.
Signed: Britton Phillips

ROBERT BARTLEY SENR.   16 January 1862   Page 621
To Wife, Elizabeth, all personal and real estate her natural life, then
to be divided. Four shares between 4 sons: John Bartley, Lorenza D.
Bartley, Thomas Bartley, and the heirs of Robert Bartley decd. to wit:
Marion I., John, Mary Ann, William H., Elizabeth R., Jacob L., Martha
Jane and Rebecca H. Bartley - 8 in number. Other children: Rachel Sults
decd., Martha Bartley, Mary Self, Elizabeth Farnsworth, Mahaly Bartley
and Ruth Collier - personal property at my wife's death. Executor:
William Cavener. Test: H.A. Bell, Samuel S. Leonidia?
Signed: Robert Bartley

MARGARET J. HENRY   4 February 1868   Page 622
Land I inherited from my father, James Henry, to be equally divided tw
between my brothers and sisters: Nathaniel M. Henry, Samuel Henry, Thomas
C. Henry, Robert Henry, Amanda Casteel and James Henry. To Susannah
Casteel, daughter of John Casteel, for the tender care of me in my
affliction - side saddle and $10. To Mary Henry, wife of Samuel - $5.
Executor: Brother - James. Dated: 4 February 1868. Witnesses: George
W. Gass, Smith R. Tadlock.   Signed: Margaret X Henry

JOHN OTTINGER SENR.   20 February 1868
Slaves, Sarah and her two daughters Julia and Mary, to be set free with
a years provisions, also to have cooking utensils, one little and one big
wheel, one loom and fixtures and the use of cotton and flax patches and
not to be molested by any of my children. Land and property to be sold
and equally divided between my seven surviving children: George, Henry,
Michael, Peter, William, Betsey Nease widow of John Neese, Mary Reese
wife of John Reese. Executors: Sons - Peter and William. Dated: 8
February 1854. Witnesses: George Jones, David Sevier.
                         Signed: John ┼ Ottinger
Codicil: To my three black girls, Julia, Sarah and Mary - a tract of land
northside of Kentucky Road where Jerry Gregg (man of color) now lives.
Witnesses: R. Humphreys, Johnathan Easterly.

RUTH McNEESE
Widow of James McNeese decd. To my daughter, Mahala Kilday wife of
John Kilday, large kittle and 47 acres land adjoining John McNeese,
Cornelius Smith Jr. et al. To grand-daughter, Ruth Ann Kilday - bedding.
To my daughter, Melinda Williams, bureau. To grandsons: George and
Benjamin F. McLain, Francis M. and Samuel W. McNeese - $5 each. Exe-
cutor: Son-in-law John Kilday. Dated: 9 April 1866. Witnesses: James
Shanks, Cornelius Smith Jr.   Signed: Ruth McNeese

JOHN HAUN
To Wife, Nancy Carroll Haun, support her natural life. To daughter,
Sarah Reed - land where she lives. To step-son, Patrick H. Kesterson,
an eaual share with my children - he and his mother are living with us
and taking care of us in our old age. I have sold where I formerly
lived to son, Seymore and son-in-law, J.B. Hurley, money to be divided.
Children: Seymore Haun, Patrick H. Kesterson, Rebecca Haun, Rachel
Kesterson, Phebe Hurley, Jane Wisecarver, Louisa Bible, Elizabeth
Courtney decd., Mary Courtney decd. Executors: Son - Seymore Haun and
Patrick H. Kesterson. Dated: 26 December 1866. Test: Lemuel Crosby,
Alfred G. Hale.
                         Signed: John Haun
Handwriting of A.G. Hale - proven by George J. Courtney 4 May 1868.

REUBEN WISECARVER   24 October 1868
To Wife, Jane, all my lands and property her lifetime, then to be sold
and divided. Heirs: John, Genetty Florence, Thomas, Adalade, Nathan,
Hunley L., Louvina. To second son, Thomas, a calf. Executors: Wife
Jane, Seymour Haun. Dated: 24 October 1868. Witnesses: James M.
Trobaugh, James C. Kinnery?   Signed: Reuben Wisecarver

ELEANOR RUTHERFORD   31 May 1862
My son, William Rutherford to pay the heirs of Thomas Crosier decd., $100;
son, Elliott Rutherford, to pay Christopher Myers or his heirs $155 (My
daughters). Daughters also to have my household and kitchen furniture.
Executor: Farmer Williams. Dated: 31 May 1862. Witnesses: George
Kenney, William Hendly.   Signed: Eleanor X Rutherford

SAMUEL BRUNER
To Wife, Rebecca, my home and where I live her natural life or widowhood.
Farm to go to last children: Andrew Jackson Bruner, Mahala, Lydia and
Anna Eliza Bruner. Son, Andrew, also to have my blacksmith tools. Farm
known as the Seneker Farm to be sold. Sons: James C., Archibald, John
decd. and Jacob H. Bruner. Daughters: Rebecca Jane Hale, Margaret
Fulkerson. Each girl gets a cow. Executor: James Shanks. Dated: 30
March 1866. Witnesses: Anthony Dodd, David D. Meare???
                         Signed: Samuel Bruner

ESTHER M. GAUNTT   7 December 1868
To my son, James B. Gauntt, 85 acres where we now live and personal
property to keep my little helpless son, Marion. To daughters, Josephine
O. and Hannah Naomi - $25 each. Daughters: Sophia Jane and Julia.
Grandson: James Caswell Ross. Executor: James B. Garrett. Dated: 7

December 1868. Witnesses: C.G. Rankin, E.A. Garrett.
Signed: Esther W.? Gauntt

F. A. McCORKLE   6 April 1869 $30,000
To my son, Robert, 1 acre on Depot Street near East Tennessee and Virginia
Railroad Depot with Marlin Hotel and my interest in 3 story brick store-
house on Main Street and 1/2 my library. To my son, Samuel V. (Minister),
where I live on Main Street adjoining the large spring and 1/3 interest in
storehouse on Summer Street. To my grand-daughter, Isabella Coffin, $500
at age 21. I give $500 each to American Bible Society, American Track
Society, American Sunday School Union, New School Presbyterian Home
Missionary Society and Bureau of Bibles for the Colony of Liberia in
Africa. Books for Washington and Tusculum Colleges. Six thousand dollars
to be invested in bonds to educate the children of Robert McCorkle. Six
thousand dollars to be used to support Samuel in his ministers duties.
Executors: Robert McCorkle, Samuel McGaughey. Witnesses: Samuel E. Snapp,
Thomas Lane.
Signed: F. A. McCorkle

DAWSON PITT   11 January 1869 $500
Children: Margrit, James, Polly, Nancy. Executor: John Kidwell. Dated:
11 January 1869. Witnesses: John Kidwell, Andrew I. Harrold.
Signed: Dawson Pitt

MARY ALLEN   24 January 1859
Children: Margaret, Robert, Elizabeth Montgomery, Martha Brisco, Isaac A.,
James, Nancy C., Daniel, Mary Eason. Daughter, Margaret not married, to
have negro girl Isabella and her increase. Executors: Son - Isaac Allen,
son-in-law Talbert Eason. Dated: 24 January 1859. Witnesses: Robert A.
Crawford, William M. Lowery.   Signed: Mary X Allen

MALINDA FULLEN   4 May 1869 $1,000
To my daughter, Malinda E. Burgner, cow, Rocky Mountain quilt, 6 teaspoons,
shawl and black bonnet. To my daughter-in-law, Eliza G. Fullen, bed and
quilt (Lady's Fancy). To my grand-daughter, Martha M Fullen, a quilt. To
grand-daughter, Margaret M. Burgner, Baltimore Belle quilt. To grand-
daughter, Caledona Collet, bed and furniture. To my son, Adam B. Fullen,
the Family Bible. Divide my dishes between all my children in this
country. Executor: Adam B. Fullen. Dated: 6 April 1869. Witnesses:
Benjamin F. Earnest, William C. Black.
Signed: Malinda X Fullen

ELIZABETH DOUD   7 June 1869 $800
The name is spelled DOUD in book and DANDS on the Will.
Children: Ellen (Hay?), May Dands, Peter Dands, Edmond and James Dands.
I owe John Ingle, Josiah Kidwell and James Brotherton. I hold a note on
son, Edmond, for $50. Executor: S.N. Crozier. Dated: 5 May 1869.
Witnesses: James P. Kenney, William Hawkins.
Signed: Elizabeth X Dands

JAMES HALL   District 17
My children to receive as near equal as possible. Small book in the hands
of E. W. Headrick for safe keeping. To eldest son, William M. Hall, land
adjoining Jonathan Pearce, D. F. Hall, Loyd Jackson and A. M. Hall, worth
$448. To son, John, 73 acres land. Son: James H. Hall Jr. Daughter:
Elizabeth. Youngest sons: Alexander and David - land adjoining son,
William M. Hall, John Vincent and William Moore. Judgment obtained
against Joseph Hall before N. Beckner Esq. of Hawkins County. I have
this day signed an indenture marriage contract to give intended wife
now, Elizabeth Crawford, 75 acres. The property to be hers. Executrix:
Wife Elizabeth. Dated: 29 September 1848.
Signed: James X Hall
Codicil: 2 August 1866. Third wife Elizabeth - land I bought of Gabriel
Morgan and deeded to me by John Hall, to Hoppers Corner. Elbert and
Risten?, boys to serve my wife till they are 21. Lands in wife's hands
at her death to return to our child Abbigail. She shall have the use of
my sugar trees. Three children by my 2nd wife, Elizabeth: Martha, Sarah

and Endimyan - land adjoining E. W. Headrick, land I bought of Jasper
Dykes including my still house. Executor: David F. Hall. Dated: 2
August 1866. Witnesses: David F. Hall, William Baskeet, Nathaniel
Mulinix, William X Moore, Thomas M. Brandon.
Signed: James X Hall

ELIZABETH A. SEVIER   15 February 1869
Money in gold to be put on interest to educate three grandchildren. To
grand-daughter, Lizzie Bell daughter of my son Alexander Sevier decd., 1
bureau. To grand-daughter, Martha Olivia Sevier daughter of my son
Alexander Sevier decd., candlestand, rag carpet. To grandson, James
Robert Alexander Sevier son of R. Sevier decd., bookcase and books. To
daughter-in-law?, Malinda Dearstone wife of Isaac Dearstone, dishes and
silver spoons. They are to cultivate farm for support of three grand-
children. To former servant, Martha Bryston wife of Anthony Bryston,
one half acre for her and her little boy, Willie. Executor: James A.
Galbreath. Dated: 15 February 1869. Witnesses: V. C. Sevier, D. Sevier.
Signed: Elizabeth A. Sevier

DANIEL KNIPP
To my son, John Knipp, all land and personal property for taking care of
me and $236 in good bankable money. Other legal heirs. Executor: David
Bible of Christian. Dated: 4 December 1868. Witnesses: James Bible,
Rufus Keesling, John Harmon.   Signed: Daniel Knipp

WILLIAM MORROW   6 September 1859 $4,000
To Wife, Elisa, everything during her widowhood - if she marries it is to
go to my brothers. My sisters to share and share alike. To my nephew,
William Broyles son of my sister Mary Broyles, a colt, saddle and bridle.
To Laura E. Low?, bed and bedding. Executor: David Morrow, his bondsmen:
Ebenezer and Adam Morrow. Dated: 12 August 1859. Witnesses: William S.
McGaughey, W. W. Drakes.   Signed: William X Morrow

ANNA BABB SENR.
Widow of Abner Babb Senr. To daughter, Rebecca Hawkins, a mare and bedstead. Daughter: Margaret Morelock. To son, Abner, bay horse and shugar
cittle (Sugar kettle). To son, Barnet, cittle. To son, Alfred, one
safe. To son, Samuel, falling leaf table. Grandson: Isaac Gray. Executor: Son - Abner. Dated: 14 February 1868. Test: Alexander Brown,
A. B. Crabtree.   Signed: Anna X Babb

POLLY JOHNSON   28 September 1869
To my grandson, Sparling Crum, horse, bedstead, dishes, cattle etc. and
clothing for services rendered to me. Children: Sparling Johnson, Nancy
Janes, Betsey Marshall wife of Samuel Marshall, Rachel Crum. Divide the
rest equally. Executor: Son - Sparling Johnson. Dated: 28 September
1867. Witnesses: Thomas Sane Sr., E. W. Headrick.
Signed: Polly Johnson

JOHN E. DODD
To my brother, William Ira Dodd, interest in my mother's estate. To my
Aunt Mary Dodd, 25 acres in 24th District. To my mother, Elizabeth Dodd,
a sorrel mare mule. Executor: O. Dated: 25 June 1866. Witnesses: A. I.
Marshall, William S. McGaughey.   Signed: John E. Dodd

JOHN FRAKER   5 January 1870   Bond $3,000
To Wife, Mary, lot where I live in Rheatown. Stock in East Tennessee and
Virginia Railroad. Children: George P., Hannah Neal. Executors: George
P. Fraker, Eli Marshall. Dated: 5 January 1870. Witnesses: William
Ellis, John Squibb.   Signed: John X Fraker

ABRAHAM G.FELLERS   18 March 1858   Bond $2,000
All property and railroad stock to be sold and equally divided between
my children except Madison, I will his part to his children. Executor:
son-in-law Lewis H. Broyles. Dated: 8 March 1868. Witnesses: O. M.
Broyles, William S. McGaughey.   Signed: A. Gfellers

PETER COBBLE   4 April 1870
Son: McKindrie, he and I have lived together at the home place and he
has taken care of me for the last ten years. He gets the home farm of
138 acres. Executor: Sylvanus Cobble. Dated: 3 April 1869. Witnesses:
Jacob Keicher, Valentine Ausburn, Nathaniel Cobble.
                    Signed: Peter Cobble, by Jacob
          Keicher - he being unable to write his name or make a mark.

MICHAEL DEARSTONE   4 April 1870 $1,200
My two sisters, Rachel and Elizabeth Dearstone, to have all property.
Widow of Abram Dearstone lives on property. Executor: John Pates.
Dated: 2 December 1865. Witnesses: Robert M. McKee, James Britton.
                    Signed: Michael X Dearstone

ANN REED   2 May 1870 $600
To Elizabeth, daughter of William and Mary Alexander, a quilt and $250.
To Elizabeth, daughter of Thomas and Martha Alexander, $200. To Thomas,
K. Alexander Jr., son of Thomas and Martha Alexander - $200. To Mary
Willis, daughter of Stephen and Sarah Alexander - $50. To Mary R.
McGaughey, daughter of John and Catharine Alexander - $50. To Ann Gray,
daughter of Edward and Jane Gray decd. - $50. To Ann E. L. McGaughey,
daughter of William and Nancy McGaughey - bedstead, sheets and pillows.
Executors: Thomas Alexander Junr., W. S. McGaughey. Dated: 25 May 1863.
Witnesses: John H. Willis, Elizabeth I. Willis.
                    Signed: Ann Reed

ABIJAH SCRUGGS ESQR.   1 January 1870 $15,000
To Wife, Betsey, widows part and dowry. Entire residue of my estate to
be divided into seven shares to daughters: Minerva and Joseph Chilton's
children (both parents dead), Sarah wife of Joseph H. Davis, Martha wife
of Samuel Moore, Mary wife of Robert E. Newman, Julia wife of Thomas Fry,
and Sons: William F. and James A. Scruggs. Grand-children: John and Caty
Chilton. Executors: William Maloney, James C. Ayres. Dated: 1 January
1870. Witnesses: James C. Ayres, Jacob Haun.
                    Signed: Abijah X Scruggs

CATHARINE D. WILLIAMS   13 June 1866
Former husband Alexander Williams. Trustees: David Sevier, James A.
Galbreath. Suits to be brought against sons and I do not want my estate
involved. To my daughter, Eliza D. Sneed, to be charged $12,000 for a house
house in Fayetteville, Western District. To my son, William D., $8000 for
land in front of Court House. To my son, Thomas L., he left involuntarily,
give him $500 above his share. To my son, Joseph A., lives with me and
helps in the business. To St. James Episcopal Church - $100. To my
grand-daughter, Fanny L. Sneed - $200 in gold. Executors: Joseph A.
Williams, James W. Deadrick, William H. Sneed. Dated: 13 June 1866.
Witnesses: Thomas A. R. Nelson, John D. McCurley.
                    Signed: Catharine D. Williams
Property damaged by war. William D. Williams to account to estate for
monies which came into his hands through acts of war or confederate notes.
Another Ex.: William H. Sneed, son-in-law, Attorney at Law. Catharine
was sole heir of William Dickson and husband Alexander Williams, deceased.
Son, William D. Williams undertook to control entire business of three
estates after his father's death, is I think liable. Seventeen Cents.
Witnesses: A. R. Wilson, V. S. Jones, William D. Williams. Dated: 17
February 1867.   Signed: C. D. Williams

SAMUEL CARTER   16 April 1863
To Wife, Mary, a roan mare. To son, Rolly, plantation on Puncheon Camp
Creek adjoining lands of my father, Nathan Carter decd., Benjamin Carter
and others. To son, James Wyly Carter, land where he now lives adjoining
William Ross, James Pearce, John Malone. To son, Anderson, 250 acres
where I live. To daughters: Nancy Linebaugh and Elizabeth Justice, $250
each. My daughter, Hiley Carter, to be supported by my sons. Executor:
Son - Rolly Carter. Dated: 16 April 1863. Attest: George Kenney, B.
Carter.   Signed: Samuel X Carter

DAVID RIPLEY (DAVID S.)   29 April 1870
Wife: Ada E. Ripley, to finish brick house, to have land I bought of
Robert Mason, decd., and land I bought of John Rhea. To my little
daughter, Idaho, the farm I live on. To my infant son, David S., old
tract belonging to my father and mother. Executor: Elbert S. Ripley.
Dated: 29 August 1870. Witnesses: James O Brien, James Britton.
                              Signed: D. S. Ripley

PETER HARMON   20 March 1868
To Wife, Elizabeth, all her lifetime. Heirs: Kennedy Harmon's heirs,
Sparling B. Harmon, John B. Harmon, William, Nelly Armitage formerly
Harmon, Joseph C., Thomas J., Lorinda Luster formerly Harmon, Alexander
and Robert Harmon. Executors: James Luster, Robert L. Harmon. Dated:
20 March 1868. Test: Charles Gass Senr., S. H. Bohannon.
                              Signed: Peter Harmon
Codicil - I include daughter, Nancy Ann, wife of George Harmon left out
in will. Witnesses: George Patterson, Simon H. Bohannon.

HILA GASS   25 November 1869 $2,800
To my daughter, Rebecca Brown, wife of Wilson Brown, One hundred dollars.
To my daughter, Elizabeth Mason, wife of John A. Mason, who kept me in
old age since the death of my father, John Ross - 325 acres in District
23. Executor: John A. Mason. Dated: 25 September 1869. Witnesses:
Robert McKee, J. B. Dobson.   Signed: Hila X Gass

JOHN FRESHOUR   2 August 1867
Wife to have her support. To son, Irenius, land adjoining Peters. To
son-in-law, John Bowers, right to water by a race, but no dam. To son,
Joseph, and daughter, Lavina, all lands in home place not given to
Irenius. To sons, John and Andrew, land in Cedar Creek. To grand-
daughters, Lidia and Nancy Bible, land adjoining Van Huss Storehouse in
Cedar Creek. Executor: B. F. Bell. Dated: 2 August 1867. Witnesses:
Robert S. Browning, James A. Ward, Jacob Neas, Andrew Renner.
                              Signed: John X Freshour

ISAAC FOX   6 February 1871   Bond $500
To daughters, Mary Jane, Eliza Catharine and Barbary Ann, one half my
plantation (110 acres), all money, pay bills and divide equally. To
children, Henry, Martha and Nancy Ann, to have the other half. Martha's
heirs to get their mother's share. Executor: Henry Fox. Dated: 16
November 1867. Witnesses: Abraham Hughes, Thomas Hughes.
                              Signed: Isaac Fox

LOUCINDA SMITH   6 February 1871 $400
To my sister, Remember Smith, bedstid and straw tick, Gouse Foot quilt.
To my sister, Elizabeth Loyd, bed, pillows, sheets and blankets. To my
sister, Martha Rush, all rest of my property. To John Rush, my small
looking glass. Executor: David Rush. Bondsman: James Shanks. Dated:
29 May 1870. Witnesses: James Shanks, Alenardia Smith.
                              Signed: Loucinda X Smith

W. C. HUNT   15 August 1870
Wife, Mary Jane Hunt, to pay debts, funeral expenses and have everything
in Fee Simple. Executor: Friend and Masonic Brother, Sylvanius Cobble.
Dated: 15 August 1870. Witnesses: Robert M. McKee, John Maloney.
                              Signed: William C. Hunt

WILLIAM W. DRAKE   5 December 1871   Bond $4,000
Three hundred acres land at Bulls Gap over which East Tenn. and Virginia
railroad runs, they are to pay $500 per year in damages and for water
rights - its not settled. This land could be sold for $30 per acre.
Children: Frances N., Martha L. Mitchell wife of F. E. Mitchell, Mary E.
C. Drake, Charles M. To youngest son, Willie B., $250 for his education,
he is to be clothed additionally. Divide all property equally between my
children. Robert Lister to plaster house, furnishing all material except
nails, lathes and studding at 22¢ a foot. Partner: Dr. James McGaughey.
Executor: Son-in-law Frederick E. Mitchell. Dated: November 16, 1870.

Witnesses: A. W. Walker, Robert McKee.

RUTH R. ROBINSON   6 March 1871 $3,000
Husband: John Robinson, to carry out my husband's will. To Ellender Ruth
Galyan - my best side saddle. John Robinson McGaughey, son of R. W.
McGaughey. Ellender R. Galyan, Elizabeth Kelly, daughters of Samuel
Kelley, part of my clothes. To two colored girls, Violet and Sharlotta,
living with me, clothes, cow, wheel and best blanket. Balance of money
to Mt. Bethel Congregation and Graveyard. Executor: John McGaughey.
Dated: 2 October 1867. Witnesses: George B. McGaughey, Samuel W.
McGaughey.   Signed: Ruth R. X Robinson

JOSEPH HAWKINS   6 March 1871
Wife, Martha, to control my estate while a widow. Brothers, William and
Phillip, to sell land left me by my brother, Thomas, in Hamblen County.
Land to be sold and invested in good land for my children. Branner land,
brothers, William, Phillip and myself bought. Last payment on Ferry Farm
to be made next fall. To children: Dudley S., John K., land I own jointly
with Lemuel Crosby and his wife, Nancy. When my sons are 21 - divide
equally. Executrix: Wife Martha. Dated: 6 March 1871. Witnesses: Isaac
D. Smith, Francis M. Easterly, Joel Thornburg.
                        Signed: Joseph Hawkins

JOSEPH WHINREY (WHINERY)   4 April 1876 $500
To wife, Jane, land on Babb Mill Road (100 acres). Two daughters, Nancy
Ann and Matilda Jane Whinery, to pay Hannah Hunt $200. To son, B. F.
Whinery, 120 acres southside Babbs Mill Road. To sons, Alex B., Lewis
B. and William C. Whinery, $50 each which son B. F. Whinery is to pay
out of his share. Executors: son B. F. Whinery. Dated: 21 May 1866.
Witnesses: James Allen, Abner Harrison.
                        Signed: Joseph Whinery

WILLIAM LANE   14 January 1871
Wife: Susan. To son, Abraham, all estate real and personal to take care
of me and his mother. To children: Rebecca White, Mary Dodd, Samuel,
Alexander and William Lane - $1.00 each. To grand-daughters, Sarah and
Susan Gass - 50¢ each. To daughter, Jane Starnes, $1.00. Dated: 14
January 1871. Attest: William Crumley, John R. Y. Crumley.
                        Signed: William Lane

JOSEPH E. BELL
To wife, Hepsibah, all property I possess, money, book accounts, notes
and judgments. Son, Benjamin F. Bell, to see that my widow is not cheated
or wronged. I am not in debt. Executor: son Benjamin F. Bell. Dated: 16
August 1870. Witnesses: Jacob P. Wells, Samuel N. Bird.
                        Signed: Joseph E. Bell

GRAVENER McNEES   4 September 1871 $1,600
Wife: Mary. To son, James B. McNees, land on Snapp's Ferry Road. To
daughter, Margaret Showman, land after the death of my wife. To heirs
of son Abner and Rebecky McNees - $125. To Harriet McNeese wife of son
Henry McNess decd. and child, Susa Alus - $125. To grand-daughter, Hiley
White - $100. To my sons, Charles and George McNeese - $200 in year 1890.
To daughter, Susan, homestead. Executrix: daughter Susan Aston? Dated:
April 23, 1871. Witnesses: John Maltsberger, James C. Jones - their Ex.
Alexander M. Smith, J. B. Hawkins, John M. Malone.
                        Signed: Gravenor McNeese

MARTHA STACY   4 March 1872 $100
(Formerly Martha Gfellers). To children: Sarah to control my personal
property, when Elizabeth is of age land to be sold and divided. Executors:
Lewis H. Broyles, O. M. Broyles. Witnesses: M. Gfellers, John Watson.
                        Signed: Martha X Stacy

CHARLES T. NICHOLS
To wife, Mary, 12 acres homeplace and personal property her lifetime.

Lands to Catharine Barlow and her children. Other children - one dollar
each if they come for it. Executor: Arthur Haun. Dated: 10 June 1870.
Witnesses: Farmer Williams, E. M. Moore.
                              Signed: Charles T. Nichols

HUGH BROWN   14 January 1871
To wife, Lucinda M., all lands and property until youngest child is of
age then to be divided between children: Robert S., James, Felix and
Archibald Brown. To children, Margaret Jane Alexander, William, Joseph
and Hugh M. - $150.50 each. My watch to William, my watch key to Joseph.
Executor: William Johnson. Dated: 14 January 1871. Witnesses: C. G.
Rankin, David Barham.   Signed: Hugh Brown

ISRAEL WOOLSEY   7 August 1871 $4,000
To my children, Fethias, James, Andrew, Sarah Brown, heirs of son Israel
decd. - Farm where I live on Lick Creek. To grandson, Alfred Smith -
$200. Executors: Fethias Woolsey, James Woolsey. Bondsmen: David Rush,
J. C. Hankins. Dated: 10 October 1870. Witnesses: Alexander Smith,
Israel Smith.   Signed: Israel Woolsey

OSCAR WILLIAMS   7 August 1871 $1,000
To wife, Matilda, all personal property and land deeded to me by Mrs. C.
D. Williams. To Horace Hunter, land on Newport Road with cabin, pay
taxes on land. He is to help my wife and his grandmother. His grand-
mother, Mary Hunter, to live in said cabin. Executor: James C. Beeks?
Dated: 20 June 1871. Witnesses: Joel Terrell, James Davis.
                              Signed: Oscar X Williams

DANIEL BEALS   15 November 1871
To wife, Ann, plantation, clay bank filly, 3 head cattle, 8 sheep, also
cane mill, sausage grinder, corn sheller, etc. To grandson, Daniel Beals,
$100. Children: Nancy Lewis, Rebecca Lewis, Sarah Solomon, Riley Beals,
Emeline Ellis, Harriett Moffett and Calvin Beals - all to share equal at
the death of my wife. Executor: Alphens Doty. Dated: 15 November 1871.
Witnesses: John Beals, Henry J. Minthorn.
                              Signed: Daniel Beals

ISAAC J. REESER - Repeat

JACOB BROYLES   7 February 1872
Children: Susan and her daughter Ann; A. F. Broyles; John S. Broyles;
Samuel, Edmund, William and Charles, sons of George J. Broyles. Children
to share and share alike. Executors: Sons - O. M. and Lewis H. Broyles.
Dated: February 7, 1872. Witnesses: Charles S. Earnest, David B.
Harrison.   Signed: Jacob Broyles

DEBORAH WHITE   1 April 1872 $200
To son, John B. White, hometract (145 acres), bureau nicely varnished.
To son, James M. White, Mountain Entry (1000 acres) and Saratooth quilt.
To grand-daughter, Jerusha L. Keen, turned bedstead. To grand-daughter,
Bell Dora White, saddle and milk pitcher. To grandson, John F. Keen,
nice new mare and saddle. To grandson, Joseph F., nice new mare and
saddle when ne is 15 years old. To son, Andrew J., $40. To daughters,
Patsey Emeline Bales, all my wearing clothes. To grand-daughter, Sarah
Maltsbarger, 1 ordinary bed. Executor: son James M. White. Dated: 9
January 1872. Witnesses: Abraham Hay, Mary D. Bruner, Catharine X
McNeese, daughter-in-law Delcenia M. White, Susannah Kitchens.
                              Signed: Deborah X White

CATHARINE BLAKE   6 May 1872
To son, Thomas Jefferson Blake, everything for taking care of me in life.
Dated: 3 April 1860. Attest: James Justice, James T. Harrison.
                              Signed: Catharine X Blake

CHARLES LOVETT SENR.   1 July 1872
All my children except Martha Jane, she is to pay John D. Lovett $80.00
she got in time of War. Executor: Elbert Murphey. Dated: 29 May 1872.
Test: J. F. Dewitt, Casson Taylor.
                              Signed: Charles Lovett

JAMES L. CARTER   5 August 1872
Wife: Mary. Three children: Russell B. Carter, Sintha Graham, James L.
Carter of Lucy Carter. Administrator: brother Robert C. Carter. Dated:
15 May 1872. Witnesses: William Armitage, Ephraim Carter.
                              Signed: J. L. Carter

DAVID F. HALL   5 August 1872
To wife, Lydia, proceeds of all Mountain land, all land I have next to
mountain - of Brandon Farm adjoining Murell Moorelot known as Lis Mosley
lot under her control. To daughter, Martha J. Baxter wife of Greene B.
Baxter, land in Washington County and Hawkins County. Interest in bees
at William Hensley's and Catharine Hall's. Wheat due me from J. K. P.
Hall. To daughter, Mary Ann wife of Amass R. Moulton, land in Washington
County. To daughter, Margaret wife of J. M. Brandon, land on mountain
adjoining Baskett. To son, William A., land. To son, John H., $700 and
blacksmith tools. To son, J. K. P. Hall, $750. To daughter, Lucinda S.
Moore wife of Brazelton Moore, part of Brandon Tract. To friend, John
Hensley Senr., part of mountain lands. To Margaret wife of William
Hensley, $50 less, one red heifer. Executor: James K. P. Hall. Dated:
22 June 1872. Witnesses: A. H. Pierce, Wilberforce Wells.
                              Signed: David F. Hall

WILLIAM YARBROUGH
To daughter, Martha Ann Bowman, all my estate. Dated: 12 August 1872.
Witnesses: M. G. Fellers, Isom A. Williamson.
                              Signed: William X Yarbrough

DAVID BRUMLEY   2 September 1872
Wife, Mary Ann and her two children, my youngest children, Sarah Ann and
Tiney Lucinda. Three hundred fifty acres in District 14 adjoining John
W. Ellis, Elkanah Ripley, James Bromley and Joana Roberts - Jeremiah
Davis lives on land. Rest of children provided for. Heirs of William
Brumley decd., Anna, Sally and David. Heirs of Nathan Brumley decd.,
Patten, Susan, Jane, Alfred, Tolbert and Sally. Heirs of David Brumley
decd., James and Sarah. To Isaac Brumley, Malinda Fulks - $1. Dated:
23 April 1870. Witnesses: Charles G. Rankin, J. W. Davis, E. R. Jones.
                              Signed: David X Bromley

WILLIAM CAVENER   4 November 1872
Wife: Mary Jane. To nephew, Francis K. Leming (to be 13 - 20 November
1872), other nephews - William A. Leming land adjoining Alexander's
corner. Executor: William A. Leming. Dated: 29 July 1872. Witnesses:
M. S. Temple, E. M. Rambo.   Signed: William Cavener

GEORGE W. MOORE   Jan. 6, 1873 - 4 May 1874 $1,600
Wife, Rebecca, to have everything as a widow. At her death to be divided
between my son, James C. Moore; grandson, George W. Moore, son of Jesse
M. Moore; and Nancy Ann Shields a girl I raised and now lives with me.
Nancy Ann Shields shared about equally. Executor: son James C. Moore.
Dated: 12 January 1872. Witnesses: Alexander M. Smith, William C. Smith.
                              Signed: George W. Moore

MARTIN HARRISON   6 January 1873
To Newton A. Harrison, all lands (80 acres more or less), a part of
William Harrison land adjoining Caleb Harrison and others in District 2.
Executor: A. J. Harmon. Dated: 23 December 1872. Test: E. M. Wright,
J. P. Wells.   Signed: Martin X Harrison

ABIGAIL HARDIN   3 February 1873
Personal property to be sold, pay debts and funeral expenses, divide

equally between my four daughters: Rebecca Jane, Mary Hardin, Catharine Johnson and Elizabeth Cradick. To daughter, Rebecca Jane, a cow and 2 heifers. To daughter, Mary Hardin, a cow and 2 heifers. I also will Clarissa Myers one dollar. To George M. D. Shanks, son of John Shanks, one dollar. His daughter, Martha Shanks, one dollar. I bought 25 acres of land myself adjoining the old homestead of Jacob Hardin. Executor: Robert P. Johnson. Test: William T. Bohannon, Oliver Hardin.
Signed: Abigail X Hardin

VINCENT ANDERSON
My stock of negroes to be divided equally amongst my children; Namely — Meyarm to be valued at half price and to choose her own master — provided there can be an equal division of said negroes, if not make it up in money. All stock and farming utensils to be sold. Household furniture to be equally divided between my boys, without a sale. All children to have land equally divided. One half acre on top of hill to be used for burying the dead. Children: Lewis has received $100, Vincent $206, John $140, Rebecca Ross $45, James $180. Executors: William Ross, Lewis Anderson. Dated: 5 May 1863. Witnesses: Jer. McMillan, Daniel L. Carter.
Signed: Vincent Anderson

JAMES W. HAROLD   5 May 1873
Divide my stock of negroes equally, if there cant be a division — make it up in money. Title to personal and real estate to descend to my son, John. Interest to my son, Charles. Provide liberally for my little daughter, Jessie. John to maintain and educate Jessie. Son, John, not to receive no percent on negroes, only on money collected by him. Executor: son John. Dated: 25 March 1873. Witnesses: George B. McGaughey, Robert M. McKee.   Signed: James W. Harrold

GEORGE TROBAUGH   1 May 1873
To wife, Barbary, house and kitchen we use under the same roof, personal property, one half grain house, one half cellar, 2 acres and $200. Son, George A. Trobaugh, to support widow. Children: George A., Lavina Jordan, Malinda Trobaugh, Elizabeth French, Polly M. Cobble, Ruthanna Hartman, Anna Ailshie, Lydia Myers. Daughter Lydia — any money from grandfather Bowers to be deducted from her share. Son, George, guardian for daughter Malinda. Executor: James Britton. Dated: 24 January 1871. Witnesses: Charles Gass, W. A. Brown.
Signed: George Trobaugh
Codicil — Britton is dead. Executor: H. C. Smith. Dated: 24 January 1873. Witnesses: James S. Wampler, James P. Cobble.

WILLIAM STANFIELD   1 June 1873
To wife, Miriam (her first husband, John Frieze), all lands and property. Children: Martha E. Stanfield while she remains single, Samuel P., Joseph decd. — his widow and heirs, William decd. — his widow and heirs, Lydia Squibb, Jane Neal decd. — her heirs, heirs of Katherine English decd., heirs of son Barton Stanfield decd. — Kitty Ann being his only child. Don't use or waste timber in any way. Executors: Samuel P. Stanfield, John Squibb (my son's son?). Dated: 31 January 1866. Witnesses: Eli Marshall, James M. Crabtree.   Signed: William Stanfield

CORNELIUS HARDIN   1 September 1873
Feeble in body, but of sound mind and memory. To wife, Annah, full possession etc., fruit to dry. Children: Nancy wife of John Gass — farm in District 12 adjoining John Gass, Lewis Harrold and others. Nancy to pay Elizabeth R. Hardin $125. Daughter, Clarissa, decd., married to John Gass and mother of five children, Cornelius H., Mary Ann, Ellender, Susan Emily and Charles Gass. Two girls married same John Gass — they are to have land on Sinking Creek near Old Galbreath Carding Machine adjoining C. G. Rankin. To daughter, Jane wife of James Gass — 92 acres. To daughter, Bethena Hardin — keep widow comfortable, 92 acre homeplace and is to furnish my wife yearly 1 sack of salt. To son, John, 51 acres. Elender's land adjoining Eliakim Hardin, Robert Harmon and Oliver Hardin. Daughter, Margaret R. Harmon. Son, Eliakim. To daughter, Anna wife of David Gray — land adjoining Joseph Foster. Daughter, Patsy O. Har n.

My four single daughters at home with me: Bethena, Elender, Elizabeth
and Patsey O., seven others. Margaret R. and her husband Robert Harmon.
Executor: son John Hardin. Dated: 20 May 1873. Witnesses: A. W. Howard,
C. G. Howard.   Signed: Cornelius Hardin

HENRY SWATZELL   1 December 1873
To wife, Sarah, land on Pigeon Creek adjoining Philip Basinger, Michael
Dearstone and others. Niece: Sarah Hybarger, daughter of Joseph Hybarger.
Brothers and sisters: Ann Hybarger, Mary Wiseman, John Swatzell, Fanny
Swope?, Jacob Swatzell, Joseph Swatzell. Dated: 19 March 1850. Wit-
nesses: Jacob Dearstone, Isaiah Dobson.
                              Signed: Henry Swatzell

NANCY PRATT   5 January 1874
Daughter, Melvina L. Pratt (alias White) - 7 head of cattle to divide with
her son, Andrew Pratt, and gray mule. To my son, Andrew Pratt, judgment
against Washington Fry and James Miter go to pay debts. Judgment against
I. J. Thornburg and Thomas English. Milton English debt. To Mary M.
Morelock - balance due me from Nathan Morelock. Executor: son Andrew M.
Pratt. Dated: 11 July 1873. Witnesses: James Shanks, Reuben Caldwell.
                              Signed: Nancy X Pratt

HENRY BOLTON   5 January 1874
To wife, Deborah, home tract (152 acres). To my neace, Nancy Ann Mays,
$100 at the death of my wife. My lawful heirs. Executors: Sons - James
H. and Thomas I. Bolton. Dated: 14 November 1873. Witnesses: Jacob K.
Pence, Limestone Dept.?; S. H. Shown, Rheatown Greene County.
                              Signed: Henry Bolton

RACHEL E. WILSON   5 January 1874
To husband, Thomas J. Wilson, my cattle, household belongings, horses.
Notes on William C. Murphey of North Carolina. Notes in hands of Henry
J. Inmen? of North Carolina. Daughter: Sarah Ingle. Son: James H.
Engar - when 21 give him a good horse, saddle and bridle. Test: M. F.
Jerls?, William Henry.   Signed: Rachel E. Wilson

REBECCA HEISKELL   2 March 1874
To my grandchild, Alice Haterson - McClellan house one half mile from
Gran Newport Road. Land per of R. A. Crawford. Executor: Rev. Samuel
McCorkle. Dated: 29 November 1873. Witnesses: John M. Brabson, George
Bell, Rebecca Bell.   Signed: Rebecca X Heiskell

JOSEPH FRAKER   6 April 1874
To wife, Nancy A., all land posessed by me. Sons, John A. B. and Joseph
M. Fraker, to have land at wife's decease and pay my daughters, Mary E.
Shanks wife of E. K. Shanks and Martha J. Armentrout, to make them equal.
Joseph A. Shanks to heir with heirs of my own body. Daughters: Sarah E.
and Florence C. Fraker. Executors: George Pickering, William A. Fraker.
Dated: 4 March 1870. Witnesses: W. G. Roberts, Lewis Cooper,
                              Signed: Joseph Fraker
Codicil - Dated: 21 February 1874 - J. W. Bowens, J. K. Armentrout, F. V.
Armentrout.

MARY M. CARTER
Two sets of tombstones, one for my husband, J. L. Carter decd., and one
for me @ $20 each. To daughter, Synthe Grimes - my wearing clothes. To
son, Russell B. Carter - all balance of my property. Executor: Isaac A.
Armitage. Dated: 27 February 1874. Witnesses: Charles Gass, Newton
King - signed in her presence at her request.
                              Signed: Mary M. X Carter

CHRISTANA NIPP
To Rufus Kesling - all my lands and personal property to take care of me
and my son, Elias. To my son, Elias - one mare, set of tools and my
still. Executor: Thomas Bible. Dated: 18 April 1868. Witnesses: James
Bible, George W. Ailshie, A. Cobble.   Signed: Christana Nipp

WILLIAM A. BAILY
Wife, Martha Ellen Baily and my heirs. Executor: T. B. Winston. Dated:
25 November 1873. Test: W. F. Reeser, J. M. Reeser.
                              Signed: William A. Baily

SAMUEL L. STEPHENS   4 May 1874
To wife, Mary Jane, all cash on hand, notes, drafts, lands in District
18. Lavenia R. Williams to have land, husband Mac Williams not to live
on it. If Lavenia R. Williams lets Mac Williams live with her again,
she shall be dispersed of land and her farm. To son, A. J. Stephens,
and daughter, Margaret E. Stephens now Waddle - land adjoining William
Crum and N. Y. East Tenn. Iron Co. To Eliza Jane Stephens Verran - land
adjoining Rollings tract now claimed by William Rollings and E. Tenn. Ir
Iron Co., to take in where George House now lives. Sons, Benjamin F.
and Isaac H. Fox Stephens, to have Mill Farm I bought of William R. and
Rebecca Farnsworth. Courdenge Mosheim to be put to the youce of schooling
- mi two youngest sons. Dated: 1 June 1873. Witnesses: H. B. Baker,
T. A. Baker.   Signed: S. L. Stephens

JOHN McGAUGHEY   1 June 1874
To son, Samuel's children - $900, land adjoining Buckingham Road. To
daughter, Jane Alexander - $600. To grandson, John R. McGaughey of
Richard - $600. Son: William R. Three grand-daughters: Hannah C., Mary
A. Kenney and Margaret E. Lyon. Son: John E. Land adjoining Mr. Morrow,
John Anderson's shop, M. S. Temple. Two grand-daughters: Nancy J. Dobson,
Martha C. Henshaw. Daughter: Margaret Rankin. Five grand-daughters of
son, David R. McGaughey. Nancy J. Dobson, that we raised. Executors:
Two sons - William S. and John E., with George B. McGaughey. Dated: 27
March 1872. Witnesses: V. S. Maloney, Charles H. Marsh, H. B. Baker,
P. S. Bradford.   Signed: John McGaughey

Codicil - To daughter, Margaret Rankin's children - Julia M., Thomas S.,
James W. and John R. B. - farm I bought on head of Holley's Creek.

JACOB BOWERS   7 July 1874
To wife, Mary, all personal property, real estate - at her death to
daughter, Sarah A. Maloney, who has been good and kind to us in our old
age. Children: Henrietta, Mary Jan, Abraham, Solomon O., Jacob decd. -
have their part. Executor: V. S. Maloney. Dated: 7 October 1873.
Witnesses: E. C. Reaves, Thomas Maloney.
                              Signed: Jacob Bowers

JESSE H. GREENWAY   7 September 1874
To my last and only wife, Elizabeth, full complete control of all my
property her lifetime - then divide between children: Humphrey, Jesse J.,
Daniel A., Moore M., Amanda C. Lamons wife of Stephan Lamons, Jeruthia F.
Bryant. Dated: 6 August 1874. Witnesses: J. S. Love, J. D. Wykle.
                              Signed: J. H. Greenway

MARY HARDIN   5 October 1874
To daughters, Elizabeth wife of David Craddick and Catharine wife of R. P.
Johnson - to have land divided so Catharine can have house. To daughter,
Rebecca J. wife of J. S. Farmer - young mare, all my cattle, 10 bushels
wheat, 12 bushels oats and rent from corn. Land adjoining Shanks,
Swatzell and Elizabeth Craddick, Oliver Hardin. Witnesses: Andrew L.
Harrold, Oliver Hardin. Dated: 28 August 1874.
                              Signed: Mary X Hardin

JOSEPH BRADLEY   7 December 1874
To lawful heirs, John K., Lucy Ann Bradley, Rebecca Knight - land equally
divided on condition they support my wife and me. Grand-children, heirs
of James Bradley decd. Mary Smith - $1. James Bradley, heir of William
Bradley decd. - $1. William Bradley Senr. - $1. Executor: S. S. Babb.
Dated: 15 July 1872. Witnesses: George A. Wattenbarger, John W.
Wattenbarger.   Signed: Joseph Bradley

ABRAHAM NAFF   4 January 1875
Wife: _____. Grandson: James S. B. Crawford. Money coming to me from
Samuel G. Oakey. Executors: Jacob Naff, Francis Robertson. Dated: 10
November 1874. Witnesses: Alfred C. Parry, Jesse Hays.
                        Signed: Abraham Naff

DAVID REED   1 February 1875
Children: Solomon, John, David P., Louisa Kirk wife of Joseph W. Kirk,
Harmon W., Mary Jane Bible, Bethany wife of Pleasant M. Guin, Patrick H.
Pleasant M. Guin to take care of my son, Patrick H. Reed, and get his
(Patrick's) part for doing so. Executors: Sons-in-law - Elbert Bible,
Joseph W. Kirk. Witnesses: William Bible, P. K. Bible.
                        Signed: David Reed

CHRISTOPHER CUTSHALL   1 February 1875
To Polly Ann, my darling and beloved wife, all property, lands her widowhood. All of my heirs. Son, Jacob, to be Executor. Dated: 10 February
1873. Witnesses: A. I. Harmon, G. W. Emmet.
                        Signed: Christopher X Cutshall

CHARLES BRIGHT   1 February 1875
Wife, Sarah, owing to her infirmity. Sons, Jacob, Charles, youngest
daughter, Nancy Jane, grand-daughter, Sarah Baxter - to all live together
as a family. To my oldest daughter, Elizabeth wife of John McCollum -
land in District 16 adjoining John Robertson, James Brown. At Sarah's
death, land equally divided amongst 5 sons. Daughters: Rebecca,
Isabella, Louisa, Nancy Jane (single girl) - $200 each at death of my
wife. Executors: Sons - Jacob and Charles. Dated: 15 April 1874.
Witnesses: Ellis Beals, John Robertson.
                        Signed: Charles Bright

ABRAHAM WILLBURN   1 March 1875
Wife, Mary, to be Executrix. Dated: 12 December 1874. Witnesses: H. L.
McMillan, Ambrose Bible.   Signed: Abraham Wilburn

JAMES FOX   1 March 1875
Children: Sarah Jane, Ruthann, Martha, Elbert and James. Railroad Stock
to Elbert S. and James A. Fox. Three daughters to have Creek Place
where Dort Hunter now lives. If Florence wife of my decd. son, Samuel
P., should have a child by him - it is to share equal at 21. James
Morris to give place he lives on to my three daughters if they marry.
Executor: Son - James A. Dated: 11 March 1872. Witnesses: M. Gfellers,
L. H. Broyles.   Signed: James G Fox
                                           his mark

THOMAS PHILLIPS   Saturday June 13, 1875   In Circuit Court
    T. W. Phillips Ex. of Thomas Phillips decd.
                vs
    H. P. McCullough and wife, Catharine McCullough
Eliza wife of G. L. Jenkens, Matilda Jenkens, land in District 6 adjoining
Thomas Jackson, Gabriel Phillips. Wife, Catharine - 200 acres during her
natural life. Son: T. W. Phillips. A. B. Keel. Susan Willsmith wife of
B. W. Willsmith. Son Thomas Jenkens and A. B. Keel and their heirs
Isabella's part and the heirs of her body by A. J. Harmon decd. - apart
from her present husband and his heirs. Executors: Son - R. W. Phillips,
A. B. Keel. Witnesses: Bedford Brown, A. H. Tittibour?
                        Signed: Thomas X Phillips
Codicil - daughter, Catharine, to have one dollar. Witnesses: E. M.
Drake, A. M. Feathers.

JOHN C. DYER   5 April 1875
To wife, Sarah E., land I bought of Hiram Proffit and wife, Nancy E.
Daughter: Martha I. Dyer. Eldridge S. Scott to have land I bought of
John Wright, Sarah A. Adams, Caswell N. Kirk and B. F. Pettit. I have
given children by my first wife, Eliza, Abraham H., Mary E. Kirk wife of
Caswell N. Kirk, Sarah A. Adams wife of James A. Adams - $800 apiece.
Executor: John Wright. Dated: 8 February 1875. Witnesses: Lemuel

Crosby, Joseph E. Dyer, H. W. Reed.

Signed: John C. Dyer

MATTHIAS BIRD   5 April 1875
To Wife, Mary Ann, one half of farm where I now live. At Mary Ann's
death to go to daughter Elizabeth. To daughter, Susan Trammel, 167 acres
land on Cove Creek adjoining John F. Parman and others, where she now
lives. To son, David Bird, 172 acres land where he lives - Jack Farm.
To son, Philip Bird's four sons, James H., Russel M., William R. and
David F. - $300 each, to have notes I hold on C. P. Fillers, Albert L.
Fillers and John F. Parman. To daughter, Cyntha E. Fry - $1000. To
daughter, Elizabeth C., one half of 192 acre farm where I now live. To
son, Isaac, Freshour farm (146 acres) and 25 acres on waters of Cove Creek
adjoining G. B. Rollins and enough bed clothing to keep him warm in cold
weather. To daughter, M. Lafollette's three sons, Matthias B., William
W. and David Lafollette - 148 acres land Jeremiah Lafollette now lives on,
on waters of Cove Creek. These three grandsons to receive $40 each as
they come of age. Executor: David Parman. Dated: 20 March 1874.
Witnesses: David Parman, J. A. Ward, Darius X Cogburn.

Signed: Matthias Bird

MICHAEL CRUM SENR.   5 April 1875
Wife: Letha. Executor: William Looney. Dated: 7 May 1872. Witnesses:
Thomas Hughes, Casson Taylor.

Signed: Michael Crum

JOHN W. (WILSON) BROWN   3 May 1875
Wife: Fannie A. Daughter: Jessie Wilson Brown. Brothers: William O.
and James P. Brown. Executor: William A. Allen. Dated: 8 April 1875.
Witnesses: Alexander Brown, T. W. McAmis.

Signed: John W. Brown

MARTHA ISABEL RICHARD   3 May 1875
Brother: Henry Richard. To my sister, Jane Richard, land we bought of
John Richard decd. and all the real estate left me by my father in the
homestead. Money to be collected of W. F. Reeser. My ca son: Abraham
Campbell. Executrix: Sister - Jane Richard. Dated: 23 November 1874.
Test: Thomas Loyd, Nancy Ann Whinry.

Signed: Martha I. Richard

SAMUEL MILLIGAN   7 September 1874
To wife, Elizabeth, all real estate in Tennessee and District of Columbia.
To son, Henry - watch and law books. To son, Charles H. - library books.
Frank I. Milligan to be loaned $500 to be repaid. Executrix: Wife -
Elizabeth. Dated: 19 April 1874. Test: C. M. Ford, R. A. Crawford,
George A. Howard.

Signed: Samuel Milligan

JACOB BEALS   7 June 1875
To wife, Keziah, the homestead during her widowhood. To son, Edie - one
red cow. To children, Nathan, Thomas and Sarah - $12 each. To son, John
- $10. To Mahlon H. Lewis - $20 cash. Children: Ellis, Daniel, Abner,
William, Jonathan, John, Rebecca Morelock, Amous, Nathan, Thomas, Sarah
Gantt and Mary Beals. Executors: Son - John, David Ellis (of Jessie).
Dated: 11 November 1870. Test: William Pierce, Samuel C. Crouch.

Signed: Jacob Beals

JOTHAM BROWN
To wife, Hannah M. Brown, her three minor children, William P., Esther C.
and Margaret M. - one yellow mare, sorrel filly, 6 hogs, 2 cows, 11 sheep,
one wagon and gearing, growing crops, wheat, oats and corn. To James E.
Brown - interest in wheat at D. B. Harrold's, note on William McKenney.
Executor: Nathan B. Smith. Dated: 10 April 1875. Witnesses: Alfred B.
Law, James B. Gauntt.

Signed: Jotham X Brown

HUGH BROADERICK
Real estate in Jefferson County and mill in Coke County to be sold.

Children: S. L. Broderick, Polly Ann McAfee, Roda E. Broyles. Son-in-law, J. F. Broyles. Witnesses: S. K. Brooks, A. C. Gregory.
Signed: Hugh X Broaderick
Codicil - other children: L. C. Rambo, W. A. Broderick, Daniel Broderick, Martha L. Remore?, Margaret J. Jones - to whom I have already given.

JOSIAH HARRISON   7 September 1875
To wife, Sarah E., all property except 1 mare. Wife, Sarah, holds bond on George W. Reynolds (640 acres land). Four children: John C., Phillip H., Maria J. Prece, Josiah - 640 acres land. Executor: George W. Reynolds. Dated: 31 August 1875. Witnesses: E. M. Wright, William Blazor.
Signed: Josiah Harrison

FRANCIS HUGHES   6 September 1875
To my brothers and sisters, Aron, Abram, Thomas and Phebe Hughes - all my estate. Executor: Thomas Hughes. Dated: 25 March 1875. Witnesses: H. D. Winters, Enoch Hopton.
Signed: Francis X Hughes

BARBARA SMELCER   4 October 1875
Barbary Smelcer and Mary Clowers, both of lawful age, appeared as witnesses to establish a Non Cupative Will of Barbary Smelcer decd, wife of Joseph Smelcer decd, who died 4 June 1875. Son, Isaac Smelcer, to have all her property for taking care of her. Witnesses: Maggie Pickering, C. W. Bible.
Signed: Barbary X Smelcer
Mary X Clowers

JAMES STARR - of Rheatown   4 October 1875
I left Missouri in early October 1873, arrived here 22 October 1873. Had deposited with Isadore Layton of Missouri a portion of my money, over $500 in silver and brought with me $600 in gold except $100 in currency, I arrived at McClains - McClain to go to Missouri for my money. I gave him $80 for trip - he got $570 in silver. We made settlement 2 June 1875. I stayed at McCollums - then to Dr. J. W. Cox for better care. I sent for my trunk, it was empty. To my five nieces, daughters of John A. B. Fitzgerald of Haywood County, North Carolina - $100 each. To John L. Gahl of Haywood County, North Carolina, the residue of my estate. Pay Mrs. Dr. Cox well. Recover money in possession of G. A. McClain. Executor: John Crawford. Dated: 23 August 1875. Witnesses: G. H. Shoun, A. N. Shoun.

MARY WHITTENBURG   1 November 1875
Wife of Jacob Whittenburg, decd. To daughter, Elizabeth Chapman, everything for caring for me. Executrix: daughter - Elizabeth Chapman. Test: James Susong, Alfred Susong, J. S. Love.
Signed: Mary X Whittenburg

GEORGE GRAHAM   6 December 1875
Wife: Clarissa Marinda Graham. Children: George Jackson Graham decd., William Alpheus, Nancy Jane, James Elbert, Samuel Alex, Andrew J., Edward F., Clarissa Marinda, Absolum Thompson, Joseph Anderson Graham. Executor: George W. Gass. If needed, sell my land at private sale. Witnesses: Joseph Write, George W. Gass.
Signed: George Graham

GEORGE HARRISON
To James Harrison and Cain Harrison - the homestead, 2 acres on wright side of woode that leads to James Justus saw mill. Wife, Polly, to have all my personal property. Balance to William, Warn, Franklin and Green Harrison and E. J. Filters. To Green Harrison - one sorl bald faced mare. Dated: 2 December 1875. Witnesses: B. W. Harrison, William Jennings.
Signed: George Harrison

JOHN A. REED
To wife, Lavina Sr., $100 her part in my entire estate, also 1 colt, one third personal property, 1 years support. Four first children, heirs of my former wife, Altamira Reed: Daniel B., Joseph M., Emily V. and William

D. Reed - my landed estate and two thirds household and kitchen furniture.
To my youngest child, David S. - my gold watch and $50. Executor: Enoch
Hartman. Dated: 8 December 1875. Witnesses: Joseph Hartman, Francis A.
Hartman.   Signed: John A. Reed

JEREMIAH PROFFITT   5 March 1876
Wife, Deborah, to have good support. To son, Joseph - $1000. Several
heirs to have the rest if there is any. Executors: Solomon and William
T. Matthews. Dated: 16 December 1875. Witnesses: James Cox, Abraham H.
Dyer.   Signed: Jeremiah Proffitt

SAMUEL D. WINTERS   1 May 1876
To wife, Mary J. Winters, the plantation I now live on. Children:
Margaret T. Geshasaur, Redah J. Wright, Charles C. C. and Caledonia
Winters. Executor: William J. Ruble. Dated: 28 February 1876.
Test: Abraham Hughes, Thomas Hughes.
                              Signed: Samuel D. Winters

ISAAC C. DOBSON   3 July 1876
Put tombstones at grave of my wife and mother. To Presbyterian Church of
Oakland in Greene County - $200, one Bible. To other organization - $100,
To Calvin W. Dobson - $10, one Bible. To Callie Buchanan - $10, one Bible.
To Isaac Siner Dobson - $10, one Bible. To Nancy Reed - a weavers loom.
I owe Samuel W. Dobson. Divide my farm between A. S. N. Dobson, John V.
Dobson, Samuel W. and Henry M. Dobson. Commissioners to make division:
Anthony Moore, Daniel Kennedy, L. M. Tadlock. Executors: A. S. N. Dobson,
John V. Dobson. Dated: 6 June 1876. Test: D. M. Dobson, G. W. Telford.
                              Signed: Isaac C. Dobson

THOMAS JACKSON   3 July 1876
Witnesses: William Hawkins, G. J. Weems. Child: Sallie Jackson. Grandson: Reed W. Jackson. To Sallie Jackson - 54 acre tract during her lifetime, then to the children of W. E. V. Jackson and children of Dr. J. A.
Rader and my daughter, Laura Rader. Little Island between Lewis F.
Rader and Harmon Reed to my daughter, Sallie. Remainder of Real Estate
to Dr. J. A. Rader to secure him harmless on Security on Guardian Bond
of W. E. V. Jackson. Executor: Daughter - Sallie Jackson. Dated: 21
June 1876. Witnesses: William Hawkins, G. O. Weems, William Keel?
                              Signed: Thomas Jackson

LUCINDA DAY
Everything to William R. Willoughby and John Barlow, divided equally.
They are to pay Dr. J. A. Rader's doctor bill. Witnesses: E. P. Barlow,
E. M. Drake, J. A. Rader.   Signed: Lucinda X Day

ISAAC PLEASANT   7 August 1876
Wife, Nancy, to have support from farm. To son, Samuel, farm I now live
on. To daughter, Susan, her support while single. To son, Thomas - $50.
Executor: Son - Samuel. Dated: 23 August 1875. Witnesses: George M.
Wright, J. K. Armentrout.   Signed: Jacob Pleasant

JOHN E. McGAUGHEY   7 July 1876
To wife, Mary A., all my personal property. To sons, Richard A., Robert
N. and George W. B. - land from my father, John McGaughey, adjoining Mrs.
Margaret Rankin, W. S. McGaughey, M. S. Temple, E. Morrison, G. B. Broyles.
Daughters: Hannah C. Britton, Ella K. McGaughey, Minnie N., Betty V. To
son, Eddi - land in District 10, 13 and 21. Executors: Robert Park,
Joseph D. Britton. Dated: 5 May 1875. Witnesses: Gon J. Broyles, George
B. McGaughey.   Signed: John E. X McGaughey

JAMES RODGERS
To wife, Elen, 505 acre plantation where I now live as a widow - at her
death to go to two sons, James and Franklin (Francis in one place), not
yet 21. Children: Jane Shanks, Louisa Basket, Susan Prats. Son-in-law,
Uruch? Hunt. Executor: Son-in-law - John Shanks. Dated: 13 March 1875.

Witnesses: A. M. Smith, Asa Bowling.
Signed: James Rogers

SUSAN CASTEEL
Sarah Elizabeth wife of John R. Casteel - have given her $1. William W.
and Jeremiah Martin Casteel. William W. took tender care of me during my
affliction. Executor: William W. Casteel, friend. Dated: 19 June 1876.
Witnesses: George W. Gass, Thomas Malone.
Signed: Susan X Casteel

JACOB JUSTICE
Wife: May. To son, John B. - land adjoining M. D. Curry, James White and
others. John B. to take care of father, Jacob Justice. Son, William,
has his part. To daughter, Jane Weems - $10. To daughter, Mary Emeline
Ellis - $10. To Mary Williams - $105. C. William Justice. Executor:
Son - John B. Justice. Dated: 11 January 1876. Test: Aulden Tucker,
John Justice.
Signed: Jacob Justice

MARY McMACKIN   7 June 1875
To daughter, Narcissa Brumley, one half my farm including house. To
daughter, Louisa E. Basket, one half my farm including cabbin stable.
Executor: William Morelock. Dated: 29 October 1868. Witnesses: William
S. McCollum, Samuel Pickering.
Signed: Mary X McMackin

WILLIAM KELLER
Pay L. D. Keller for taking care of me. Divide rest between my brothers
and sisters. Executor: R. K. Waddle. Dated: 9 September 1876. Test:
John Keller, S. D. B. Keller.   Signed: William X Keller

MARGARET BOWERS
Grand-children living of my son Andrew S. Bowers decd. - to share and
share alike. Children of my daughter, Lavina S. wife of David C.
Johnson. Daughter, Mary M. wife of Dr. Benjamin F. Bell, to have
nothing - I have given to them. Executors: Samuel Stephens Jr.,
Andrew S. Freshour Esq. Dated: 15 December 1871. Witnesses: E. W.
Headrick, S. E. Snapp.   Signed: Margaret X Bowers

DANIEL L. CARTER   27 October 1876
To wife, Sarah, one third rale estate, horse with gears, one windmill,
all cattle except one red bull. To son, John P. Carter - wagon and black-
smith tools. To daughter, Martha Carter - 1 bay mare. Children: William
B., D. M. (Daniel), Alfred, Margaret - $200, Martha - $100. Children:
Mary, Eliza, Lewis and James - the balance. Executor: William B. Carter.
Dated: 5 September 1876. Witnesses: J. D. Anderson, Jeremiah McMillan.
Signed: Daniel L. Carter

DELILA MARSH
Son John - farm I live on in Washington County - other heirs. Son Lewis -
his part in farm in Missouri and Greene County. Other children: Martha
A. Maloney, Elizabeth Miller, Harriet McCord, Hannah Likens, Mary Ann
Trivell, James H. Marsh and Rebecca Caroline Hannah. John Hannah lives
on home place. Executors: Son - Lewis Marsh, William B. McCord. Dated:
5 December 1868. Witnesses: William B. Hudson, Rebecca Hudson.
Signed: Delila Marsh
(This is the farm where Greene Valley is now - the old bridk house is
still standing. Delila was widow of James Marsh I believe. G.F.B.)

GEORGE ROBERTSON   6 November 1876
Daughter, Margaret - to pay heirs $400 each and to have home farm l
purchased of John Collier in 1828 (69 acres), also land I purchased of
M. Bright adjoining John H. Hays, S. H. Baxter. Children: Ann, Jane
Rush. Three grandsons: Charles and Nathan Pierce, Isaac Bales.
Children: James R., Deborah, Jane Margaret Hays, Rebecca Phillips,
Mary Robertson, Adaline Register, Jessa and Allen Robertson, Mahala
Collier, Martha Campbell. Executor: Francis Robertson. Dated: 12 May

1872. Witnesses: A. G. Register, Nathan Hays.
Signed: George X Robertson

R. E. KINGSLEY - of Whitfield Co., Georgia   6 November 1876
On Eve of going into the army in Middle Tennessee. Bury me beside my
brother, Eugene. Put a cheap neat monument and non rail at my grave.
If they see fit to remove Eugene to Cumberland Shed where Walter Broyles
is buried - I want to be buried there. Wife: Nannie. Sister: Fannie.
My children to have their part when they come of age. Executors: wife
Nannie and her father, James Worley. Dated: 28 December 1862. Witnesses:
B. F. Prater, John S. James.   Signed: R. E. Kingsley

JOSEPH BURRIS
Pay debts. Mary Catharine Scott, wife of Reuben Scott, and her children
to have remainder of my estate after debts. Executor: Reuben Scott.
Dated: 8 September 1876. Witnesses: Robert M. McKee, E. B. Smith.
Signed: Joseph X Burris

MARTIN WELTY
Wife, Sarah E., to have land. To grandson, Jeremiah M. Casteel - $100
and a mare at Sarah's death. Margaret An Casteel's heirs, Susannah
Casteel heirs, Elizabeth Brown and her heirs. Make deed to Joseph
Susong for land I sold him, also make deed to James Graham for land I
sold him. Executors: William Casteel Sr. & James D. Brown. Dated: 19
June 1876. Witnesses: William Brumley, James X Graham.
Signed: Martin Welty

SARAH E. WELTY   5 February 1877
To grandson, Jeremiah M. Casteel, 1 pare high posted bedsteads with his
name on, feather bed and blanket, wool carpet, chiney, straw tick, tea-
cups and saucers. Executors: William Casteel, James D. Brown. Dated:
15 December 1876. Witnesses: James X Graham, Samuel Reynolds.
Signed: Sarah E. X Welty

CHARLES R. GASS   5 February 1877
To my mother, Laura A. Gass, land my father, William Gass, owned.
Sister: Jennie B. Gass. Brother: George R. Gass. Other sister: Mary
E. Gass. Dated: 15 June 1876. Witnesses: William McAmis, Charles R.
Gass of John.   Signed: Charles R. Gass

MARTHA BARTLEY   5 March 1877
To my sister, Mahala Bartley, all my real and personal estate her life-
time, then to the heirs of Ruth Collier. Executrix: Sister - Ruth Collier.
Dated: 19 September 1872. Witnesses: Catharine Howell, J. W. Howard, A.
W. Howard.   Signed: Martha Bartley

ABRAM WEEMS   3 September 1877
To wife, Elizabeth, 275 acre landed estate and personal property. Her
boys: Abram, George, Andrew, Thomas, John and James to pay her girls:
Catharine Dodd, Margaret Ragsdill, Eliza Weems and Matilda Weems - $200
each. My children: William, Nancy, Sarah, Martha and Mary Ann - have
received their portion in lands known as Benjamin Goodman Lick Creek
Distric 7. I give three fourth acre land around Wesleys Chapel Church
to Methodist Episcopal Church South as long as it is used for church and
schoolhouse. Executor: George E. Kenney. Test: Samuel McLain, William
W. Malone.   Signed: Abram Weems

JOHN ASTAN   3 September 1877
Wife, Mary B. One of the three children to live with my wife. Samuel R.
Astan, John Astan, John Henry Stanton. All heirs to share except William
H. Astan and the heirs of James M. Aston - they have their part. Exe-
cutor: Son - Washington J. Astan. Dated: 23 July 1877. Test: Francis
Robertson, W. F. Reser, W. M. Kelley.
Signed: John Astan

HANNAH THOMASON   3 September 1877
To son, John Thomason - land at Gravy Falls Spring running a strate
course to Yokley hollo. To son, Hail B. Thomason - rest of land. To
daughter, Susan Babb - kettles etc. Kettle belonging to Granny Hoggatt.
Witnesses: Andrew X Malone, James H. Brown.
                              Signed: Hannah X Thomason

WILLIAM MILBURN   1 October 1877
Children of my first wife, Martha Milburn - home farm in District 15
adjoining Joseph Fraker, J. Milburn, William Fraker, Baskett, Jonathan
Milburn and Andrew McMackin. Present wife, Sarah Ann. I give to George
C. Milburn - overcoat. To J. P. Milburn - watch. To Flora E. Milburn -
bureau and $700. Build Sarah A. Milburn a house 18 ft. wide x 32 ft.
long, 2 stories high. Executor: W. E. F. Milburn, Ex. and Attorney.
Dated: 21 September 1877. Test: J. P. Milburn, J. W. Vicary.
                              Signed: William Milburn

JAMES MURPHEY   4 February 1878
Wife: Jane. After her death divide land between Isaac C., Joseph C. and
Rebecca P. Murphey equally. To my daughter, Mahaly Jeffers - $50. To
two of William Murphey, decd. - books and novely $25 each. To George J.
Murphey - $300. To Dianah C. McNeese - $75. To Betsy Jane Ball, my
daughter - $75. To Nancy Baley, my daughter - $10. Executors: Isaac
C. Murphey, H. J. Frazier. Dated: 14 January 1878. Test: L. B. Ball,
Abner J. Frazier.   Signed: James Murphey

CATHARINE DODD   February 4, 1878
To Martha M. Sisk - 2 beds and other things equal to other children. To
Catharine L. Sysk - bed, cow, saddle and half as much bed clothing as I
gave my own children. To Samuel R. Dodd - 2 bedsteads, as much as I gave
my daughter. Dated: January 19, 1878. Test: S. X Seton, J. A. Leming.
                              Signed

ELLEN ROSS   4 March 1878   Non Cupative
Two youngest daughters, Nancy and Mary Eliza Ross, to have all property
belonging to her. Dated: 2 December 1877. Witnesses: Hannah M. Sexton,
George W. Ross.   Signed: Hannah M. Sexton

SARAH ROSS   1 April 1878
Widow of Allen Ross, Decd. Daughters: Hannah Harmon, Elizabeth Cavener,
Margaret Anderson, Nancy Keller, son William Ross - one dollar each. To
Sarah Elizabeth and Mary Jane Ross, my grand-daughters and daughters of
James and Margaret Ross - $100 each. Son, James Ross, to get remainder.
Executor: James Ross. Dated: 1 February 1875. Teste: S. M. Bird,
George E. Kenny.   Signed: Sarah X Ross

HENRY BIBLE   2 April 1878
To wife, Isibell J. Bible - use of all property, 181 acres land in
District 8 - then to go to son, William S. Bible. To daughter, Margaret
E. Bible - $200. Have already paid daughters, Louisa J. Hartman and
Susannah Cobble. To the heirs of my son, James Bible - $200. Jonathan
Bible, guardian to Charles L. and Barbary E. Bible. Sons: A. J. Bible,
Charles S. Bible, Christian W. Bible - have received $300. Two youngest
children: Margaret E. and William S. Bible. Executor: Son - A. J. Bible.
Dated: March 22, 1878. Test: D. R. Gass, Christian Bible, Charles M.
Collette.   Signed: Henry Bible

ELIJAH W. HEADRICK   3 June 1878
To wife, Juretta A. Headrick, house, personal property, rent and profits
of my farm near town, 20 bushels wheat, 30 bushels corn, 2 horse loads of
hay perannum, $100 per year and her firewood. To my son, O. B. Headrick,
land adjoining J. G. Reese, J. A. Brown. To my daughter, Clementine T.
Tipton, house in town. My four children: William L., Orvil B., Lewis B.
Headrick and Clementine T. Tipton. My grandson, Walter, son of L. B.
Headrick, to get my $100 gold watch. To grandson, Lewis Walter Tipton -
$50. To grandson, Robert, son of O. B. - $25 for being a good boy. If
any of my sons names a son Elijah Walter, he is to get $150. To my son,

O. B. - my surveyors chain, compass and instruments. To J. B., son of my
son, W. L., Robin, son of O. B., Lewis W. Tipton - to get my E. T. & Va.
Railroad Stock. George W. Tipton. Executor: son - O. BO Headrick.
Dated: 12 April 1871. Witnesses: William S. McGaughey, Robert M. McKee.
Signed: E. W. Headrick

WESLEY BENSON   3 June 1878
Wife: Mary Catharine. Two younger children: Lincoln and Easter Benson.
Guardian for wife and children: Emory Telford. Dated: 12 August 1876.
Attest: Wils McAmis, Andrew Marvel.

MAGDALEN NEAS   1 July 1878
To Elizabeth Neas, widow of my brother, John Neas decd., and her son
Henry Neas - all and every part of my estate. Executor: Thomas Neas.
Dated: 13 November 1871. Witnesses: Paul Neas, Noah Neas.
Signed: Magdalen X Neas

BENJAMIN WADDLE   1 July 1878
Lydia, wife of Jonathan Waddle, to have corner cupboard and one bureau
standing under clock. Written by W. A. Harmon and signed by us 3 June
1878 - G. S. Sentelle, S. D. Waddle. Dated: 22 April 1878

SARAH LENTZ   5 August 1878
Formerly Sarah Farnsworth. Only living daughter, Elizabeth B. Willis, to
have farm I live on - I heired it from my father, John Farnsworth. Only
living son, Henry M. Lintz - $10 to be paid by Elizabeth. Executor: S. K.
Brooks. Dated: 16 April 1878. Witnesses: W. V. Bell, Charlie C. Hartsell.
Signed: Sarah Lentz

ELVIRA M. STULTS   5 August 1878
Formerly Elvira M. Bible. To husband, Philip Stults, all my land in
Laurel County, Kentucky. Dated: 27 May 1878. Attest: W. A. Harmon.
Signed: William Stults
Elizabeth X Smith

J. F. GASS   5 August 1878
To wife, Nancy, her support. To Sarah Jane McAmis, daughter of Nancy
McAmis - 50 acres land willed me by my grandfather, John Gass - I am
fully satisfied she is my daughter, born out of wedlock and I have
married her mother, Nancy Jane McAmis - I make her my legal heir. To
daughter, Mary Allis Gass - 37 acres with mill and mill seat. Executor:
George W. Gass. Dated: 20 April 1878. Test: Elijah Kidwell, J. E.
Hankins.   Signed: J. F. Gass

ELIZABETH FALLS   4 November 1878
To grand-daughter, Minerva Elizabeth Falls - land near Gillespie Falls.
Son, William M. Falls, her guardian. Executor: son - William M. Falls.
Dated: 20 March 1861. Witnesses: John Crabtree, Absalom Stonecypher.
Signed: Elizabeth X Falls

JACOB JUSTIS   4 September 1876
To wife, Mary, 1 gray mare, 3 head cattle and 4 sheep. To my son, John
B. Justis - farm adjoining M. D. McCurry, James White and others for
taking care of his father and mother, Jacob and Mary Justis. Son:
William Justis. To daughter, Jane Weems - $10. To daughter, Nancy
Emaline Ellis - $10. To daughter, Mary Williams - $105. To daughter,
Catharine Williams - $105. Executor: son - John B. Justis. Attest:
Aulden Tucker, John Justis.   Signed: Jacob Justis

JOHN HAROLD   1 January 1879
To my sister, Jenie Harold - one third of my estate and personal property
and land of my father's estate when she is 21. To my brother, Charles
Harold - other two thirds. Father: James W. Harold, decd. I am Exec.
of my father's estate. Executors: James G. Reeves, Robert M. McKee.
Dated: 19 April 1876. Witnesses: George L. Farbyer, Paymaster; John S.

Wharton, Capt. 19 Inf.; J. W. Fisher, New York City Army Building.
Signed: John Harold
1st Lieu. 19th Infantry

SETH BABB   3 February 1879
Wife, Mary, to have ample support. My two sons, Samuel and Charles Babb,
to have land. Children by my former wife, Cintha Crawford decd.: Jane
married to Alexander Brown, Mary married to David W. Bright, James Babb
decd. and William Babb. Alexander Babb left years ago without heirs.
Son, Elbert Babb, to have William Stonecypher farm sides of graveyard.
To grandson, Leander Babb - $50. Executor: Son-Samuel. Dated: 10
December 1878. Test: John A. White, B. G. Middleton.
Signed: Seth X Babb

MARGARET CARTER   3 February 1879
To grandson, Benjamin A. Carter - 1 bureau, 29 pieces of china, note on
William Ross. Grandsons: John B. Carter, Thomas A. Carter. Executors:
Grandsons - Benjamin A. and John B. Carter. Dated: 22 April 1878.
Test: John C. Burger, L. N. Sayler, J. K. P. Saylor.
Signed: Margaret X Carter

PETER KEY   8 April 1879
To wife, Sarah, all my estate. If I outlive my wife, I bequeath to
Emma Kidwell, daughter of William A. Kidwell - everything. Executor:
D. R. Gass. Dated: 11 June 1878. Test: Jer McMillan, Hiley X
McMillan, James W. Cloyd. Signed: Peter X Key

JOHN NELSON   7 April 1879
To my daughter, Sarah Nelson, all my property her natural life for caring
for me. To my daughter, Luvina married to William Willis - an equal
portion. Son: David Nelson. Executor: Joseph Burgner. Dated: 11
February 1879. Test: M. Gfellers, Anderson S. Broyles.
Signed: John X Nelson

CLAIBURN WEBB   5 May 1879
Wife: Annie C. Webb. To my son, William C. Webb, 106 acres land for
giving my wife and me a plentiful and decent support and pay to three
daughters: Annie L. Linbaugh - $25, Mani? Malone - 50 acres, Hannah E.
Webb - $25 when she is 21. To daughter, Marina B. McNees - 50 acres.
To daughter, Margaret L. Crumley - 50 acres land and a home at my house
as long as she remains chaste. Dated: 9 September 1876. Test: E. E.
Bebber, P. B. Welsh. Signed: Claibourn Webb

SAMUEL HENRY   5 May 1879
To wife, Mary B. Henry, homestead of 18 acres and mill, 50 acres adjoin-
ing Fairground when the right is secure by Chancery Court. All my heirs.
Executor: Widow. Dated: 24 March 1879. Attest: John T. Davis, James
Henry. Signed: Samuel Henry

SARAH E. MILLER   7 July 1879
Virginia, youngest daughter of Virginia (now dead) and W. G. Smith her
husband, was left by her mother in an extremely helpless situation.
Other children and grand-children. Executor: Dr. William A. Harmon.
Dated: 25 April 1879. Test: Mary T. Bryant, George E. Jones, James H.
Robinson. Signed: Sarah E. X Miller

MARY A. BRANDON   4 August 1879
To daughters, Sarah Manda and Nancy Ann - personal property as long as
they are together. Son: William Franklin, decd. Daughter: Elizabeth
Jane Baley - her children, William H. Bailey, Franklin and Dora Bell
Bailey. Executor: James E. Smith, my friend. Dated: 4 June 1879.
Witnesses: James A. Middleton, John S. Hays.
Signed: Mary A. X Brandon

ISAAC D. SMITH   1 September 1879
All to go to his children by his present wife. Executor: Brother -
William D. Smith. Dated: 1 March 1876. Test: John C. Bible, H. D.
Maloney.   Signed: Isaac D. Smith

JOHN E. KIDWELL   1 September 1879
Divide $300 between Katie and Fannie Kidwell - $150 each. Divide $400
between Allis and Eullie Kidwell - $200 each. Elijah Kidwell to have
land and pay others the difference. Witnesses: W. A. Kidwell, J. K.
Harper.

NEWTON HARVEY MASONER   3 November 1879
Wife: Sarah. Grandchild, Ally Ragan Pedagrous Masoner, to share equal
with my children. Executor: Son - T. F. Masoner. Dated: 16 September
1879. Witnesses: William D. Gorman, J. P. Easterly, J. P. X Harris,
Robert X Harris, John I. X Harris.
                       Signed: N. Harvey Masoner

JAMES LAUDERDALE   3 May 1880
To wife, Elizabeth, one year support, 35 acres land adjoining William J.
Lintz during her widowhood, no longer. To my son, Jacob - $75. To my
son, John - $75. To my daughters: Lucinda Huff decd., her heirs - $50;
Martha Howell - $50; Sarah Snider - $50; Isabella Catron - $50; Harriet
Farnes - $50; Elizabeth Greenlee - $65; Mary E. Nease - $65. To grand-
daughter, Ellen Lauderdale - $20. Executor: George Nease. Dated: 10
June 1873. Witnesses: William J. Lintz, L. C. Ottinger.

JESSE PAINTER   3 May 1880
As to debts: Thank God I owe none. To my son, George M. - 80 acres, to
care for me. To my son, Newton - 77 acres. Sons, George M. and Newton,
to pay son, Joseph H. $600 - also to pay daughters: Susannah Broyles and
Sarah Bitner - $200 each. Three grandchildren: Joseph E., Ozy and
Tennessee Margarette Walter? My three sons: Daniel K., William R. and
Ozzy Painter - previously provided for. Dated: 13 January 1872.
Attest: A. F. Broyles, Daniel K. Painter.
                       Signed: Jesse Painter

WILLIAM RADER   3 May 1880
Wife: Barbary. I want a set off against my son, John Rader - he borrowed
$200 of me two years ago and never paid. Five children by first wife,
Anna Cobble: Daniel, William, James and 2 daughters. Andrew Rader,
decd., children to wit: Franklin, Elliott. My son, Henry Rader's heirs:
J. L., Ruben Lafayette M., Mary. My son, Joseph, to have a set off of
$500 less than the others. Son: Matison. Daughter: Sarah Hartman.
Margaret Campbell. Dated: 16 March 1878. Test: D. B. Reed, S. Wampler.
                       Signed: William Rader

ADAM MORROW   7 June 1880
To wife, Margaret - 160 acres on Holleys Creek adjoining J. H. Willia,
McGaughey heirs and David Morrow in District 13, deeded to us by Thomas
Murphey. To my four sons: John, Thomas J., Joseph A. and James W. -
Dobson farm containing 100 acres adjoining David Dobson, David Morrow
and J. R. Lowe, also railroad farm of 113 acres on Greeneville to
Bristol Road adjoining Bonham Ellis and Moore. Daughter: Margaret E.
Morrow. Executors: son - John and Joseph. Dated: 26 May 1880.
Witnesses: John W. Willis, Thomas S. Ranken.
                       Signed: Adam Morrow

JOHN STINE   5 July 1880
Wife, Phebe, to have all her lifetime. To my daughter, Sarah Stine -
$400, 2 head cattle, 4 sheep and to care for Phebe and me. Son, Rufus,
to care for farm and have it at our deat at $10 per acre. To my son,
David Stine, pension note pending in Washington D.C. Son: Christian.
Daughter: Catharine Brown. My eldest daughter: Lydia Casteel, decd.
Executor: son Rufus. Witnesses: George W. Gass, C. G. Johnson.
                       Signed: John X Stine

HARRIET CUMMINGS - now of Greene County
Grandfather, Jackson Hale or Emasharet Hale. My husband, A. B. Cummings,
to care for my infant child, Charles Cummings. Executor: A. B. Cummings.
Dated: 6 April 1860. Witnesses: William Girtner, James V. Anderson.
Signed: Harriet Cummings

MARY A. HALE
My son, Milton, to have everything. My grandson, A. G. Cox of Missouri,
to get one dollar. Executor: Dr. J. P. Casteel. Dated: 28 April 1877.
Attest: John Hawn, Joacim Bible, S. P. Hale.
Signed: Mary A. X Hale

HENRY BRUBAKER
Put a tombstone at my daughter, Sarah's and my graves. My widow to have
one fourth profits of farm. Six sons: Peter, Jacob, John, Jonathan,
Joseph and Henry and the heirs of my daughter, Sarah. Executor: son
Jacob. Dated: 10 April 1880. Witnesses: Robert Smith, George W. Fenk,
James K. P. Saler. Signed: Henry Brubaker

FELIX W. WELLS
Wife: Anne C. Wells. Sons: Samuel H. and William C. S. Wells - to have
everything at our deaths and to pay to other heirs. Sons: George H.,
Gustavus B., and daughter, Mrs. Mary M. V. Lee - $200 each. Son, Morris
H. Wells - $300. Daughter, Mariah B. Agnew - in independant cercum-
stances, wants her part to go to her brothers and sisters. Executors:
Samuel H. and William C. S. Wells. Dated: 21 August 1871. Witnesses:
William Hawkins, John E. Carter, Edward G. Page.
Signed: Felix W. Wells

JAMES GASS - of James
To wife, Mary E. Gass - $1. Brother: Thomas. To brother, Caswell V. -
$5 and a sarle (Sorrel) filly. Adamay Anderson. Two sisters: Mrs.
Rebecca Mercer, Miss Nancy Gass. Dated: 8 May 1880. Witnesses: C. V.
Harmon, Rufus Lucky. Signed: James Gass

JAMES GRAHAM   2 August 1880
To wife, Margaret, everything her lifetime, then to be divided equally
between my legal heirs. Executor: J. D. Brown. Dated: 25 June 1880.
Test: Peter Luster, William Brown. Signed: James X Graham

THOMAS N. BROOKS
Pay my honest debts by selling land. Widow and minor orphans. Nancy
Josephine wife of Fox Stephens, Charly Francis, Michael Henry, Sarah
Louisa, Emma Florence, Joseph Newton, Martha Carolina, Susah Elizabeth,
Frances Elen, Laura Allice and Margaret Sophiah. Executor: S. K. Brooks.
Dated: 11 June 1880. Test: B. F. Harrison, N. A. Harrison.
Signed: Thomas N. Brooks
Executor to pay $600 due Conrad Girdner to secure note to A. J. Harmon.

POLLY A. HARMON
Father, John Gass, to put tombstones (worth $50) at mine and my husband's
graves. I gave to Robert Harmon - property. Executor: my father John
Gass. Witnesses: William McAmis, J. C. McAmis.
Signed: Polly A. X Harmon

MARY J. SHAW
To my husband, S. W. Shaw - land in 1st District adjoining John Pierce,
John Wilhoit, Isaac Earnest and others, Entry made by James Jennings,
No. 2689, February 22, 1848 adjoining Williamson. Executor: husband -
Solomon W. Shaw. Dated: 12 August 1878. Attest: Granville Rader,
Thomas A. Shaw. Signed: Mary J. Shaw

ELIJAH PRUIT (PRUITT)
Wife: Anna. I gave daughter, Barbara Ailshie - 400 acres. Son, Fountain
Pruett, to stay on with Anna and get land. Son, Thomas Pruett, 550 acres

land (Debusk Land). To daughter, Theny Forby - 110 acres. To daughter, Susan Jane - many things and great expense. Dated: 22 May 1880. Test: Jefferson Davis, D. B. Reed.   Signed: Elijah Pruit

ADAM NEASE
My three sons: Adam Jr., Reuben and Thomas F. Nease - to have home farm. My sons: John H. and Andrew Nease - to have Renner Farm. My five daughters: Sarah, Regina, Catharine Nease, Mary wife of Eli Rader, Barbara wife of Joseph Rader - $240 each. Dated: 31 October 1868. Test: Andrew Rader, Henry Nease, Pall Nease.   Signed: Adam Nease

JOSEPH A. FOSTER   7 March 1881
All children go together and pay out what I owe J. C. Hankins on land I now live on. Wife: Marian Foster. To my son, Joseph A. - 20 bushels sowing wheat of John Gass and a Oliver Chill Patter Plow. Son: Andrew J. Foster. Daughter: Mary Foster. Mill to be repaired. Executors: Joseph A. Junr. and Harrison Foster. Dated: 23 December 1880. Test: G. W. Gass, Mary A. Gass.   Signed: Joseph A. Foster

JENNIE B. GASS   4 April 1881
Land to step-father, William Gass. Dated: 20 November 1880. Test: John Kidwell, Cornelius H. Gass.   Signed: Jennie B. Gass

POLLY DUNCAN   4 April 1881
To Alfred Duncan, a man of color, my plantation called Boo Place, a place Joseph Duncan, decd., purchased of William Dodd and all personal property for supporting me. Executors: William Ford, Jacob Crabtree. Dated: 21 October 1869. Witnesses: David W. Bright, John F. White.
                    Signed: Polly X Duncan

JESSE ROBERTSON   4 April 1881
To my grandson, Archibald B. Baxter - 100 acres. To my grandson, F. T. Baxter - 185 acres. To my two grand-daughters, Ellen and Dialtha Robertson - $300 when they come of age. My heirs: Deborah J. White, John C. Robertson, Joseph Robertson - having heretofore been provided for. Executor: John Crawford Robertson. Dated: 10 March 1881. Witnesses: James Collier, William A. Horton.   Signed: J. Robertson

SAMUEL P. STANFIELD   1 August 1881
To wife, Elizabeth Lavenia, everything her lifetime - then to go to my son, Charles G. Stanfield. Executrix: wife Elizabeth Lavenia Stanfield. Dated: 10 March 1881. Witnesses: Eli Marshall, James B. Grant.
                    Signed: Samuel P. Stanfield

JANE M. BROWN   1 August 1881
To my three children, W. C., F. T. and Laura E. Brown - all my personal property. Emma Wagner. Dated: 10 May 1881. Witnesses: D. M. Dobson, T. W. McAmis.   Signed: Jane M. X Brown

THOMAS HUGHES   5 September 1881
To my brothers and sisters, Aaron, Frances, Abraham and Phebe Hughes - all property and all money in hand and out of hand to do as they please with. Executor: Abraham Hughes. Dated: 5 March 1875. Witnesses: S. D. Winters, Enoch Hopton.   Signed: Thomas Hughes

JESSE HOLT   5 September 1881
To my wife, Elizabeth Holt, all real and personal estate her widowhood, but if she should squander it Executors see to it, stop it. All my heirs: Jacob, Margaret wife of Andrew Nease, Nancy wife of John N. Nease, James decd., Sary An wife of Joseph Blaser, Maryan wife of Andrew Peters, Catharine wife of Joseph Nease, Emaline wife of Leonidas Bowers, James H. Holt. Executors: Sanalaws? - Leonidas Bowers and Andrew Peters. Dated: 27 June 1881. Witnesses: Thomas Nease, Isaac F. Rader.
                    Signed: Jesse X Holt

BENJAMIN F. GREGORY   5 December 1881
To my wife, Catharine, all my effects as long as she remains my widow.
If they wish to emigrate, sell land to buy more land and pay traveling
expenses. Seven Children: John B., James M., Martha L., Alexander C.,
Andrew N., Sarah C. and Mary J. Gregory. Executor: S. K. Brooks.
Dated: 6 September 1881. Witnesses: Isaac Seaton, A. C. Gregory and
Michael L. Girdner.   Signed: Benjamin F. Gregory

SAMUEL McNEESE   5 December 1881
To my sons, Elihu and Jacob - 180 acres land where I now live in District
20. To my grandchildren, heirs of Sam Henry McNeese, decd. - $50. To my
daughter, Eliza Jane Holland, widow of William Holland - note on her late
husband payable to Sarah McNeese from whom I acquire the same by inheri-
tance. Daughter: Nancy Ann Thompson. Two wind mills and cider mill and
corn mill to son, Elihu. Executor: Son - Elihu. Dated: 3 May 1881.
Witnesses: Jeremiah Downy, John A. Downy.
                              Signed: Samuel X McNeese

WILLIAM C. MALONEY   20 January 1882
Wife: Louisa. Children: John A., Nannie, H. D. Land on Warrensburg Road
purchased from Hale adjoining David Bible, H. D. Maloney, J. C. Ayers,
upper island in river. To my grandson, Willie Johnson - land in Cocke
County on south side of river adjoining Scruggs, Bear Creek, McMillan.
Iron railings to be placed around graves on the hill and graves near
house of my children. Pay J. B. Johnson $300 on account of Willie
Johnson. Surveying instruments to sons Hugh and John. Executors: John
A., H. D. Maloney - sons. Dated: 9 December 1881. Witnesses: Samuel O.
Ayers, R. M. Easterly.
                              Signed: W. C. Maloney
Codicil - my one half of Bewley Farm to H. D. Maloney. Land to my
daughter Nannie Herring. Send Willie Johnson to school 2 years maybe
3 years at my expense. Land on top of Birds Hill to go to three farmers
for the purpose of getting limestone rock. Witnesses: J. H. Coulter,
R. M. Easterly, Samuel O. Ayers.

SUSAN FOWLER   6 March 1882
To Margaret and James Hamton and their heirs - land at head of Middle
Creek in Districts 1 and 22. Dated: 1 February 1881. Witnesses: Elbert
M. Reaves, William M. Jennings.   Signed: Susan X Fowler

SAMUEL S. HAWKINS   6 March 1882
To daughter, Sarah wife of Samuel Babb, her son Archibald - $100 now,
$100 at death of daughter, Rachel, deed gift of 100 acres land. Samuel
Babb has left his wife and family - help them as much as possible. To
daughter, Jane wife of James H. Thacker - land by conveyance. To Jane's
daughter, Sarah Frances - $100. To son-in-law, James H. Thacker - $100.
Son, James, if still living, must present himself in the state of
Tennessee and sign receipt for his part of my estate which is $1000.
Daughter, Rachel Hawkins - not capable of managing for herself, others
to assist her. Polly Ann Davis and Jane Thacker to council with Rachel.
To grand-daughter, Margaret, daughter of Jacob Hawkins - $300. To my
grandsons, Samuel D., John N., James H. and Charles S. Thacker, sons of
my daughter Jane and J. H. Thacker - $900. Land on Raccoon Branch
adjoining Samuel Davis. Executor: Charles A. Bright. Dated: 15 August
1881. Test: S. B. Davis, O. M. Kilday, Jacob Bright, G. T. Weems, S. A.
Starnes.   Signed: Samuel S. Hawkins

GEORGE B. SIMPSON   4 April 1882
To my wife and daughter, Mary Simpson - Simpson farm adjoining Ham Shoun,
John Crawford, Alen Beals et al. Note on son, John, to be delivered to
him when he pays my debt. My heirs. Executor: Thomas I. Doyle. Dated:
3 April 1880. Witnesses: Jeremiah T. C. McCaleb, W. A. Beals.
                              Signed: George B. X Simpson

WILLIAM BRANNON   3 April 1882
Wife: Catharine, which was Catharine Wykle. Dated: 7 April 1880. Test:
Alfred Susong, John Brannon.   Signed: William X Brannon

T. J. MORROW
To wife, Eliza J. Morrow, all property including land in Boone County,
Missouri (40 acres). Executrix: Wife - Eliza. Dated: 27 March 1882.
Test: William S. McGaughey, David Morrow.
Signed: T. J. Morrow

MARY M. WHITEHURST
Thomas W. Whitehurst, Wellington W. Whitehurst and Mariny to have home-
stead. Lou E. Ricker wife of Daniel Ricker and India J. Waddle wife of
J. F. Waddle - to have money for land to purchase shares. Executors:
Thomas W. Whitehurst, John F. Waddle. Dated: 20 March 1882. Test: F.
K. Ricker, Eliza X Ricker. Signed: Mary M. Whitehurst

CONRAD GIRDNER   5 June 1882
Eight children or heirs to share equal. Executor: William R. Gibbs.
Dated: 19 April 1873. Test: Charles Jones, Jacob Cutshall.
Signed: Conrad Girdner

NANCY A. BRANDON   5 June 1882
To friend, James A. Middleton, all personal property, meat of 1 hog, 11
bushels wheat and $200 willed me by my mother, Mary A. Brandon decd.
Brother: William F. Brandon. To brother-in-law, George W. Baily - $1.50.
Executor: Cornelius Mays. Dated: 16 January 1882. Witnesses: Noah
Bishop, John Crawford. Signed: Nancy A. Brandon

SPARLING BOWMAN   4 September 1882
District No. 22. Wife, Catharine, to have all lands etc. as long as she
remains my widow. Six youngest children: Mary Seton, Martha Jennings -
each 15 acres including Cooly Farm, remainder to daughters, Sarah Jane
Jones, Elizabeth Bitner, Selma Bowman and son, Thomas J. Bowman. Executor: S. H. Price - if he cant, I choose David Parman. Dated: 21 July
1882. Test: John W. Ruble, Hiram H. Ruble.
Signed: Sparling Bowman

VIOLET DIXON   September Term 1882
Husband, Simon Dixon, to have my property - at his death to go to grand-
children, Florence Linn, Walter Linn. One acre to John Jones, step-son
of Isaac Barnett, a boy I partly raised. Executor: Samuel Babb. Dated:
16 August 1882. Witnesses: John Kidwell, Samuel Babb.
Signed: Violet Dixon

MARY M. CARTER   October Term 1882
To Mary B. Bowman and her heirs - all my farm (40 acres) 24 District
adjoining Cooter, A. C. Gregory, Johnson farm, John Cooter. To my
brother, Nathan Smith - $400 coming to me through Joel Stryner, also
my desk, sausage grinder, fire shovel and family Bible. Executor:
John Gray. Dated: 20 June 1882. Witnesses: S. K. Brooks, L. D.
Johnson. Signed: Mary M. X Carter

ESTHER PETERS
To my son, John, all household property, my windmill and large copper
kettle, 2 cows and interest in my cane mill for taking care of me.
Executor: A. L. Maupen. Dated: 19 November 1881. Test: L. A. Ford,
T. J. Humphreys. Signed: Esther X Peters

A. P. CAMPBELL (ADAM P.)   6 November 1882
To my wife, Margaret L., land - at her death to son, Lemy P., provided
he stays with his mother and takes care of her. Land in 16 District
north side of Lick Creek adjoining William Jones, Jacob H. Campbell,
Joseph Ervin, Nancy A. McLain. Other land of 10 acres to my older
heirs who are of age. Executor: Jacob H. Campbell, son. Dated: 24
October 1882. Test: David Forrester, Isaac Crawford.
Signed: A. P. Campbell

130

NANCY SHANKS   10 October 1882

Nancy Shanks died 24 September 1882. Will all things to Mary Crawford for taking care of me, it will not pay her for her truble. Darkis Hunt and W. K. Seer heard the decest make the statement. Test: B. F. Whinery.

Signed: Darkis X Hunt

W. K. Speer

JOHN J. BROYLES   4 December 1882

Son, Nelson S. Broyles - to lease farm and pay us one fourth. To my wife, Elizabeth, 100 acres Greene County, 45 acres in Washington County, 75 acres adjoining Grays. Children: Clary M. Seaton; children of deceased daughter, Mariah S. Hoyle - John J., Windfield S., Mariah P. and Grace C. Hoyle; Nelson S. Broyles; Martha E. Click; deceased son Ephraim B. Broyles, his daughter Kissiah E. Bitner; King H. Broyles and Anderson S. Broyles. Martha E. Click to pay rest of note signed by Samuel Click. Mariah Hoyle's heirs - note signed by Michael Hoyle. Executor: son Nelson S. Broyles. Dated: 24 August 1872. Test: S. A. Broyles, A. S. Johnson.

Signed: John J. Broyles

CHARLES GASS   January Term 1883

To be buried by wife in graveyard at Harmon's - present wife to be buried same row if she desires - tombstones to be placed at our graves. To wife, Elizabeth, the property I got with her, one half bed clothing she has made since we married, $100 and 1 years support. To Rufus Lucky - 80 acre Reynolds plantation. Land I bought of Clement Reynolds and James Harmon (of Bingman Harmon) - to John Gass. Gass girls: Nancy and Rebecca. Executor: Rufus Lucky. Test: A. Gray, Mordecai L. Harmon.

Signed: Charles Gass

Codicil - Five heirs: James, Nancy, Rebecca, Thomas, Caswell Gass lawful heirs of James Gass, decd. 27 February 1877.

SOLOMON GOOD   March Term 1883

Wife, Anna, to have her pick of my personal property. My daughter, Manerva, to have her support from my farm (200 acres) provided by son, Joseph and daughter, Julia Good. To my daughter, Margaret Dobson, farm in Hamblin County. To William Good - $300 in personal property. Mary Price, Nathan Good, Battie Simson and Jacob Good have their part. David remaining between all my heirs except the heirs of my daughter, Mary Price. Executors: My sons - Nathan and Joseph Good. Dated: 28 February 1882. Test: N. M. Good, J. H. Good, John A. Senaker.

Signed: Solomon Good

THOMAS SHAW   March Term 1883

Wife: Elinder. My three sons, S. M., Solomon Y. and John P. Shaw to have all my land by each paying Elinder $43 and to pay son, Thomas G., $20 at my wife's death. Executor: John P. Shaw. Dated: 2 December 1882. Witnesses: G. S. Sentell, J. S. J. Wilhoit.

Signed: Thomas A. X Shaw

ELIZABETH VESTAL

Daughter: Laura Vestal. Sister: Mary Vestal wife of C. M. Vestal - land I bought with money from my father's estate in Districts 8 and 12 adjoining heirs of John Rhea. Division of money to include Martha L. Anderson and James Anderson. Son, James Vestal, went west 15 years ago, if he returns he is to get $20. Executor: C. M. Vestal. Dated: 14 July 1882. Witnesses: R. L. Dobson, Frank Mercer.

Signed: Elizabeth X Vestal

SARAH MARTIN   April Term 1883

To my nieces now living with me: Mary A. B. Blanton and Nancy L. Blanton, if they care for me - land bought by W. E. Blanton and myself of William Guthrie - if they do not stay and care for me, their part is no longer binding. Dated: 20 August 1881. Witnesses: H. R. Jones, G. T. Pope, J. C. Hill.

Signed: Sarah X Martin

JOSEPH RENNER   May Term 1883
Wife, Elizabeth, to have full control of everything and get 100 bushels
corn, 50 bushels wheat, one half meadow hay - at her death everything to
be advertized and sold.   All my legitimate heirs. Executor: son Andrew.
Dated: 7 February 1880. Test: Andrew Freshour, P. G. Humphreys.
                              Signed: Joseph X Renner

NANCY CRAIG   May Term 1883
My niece, Louisa Craig, daughter of John Craig, to receive everything
after debts are paid, all my silverware, Queens ware, glass and china
ware, jewelry and clothing. Executor: J. R. C. Parks. Dated: 16
August 1879. Witnesses: Henry G. Wells, Charles W. Wells, M. E.
Temple.   Signed: Nancy Craig

A. W. WALKER   May Term 1883
To be buried by my wife, Lizzie, who lies in Old Graveyard in Greeneville
in the rear of V. S. Maloney's enclosure. To wife, Elen C. Walker - 100
acres property adjoining P. G. Rosenblatt, C. L. Sevier, Fred Starns, Ed
Turner, A. N. Pettibone, widow John Brown and L. W. Tipton. Five children to share and share alike. Wife, Elen, sale executor. Dated: April
4, 1883. Test: W. C. Welles, A. N. Shoun.
                              Signed: A. W. Walker

JAMES A. P. WEEMS   June Term 1883
To my two children, Laura Taylor and Patton Click - all my estate when
they arrive at age 21. My brother, Thomas N. Weems, store burned at
Rheatown - to have use of my Shaw tract. Executor: William J. Weems.
Test: James Luster, James H. Morrison.
                              Signed: J. A. P. Weems

WILLIAM BROWN
To daughter, Rutha Emily Grant - all my personal property now in her
possession, $100 in railroad stock and 196 acres land adjoining G. H.
Shoun. To daughter, Lasandra Jane Brown - personal property and $400
and one half interest in 228 acres. To daughter, Rachel H. Brown -
$220 in Railroad Stock, other half of 196 acre farm. Executor: Eli
Marshall. Dated: 7 October 1880. Witnesses: Clay Shoun and George
H. Shoun of Rheatown.   Signed: William Brown

RACHEL DAVIS
Mary T. Hayes account to be paid. One half rest to go to William C.
Fraker, other half to be equally divided between the heirs of John Hays
wife Elizabeth J. Hays. Executor: J. H. Crawford. Dated: 29 June 1883.
Test: J. R. Collens, Alfred Justice.

MARY J. FELLERS   Non Cupative
Her father, James G. Fellers to have everything. Dated: 2 July 1883.
                              Signed: F. E. Painter
                                      Jasper N. Price

VASTA ETTER   August Term 1883
To daughter, Lavinia E. Etter, to have 64 acres land where house is with
spring and garden. To son, Franklin Etter, 30 acres, pay debts and pay
son, George Etter, $320. To daughter, Martha C. Haun - one sixth. To
daughter, Sarah C. Trobaugh - one sixth. To daughter, Mary J. Bible -
one sixth of land. Franklin Etter to be guardian to daughter, Lavinia
E. Etter, and if he is kind to her he gets her property at her death.
Executor: Franklin Etter. Dated: 11 June 1883. Witnesses: William
Bible, N. W. Bible.   Signed: Vasta X Etter

SOLOMON MILLER   August Term 1883
Wife, Sarah, to pay debts and have everything her lifetime. Children:
M. F. Miller, J. A. Miller, L. N. Miller and Almeda L. Miller - to share
equally at Sarah's death. Executors: M. F. and L. N. Miller. Dated: 26
June 1882. Witnesses: William C. Miller, Robert Million.
                              Signed: Solomon Miller

PETER OTTINGER   September Term 1883
To sons, William and Calvin - land valued at $6 and $10 per acre adjoining William Huff and C. Smelcer. William also to receive $124. To
daughter, Catharine Inman - $50. To daughter, Martha Lauderdale - side
saddle and a cow. To daughter, Mary Winters - bay horse, side saddle,
$25 and $16 for waiting on me. To son, Morgan Ottinger - $95. To son,
Isaac Ottinger - $124. I gave my son, Marshall, $80 when he went west.
To grand-daughter, Margaret Faubion now Smelser - one side saddle. To
grand-daughter, Ellen Lauderdale now Ellen Scott - $70 in place of a
horse. Grandsons: Clark Winters, Edward Winters, Hidemount Winters.
Executors: son Calvin Ottinger, son-in-law Shade Inman. Dated: 30 July
1883. Witnesses: Abraham Rader, John A. Ottinger.
                         Signed: Peter X Ottinger

HOWEL THOMASON   September Term 1883
To wife, Rebecca, beds, furniture etc., all the property she brought here
with her. To Nora Proctor, my wife's grandchild - $70 to buy a horse
when she is 13. Our property to be sold and the money put on interest
for my wife's use - money not to be used by Matthew Simmons and his wife,
Laura, for themselves. Executor: James H. Brown. Dated: 13 August 1883.
Witnesses: John Crumly, Abram Crumly.
                         Signed: Howel Thomason

JAMES JUSTICE   1883
My wife to have all the water power, the rase not to be interfered with,
one half mills, machinery, threshing maching and one half bees and hogs,
other half to pay my debts. To B. B. Broites - one sawmill. Executor:
William Jennings Esqr. Dated: 17 July 1883. Test: B. P. Snapp, Isaac
R. Tignor, William Jennings.   Signed: James Justice

STEPHEN WADDLE   1883
To Charley D. Waddle - sorrel mare, wagon, harness and turning plow. To
Nancy Ann Waddle - 1 heifer. Executor: S. D. Waddle. Dated: 19 July
1883. Witnesses: G. S. Sentell, S. D. Waddle.
                         Signed: Stephen Waddle

WILLIAM GUTHRIE   July 12, 1883
To son, M. L. Guthrie - $75. To daughter, Martha Knight - $25. To
daughter, Nancy Dykes - $25. To daughter, Miriam Crocker - $75. To
daughter, Adaline Blanton - $50. To daughter, Lucinda Casteel - $50.
All to be paid 5 years after my death. Niece: Mahala Jones. To son,
William Thomas Guthrie - all personal property for taking care of us.
Wife: Clementine. Executors: D. R. Gass Esq., son W. T. Guthrie.
Test: C. L. Pope, J. T. Pope.   Signed: William Guthrie

AARON HUGHES   November Term 1883
To my brother, Abraham - all real and personal and mixed property and all
money. Executor: L. W. Smithson. Dated: 21 August 1882. Witnesses:
James Jones, James Hawes.   Signed: Aaron X Hughes

JOSEPH NEWBERRY   November Term 1883
Administrator, son Isaac N. Newberry, to care for wife, Elizabeth, and
at her death is to receive land and property. Dated: 5 October 1883.
Test: M. P. Hampton.   Signed: Joseph Newberry

JEREMIAH McMILLON
To wife, Hiley, all property her natural life then to whoever she may
direct. Dated: November 21, 1883. Witnesses: A. M. Cash, Peter Myers,
D. R. Gass.   Signed: Jeremiah X McMillon

SAMUEL WHITE   29 October 1883
Wife: Nancy Ann. Executor: T. C. Mercer. Test: Alexander Brown, Phillip
Dunn.   Signed: Samuel X White

JAMES EVANS   January Term 1884
To wife, Mary E. Evans - one fourth. To daughter, Nancy - one fourth of
my estate, $320 and all property Mary brought or bought with her own
money. Property to be divided into 4 equal parts. Four persons to be
my heirs: youngest daughter Nancy E., five grandchildren of my daughter
Angeline J. Dobson: Thomas, William, Eula, Nena Belle and James E.
Dobson - 1 part. Deceased daughter, Margaret P. Allen's 1 child,
Margaret E. Allen - 1 part. Angeline (or Duck) Allen, daughter of my
daughter Florence Allen - 1 part. Grandchildren: Fannie E. Campbell,
Eula M. Campbell and Sarah M. Campbell, children of my deceased daughter
Emily E. Campbell - one fourth my estate. All minor heirs must have
guardians. Executors: William W. Easterly, James Henry. Dated: 28
August 1883. Witnesses: R. Bowers, W. C. D. Hutton.
                          Signed: James Evans

CATHARINE TIMMONS
James Warde and wife Barbary - to have all lands etc. until my youngest
child is 21 for waiting on me and my two children, who are dead - then
to my heirs. Executor: Thomas Neas Senr. Dated: 13 June 1880.
Witnesses: D. L. Woods, Andrew Renner.
                          Signed: Cathrin X Timmons

REBECCA BRUNER
To son, A. F. Hughes - $700, his sons, W. A. Epps and T. Benson - $3
each. To daughter, Nancy V. married to A. C. English, their children:
Archibald A. - $120.66 2/3 cents, James, Rebecca M. - $50, and Nancy V.
English - $25. To son, A. J. Bruner - $280, his daughters, Rebecca E.
and Eliza J. Bruner - $6. To daughter, Mahala married to John H. Craw-
ford - $212.66 2/3 cents. To daughter, Lydia, married to Simon P. West -
$240, her daughter, Rebecca F. West - $5. Daughter, Analya, married to
Jacob White. Executor: A. F. Hughes. Dated: 1 June 1880. Witnesses:
James H. Bolton - Clear Creek, Tenn., N. B. English - Clear Creek, Tenn.
                          Signed: Rebecca Bruner

J. C. LOTSPEICH   Term 1884
To wife, Maggie J. Lotspeich - house and lot where we live. Land in
town of Greeneville south side Irish Street adjoining Joseph Hacker and
heirs of Charles Marsh. Executrix: wife Maggie J. Lotspeich. Dated: 5
December 1883. Test: D. R. Britton, W. A. Allen.
                          Signed: J. C. Lotspeich

GEORGE W. SMITH   1884
To wife, Elizabeth, all real and personal property during her natural
life. Three Daughters: Rebecca, Catharine and Margaret. Executor:
William McAmis. Dated: 13 June 1881. Witnesses: N. B. English, William
McAmis.
                          Signed: George W. X Smith

SARAH M. HANKINS   April Term 1884 at Jeffersonville, Indiana
Sarah M. Hankins late of Clark County, Indiana. To Abram Courtney of
Clarke County, Indiana - all my property and my interest in my brother,
John C. Hankins decd., of Greene County, Tenn. Witnesses: Laurent E.
Douglas, Mattie E. Green, Nannie L. Green, Sarah G. Penney. Dated: 6
March 1884.   Signed: Sarah M. X Hankins

DAVID DEVALT   May Term 1884
To son, Frederick - $1200. To son, John - 92 acres. To daughter, Sarah
R. Hannah - $820. To daughter, Louisa V. Easterly - $820. To daughter,
Mary Devalt - $700 beside her equal part for caring for her mother and
me. Executor: J. P. Easterly. Dated: 15 April 1884. Witnesses:
Bernard Cooter, Charles Cooter. Signed: David Devalt

MATTHEW COX   May Term 1884
To wife, Nancy, land and personal property. To son, Elisha Cox - farm
on Roaring Fork adjoining Patton Brumley, J. A. Armitage and Duff
Anderson. To daughter, Adaline Cox - land adjoining James Anderson,
house at wife Nancy's death. To daughter, Margaret Myers - part of home

farm on Roaring Fork. To daughter, Nancy A. Swatzell - land. To Eli
Ensor who lives with me - $25 when he is 21. Executor: John Harden.
Dated: 29 March 1884. Test: J..A. Harmon, James C. Park.
Signed: M. Cox

JOHN SQUIBB   May Term 1884
To wife, Lydia, entire homestead, farm and personal property her natural
life - at her death to my youngest son, Charles F. Squibb. To my invalid
daughter, Sallie - $500. At the death of my wife send Sallie to daughter
Martha Keckley, now in Washington Territory. Sons: Joseph M., James Foy
and Caleb Alexander - notes I hold on them. To son, John Wesley - $100.
Two grand-daughters: Virgie and Carletta Ellis - $50 each. Executor:
Eli Marshall. Dated: 24 November 1883. Witnesses: E. S. Ripley, Eli
Marshall.   Signed: John Squibb

GEORGE M. GASS   May Term 1884   District 11 - on Lick Creek
Wife: Martha Emaline. Youngest son: Joseph Elliott Gass. Executor:
George H. Gass. Dated: 21 April 1882. Test: Jacob Smith, George E.
Kenney.   Signed: George M. Gass

THOMAS LANE   June Court 1884
Wife, R. D. Lane - to reside with Elizabeth Snapp, my daughter, for
board of my daughter and her family for 6 years - after 6 years Elizabeth
is to receive $100 per annum. Children: Elizabeth Snapp, Alexander A.
Lane decd., Kate Jones, Eliza Marsh, Thomas J. Lane, William F. Lane,
Robert J. Lane, heirs of Alexander A. Lane decd.: Edgar, Wendell, Willie
and Andrew Lane. I have advanced sums to my children. Collect interest
on my U.S. Bonds and use for support of my widow. Property consists of
farm at Tusculum, property near railroad, Tanyard and store Wilhoit
Stand on Buckingham Road. Executors: Sons - Thomas J., William F. and
Robert J. Lane. Witnesses: A. N. Shoun, James C. Parks.
Signed: Thomas Lane

JOHN W. MATHES   August Term 1884
Wife, E. J. C. Mathes, to have land, notes and bonds to support our
children. Two thousand dollar note on W. J. Haney for Mill property.
I owe my father, E. Smith Mathes, $800. Purchase money for Mill Property
to be paid. Pay my wife for her money which I have used. Executrix:
wife. Dated: 16 June 1884. Witnesses: Z. S. Mathes, E. Smith Mathes.
Signed: John W. Mathes

JAMES H. DINWIDDIE
My son, John C., left home at age 16 to learn a trade - to receive $100.
My son, James M., to maintain his parents in a decent mannor and pay
son, Jacob W., and daughters, Ann, Amanda M. and Margaret Ann - $200
each. To Calvin's boys - $50 each. To Elizabeth Jane Sheffey's child-
ren: Amanda, Mary, Andrew J. and James - $50 each. Executor: son Jacob
W. Witnesses: S. A. Armstrong, A. C. Fraker.
Signed: James N. Dinwiddie

REBECCA WHITE
To my grandson, Jacob White, who lives with me - wagon, gearing etc. To
my son, John White - a horse wagon and windmill. To grand-daughter, Mary
Catharine Gass - small spinning wheel. To daughter, Ibby Gass - one loom.
To grand-daughter, Hily Gass - bedstead. Executor: A. J. Frazer. Dated:
6 March 1880. Test: A. J. Frazier, James N. Brown.
Signed: Rebecca X White

POLLY ANN CLIFFORD
One dollar each to my children: Mitchell Clifford, Sarah wife of John
Wisecarver, Esh Rebecca wife of Elias House. Other children: Martha A.
wife of Millard Lemons, Julia wife of J. D. Haun. Youngest daughter,
C. C. C. Clifford, has taken good care of me. Executor: R. A. Keicher.
Dated: 4 August 1884. Witnesses: James N. Swatzel, J. L. Newman.
Signed: Polly Ann X Clifford

RACHEL GALION
To my grandson, Houston Monro Galion - bedstead and clothing. To my son, John R. Lowe - all the remainder of my property and money. Dated: 28 February 1880. Witnesses: John H. Willis, James Jones.
Signed: Rachel X Galion

JOHN A. MASON   8 August 1884
To wife, Elizabeth Gass Mason - all property. My brother, George Mason, to have a home with my wife and son, David, provided he helps keep up the place. Executor: son Robert Mason. Witnesses: James C. Park, J. W. Willis.
Signed: John A. Mason

RUSSELL B. CARTER
To wife, Mary, 26 acres in District 13 adjoining John Moore, John Morrow and others. Dated: 7 July 1884. Witnesses: Cyntha Graham, Thomas X Yeakly.
Signed: R. B. Carter

MAHALY RUSTIN
My interest in my brother, Thomas Pierce decd., estate, who lived and dide in Washington Territory - collect and divide between my nephew, John C. Price, and niece, Lurinda J. Moore, for taking care of me. Executor: E. M. Moore. Dated: 3 July 1884. Test: Henry Dryman, E. M. Moore.
Signed: Mahaly X Rustin

GEORGE BUCHANAN
Wife, Adaline, and I to be supported. To son, John Buchanan, 55 acres on Gap Creek and all personal property at his mother's death. To son, George Buchanan, horse when he is 21. Three girls to be supported by John. Dated: 7 April 1884. Witnesses: Felix Buchanan, M. M. Couch, J. H. Eakens.
Signed: George Buchanan

ROBERT B. WINSLOW - near Rheatown
To my daughters, Julia and Eliza - my 80 acre farm for serving us so faithfully in our old age. Other children: Sarah McCoy, G. A. Winslow, S. B. Winslow and Mary A. Bonner - have already been helped by me. Dated: 31 July 1884. Test: William Obaugh, Philip A. Doyle.
Signed: Robert B. Winslow

GEORGE W. GASS
To wife, Mary An Gass, all real and personal estate her lifetime to use and control as she pleases. Wife not to waist estate, if she does waist estate she is to be called into Court and make a full inventory. Children: John M., Marian Wilburn Gass, Laury Catharine, William H., Sarah N., Mary Jane and Emey Elsey Gass - all to receive an equal share. Executrix: wife Mary An. Dated: 30 January 1883. Test: James D. Brown, Elijah Kidwell.
Signed: G. W. Gass

JOHN S. REED
To wife, Elizabeth A. Reed - entire control of my whole estate until my children come of age, then there is to be an equal division, my wife getting a childs part. Children: Mary E., William M., John F., Charley S., Ethel and Thomas Stewart Reed. Executor: George A. Baily. Dated: 15 November 1884. Test: A. J. Bruner, W. L. Jeffers.
Signed: J. S. Reed

ELIZA ANN BULLEN
Husband, Loyd Bullen, getting old and too feeble to provide for himself - to have my estate but not to use it to pay his debts. On his death to go to my children, Martha J. and George Bullen. If George's wife, Rebecca, outlives him, it is to be hers. Elizabeth An Rose decd., her children, Loyd M., John R., Mary An and Jeff D., Laura J., their father James H. Rose not to have any control. Executor: C. G. Rankin. Dated: 28 September 1882. Test: J. M. Rhea, John Clem.
Signed: Eliza Ann Bullen
Codicil - Daughter, Martha, married John Ross. My bounty is intended for

my children alone. If any heir should question this will, their right is
forfeited. Dated: 22 July 1884. Test: James C. Robinson, Ellen Robinson.

MARY ANN MALONE (Verbally)
In presence of James G. Alexander and James Gass, witnesses. Place my
body in plain cheap cloths and place me in a cheap coffin (home made).
My nephew, Lafayette P. Easterly, to have money in his possession and
amount due me in Aunt Sallie Miller's estate.

JAMES B. BROWN   August Term 1885
Of the city of Roane, Floyd County, Georgia. To son, Albert Leroy - gold
watch and chain. To my wife, Clamantha Jane - all property her lifetime.
Executor: Dr. E. B. Smith. Dated: 22 June 1885. Witnesses: J. R. Brown,
F. J. Brown.   Signed: James B. Brown

SARAH ANN COOPER   Verbal Will
Widow of Daniel C. Cooper - died April 15, 1885. Said on her death bed,
"I want Lizzie to have it all," when asked about her property. Witnesses:
Louis Kiser, H. S. Borden.

HENRY P. DEAN
Wife, Susannah, to be supported. Son, Hiram, gets all at wife's decease.
Grandson, Henry D., to remain on farm. All my children to receive one
dollar each. Executor: son Hiram. Dated: 4 April 1884. Test: Edward
Walker, E. B. Couch.   Signed: Henry X Dean

PETER HARMON
Sell at public outcry enough to pay debts. Land on Lick Creek to be
divided between my five children: 1. Rachel Everhart decd., to her children; 2. Elizabeth Simpson decd., to her children; 3. Eliza Everhart;
4. Harriet Carter; 5. William A. Harmon, my son. To my eldest son,
Isaac A. Harmon - 30 acres. To my third son, Peter M. Harmon - land.
To daughter, Emma Simpson - 53 acres. To daughter, Margaret Jones - 20
acres land on Big Ridge. To my youngest daughter, Nancy K. Harmon - 50
acres where I now live. Executor: son Isaac A. Harmon of Hamblin County,
Tennessee. Dated: 4 April 1885. Test: William A. Harmon, F. D. B.
Harmon.   Signed: Peter Harmon
                                           of Isaac

CHARLES HAWKINS
To wife, Elizabeth, 170 acre home place I bought of Thomas Bailey Senr.
At her death to go to son, George A., if he takes care of her. Sons:
Jesse, John and William - these three sons get my other lands, but can
use timber on Old Home tract for rails and firewood. Eldest son: James.
Executor: George A. Bailey. Dated: 7 March 1885. Test: R. K. Bailey,
Jacob Linebough.   Signed: Charles X Hawkins

FRANCES WILLIS
All my property to my daughter, Martha Harold, wife of William C. Harrold.
Executor: son James H. Willis. Dated: __ October 1884. Test: W. R.
Harris, J. F. Love.   Signed: Frances X Willis

SUSANNAH MARGARET STANLEY - Independence County, Arkansas
To Francis M. Dodd - all I have it he takes care of me while I live.
Dated: 19 January 1885. Attest: J. I. Jackson, William Crumley, James
Gambill.   Signed: Susannah Margaret Stanley

MARY ANN BUTLER
Husband, James N. S. Butler - to control and maintain my farm and give
my grand-daughter, Margaret L. Smelcer, a home during her natural life.
After husband's death, farm to be divided between my son, John L. Butler,
and my daughter, Margaret J. Cloyd. E. C. Cloyd, farm renter, to remain
if he wants to. Timber not to be wasted. Executor: G. M. Smith. Dated:
10 February 1886. Attest: G. M. Smith, A. J. Leonard.
                                Signed: Mary Ann Butler

JAMES LOTSPEICH   May Term 1886
To wife, Elizabeth, $500 out of my estate, note on W. W. Easterly for
$300, another for $500 and money on hand. Balance to be divided to
heirs. Executor: son A. W. Lotspeich Senr. Dated: 6 May 1884. Attest:
William Bible, Charles Jackson.   Signed: James Lotspeich

ELLIOTT H. RUTHERFORD   May Term 1886
To wife, Mary - 18 acres land on Big Gap Creek, which belonged to my
mother, Elinor Rutherford, I bought of heirs namely: Farmer Williams and
wife Mary, William Price and wife Nancy, P. M. Kirkpatrick and wife
Harriet, Jonathan Brubaker and wife Margaret, heirs of Benjamin Carter
and wife Eliza and heirs of John Rutherford and wife Sarah - Carter Heirs.
To Alice Dodson of Hawkins County, daughter of Patsy Ann Dotson, formerly
Ward - Alice Dodson being a child Emily Kirkpatrick is raising, the late
wife of Carn Kirkpatrick, formerly Emily Kenow the wife and widow of
Thomas Kenow of Hawkins County, a daughter of William Sharp decd.
(William Sharp, Revolutionary Soldier. G.F.B.) Executor: Edward Dodd.
Test: Samuel N. Crozier, David F. Park.
                         Signed: Elliott H. Rutherford

ELENDER GASS
To my father, John Gass, who took care of me in sickness and health - all
entries I have in $1250 that my grandfather Hardin willed to his dater
Clarissa Gass. Dated: 17 March 1886. Test: R. C. Harmon, John Harden.
                         Signed: Elender X Gass

JOHN ALEXANDER
To my sons, S. K. and R. B. - farm where I live divided as Mill Tract and
Farm Tract and each son to pay to: son John F. - $200, daughter Lydia M.
Dodd - $200, daughter Elizabeth Jones - $200 and daughter Minnie B.
Oliphant - $200. Executors: son S. K. and son Robert M. Alexander.
Dated: 10 September 1885. Test: Thomas Alexander, D. D. Alexander.
                         Signed: John Alexander

MARTHA HUNTER
To my two neices, daughters of James H. Fox: Ida M. and Jennie E. Fox -
$100 each in gold. To my sisters: Sarah J. and Mary R. Fox - all the
balance of my property. Executrix: sister Sarah Jane Fox. Dated: 1
April 1886. Test: M. J. Fellers, James A. Fox.
                         Signed: Martha X Hunter

JESSE REYNOLDS
Brother, Joshua Reynolds, Executor of Estate - to take money and interest
in land, to get all - then at his death to go to Joshua Benjamin Reynolds
never to be sold as long as these two live. At Joshua Benjamin Reynold's
death, to go to his nearest heir. Dated: 20 May 1886. Test: J. D. Brown,
J. B. Gass.   Signed: Jesse Reynolds

WILLIAM MYERS
To my son, S. F. Myers - 84 acre farm in 8th District. To my son,
Alexander - $400 and household furniture, pay his $100 debt out of the
$400. My watch which belonged to my deceased son, Robert, to S. F. Myers
to keep in the family. Executor: S. F. Myers, son. Dated: 24 August
1886. Test: Samuel G. Shields, S. D. Park.
                         Signed: William Myers

JANE M. REMINE
To my grandchildren, Daniel E. P. Burgner, Elizabeth C. Burgner - $10
each or 1/50 of estate. My sister, Elizabeth C. Wilson - to have a
comfortable room her lifetime. My daughter, Nannie J. Remine, Executrix
of Estate - to receive residue of estate. Dated: 10 January 1880. Test:
Robert M. McKee, John N. Cooter.   Signed: Jane M. Remine.

CATHARINE COLLETT
To my son, Charles M. Collett, Executor - 37 acre farm he lives on known
as Mat Rader Farm and $100. To my daughter, Martha Elizabeth Johnson -

48 acres next to the Railroad. To my daughter, Melvina Kelton — 48 acres with house. Three heirs to share equally in the rest. Dated: 4 June 1886. Test: D. R. Gass, Jacob Baughard.

Signed: Catharine X Collett

ABRAHAM HUGHES
To my neice, Mary E. Smithson (Mary E. Hughes) and her heirs — all my property, real, personal and mixed. To my sister, Phebe — $8 per year from storehouse rents and the upper end of our dwelling for her use. Executor: L. W. Smithson. Dated: 30 September 1886. Test: William Looney, M. P. Hampton.

Signed: Abraham Hughes

MISSOURI A. BROYLES
To my sister, Annice C. Broyles — real estate. To my sisters, Martha and Julia Broyles — bedstead. See that Flora and Walter Dunham learn to read and write and carry on their business. To Flora — bed. To Walter Dunham — bed. Executor: Will A. Broyles. Dated: 8 July 1888. Test: W. S. Gray.

Signed: Missouri A. Broyles

RACHEL DAVIS
Children: Susan Horton — $1 in full, Polly A. Hice — $1 in full, seven children of Samuel Davis decd. — $1 equally divided, Henry — to move his house close to mine, he and Harry — to take care of my husband John Davis and me. Executor: Charles A. Bright. Dated: 16 August 1884. Test: Elihu McNeese, Samuel H. McNees.

Signed: Rachel X Davis

LAURA VESTAL
To my aunt, Martha L. Anderson — all my property. To James F. Anderson — $200 when he is 21 if he stays with C. M. Vestal or Aunt Martha Anderson. Uncle C. M. Vestal, Executor. Dated: 6 February 1885. Witnesses: W. W. Deadrick, William Armitage.

Signed: Laura Vestal

JOHN BROWN
To wife, Sarah, sufficient means for the comforts of life from the farm. My sons, G. F. and J. W. — to share equal in all my property. To my daughter, Electra Brown — $500. To my daughter, Mary Williams — $300 paid by G. F. To my daughter, Jane C. Haynes — $300. To my daughter, Lula E. Brown — $300 and my piano. Executors: sons — G. F. and J. W. Brown. Dated: 17 July 1884. Witnesses: John Woody, Joseph A. Dobson.

Signed: John Brown

E. F. MERCER, SENIOR
Wife, Catharine C. Mercer — to be in control of land as is until son, Erby, is 21. Daughter, Mary E. Mercer, to be made equal with her sister and have a home. Son: Erby. Put head and foot rocks at my grave. Executors: D. W., Thomas S. and William Mercer. Dated: 8 February 1887. Witnesses: J. A. Harmon, Hugh Mercer.

JOHN GRAY — Rheatown
To my nephew, John Alexander Duncan, and his wife Lizzie Duncan — land in Rheatown, horses, wagons, gearing and whatever I might have. Executor: James Russell. Dated: 19 February 1887. Witnesses: Clay Shoun, W. M. Dukes, James Russell.

Signed: John X Gray

JOHN WOLOVER
To wife, Catharine — all land and tenements — at her death to son, Willie Cleaveland. No Executor. Dated: 19 July 1887. Witnesses: Thomas Henderson, George French.

Signed: John X Wolover

SAMUEL COCHRAN
To wife, Eliza Jane Cochran — my farm and all my stock — at her death have an equal division. Don't waste my forest timber. Children: Martha Emeline, Margaret Jane, James Alfred, Mary Ann, Eliza Amanda and Alpha Elizabeth. Executors: James Henry Senr. and wife Eliza Jane.

WILLIAM ROSS
Wife, Addie, to have all property that except that in possession of son, James for securing my note to William Armitage. Executor: R. H. Beals. Dated: 11 July 1887. Witnesses: J. M. Rhea, Alexander Brown.
Signed: William X Ross

RUFUS K. HARMON
To son, Isaac A. - 146 acre farm where I live in the 23rd District, to erect 2 pairs tombstones, $36 for both. To daughter, Alice - $100 and sewing machine. To son, Martin - $300 no more. To daughter, Sarah Hughes - $300 no more. Deceased daughter, Talitha Everhart - her children $50 each. To James W. and Rufus Everhart - my interest in threshing machine. Executors: sons - Martin and Isaac A. Dated: 27 August 1887. Witnesses: James C. Park, W. J. Doyle, A. Gray.
Signed: Rufus K. Harmon

TENNESSEE FARNSWORTH
To wife, Peggy - all property, pay Dr. Girdner and H. J. Steelman if she has the money. To Martha Ellen Whittenberg. Executor: William A. Leming. Dated: 6 February 1886. Test: William Cannon, S. K. Brooks.
Signed: Tennessee X Farnsworth

ALEXANDER J. KELLER - Noncupative Will
Alexander J. Keller died at residence of his mother, Sarah Keller, 22 day July 1887. Brother: Edgar. Mamie Holliway, daughter of Mrs. Florence Holloway. Dated: August 2, 1887. Attest: A. N. Shoun, Thomas J. Lane.
Signed: J. B. Rankin
E. B. Smith

MARY MARIAH HENEGAR
To my brother, Franklin Henegar - enough of my wearing clothes for a keepsake. To my neice, Irella Feazel - all lands and property for taking care of me, bed, 5 quilts and 2 blankets for her daughter Lucy. Executor: Newton Smelser. Dated: 1 February 1883. Attest: J. P. Easterly, C. W. Blair.
Signed: Mary M. Henegar at residence
Little Chuckey, Tennessee

SAMUEL P. MYERS
To wife, Emeline - to get land, notes and accounts - then to James L. Harmon and his heirs. James L. Harmon is to cultivate land and pay my wife 1/3. To have handsome tombstones at head and foot of mine and my wife's graves. Executor: James L. Harmon. Dated: 13 August 1887. Test: William A. Harmon, S. P. Chambers.
Signed: Samuel P. X Myers

B. F. EARNEST
Wife, Macy - to have all personal property and property in Knoxville and Texas for her support and to educate my children (not named). Dated: 20 September 1887. Test: A. S. Johnson, J. R. Earnest.

SHADRACH CHASE   24 September 1887
My son, John S. - to have my farm his natural life, then William B. Hale to have $100, then land and all property to go to my four girls: Nancy E. Riggs, Mary A. Babb, D. A. Babb and M. E. Chase. Executor: John B. Chase. Attest: John B. Chase, Charles R. Baxter.
Signed: Shadrach Chase

ROBERT C. GRAY
Property to be divided eight ways. Eight children of my two sisters, Mary Walker decd and Elizabeth Hayes decd.: Betsey Tunnell, Harriet A. H. Hayes, Mary A. C. Brimingstool, Samuel Whitfield Walker, Alexander B. Walker, Catharine Pickering, Robert G. Hays, Mary Ann Brumley decd. - to have all my personal property. Heirs of Mary Ann Brumley decd.: Sarah Elizabeth, Mary Catharine and Adeline Brumley - these children 1/8 of my property. Betsey Tunnell decd., children now living: Mary C. Tunnell,

Harriet A. H. C. McNeese. Executors: Michael Morelock and George Pickering. Dated: 20 March 1880. Attest: Joseph Robertson, Clay Shoun.
Signed: Robert C. Gray

SARAH A. RUTHERFORD
To my three daughters, Nancy V., Harriet Cordelia Rutherford and Willie
Ann Ross Rutherford - all my property. Daughters: Jane and Mollie. To
son, Richard Rutherford - colt. My six children to divide personal
property. Land on Lick Creek 16th District. Executrix: Nancy V.
Rutherford. Dated: 7 January 1888. Attest: G. W. McNeese, O. M. Kilday.
Signed: Sarah A. X Rutherford

GEORGE A. SMITH
My wife in charge of everything until her death then to my children. To
son, Caleb B. - 50 acres with mill. Remainder of land to these children:
John B., Susan J., Hannah E., Julia A., Sarah E., Martha F. and Minnie B.
Smith - share and share alike. To Mary E. James - $25 at my wife's de-
cease. To son, William A. - $700. Executors: John B. and Caleb B. Smith.
Dated: 20 January 1888. Test: J. S. J. Wilhoit, S. D. Waddle.
Signed: George A. X Smith

G. H. SHOUN - of Rheatown   66 years old
To wife, Thodocia - all property, real, personal and mixed - at her death
my two sons to divide equally themselves. To my oldest son, A. N. Shoun -
my fine gold watch and fob, $100 Aetna Life Insurance Policy. To my
youngest son, E. C. Shoun - $100 from Life Policy. Land in Shady Johnson
County, Tennessee worth $400, when I put a house on it, it will be worth
$500. Executors: A. M. and E. C. Shoun. Dated: 22 February 1888.
Attest: T. Stanley Smith, J. R. White.
Signed: G. H. Shoun

JOHN RICKER
To wife, Delila - all property her widowhood. Children: Margaret Ricker,
Nancy Ann - note on her husband William Cutshall, Martha, Elijah, David
S., Susannah, Daniel P., Fredrick, Eve, Mary Jane, Malinda Ricker, John
K., Sarah Caroline Ricker - owes thirty dollars note signed by Emanuel
Waddle. Property to be sold and all children to receive equal parts at
Delila's death. Executor: William R. Gibbs, he is not to give bond.
Dated: 10 February 1887. Attest: John X Ricker, Delila X Ricker.
Signed: John Ricker

LEMUEL CROSBY - Lick Creek near Hamblin County
Wife, Nancy, to have what came by her and land in Hamblin County in fee
simple, to have rest of property and give to children as she thinks right
as long as she lives. At her death sons, Andrew and Caleb, to have land
on westside Lick Creek in fee simple. To daughters, Sarah Rader and
Eliza Jane Jones - farm where I live on Greeneville Road. To Sarah
Wright decd. - her children and Elizabeth Wright - balance of land on
southside of Greeneville. To Mary Pangle wife of James Pangle - land in
Hamblin County - if Mary should die without issue, property to go to
Christian Pangle. Executors: sons - Andrew and Caleb. Dated: 15 February
1884. Attest: William Hawkins, W. A. Rader.
Signed: Lemuel Crosby

JOHN MALONE
To my sons, William and Harvey B. - all my 126 acres land in District 21
and they are to pay my sons, George and John D. - $15 each when conven-
ient. Executors: sons - William and Harvey. Dated: 24 March 1887.
Attest: J. A. Brown, W. M. Dugger. Signed: John X Malone

JOHN HARMON
To wife, Mary Magdalene - all I possess during her natural life if she
should outlive me. At our deaths all land to go to son, Granville D.
for taking care of us and paying my just debts. Daughter, Amanda E. -
to have what she owns. Six other children: W. R., J. R., A. J., D. J.,

A. G. and Sarah Knipp. M. I. Roberson, M. E. Harmon. Executor: Daniel
J. Harmon. Dated: 12 April 1878. Attest: Rufus Bowers, John F. Hunt.
Signed: John Harmon

BLACKSTONE McDANNEL
I have disposed of my land as deeds of gift. My son, Joseph W., to put
foot and headstones at our graves and pay my debts. To son, John L. of
Jefferson County - 1/3 of note I hold on him. To Mary Elizabeth (Mamie)
McDannel, only child of my dead son James - 1/3 of note. Other 1/3 note
to minor children of my deceased daughter, Sarah J. Dukes: Minnie, Henry
and Annie Dukes - John L., Mary Elizabeth, Ninnie, Henry and Annie have
received their parts. Executor: son Joseph W. Dated: 23 June 1887.
Attest: J. C. Park, W. N. Piper. Signed: Blackstone McDannel

THOMAS J. REEVE
To wife, Rebecca, all property her lifetime, then to be sold and equally
divided. My sons, F. A. and M. P. - have received $100 each. Daughters:
Louisa V. Marsh - $80, Sarah A. Broyles' children - $100, Narcissa E.
Seaver and children - $100, Kitty J. Lyon - $100, Mary R. Reave - $100.
To make my daughters equal with my sons. Executor: son M. P. Reeve.
Dated: 11 December 1888. Attest: M. Gfellers, G. F. Morelock.
Signed: Thomas J. Reeve

SALLY MOORE
After all debts are paid, I give everything to Trustees of Blue Springs
Methodist Church South - to be used by the church. Executor: Andrew
Bible. Dated: 26 June 1888. Attest: Henry Bible, D. A. Gass.
Signed: Sally X Moore

JAMES M. WHITE
To wife, Rachel, all land and property in 16th District known as Davis
Farm during her widowhood. At her death all to be sold and equally
divided. Children: Marthy Park, Margaret Ann Weems, George, John F. and
July. Executrix: wife Rachel. Dated: 8 May 1888. Attest: John B.
White, W. A. Pierce. Signed: James White

MARGARET R. GRAY
To husband, D. T. Gray, personal property and land in First District
adjoining Jesse Reaves. Executor: T. N. Gray. Dated: 19 July 1888.
Attest: D. W. Duck, A. F. Morgan. Signed: M. R. Gray

THOMAS L. WILLIAMS
To John Henry Williams - all property except notes and bonds, land ad-
joining Allen in District 13. To children of Jamison Williams: Thomas
C., Alex S., George, James M., Mollie Ervin daughter of Mollie Ervin nee
Williams, Caledonia J., Lou Ellen, Sallie and Nettie - balance of Ross
land, notes and bonds equally divided. David W. Williams, excluded from
this will, I have already given to him. To Robert and Carolyn McLinn's
four children: Mollie, Charlie, Ellen and Benjamin - my 44 acre William
Huffman tract. Executor: James M. Williams. Dated: 7 July 1888.
Attest: R. N. Collum, A. B. Collum. Signed: T. L. Williams

GENETT WISECARVER
After paying my debts and funeral, divide equally to my brothers, Nathan
and Honley Wisecarver, they have taken care of me. Dated: 13 April 1888.
Attest: Joseph Day, J. T. Purgason. Signed: Genett Wisecarver

NANCY SHEFFEY
To Jessie and Sallie Sheffey - $1 each. To son, James F. - balance of my
property including land where I now reside adjoining Fairgrounds. I purchased this of John Jones, until he is 21, he is to take good care of
land and receive rents and profits from it. Executor: W. H. Piper.
Dated: 14 September 1888. Attest: Jennie Brannon, Carrie Piper.
Signed: Nancy X Sheffey

FANNIE L. SHIELDS
To my mother, Mrs. R. L. Brown - $1000. To my brother, Hairy D. Brown - $1000. To my sister, Mollie Traynor - $500. To my husband, Samuel G. Shields - all the rest, remainder and residue of my estate. Executor: husband - Samuel G. Shields. Dated: 28 July 1888. Witnesses: A. N. Shoun, E. B. Smith.   Signed: Fannie L. Shields

AZOR KOONTZ
To daughter, Mary E. Britton - 32 acres land on Frank Holleys Creek adjoining Julia and Joseph Good. To daughter, Julia Brittain - 28 acres on Frank Holley Creek adjoining Christian Bible and E. W. Piper. To son, William M. Koontz - 80 acres, the remainder of my home tract deeded to me by Solomon Good - he is to take care of my wife and me our natural lives and pay Daniel Y. Koontz $325. Executor: son William M. Koontz. Dated: 2 April 1884. Witnesses: William S. McGaughey, S. W. Leming.
                    Signed: Azor X Koontz

WHITFIELD MOONEY
To wife, Adeline Mooney - all my landed estate her lifetime, then to be equally divided between my children by my last wife, Adeline Mooney. Dated: 16 July 1888. Witnesses: A. M. Cash, W. E. Keller.
                    Signed: Whitfield X Mooney

CICEROE HAYNES, decd.   Will has been lost.
   Annie W. Haynes   ⎫
        vs   ⎬ Decree
   Bessie Roe Haynes ⎭
      Cicero Haynes died in July 1888 - W. E. F. Milburn is guardian of minor child. The will was written by A. B. Wilson, signed by Cicero Haynes and witnessed by C. G. Howard and L. C. Haynes and was as follows:
      All property to go to my wife, Annie W. Haynes and child, Bessie Roe Haynes - to be equally divided. My child's part is to be invested by my executors and kept for her use when she is 21 or marries. Keep taxes paid on my land in Polk County, Florida and sell when proper. Executrix: Annie W. Haynes, wife. Dated: 23 November 1888. Witnesses: C. G. Howard, L. C. Haynes. W. E. F. Milburn's bill is $30.00.

SAMUEL WILHOIT
My wife to have all my lands and property while she lives. Joseph Wear to have the house where he lives and 1 acre ground around it, also 30 acres more up next to Old William Stills. At the death of my wife all property is to be sold and equally divided between my heirs after counting out the amounts their notes call for, which I hold on them. Notes not to draw interest: Emanuel Wilhoit - $50 note, Daniel Wilhoit - $70, Samuel L. Wilhoit - $100, Susannah Greer - $300, Caroline Miller - $180. Executor: W. R. Gibbs, and I give him orthority to sell and collect and make right without asking the law or court for any authority. Dated: 23 March 1882. Witnesses: John P. Wilhoit, David A. Parman.
                    Signed: Samuel X Wilhoit

JAMES ALEXANDER DIXON
To wife, Margaret Jane - all my real and personal property her lifetime provided she remains my widow, then to be divided between my three youngest ares after mi dets and funeral expenses is paid. Dated: 24 November 1888. Witnesses: A. B. Morelock, T. L. Mercer.
                    Signed: James X Alexander Dixon

MARY SNYDER
My 40 acres land where I live and all personal property to my daughter, Caroline Colyer, absolutely. Five dollars each to John and Henry Snyder. Dated: 7 May 1885. Witnesses: O. B. Headrick, J. L. Bartley.
                    Signed: Mary X Snyder

CATHARINE ZIMMERMAN
To my grand-daughter, Mollie Hardeman, living in Missouri, Colwell Co. -

$50. To my grand-daughter, Florence Estes, living in Missouri, Colwell Co. - $50. To my grand-daughter, Fannie Miller, she a resident of Oregon State - $50. To Mary Jane Reesor - my buggy, bed and bed clothing to be divided between the children of W. F. Reesor. Executor: S. B. Winslow. Dated: 17 December 1883. Test: W. F. Reeser, W. B. Reeser.

Signed: Catharine X Zimmerman

SALLIE CARTER
Wife of Daniel L. Carter, deceased. I prefer a neat home made coffin and have tombstones at my grave. To my son, William B. Carter - 9 acres on Lick Creek, District 23, transferrable only to the heirs of my body. My daughter, Eliza Armitage and my son, John P. Carter, have instructions to dispose of my household goods, none to be sold at public outcry. Son, John P. Carter, to dispose of livestock. To each of my grand-children, heirs of my daughter Mary A. Bible: David and Foy Bible - a trust of $25 plus interest to be paid when they are 21. To my grand-children, Eliza A. and Louie A. Martin - $25 in trust of their father, Romeo Martin. To Carters Station Methodist Episcopal Church - south at Carters Station in trust $100. What money is left to be divided between these my children: Margaret Thompson, Lewis A. Carter, James R. Carter, Alfred Carter. I give $100 for paling or a picket fence around the graveyard where my husband and others are buried. Executor: son John P. Carter. Dated: 24 November 1888. Witnesses: William T. Guthrie, William E. Blanton.

Signed: Sally Carter

JOSEPH R. BROWN
To wife, Eva J. Brown, and her heirs by me - all property I own at the time of my death and keep the house for our heirs. My brothers: William H. and Hugh M. Brown - to inherit equally if they outlive my wife and children. Dated: 31 January 1889. Witnesses: T. J. Moore, L. P. Speck.

Signed: Joseph R. Brown

JONATHAN BEALS
To wife, Eliza Jane - all proceeds from crops for 1889. If her support is exhausted my hears shall help her. To son, Jonathan - $60 if he is ever found. My real estate to go to my hears: Lewis R. Beals, Harvey and Henderson Beals, M. J. Whitaker formerly Beals, Clark, Jonathan A., James P. and E. J. G. Beals - equally divided. Son, W. A. Beals, to have the farm where he now resides. Executor: son Clark Beals. Dated: 8 January 1889. Witnesses: J. M. Rhea, L. R. Beals.

Signed: Jonathan Beals

LUCINDA PHILLIPS
To son, John H. Phillips - lifetime support on my farm that I now live on, joining the land of Jackson Phillips, Huts Basket and others in District 17. Dated: 30 January 1886. Test: L. A. Rector, A. J. Carter.

Signed: Sinda X Phillips

ALBERT T. SWANAY
Wife, Susannah, shall have her maintenance from farm and mills her life-time. To son, A. B. Swanay - 6 acres shere house and store house stand, one half of my Grist Mill and one third my sawmill. To son, W. F. Swanay, one fourth grist mill and one fourth my sawmill until he is 21 years old. To my grand-daughter, Fletia A. Swanay, daughter of John Swanay decd. - one fourth interest in my grist mill. To daughter, Mary E. Shipley - lot in Rheatown and one third sawmill. Executor: A. B. Swanay. Dated: 8 April 1889. Witnesses: John Whitehead, M. C. Hair, S. H. Baxter.

Signed: A. T. Swanay

WILLIAM GIRDNER (Doctor at Cedar Creek. G.F.B.)
To have a neat tombstone at my grave. To wife, Mary Jane - the farm where we now live to do as she pleases, all notes payable to her, $10 from the sale of my Iron Safe, all farming implements, all livestock, poultry, except my riding horse, saddle and bridle. One fourth of my estate to be in trust for support of my son, Robley D. Girdner, now in the asylum. One fourth of my estate to daughter, Laura Horton, of Ozark, Arkansas. One fourth of my estate to son, John H. Girdner, of New York

City. One fourth of my estate to the guardian of my grand-children, who
are minor heirs of my daughter, Emma Broyles decd., namely: Sidney E.,
Horace and Ethel Broyles. William G. Broyles of Cedar Creek to be
guardian of my son, Robley, and also guardian of Sidney E., Horace and
Ethel Broyles. Executor: James A. Park of Greeneville. Dated: 13
February 1888. Witnesses: William F. Lane, J. T. Brown, C. W. Wells,
M. C. Myers.

                          Signed: William Girdner
Codicil - July 20, 1888
     Son, Robley, has died intestate - his part to go to my daughter, Laura
Horton, John H. Girdner and the remaining one third to the heirs of my
deceased daughter, Emma Broyles, namely: Sidney E., Horace and Ethel
Broyles equally. Witnesses: Joseph Medlock, Thomas Medlock.

EZEKIEL CARTER   26 October 1832
Will not found. Executors: Ezekiel Carter, Jacob Carter.

SAMUEL KELLER   7 January 1858 $20,000
Executors: John Keller, Samuel J. Keller. Witnesses: George Lady,
Matilda Carter, Cornelius Harden. I did not find will - G.F.B.

ANDREW McPHERAN SENR.   4 May 1874 $400
Executor: Thomas McPheran - his bondsmen: A. W. Walker, James W. Cloyd.
(De Bonrs non?) with will annexed.

WILLIAM GALBREATH   1799
Wife: Margaret. Daughter: Elizabeth. Executors: brothers - James and
Alexander Galbreath, John Liggett, James Denniston. Witnesses: Agnes
McAmis, Samuel Wilson.   Signed: William & Galbreath
                                                    his mark

JOHN HOWARD   Deceased 1797
Wife: Hannah. Youngest daughters: Patty, Joanna. Executrix: wife
Hannah, daughter Joanna. Dated: 12 August 1797. Witnesses: Andrew
English, John Woolsey, Elizabeth English.
                          Signed: John Howard
                                         his mark

DANIEL DUNN   23 April 1822 $7,000
Executors: Daniel and Levi Dunn, George Wells, Gilbert Woolsey. Executor
bond will in book.

THOMAS DAVIS   8 November 1866
Executors: James Davis - his bondsmen: Jacob Kerbaugh, Christian Bible.

THOMAS ELLIS   1798
Three sons: Thomas, David, Reese? Wife: Margaret. Executors:.wife
Margaret, Ellis Ellis. Dated: 30 May 1798. Witnesses: John Jones,
Isaac Todhunter.   Signed: Thomas Ellis

MOSES HUGHES, decd.   31 October 1833
Agreement between heirs who met 1 November 1833. Heirs - Children: John,
Aaron, Francis, Hezekiah, Abraham, George, Thomas, Christener Hughes
Kennedy wife of James Kennedy, Polly Hughes, Phebe Hughes, Moses Hughes
Junr. Witnesses: John P. French, Alexander Bailey.

ISAIAH VANSANDT   1789   Greene Co., North Carolina (later Tenn.)
Children: John, George. To my son, Thompson Vansandt - land in Cove. To
Margit, my wife - land and mill. Daughters: Mary, Margaret. Sum of hard
cash being in Bucks County in the State of Pensylvaney, to go to my
children: Elijah, Elisha, Ezekiel, Joshua, Elizabeth, Rachel and Sarah
Vansandt. Executors: John Lescollet, John Wilson. Dated: 8 August 1789.
Witnesses: John Lescollet, John Wilson, Samuel Hutchison, Joseph Tyler,
William Wilson, Rouben pompson (Thompson?)
                          Signed: Isaiah VanSandt

BENJAMIN VanVECTOR   27 January 1823 $1,800
Children: Joseph, daughter Curtiti is? wife of Charles Parler?, daughter
Phebe wife of Joseph Melvin decd. Executors: William Dodd, John Ander-
son, George Brown. Dated: 26 November 1822. Witnesses: William Carter,
Joseph Brown.   Signed: Benjamin X VanVector

RUFUS J. KIDWELL
I will and devise my entire estate of whatever character or discription
it may be to my wife, Emeline Kidwell, absolutely and unconditionally -
subject only to the payment of my just debts. I desire that there be no
public sale of any of my property. Executrix: wife Emeline. Dated: 31
July 1875. Witnesses: Robert McFarland, William McFarland.
                                 Signed: Rufus J. Kidwell

DAVID BIBLE
Wife, Dianon Bible - all my land and personal property during her life
and at her death to be equally divided between my two grand children,
Lillie E. Jones and Daniel F. Jones, in the event either one of them
dies before their grand mother, leaving no issue, the whole estate is
to go to the surviving child. Executrix: wife Dianon. Dated: January
12, 1889. Witnesses: C. F. Brown, Thomas Fry, R. M. Jones.
                                 Signed: David X Bible

MOSES SEATON
I Moses Seaton being of sound mind and disposing memory. I have 70 acres
of land in Greene County. My son, Brown Seaton, to have and controll the
land allowing my beloved wife, Mollie Seaton, her lifetime support and
interest in said land. At her death to go to Brown Seaton in fee simple,
and to pay other children: Orlena Fox - $100, Winy Williamson - $100.
To Hattie Seaton - $200, one horse, saddle and bridle. Executor: son
Brown Seaton. Dated: April 17, 1889. Witnesses: J. W. Donnelly, R. E.
Berry.   Signed: Moses X Seaton

ZACHARIAH BROWN
To wife, Mary Brown, farm that we now live on as long as she lives and
personal property. At Mary's death personal property on hand to be sold
and the proceeds equally divided between: my daughter, Elizabeth Hickman;
the heirs of my daughter Nancy A. White; and my son, John S. Brown. To
son, John A. Brown - my farm after death of my wife, Mary Brown, by him
paying my daughter, Elizabeth Hickman - $100, and the heirs of Nancy A.
White - $100. Executor: James B. White. Dated: 29 July 1886. Test:
William S. White, F. E. Murr.   Signed: Zachariah X Brown

W. F. RESER SENR.
To wife, Chilnese, all my lands, household and kitchen furniture, all my
stock, horses, cattle, sheep and hogs and all farming tools during her
natural lifetime. At her death, personal property to be sold divided
equlla among the children, as the heirs of my bodda. If two or more of
the heirs want the land or farm on which I now live - they may buy it by
paying to wit: Jacob M. Reser - $500; William B. Reser having got his in
land that is the $500 and to is to pay $400 to me for what land he has
got apart of which is paid; James A. Reser - $100; Samuel P. Reser - $100.
Each of the guerls to have $400 - Francianno P., Elizabeth C., Louisa B.,
Emma C. and Mary. Lou and Mary to have a home while they remain single.
Dated: 25 March 1882.   Signed: W. F. Reser

JANE M. GRACE
To be buried in a good and respectable maner. Administrator to buy three
sets of Tomb Stones properly lettered, one placed at my grave and one at
my husband, William Grace's grave, and one at my son, James Grace's
grave. Farm to be sold and two daughters to have $100 each. To son,
Alfred - the remainder. To daughter, E. C. Cloyd - one beurau and small
chest, one bed, 2 sheets, 2 blankets, one comfort, 1 quilt or county
pane, one bolster and set of pillows, two green chairs, one wash bowl and
Family Bible. To grand-daughter, Betty Cloyd - one Laura Loaf quilt. To
my daughter, E. J. Ottinger - one bed, 2 sheets, two blankets, one comfort, one quilt, one coverlid, one trunk and two green chairs, one

146

looking glass, one brass kettle, my Lady Basket and side saddle and Book
of Psalms. Crockery Ware and Cuberd Ware to be divided between two
daughters. To son, Alfred - my large Testament, small table and personal
property. Dated: May 9, 1888. Attest: A. M. Sheffey, Susan Shawe.

Signed: Jane M. X Grace

WILSON WATTENBARGER

To wife, Cerena E. J. Wattenbarger, household furniture, one cow, one
heifer, proceeds of my Estep Farm furing the widows natural life, or
while she remains my widow. At her death or remarriage to go to Laura
C. Jones and G. A. Wattenbarger. To Laura C. Jones - a two year old
colt when she is 12. To my son, E. B. Wattenbarger - tract of land on
Cove Mountain and one four horse wagon. To my son, G. A. Wattenbarger -
all machinery, land laing on south east side of Pin Mountain, two horse
wagon, Blacksmith tools, one black colt and my part in cider mill and
cross cut saw. To my son, J. W. Wattenbarger - 200 acres land, one set
tanyard tools. To my son, J. E. Wattenbarger - $400 cash or cash notes
and one mule coalt. To grandson, J. W. Wattenbarger Jr. - note on G. W.
Yokley for $51.56 and G. A. Wattenbarger to pay him $48.44 making $100
in all. Executors: sons G. A. and J. W. Wattenbarger. Dated: June 3,
1886. Attest: A. F. Tucker, J. R. Malico.

Signed: Wilson Wattenbarger

REBECCA MOORE

To be buried in a nice walnut coffin and a walnut case and to have marble
Tomb Stones put up to my grave and my husband's grave. To son, Jessee
Moore - $6 in full of all his part. To my grandchildren, children of my
son, James C. Moore decd., viz: Ulysses, Robert, Rebecca F. Moore - $2
each. To grandson, George W. Moore - plantation whereon I now live, all
farming tools, all horse stock, sheep, cattle, hogs, all household and
kitchen furniture, bedding and bed close - he has stayed and helped me
a long and I expect him to stay and take care of me while I live.
Executor: Charles A. Bright. Dated: 7 March 1881. Witnesses: Emma
Loyd, Michael Bright.   Signed: Rebecca _B_ Moore
                                                 her mark

JAMES JOHNSTON

To be buried by the Masonic Fraternity of Greene County. To wife, Eliza
H. Johnston and to my son, James Johnston - equally share and share alike
all my property of every kind, real, personal and mixed except the
Bridgeport and Mill Property. To my daughter, Bettie Allen wife of
William Allen - $500 paid by my wife and son James. To grand-daughter,
Eliza Woodson - $500. To grandchildren: James Johnston, Mary Blakemore,
Retta Leach and Maggie Johnston, the son and daughters of decd. son,
Crockett Johnston - all real estate in Cock County, Tennessee known as
the Bridgeport Mill Property - divided between them equally. I have
given my son-in-law, David Russell, and his children and to my son, John
F. Johnston, their full share. To John Dugan - a horse, saddle and
briddle, if he remains with me and my wife until his father needs him
and is a good and obedient boy. If my son, James Johnson does not treat
his mother kindly and take good care of her, he shall forfeit all his
interest in my estate. Execytors: wife Eliza H. Johnston and son James
Johnston. Dated: June 1, 1887. Test: Richard G. Gammon, James Allen.

Signed: James Johnston

ANDREW RADER

To my wife - $600.50, one bureau and safe, all she brought with her when
we married and all she has made in the house since she came hear. I want
to be buried at Timber Ridge by the side of my first wife, and berry me
in a coffin just like your mother was buried in and put up Toom Stones
about same quality of hers. All my money and personal property eaculey
divided between: William Rader, George Rader, Andrew Rader, Carline
Taylor and Lyda Bordon. I want iron palings aroung my first wife's
grave with room for myself. Executor: son William Rader. Dated:
September 4, 1889. Witnesses: J. G. Greer, W. P. Bradford.

Signed: Andrew Rader

EZEKLE ADAMS

To wife, Rebecca L. Adams, all my property both personal and real estate during her life. To son, J. B. Adams - 11 acres on south side of Little Chucky Creek adjoining J. A. Maloney. To my four children: William T., R. F., C. D. and A. J. - $1 each. To my daughter, Mrs. M. A. Marshall - remainder of the upland field on which she now lives (5 acres). To my daughter, Bettie Adams - all the remainder of my property both real and personal at the death of her mother. Executrix: wife Rebecca Adams. Dated: 12 July 1889. Witnesses: Robert M. Jones, J. C. Ayers.

Signed: E. X Adams

ADALINE E. SNAPP

All my children except my youngest daughter, Mary A. Snapp, are well settled in life and have no need of assistance. To daughter, Mary A. Snapp - house and lot where I now live, one other lot adjoining thereto in District 10, fronting Main Street in town of Greeneville - beginning on the North East corner of the lot upon which Dr. J. B. Gilleyland now lives, thence with his line, and the line of the lot now owned by John H. Doughty to the Eastern edge of Irish Street, thence with the calls of my deed along the verge of the Rail Road to corner between Snapp and Dr. W. F. Fowler, thence Eastward with Fowler line to edge of Main Street, thence with said street to the beginning - also all my personal property of every kind including notes, due bills and accounts. Executrix: Mary A. Snapp. Dated: 21 April 1886. Witnesses: A. W. Taylor, W. A. Harmon.

Signed: A. E. Snapp

CLAIBORNE SELF

To wife, Winny Self, $600, all stock - horses, mules, colts, hogs, cattle and sheep, all poultry, farming emplements, all grain on hand, all growing crops, all household and kitchen furniture, one tract land including homestead lying on both sides of Lick Creek (176 acres) adjoining Rebecca Rollins, T. F. Self, I. Hays, also one other tract on the south side of Lick Creek adjoining Jones Rudder, J. K. Haun, Ellen McGuffin (20 acres) during her natural life or widowhood. To Louis McGuffin and wife - all the above tracts, if they stay with, be kind too and take good care of me and my beloved wife during our natural lives. To sons, James P. T. and D. K. Self - portion of the homestead lying north side of Lick Creek, equally divided. To daughter, Sallie Senaker, and her heirs - land on North side Lick Creek at or near the Slaty Ford (20 acres). Sell all lands not heretofore disposed of at Private or Public Sale - pay debts and divide equally between all my heirs, except Thomas F. Self, I have given him as much as I allowed. Executor: James W. Cloyd. Dated: 19 November 1888. Witnesses: G. B. Rollins, I. B. Brown.

Signed: Claiborne Self

THOMAS NEASE

Wife, Elizabeth Neas, to have full possession and control of all personal and real estate during her natural life or widowhood, with exception of 40 acres land I will to my son, Jerome. To John A. Neas - land. To son, Jacob Nease - land. Remainder of estate to be sold to highest bidder. Executors: son John A. Nease and Jacob W. Neas. Dated: 21 October 1889. Witnesses: William A. Love, A. W. Holt.

Signed: Thomas X Neas

MARY PANGLE

The body of my son, George, who was buried in Georgia, to be brought to the family burying ground and entered by my side and that the two graves be enclosed by a good iron fence and suitable tombstones be placed in our memory. To nephew, E. C. Rader - my bureau. To neices, Kitty and Lilly Wright - each to have a bed with the clothing. Any other property to be divided between my brothers and sisters. To Mary Graham, now in Washington Territory - $100 to be placed in Lookout Bank at Morristown, Tennessee at interest until she is 21. To my husband, James Pangle - $100 if he returns within the next 7 years. Sister: Susan. To the Concord Ladies Mission - $20. Executor: my brother Andrew Crosby. Dated: 5 June 1889. Test: John Wright, Jr., William Hawkins.

Signed: Mary Pangle

MARY VESTAL
To my sister, Martha L. Anderson - all my property both real and personal
to have and to hold unto her, her heirs and assign forever. Dated: 5
January 1885. Witnesses: C. M. Vestal, Isabel F. Brinkman.
                              Signed: Mary X Vestal

PIERCE B. HARRIS
To Mrs. Mary Ballard - all my real and personal property her lifetime -
her kindness to me at all times and particularly during my sickness has
been unfaltering. Reading Room on my town lot to be maintained so long
as it may prove of benefit to the people - but not to be maintained out
of money from estate. If Reading Room ceases to benefit the people, to
be sold including lot - $200 to be paid to Miss M. Collins, 41 West 11
Street, New York, N.Y. Dated: 4 October 1887. Witnesses: Robert M.
McKee, Sam M. McKee.   Signed: P. B. Harris

THOMAS DAVIS   8th District
Being of sound mind and disposing memory, but having nearly attained my
"Three-score years and ten." To my daughter, Sarah Harmon - $500, I
have paid her $1000 making $1500 in all. To my daughter, Margaret
Adaline Bible, and her heirs - 100 acres land where she now lives con-
veyed to me by William Evans, also 77 acres conveyed me by James Davis
adjoining Thomas Hartman, Dr. A. J. Hartman, James Rader and others.
To my son, John T. Davis, and his heirs - farm where he lives (132 1/2
acres), also 77 acres on lower end of the "Home Farm". To my daughter,
Martha C. Smith - part of the "Home Farm" (172 acres). To Alexander
Holder, a boy about 12 now living with me - $150 when he is 21. Sell
remainder of my estate and divide money equally between my children.
Executor: James C. Park of Greeneville. Dated: 25 January 1890.
Witnesses: D. W. Mercer, S. D. Park.
                              Signed: Thomas Davis
Codicil - The ninth clause of said will be modified - household and
kitchen furniture to be divided equally between my four children: Sarah
Harmon, Adaline Bible, John T. Davis and Martha C. Smith. Dated: 18
February 1890. Witnesses: H. N. Baker, H. J. Hartman.

ABRAHAM CARTER
To my daughter, C. J. H. Leib, and her heirs - upper end or part of my
farm so as to include the buildings and improvements where I now live
and 1/2 of the acres of my farm, 1/2 of the bottom land and 1/2 of the
upland. To my grandchildren: Eugena P. Walker, T. S. Walker, Mand R.
Walker and Della M. Walker, children of Rev. T. S. Walker - the other
half of the acres of my farm. To Sally A. Reed - one dark brown mare
colt now about 9 months old, one muly cow now about two 1/2 years old
and one bed and necesary bed clothing. To my daughter, C. J. H. Leib -
all balance of my personal property. Executor: George F. Leib. Dated:
3 January 1890. Witnesses: H. A. Carter, T. L. Mercer, George E. Kenney.
                              Signed: Abraham Carter

CORNELIUS MAYS   17th District
To wife, Nancy Mays, all household and kitchen furniture, my farm or
lands and improvements on which I now reside during her natural life.
Said land on Lick Creek adjoining Allen, Bolton, White and others. At
my wife's death, the land or farm to be equally divided between: W. T.
Mays, J. J. Mays, Lydia C. Bolton and Debbie I. Mays. To daughter,
Isabella N. Mays - all my mountain land. My beloved old Mother to
continue to live with the family during her natural life. Executor:
son W. T. Mays. Dated: 4 April 1889. Attest: Lewis White, William
Blazer.   Signed: C. X Mays

ISRAEL SMITH of Jeroldstown
To my beloved wife, Sarah, all my household furniture, all live stock
and farming implements and all my lands her natural life or widowhood.
My bay mare, Nerva, to be kept on the place as long as she is service-
able. To my two daughters, Florence S. Smith and Emily T. Smith - all
my lands, also to pay James B. Parker, Margaret Ann Brown, Mary E.
Morrison and Alexander H. Parker, each respectfully $15. Executor:

D. T. Woolsey. Dated: 17 January 1890. Witnesses: D. T. Woolsey, R. J.
Fink.   Signed: Israel Smith

NANCY GASS
To James Roy Mercer and Caswell V. Gass, my brother - intire farm in-
cluding homestead. To Elbert F. Mercer - interest in the 10th District
and lot in Greeneville. To the New Bethel Cumberland Presbyterian
Church - $20. Executor: E. F. Mercer. Dated: 18 April 1890. Atest:
D. W. Mercer, Rufus Lucky.   Signed: Nancy Gass

W. W. SMITH
To wife, Edna D. Smith - $100, all the personal estate that belonged to
her when we married, one white milk cow, one brindle milk cow, two hogs,
two horses, one harrow, one single plow, one churn, one cast kettle, one
washstand, all my dishes, all my cooking vessels, all chickens and all
grain for 1890. To my three children: George E. Smith, Girtie J. Smith
and Oscar P. Smith - my bedsteads, all bedding, and remainder of my
personal estate equally divided. To son, George E. Smith - $125. To
daughter, Girtie J. Smith - $125. To son, Oscar P. Smith - $125. Executor: J. C. Doty. Dated: 19 March 1890. Attest: J. T. Barham, G. H.
Huffman.   Signed: W. W. X Smith

ELBERT S. SMITH
To wife, N. J. Smith - one mare, two coults, 1 two horse wagon, 1 harrow,
farming tools, all house and citchen furniture, 1 buggy, 1 harness, two
cows and calfs, house where I know live and barn, all out buildings and
1/2 my farm during hir widdowhood or natheral life. At her death to go
to my son, Franklin. To sons, William and George Smith - other half my
farm. Dated: 27 November 1889. Atest: William McMackin, D. A. Smith.
                               Signed: Elbert S. X Smith
                                       N. J. Smith

KENNEDY BOWMAN
All my real and personal property controld by me to be equelly devided
between all of my children after all of just dets is paid. Also Kenny
Bowman and wife, Poley Bowman, to hold the same duern ther nacherl lif
to do as ther pleas with the same. Jacob and John part to be laid off
where tha liv to William Bowman, Sparling Bowman, Cathern Jennings,
Elizabeth Gant, Gacobe Bowman, John Bowman. Dated: 23 November 1876.
Witnesses: James L. Fannon, William Jennings.
                               Signed: Kennedy X Bowman

JOHN F. STURM
To wife, Emaline Sturm, all my property, real, personal and mixed,
collect all debts, claims and accounts due me, and have complete control of my business. Executrix: wife Emaline Sturm. Dated: 20 May
1890. Test: J. M. Piper, N. T. Howard.
                               Signed: John F. Sturm

WILLIAM OTTINGER   23d District
To wife, Elizabeth Ottinger, all fixtures, books, household goods,
furniture, chattels and effects, all live stock, grain, farming implements, dwelling house with tract of land, 155 acres purchased of W. T.
Guthrie. To son, William Scott Ottinger - 1 bay filly, 3 steers and
about $70 cash. Executrix: wife Elizabeth Ottinger. Dated: May 1,
1890. Witnesses: William T. Guthrie, Peter Myers.
                               Signed: William Ottinger

JOHN HARMON of Jacob
To daughter, Polly Ann Turner wife of William Turner - 22 acres land off
farm on which I reside in District 19. Remainder of land to be divided
between my two sons, Jacob L. Harmon and Moses P. Harmon, so that the
latter receives 50 acres more, also to pay as follows: son Harrison C.
Harmon - $300, daughter Catharine Haun wife of John Haun - $300, daughter
Martha E. Haun wife of Lewis M. Haun - $300, daughter Sarah J. Huff wife
of Jonas Huff - $300, daughter Louisa A. Bible wife of _____ S. Bible -

$300, grand-daughter Amanda Adaline Ailshie daughter of my son Andrew J. Harmon decd. and wife of Washington Ailshie - $150. To my beloved wife, Sally, all above property, $50 in cash, and all personal property if she survives me, until her death. Executor: Rev. J. C. Barb. Dated: 13 December 1881. Witnesses: William Hawkins, N. E. Hawkins, W. F. M. Harmon.   Signed: John Harmon

LEWIS H. BROYLES
To my daughters, Margaret Ellis and Mary Bird - all my household and kitchen furniture, rest of my personal property, my home farm, and my half interest in the farm known as the Wincle Farm in Washington County. To King Broyles, colored - $25 to be paid to him as he needs it. Executors: sons-in-law L. Ellis and C. H. Bird. Dated: 18 November 1889. Attest: I. R. Earnest, O. M. Broyles.
                         Signed: Lewis H. Broyles

ENOCH P. MURRAY   4th District
To wife, Lavina Murry - all my estate both real and personal including money during her natural life. To son, Thomas - my entire real estate including the home place where I now live and different parcels or tracts on Lick Creek, for which he is to pay $2500. Sons: Hugh and Thomas. To my grandchildren of my deceased daughter, Narcissa, viz: Nannie, Wassie, Macomb, Coy, Julia, Robert and Pearl Lane - one third of my estate - I appoint V. S. Murray, their guardian. Executor: son Thomas Murray. Dated: 10 April 1890. Witnesses: H. D. Maloney, P. M. Bewley.
                         Signed: Enoch P. Murray

WASHINGTON WHITE
To wife, Martha White - all my household furniture, farm and stock, 1 cow and calf, 1 sow and 7 pigs, use of my dwelling house and lands during natural life or as long as she remains my widow. To daughter, Sarah Slagle - my house and land in Greene County, District 16. Executor: son Hail White. Dated: 29 March 1888. Attest: Sarah E. Smith, Orlin L. Smith, J. W. Tucker.   Signed: Washington White

G. F. COX   17th District
To wife, Martha E. Cox - all my personal property, all real estate consisting of farm where I now live adjoining William Pierce, A. J. Pullman and others. Dated: July 9, 1890. Witnesses: T. M. Wells, G. W. Basket, S. M. Brandon.   Signed: G. F. Cox

JOSEPH ALBRIGHT
The tools to be divided equally between William M. Albright and Joseph L. Albright and that Joseph was to have the Rosewood plowplane and Louisa S. Albright is to have house and lot and house furniture and that William Albright was to do with the machinery as he thought best, the rest have thare part. Dated: February 10, 1880. Witnesses: Louisa S. Albright, William M. Albright, Bettie Rader.
                         Signed: Joseph Albright

GRAVENOR DICKENSON
All my effects boath real and personal to A. B. Adams and wife, Sarah G. Adams, for taking care of me while I live, also my wearing apparel, bead cloathing, 2 stands of bees, household and kitchen furnature, house and lot (2 acres) in 15th District adjoining Mara B. Aston, Widow Okay, Thomas A. Pleasant. Dated: June 4, 1890. Witnesses: R. A. Taylor, S. R. Aston.   Signed: Gravener X Dickenson

SARAH KEY
Wife of Peter Key. To Emma Kidwell, daughter of William Kidwell - all residue of my estate both real and personal. Executor: D. R. Gass. Dated: 11 June 1878. Witnesses: Jere McMillen, Hiley X McMillen, James W. Cloyd.   Signed: Sarah X Key

SARAH WHITE
To my beloved neice, Emma E. Barham, my real estate in District 14 ad-

joining E. E. Bebber, W. W. Smith and others, known as the Ingle Lot. To
my beloved grate neice, Sarah Lula Barham - 1 bed to be complete. To my
beloved nephew, John F. Barham - all the residue and remainder of my
personal estate consisting of cattle, household and kitchen furniture
with all my bed clothing and personal clothing. Executor: nephew John
F. Barham. Dated: 30 March 1889. Attest: Henderson Beals, W. A. Beals.
Signed: Sarah X White

WILSON McAMIS
To my dearly beloved wife, Jane McAmis, my black horse, two horse wagon,
hack and hack harness, all my household and kitchen furniture except one
bedstead and bedding which I bequeath to my grand-daughter, Sarah Elizabeth Jan McCamis. To my son, Jacob H. McCamis - all my farming tools.
To my grandsons, William E. McCamis and John D. McCamis - all my car-
penter tools equally divided. To my son, Ephraim D. McCamis - $100. To
my daughter, Sarah Bowers - $100. To my daughter, Elizabeth G. Hubbard -
$100. To my son-in-law, A. C. McCurry - $100 and $1 apiece to each of
the heirs of my daughter, Mary Jane McCurry decd. To my grand-daughter,
Corda F. McCamis - 1 cow of good stock or $20 when she arrives at the age
of 18. Wife, Jane, to have full controll of all real estate during her
natural life - then to my son, Jacob H. McAmis and his wife, N. A.
McAmis. Executor: W. D. B. Doty. Dated: 4 October 1890. Attest: J. R.
Kilday, John D. McCollum. Signed: Wilson McAmis

MARTHA L. ANDERSON
To James F. Anderson - $200 when he attains age 21. To C. M. Vestal -
all my estate both real and personal such as the town lot I now live in
Greeneville adjoining President Johnson residence, the old John Morris
property and on McKee and Water Streets, also the old Vestal farm in
Districts 8 and 12 adjoining heirs of John Rhea Sr. decd., John Harden,
Charles Gass and others. Executor: C. M. Vestal. Dated: May 1, 1887.
Witnesses: B. D. Harrold, L. W. Tipton.
Signed: Martha L. Anderson

MARTHA L. ANDERSON
Revoking all other wills. Sell farm on Rogersville Road about 2 miles
from Greeneville adjoining the Rhea and Wykell heirs, McCurry, John
Bohanan, Robert Harden and others, containing 130 acres. Proceeds from
sale to go to C. M. Vestal. To Mary Brown, wife of H. H. Brown - all my
real estate on Main Street in Greeneville, bounded by Main Street, J. F.
Fields, McKee Street, W. F. Lane and the Johnson property, on which are
the Mansion house, kitchen, barn and other out houses - in consideration
of her care and attention to me in my affliction. To my neice, M. A.
Carter, wife of N. W. Carter - all household goods and personal property.
Executor: Samuel Babb. Dated: October 15, 1890. Witnesses: V. S.
Britton, Peter Barham. Signed: Martha L. Anderson

REMEMBER SMITH
To my son, Andrew Jackson Smith - all real estate after my deth, my bay
mare, 1 bed and bedding and all farming tools. To my daughters, Rebecca
Jackson, Malinda Jane Shanks, Margaret An and Mary Smith and my grand-
daughter, Cordy Smith - all my household and kitchen furniture equally
divided. Executor: son A. J. Smith. Dated: 10 September 1881. Attest:
John Shanks, William McAmis. Signed: Remember X Smith

MARGARET MORELOCK
My landed estate consisting of $1040.00 to be divided as follows: David
Morelock - 1/4, William A. Morelock - 1/4, Samuel B. Morelock - 1/2, he
paid Abner for his share. Dated: 19 April 1890. Witnesses: W. B.
Morelock, John R. Coffey. Signed: Margaret X Morelock

ELIZABETH COSBY
My money, land, interest in an Iron Ore Bank left me from my father's
estate, also a note on my brother, James, of $1400, one on Jimmy Allen
Jr. for nearly $300. My sisters: Nancy E. Lowery, Margaret E. Noel,
Mary J. Eason, To the Foren Missions of the Methodist Protestant Church.
To my sister Martha A. Briscoe's daughter, Mattie A. Briscoe. To my

brother, Isaac A. Allen's daughter Lizzie Allen. Dated: 22 September 1884. The reason I have not specified my brother, James, is that I do not expect to collect much of the debt he ows me.
Signed: Elizabeth Cosby

REBECCA HICKS

To my daughter, Emma Hicks, during her natural life - my sewing machine, then to daughter, Dice. To my son, James - one feather bed, 3 best calico quilts, 1 blanket, 1 luisy? quilt, 2 sheets new domestic ones, 2 pillows and $5 cash. To my daughter, Dice - 1 bureau to be kept in possession of Lucretia Ball until she attains the age of 14. Sell remainder of property and proceeds to be divided equally between my three children. All given to my son, James, by his grandfather, Washington Smith, be and remain his forever. Executor: J. E. Pierce. Dated: 23 October 1890. Witnesses: D. F. Woolsey, R. J. Turk.
Signed: Rebecca X Hicks

E. K. WEEMS

James R. and Isaac N. Weems, each have received the portion I desire them to have of my estate. To my sons, Benjamin L. and William W. Weems - the farm known as the Hawkins Farm adjoining A. W. Carter and others. Benjamin L. Weems is to pay my son, Thaddeus R. Weems, $500 - but in the event that Thaddeus should die without heirs before this will goes into effect, then the said Benjamin L. is to pay four daughters, namely: Carrie R., Corra F., Lucy B. and Maud M. Weems - $100 each. To my sons, Edmond J. and Charles B. Weems - farm known as the homestead farm of my father, John Weems, adjoining Dr. John Linebaugh and others (200 acres), also to pay Martin D. Weems $100 each and to pay Elizabeth M. Yokley $50 each. To my son, Dewitt T. Weems - farm I now live on adjoining M. L. Bailey and others (37 acres), also 10 acres on the south side of Lick Creek adjoining William Linebaugh. To three youngest girls: Corra F., Lucy B. and Maud M. - horse, saddle and bridle, cow and good common bed. To daughter, Carrie R. Weems - 1 horse, saddle and bridle, cow, good common bed and parlor oregan. Any property still on hand to be equally divided between Narcissus McCurry, Steller Hawkins, Carrie R., Corra F., Lucy B. and Maud M. Weems. Executor: W. W. Weems. Dated: 2 March 1889. Attest: George E. Kenney, George A. Bailey.
Signed: E. K. Weems

BEALS (cont.)
Daniel (cont.) 112, 118
E. J. G. 144
Ebby 68
Edie 118
Elbert 97
Elihu 2, 75
Elisha 43
Elizabeth 42, 47, 56
Eliza Jane 144
Ellis 87, 101; 111, 118
Emeline 112
Enoch 97
George M. 97
Hannah 42, 47, 56, 75
Harriett 112
Harvey 144
Henderson 144, 152
Isaacs 27
Jacob 42, 43, 47, 55,
    56, 68, 75, 97, 118
Jacob Senr. 42
James 68
James P. 144
Jane 42, 43, 97
John 43, 97, 112, 118
Jonathan 103, 118, 144
Joseph 42, 75
Keziah 118
Lewis R. 144
Louisa 97
Lydda 87
M. J. 144
Martha 42, 43, 68
Mary 56, 118
Mary Ann 97
Nancy 112
Nathan 97, 118
Newton 97
Polly 43
R. H. 140
Rachel 47, 56, 75
Rebecca 42, 68, 83, 112,
    118
Riley 112
Samuel 42, 43, 68, 103
Sarah 47, 97, 112, 118
Serene 97
Solomon 2, 27, 68, 75
Solomon Senr. 42
Stephen 42, 68
Thomas 43, 53, 118
Thomas A. 97
W. A. 129, 144, 152
William 47, 48, 118
BEARD, Peggy 7
William 95
BEATY, James 8
James Jr. 4
BEAYLES, Jacob 42
BEBBER, E. E. 125, 152
BECKNER, N. 107
BEEKNER, Abraham 66
Elizabeth 66
BEEKS, James C. 112
BELL, Alphiar 37
B. F. 110
Benjamin F. 93, 94, 111
Benjamin F., Dr. 121
David M. 36
Eliza Jane 37
Elizabeth 2
Elizabeth Dixon 2
George 2, 40, 52, 115
H. A. 105
Henry 20
Hepsibah 85, 111
James 2
James C. 35
Jane 9
John 2, 5, 43, 45
Joseph E. 111
Katherine 2

BELL (cont.)
Lucinda 93
Mary Ann 2
Mary M. 121
Nancy 37
Polly Ann 36
Rebecca 115
Sally M. 36
Samuel 2
W. V. 124
William 13
William Senr. 36
Wilson Allen 2
BENHAM, Robert 5
BENSON, Easter 124
Lincoln 124
Mary Catharine 124
Wesley 124
BERD, Andrew 23
BERRY, Jenny 38
John 38
R. E. 146
Thomas 67
William 42
BESE, William, Capt. 98
BETSEY, Eliza 37
BEWLEY, Jacob M. 61
P. M. 151
BIBLE, A. J. 123
Abraham 41, 71, 72, 79
Adam 39, 41, 47, 56,
    95
Ambrose 85, 104, 117
Andrew 71, 142
Ann 41
Barbary E. 123
Betsey 60
C. W. 119
Charles L. 123
Charles S. 123
Christian 41, 75, 79,
    95, 108, 143, 145
Christian W. 123
Christly 72
David 72, 108, 129,
    144, 146
Dianon 146
Dolly 95
Elbert 117
Elizabeth 39, 41, 72,
    95
Elvira M. 124
Foy 144
George 41
Henry 92, 95, 123, 142
Isaac 71, 41
Isibell J. 123
Jacob 53, 63, 41, 71,
    93
James 108, 115, 123
Joacim 127
John 41, 72, 95
John C. 126
Jonathan 123
Lewis 41
Lidia 110
Louisa 106
Louisa A. 150
Louisa J. 123
Magdalene 95
Margaret 41, 53, 71, 95
Margaret Adaline 149
Margaret E. 123
Mary A. 144
Mary J. 132
Mary Jane 117
N. W. 132
Nancy 110
Noah 71
P. K. 117
Paul 92, 95
Phillip 53
Phillip Henry 69

BIBLE (cont.)
Rachel 95
S. 150
S. Harrison 79
Solomon 95
Susan 95
Susannah 71, 123
Thomas 115
William 71, 117, 132,
    138
William S. 123
BIDDLE, James 56, 65
Mary 105
S. J. 83
BIGGS, Elbert 94
I. 101
James 23, 91
Jane 91
Margaret 91
Sarah R. 91
BIGHAM, William 12
BILLINGSLEY, Elijah 32
John, Sr. 2
BIRD, C. H. 151
Cyntha E. 118
David 66, 102, 118
Elizabeth 118
Isaac 118
J. B. 77
James H. 118
John 1, 105
John, Senr. 35
Mary 98, 151
Mary Ann 118
Matthias 98, 118
Philip 118
Polly 56
Russel M. 118
S. M. 123
Samuel N. 111
Susan 118
William R. 118
BISHOP, Noah 130
BITNER, Elizabeth 130
Kissiah E. 131
Sarah 126
BLACK, Christopher 96
Clark 96
Elenar 31
Elender 91, 92
Elizabeth 31
Elizabeth Ann 96
Joseph 31, 96
Lewis 96
Margaret 31
Marthy 31
Mary Ann 62
Rachel 31
Rebecca Ellen 96
Susannah 31
William 31, 96
William C. 107
BLACKWOOD, Andrew 3
Ann 3
Elizabeth 3
John 3
Martha 3
Mary 3
William 3
BLAIR, C. W. 140
John 1, 9
John, Col. 14
Joseph 32
Mary 90
William 32
BLAKE, Catharine 112
Thomas Jefferson 112
BLAKELY, John 62
BLAKEMORE, Mary 147
BLANKENBECKLER, Jesu 21
BLANTON, Adaline 133
Mary A. B. 131
Nancy L. 131

BRITTON (cont.)
James, Maj. 63
John A. 86
Joseph D. 120
Mary E. 143
V. S. 152
William 58, 102
BROADERICK, Daniel 119
Hugh 118, 119
Polly Ann 119
Roda Z. 119
S. L. 119
W. A. 119
BROILS, Lucinda 78
BROITES, B. B. 133
BROMLEY, James 113
BROOKS, Asbury 81
Charity 81
Charly Francis 127
Elizabeth 81
Emma Florence 127
Frances Elen 127
Henry 8, 102, 103
Jacob 102
Jacob F. 31, 81
Jesse 81
Joseph Newton 127
Laura Allice 127
Margaret 11, 81
Margaret Sophiah 127
Margrethe 25
Marien W. 103
Marion 102
Martha Caroline 127
Mary 81
Michael Henry 127
Nancy 81, 103
Nancy Jane 100
Polly 8
Rachel 81
S. K. 119, 124, 127,
    129, 130, 140
S. R. 11
Sarah 67, 81
Sarah Louisa 127
Stephen 7, 11, 25, 27,
    28, 31, 32, 38, 81
Susan Elizabeth 127
Thomas H. 102
Thomas N. 127
W. P. 11
William 81
BROTHERTON, Andrew I. 72
Benjamin 49
Easter 76
Elizabeth 67
George 49
Henry 49, 67
James 49, 51, 72, 107
James M. 76, 79
Jane 76
Jinny 49
John 49
Rodah 72
William 41, 49, 72
BROWN, Albert Leroy 137
Alexander 60, 78, 98,
    108, 118, 125, 133,
    140
Archibald 112
Bedford 117
Betsey 53
C. F. 146
Catharine 2, 126
Clamathan Jane 137
David 68
David, Junr. 59
David, Senr. 59
Electra 139
Elija A. 98
Elizabeth 98, 122, 146
Emma 85
Esther C. 118

BROWN (cont.)
Eva J. 144
F. J. 137
F. T. 128
Fannie A. 118
Felix 112
G. F. 139
George 66, 146
H. H. 152
Hairy D. 143
Hannah 2
Hannah M. 118
Harriet P. 1
Hugh 112
Hugh M. 112, 144
I. B. 148
Isaac 53, 59
J. A. 123, 141
J. D. 127, 138
J. R. 137
J. W. 139
J. T. 145
James 21, 31, 35, 53,
    54, 85, 117
James Junr. 16, 21
James Senr. 16, 25
James B. 137
James C. 98
James D. 122, 136
James E. 118
James H. 123, 133
James N. 135
James P. 118
James Thomas 85
Jane 85, 125
Jane M. 128
Jessie Wilson 118
Jetham 59
John 31, 53, 59, 85,
    132, 139
John A. 12, 40, 91, 146
John H. 98
John L. 1
John S. 146
John W. 98
John Wilson 85, 118
Joseph 23, 40, 59,
    112, 146
Joseph R. 144
Jotham 118
Lasandra Jane 132
Laura 85
Laura E. 128
Lucinda 98
Lucinda M. 112
Lula E. 139
Lydia 59
Margaret 53, 98
Margaret Ann 149
Margaret Jane 112
Margaret M. 118
Marthy 59
Mary 31, 139, 146, 152
Meriam 53
Milly 13
Mirrian 31
Morton V. 98
Nancy 2, 59
Nancy A. 146
Phebe 59, 90
Polly 2, 53, 59, 98
R. L. 143
Rachel 53
Rachel H. 132
Rebecca 2, 110
Richard W. 98
Robert 85, 98
Robert S. 112
Ruth 4, 6, 53
Rutha Emily 132
Sally 98
Samuel 2, 53
Sarah 68, 98, 112, 139

BROWN (cont.)
Solomon 2, 53
Sylvanus 59
Thomas 2, 28, 31, 53
Thomas H. 2
Thomas Parsons 1, 2
W. A. 114
W. C. 128
W. R. 72
William 2, 35, 45, 47,
    51, 53, 56, 59, 73,
    98, 112, 127, 132
William C. Maloney 85
William H. 144
William L. 98
William O. 118
William P. 118
William R. 77
William S. 98
Wilson 110
Violet 51
Zachariah 146
BROWNING, Benjamin 29
Nathan 29
R. D. 87
Rebeckah 18, 29
Robert S. 110
Roger 18, 29
BROWNLOW, Thomas, Junr. 46
BROYLE, Adam 38
Cain 11
Elias 38
John 38
Mary Magdalena 38
Nancy B. 38
Polly 38
Sally 38
Thomas 38
William 38
BROYLES, A. F. 112, 126
Adam 38
Alexander 56
Anderson S. 125, 131
Annice C. 139
Barbary 32
Bobby 3
Clary M. 131
Charles 112
David 69
Delilah 1
Edmund 112
Emma 145
Ethel 145
Elender 69
Elizabeth 1, 3, 56, 69,
    131
Ephraim 1, 73
Ephraim B. 131
Eve 73
Ezekiel 1
Frances A. 69
G. B. 120
Grace 73
George J. 112
Gon J. 120
Horace 145
J. F. 119
Jack 69
Jack F. 69
Jacob 1, 3, 112
Jacob F. 69
James 1, 3
James F. 57, 77, 103
Jeremiah 1
John 1, 3, 35, 69
John I. 73
John J. 131
John S. 3, 112
Julia 139
Keziah 1
King 151
King H. 131
L. H. 117

COURTNEY (cont.)
Fielden 101
Fielding 45, 70
George Senr. 70
George J. 106
George W. 70
James 45, 70, 101
John 70, 73
Joseph 5, 101
Margaret 101
Marshall 46, 48, 70
Martial 45
Mary 106
Mourning 70
Nancy Adeline 101
Sarah 45, 70
Stephen 70
Susan Victory 101
William 70
William S. 101
COX, A. G. 127
Adaline 134
Ann 5
Ann M. 84
Eliakim 5
Elisha 134
Elizabeth 95
Ephraim 95
G. F. 151
Gene 5
J. A. 66
J. W., Dr. 119
James 120
L. A. 67
Leah 5
Lemuel 93
Margaret 134
Martha E. 151
Mary Ann 97
Matthew 5, 58, 134, 135
Mehalah 5
Nancy 94, 134
Polly 104
Samuel 5
William 5
COYLE, Sarah 44
CRABTREE, A. B. 104, 108
Anney 3
Barnet 3, 15, 81
Betty 3
Crawford 104
Daniel 3
Ester 61
Henry 3
Jacob 128
James 3, 58
James M. 114
John 3, 15, 58, 64, 66,
68, 81, 99, 104, 124
Peggy 3
Polly 3
Ruth 104
Sarah 104
Susanna 3
William 3, 61
CRADDICK, David 103, 116
Elizabeth 116
William 30, 70
CRADDOCK, Charity 70
David 70
James 70
John 70
Lucinda 70
Madison 70
Melinda 70
Newman 70
Rachel 70
Rebecca 70
Robert 70
William 70
CRADIC, Margaret 94
CRADICK, Elizabeth 114
CRAIG, Benjamin 13

CRAIG (cont.)
Eleanor 88
James 88
Jane 88
Jane I. 88
John 12, 88, 132
Louisa 132
Mary 88
Nancy 88, 132
Robert 88
Samuel 88
CRAIGMILES, Bathsheba 12
Joseph 12
Pleasant 12
William 12
William N. 52
CRANE, K. T. 40
CRAVENS, Ann 4, 16
William 4
CRAWFORD, Adam 4
Alec 4
Barbara 4
Benjamin 4
Catrene 4
Cintha 125
Dianna 61
Eliner 5
Elizabeth 4, 49, 58,
73, 84, 107
George 4, 61
George G., Dr. 49
Hamilton 61
Isaac 61, 130
Isabel 59
Isabella 4
J. H. 132
Jackson 61
James 5, 22, 61
James S. B. 117
Jane 61
John 4, 5, 24, 61,
62, 103, 119, 129,
130
John H. 134
Mahala 134
Margaret 5
Mary 4, 131
Nancy 61
Nicholas 4
Peter 4
R. A. 115, 118
Rhoda 61
Robert 4
Robert A. 9, 74, 107
S. P. 21, 93, 98
S. P., Dr. 98
Samuel 5, 61, 103
Susannah 4
William 4, 5, 59, 61,
80
William G. 58
CRAY, Robert C. 66
CREAMER, Alexander 71
Ann 71
Martha M. 84
William 71
CREMER, Thomas 53
CREZELIUS, Elizabeth 41
Isaac 41
CRITTENDON, Amelia 97
Martha Jane 97
Prior 97
CROCKER, Miriam 133
CROCKET, Robert 16
CROCKETT, Robert 4
CROSBY, Andrew 141, 148
Anne 4, 5
Caleb 141
David 4
Edward 4
Eliza Jane 141
Elizabeth 4, 6
Frances 4, 5

CROSBY (cont.)
George 4, 5, 6, 18,
15, 45
Jane 4, 5
Jeremiah 4
Jinny 4
John 4
Lemuel 60, 67, 86, 87,
95, 97, 98, 106, 111,
117, 118, 141
Lyddax 5
Lydia 18
Marget 4
Marjey 4
Mary 4
Melone 4
Nancy 4, 5, 111, 141
Naomi 4
Peggy 4, 5
Peter 4
Rachel 4
Rebeckah 5
Ruth 4
Sally 5, 18
Samuel 60
Sarah 4, 141
Susanna 4, 5
Thomas 4, 5, 18
Uriel 4
William 4, 5, 6, 18
CROSIER, Thomas 106
CROSSWHITE, Abraham 5
George 5
John 5
Lucy 5
Mary 5
Mevy 5
Milly 5
Polly 5
Sary 5
CROUCH, George M. 82
Martha 89
Nancy 82
Samuel C. 118
CROW, Benjamin 9
CROZIER, S. N. 107
Samuel N. 138
CRUM, Jacob 87
James 102
John 10, 32, 87
Letha 118
Margaret 10, 87
Margit 32
Michael 32
Michael, Senr. 118
Nancy 87
Rachel 108
Sarah 87
Sparling 108
William 87, 104, 116
CRUMLEY, Abraham 31
Elizabeth 20
Jane 50
John R. Y. 111
Lydia Jane 103
M. B. 88, 99, 103
Margaret L. 125
Mary Elizabeth 103
Nancy 103
Phebe Catharine 103
Rody 101
Sarah Alis 103
William 17, 67, 91, 111,
137
CRUMLY, Abram 133
John 133
CRUMP, Benjamin 5
Edmond 5
Isaac 5
Margaret 5
Nancy 5
CULBASON, Mary 16
CULVER, M. J. 91